Teaching language and communication to the mentally handicapped

SCHOOLS COUNCIL CURRICULUM BULLETIN 8

Teaching language and communication to the mentally handicapped

report of the Schools Council
Education of Severely Educationally
Subnormal Pupils Project

KEN LEEMING WILL SWANN
JUDITH COUPE AND PETER MITTLER

Foreword by MARY WARNOCK

Evans/Methuen Educational

*First published 1979 for the Schools Council
by Evans Brothers Limited
Montague House, Russell Square, London WC1B 5BX
and Methuen Educational
11 New Fetter Lane, London EC4P 4EE
Reprinted 1980*

*Published in the US as
Teaching Language and Communication to the Mentally Retarded
by Methuen, Inc.
733 Third Avenue,
New York, NY 10017*

© *Schools Council Publications 1979*

*All rights reserved. No part of this publication
may be reproduced or transmitted, in any form
or by any means, electronic, mechanical, photocopying,
recording or otherwise without the
prior permission of the publishers.*

Schools Council Education of Severely Educationally
Subnormal Pupils Project.
Teaching language and communication to the mentally handicapped.
(Schools Council. Curriculum bulletins; 8 ISSN 0533-1633).
1. Mentally handicapped children – Education
– England – Language arts
2. Schools Council Education of Severely Educationally
Subnormal Pupils Project
I. Title   II. Leeming, Ken   III. Series
371.9'284   LC4616

ISBN 0 423 50680 3 (hardback)
ISBN 0 423 50660 9 (paper)

*Phototypeset in V.I.P. Times by
Western Printing Services Ltd, Bristol
and printed in Great Britain at the
University Press, Cambridge*

Contents

Foreword   xi

Introduction   1
Planning for development   2
The project   3
A guide to this book   6
References   8

I **A survey of language abilities**   9
Structure of the survey   9
The schools and the children   10
The language questionnaire   12
English Picture Vocabulary Test   16
Organization of survey   16
The individual session with teachers   16
Scoring of language questionnaire and EPVT   17
Results of language questionnaire and EPVT   18
Language abilities and age   23
Language abilities and identifiable groups   29
The survey as an assessment technique   33
The survey as a guide to curriculum planning   34
Summary   35
References   38

II **Aims and the curriculum**   40
A model of the teaching process: some definitions   40
Aims and education: the teachers   44
Aims and education: the parents   50
A study of the curricula of five schools   54
Autonomy   61
Summary   65
References   65

vi CONTENTS

III Defining teaching objectives: a study of six teachers 67
The intervention study 68
Planning lessons 69
Implementing the plan 80
Evaluating and modifying the plan 89
References 92

IV Curriculum content: sources, concepts and objectives 93
Sources for a curriculum framework 94
The communication process 100
The curriculum framework – introductory note 110
Stage I. Children at or below the one-word level 110
   Meanings 111
   Teaching the medium for communication 125
   Using the Stage I curriculum – an example 128
Stage II. From one to two words 131
   1. Extending relational meanings 132
   2. Combining substantive meanings 133
   3. New meanings 135
   Words or meanings 136
   Forms at Stage II 137
   Prerequisites for Stage II 138
   Generalizing Stage II objectives 140
   Using the Stage II curriculum – an example 142
Stage III. Extending meaning and structure 144
   Basic teaching strategies – Stage III 145
   Aspects of the Stage III curriculum 146
Language in use 155
Conclusions 159
References 160

V Observational methods 164
Levels of observation 166
A framework for observation – a worked example 167
Do we have the time? 172
Using the approach in the classroom – three examples 173
   Ruth 173
   Peter 182
   Linda 186
Using the approach outside the classroom – two examples 188
   Working with a mother 188

Working with staff in a residential home   195
Summary   201
References   202

VI **Teaching vocabulary**   203
Tests of common nouns   204
A test of verbs – movement   209
Spatial test results   210
Summary of results   211
Designing vocabulary tests   212
Teaching new vocabulary   221
Summary   236
References   237

VII **Non-verbal communication**   238
A study of two children   239
  Ian   240
  Susan   252
Summary   265
References   267

VIII **Using questions in the classroom**   268
Questioning and picture materials   269
The questioning procedure   275
Putting the procedure into practice   277
Further applications and developments   284
Conclusions   290

IX **Using language curriculum packages**   292
Content, method and material   292
Implementing a curriculum package   293
Peabody Language Development Kit – Level P   294
Jim's People   302
Distar Language I   310
Language and How to Use It – Beginning levels   320
Using language curriculum packages – general issues   324
Conclusions   327
References   328

X **Postscript**   330
Teacher workshops   331
Sharing knowledge and skills   333

Schools as resource centres 334
Special education outside schools 334
Partnership with parents 335
References 336

Appendices 339
A   The language survey – additional tables   341
B   Words used in vocabulary survey   346
C   Examples of tests for play and pastime vocabulary   349
D   Examples of detailed programmes for teaching body-part and spatial vocabulary   350
E   Communication Behaviour Rating Schedule   372
F   Pictures used in the questioning procedure tests   380
G   Categories for analysis of utterances in questioning procedure tests   385
H   Questioning – skeleton procedure form   388

Project team, consultative committee and participating schools   391
Index   393

Videotapes

Three 30-minute, black-and-white videotapes were made by the project team which show some of the work described in the report. 'Setting language objectives' shows part of the intervention study in Chapter III; 'Teaching new words' features two teachers using the vocabulary teaching approach advocated by the project in Chapter VI; and 'Communication before speech' illustrates the two examples of teaching non-verbal communication described in Chapter VII. The videotape programmes, edited with the help of the University of Manchester Audio Visual Service, are published by Drake Educational Associates, 212 Whitchurch Road, Cardiff CF4 3XF.

The purpose of education for all children is the same; the goals are the same. But the help that individual children need in progressing towards them will be different. Whereas for some the road they have to travel towards the goals is smooth and easy, for others it is fraught with obstacles. For some the obstacles are so daunting that, even with the greatest possible help, they will not get very far. Nevertheless, for them too, progress will be possible, and their educational needs will be fulfilled, as they gradually overcome one obstacle after another on the way.

Special Educational Needs

Foreword

Special education has changed radically in the last decade. The revolution began in 1971 when all children in England and Wales (with Scotland soon following), however severe their handicaps, were brought into the educational system. From this time, education has been seen officially as a right of all children, and thus as a genuinely common good. It was a natural next step, therefore, that in 1974 a committee was set up by the Government to inquire into the present state and future development of the education of all handicapped children in England, Wales and Scotland. In the report of the Committee of Enquiry, *Special Educational Needs*, published in 1978, an attempt was made to widen the concept of special education. For all education was conceived as having broad common aims: independence, and imaginative understanding of the world. Education, it was argued, becomes 'special' when there are special obstacles to be overcome in the progress towards these distant goals. An educational need is determined by the provision which must be made for a child if he is to overcome his particular obstacles (or begin to); and a need is 'special' if the provision must be special. Thus many children now in ordinary schools were thought to have special needs of one kind or another. Equally, and more obviously, the mentally handicapped have special needs of a different kind, since the obstacles in their path are different and more daunting. But the progress, if it is genuinely educational, will be in the same direction for all children. There could be no more vivid and moving illustration of these concepts than the cases of Ian and Susan, recorded in Chapter VII of this book.

The report of the Committee of Enquiry was not itself revolutionary. It called attention to the best practice already in existence, and it did little more than bring together ideas already influential in determining the direction of special education, and base its positive recommendations on these ideas. There was one area in which, conspicuously, the Committee had to leave the work to be done by others, and this was the crucial area of curriculum development. The Schools Council had already in its special education programme set up a number of projects which the Committee looked at –

these were concerned with the special needs of deaf children, blind and partially sighted children, disturbed children and slow learners – and teaching materials and reports from some of them have already begun to appear. It is of the greatest importance that such a detailed study as *Teaching Language and Communication to the Mentally Handicapped* is published and its content thoroughly assimilated and argued over by teachers practising in the field, and those responsible for training students. For it is no use thinking of *education* of the handicapped, as opposed to a more generalized care of them, unless an educational curriculum can be specified. To educate a child is to help him to progress; but there can be no progress without clear direction.

There is still a great need for a change of attitude towards this positive concept of education. Many people, though they may not admit it, still think that education is a matter of learning to read, write and calculate, and that for those children who will never be able to do these things, education is impossible. Again, many people believe that education is what goes on at school, so for those children who are below even nursery-school age there can be no question of education. One of the most important things demonstrated by the Hester Adrian Research Centre at Manchester University, under Professor Mittler's direction, is the general point that work with very young children and their parents is not only immensely valuable, but is specifically educational. For the severely handicapped must be taught things which are learned spontaneously by most children. By far the most important thing which they have to be taught is communication, non-verbal and, if possible, verbal. Such teaching *is* education, since without it no progress, however, small, can be made along the road towards the common educational goals. But teaching, even of babies, will be labour lost – it simply will not work – without curricular objectives, clearly set out.

It is essential that this view, both of the demands of education and of its central importance to the severely handicapped, should be understood and accepted by teachers themselves, and also by parents and by the other professionals who will be concerned with the welfare of the handicapped child. Unless all professionals understand what is meant by the education of the severely handicapped, such children may not get to the full what is now their legal right. And unless parents understand it too, they will not be able either to co-operate in the educational process, or to insist on special provision suitable for their children.

For these reasons it is to be hoped that the content of this book will be disseminated beyond the teaching profession itself. And there is another reason: the whole argument of the book demonstrates most perspicuously the necessary connexion between theory and practice. It is impossible to read it without being made to consider both the notion of human behaviour and how it is influenced, and the fundamental nature of language itself. There is no field more absorbing for psychologists and philosophers; it is a field in which, increasingly, universities should interest themselves. There is an urgent need, which the Committee of Enquiry pointed to, for more research, more university chairs, and more graduates of the very highest calibre to man both the research projects and the teaching profession. This book, and the Schools Council project of which it is the outcome, provides an outstanding example of the kind of work which is needed. I hope that it will be read not only by those concerned with special education, not only in university departments of education, but in departments of psychology and philosophy as well. Only so will its implications for the future be fully grasped.

MARY WARNOCK
Chairman
Committee of Enquiry into the Education
of Handicapped Children and Young People (1974–78)

Acknowledgements

So many people contributed to the project and to the writing of this book that it is impossible to mention them all by name.

But our thanks must go first and foremost to the headteachers and staff of all the schools that took part in the project, and to the many children in the schools with whom we worked and from whom we learned so much.

Among the many others whom we wish particularly to thank are John Tomlinson, Director of Education for Cheshire, and his colleagues, John Davis, Alan Gorton and Robin Totty; George Bradbury, Headteacher of Greenbank School, Hartford, for allowing us to use part of his new school as project headquarters; Geoffrey Thornton and Stephen Steadman who helped us greatly by their critical discussions of the project's aims and methods. We should like to thank the members of the project's consultative committee, and particularly its chairman, Mike Gore, for their guidance and support. Of the many staff of the Schools Council who helped us at various times we are particularly grateful to the project's curriculum officer, and for the skilled and sensitive editorial help we received from our editor in the Council's Publications Section. We should also like to thank R. MacKenzie and J. U. West for the drawings used in the questioning procedure tests, reproduced in Appendix F. But our greatest debt is to our secretary, Ann Rawson, who was a tower of strength to all of us.

Introduction

Teaching mentally handicapped children brings us face to face with some of the most baffling and fundamental questions of human development. How does a child learn language? What is language and where does it begin? Can it be taught at all, and if so how? Where do we begin?

Teaching a child to understand and use his own language is perhaps the most exciting challenge that can confront a teacher. After all, neither our training as teachers nor our experience as parents adequately equips us for such a daunting task. Most children enter the educational system with well-developed language abilities, and while there is much that the teacher can do to help the child to use and extend his language abilities, it is only when the teacher begins to work with mentally handicapped children that she will need to take up the challenge of helping the child to learn his own language for the first time.

Although we have only just begun to grapple with these problems, both teachers and research workers are beginning to make some progress in understanding some of the elements of the problems facing them. It is, for example, becoming obvious that we cannot just sit back and wait for language to develop. If we want children to learn language, we shall have to find the means to teach them. Exposing them to a linguistically stimulating environment is merely to create the context for teaching. It is no substitute for direct teaching.

This book is about the teaching of language and communication. It offers a working model which derives from both theory and practice, and tries to build a bridge between them. It provides detailed examples of teachers putting principles into action and illustrates how teachers and children work together. This is perhaps the main justification for its length; we did not feel justified in discussing principles of teaching without providing illustrations of teachers putting principles into practice. We hope this will help readers to get the feel of the work of the teachers in their classrooms, as well as on the working parties which lay at the heart of the project.

Planning for development

One important difference between mentally handicapped and other children lies in the necessity to plan for development. We cannot afford to wait for learning and growth to occur naturally; we often have to plan to develop skills and abilities that other children achieve without special teaching. Success in this challenging field therefore depends on the extent to which those taking part are able to define and agree on their objectives, and, in a wider sense, to apply the elements of the teaching model that forms the core of the approach described in this report. Without specific objectives, as distinct from general aims, without appropriate organization and methods, such developments are in danger of drifting into well-meaning but undifferentiated activities.

But we are far from advocating that the teaching model which we outline here should be applied as a kind of educational strait-jacket to every aspect of the child's life. We do not see prescriptive teaching or an approach that emphasizes measurable objectives as a way of life or even as a total system of education. But we do see behavioural principles and methods as central to the development of a systematic approach to teaching. Because a behavioural approach provides a rich storehouse of powerful techniques for achieving the goals of education, we believe that all teachers should be skilled and competent in their use. These methods and technologies by no means undermine either the aims of education in general or the teacher's autonomy. Indeed, they enable the teacher to think more systematically about how general aims and goals, either for children or for themselves, can be translated into reality.

Nor do we see behavioural methods as necessarily incompatible with other approaches. In the context of education, we believe they should be used for educational purposes – that is, to further the development of skills and abilities in children. But they are only one means to that end, and there is no reason why other means should not be used at the same time.

It is sometimes assumed that advocates of a systematic approach are opposed to free play, to 'discovery methods' and to creative activities in special schools. This is certainly not the view taken here. Although we lay a great deal of stress on a behavioural approach, we are more concerned with the content of what is to be taught and with the precise definition of objectives, than with reinforcement. We have emphasized the reinforcement that comes from successful completion of a task, rather than from the delivery of external rewards. A systematic approach to teaching children to swim, dance, throw a pot, use a paintbrush, or put a spin on a tennis ball, is merely a means to the end of children enjoying new skills and experiences, and using these to extend their interests and as a basis for new learning.

The project

The project had its origins in a special education working party set up by Cheshire Education Committee soon after responsibility for the education of mentally handicapped children was transferred from health to education authorities in 1971. This working party prepared a report containing a large number of practical suggestions for the extension of special education services to the new special schools. But they also underlined the importance of a careful consideration of teaching content and methods and thereby laid the foundation for the first extensive curriculum development study undertaken in the field of severe mental handicap in this country. It is the results of this study that we report here.

The project was based on a wide network of collaborating agencies and individuals. Cheshire laid the foundations by conceiving the idea. By asking Peter Mittler to direct the project and prepare a set of proposals to submit to the Schools Council, Cheshire sought to forge a working link with the Hester Adrian Research Centre at Manchester University and in particular with the Social Science Research Council Language and Communication project. The two projects were planned in parallel, worked under joint direction, and were deliberately designed to complement one another. Although the SSRC project also involved classroom research and the teaching of language skills, the Schools Council project was more closely concerned with curriculum development and with working directly with a large number of teachers. The two projects benefited greatly from each other's work, held regular meetings to discuss findings and methods, and developed a variety of working links, but each project retained its own autonomy. A preliminary report of some aspects of the SSRC study was published in 1976.[1] Details of other project publications and reports are available from the Hester Adrian Research Centre, Manchester University.

It became clear at an early stage of planning the Schools Council project that it would be sensible to try to achieve complete coverage of a given geographical area and to include all the schools for severely educationally subnormal (ESN(S)) children within that area. With the reorganization of local government and the appearance of new boundaries in April 1974, several schools previously in Cheshire became the responsibility of new local education authorities; nevertheless, the full co-operation of all the relevant

LEAs and their staff made it possible to achieve the aim of complete coverage of an area which included the whole of Cheshire, Manchester, Stockport and parts of Trafford, Tameside and Wirrall. There were therefore nineteen schools involved in the project, containing about 1400 ESN(S) children, about 150 teachers and about the same number of care staff working in classrooms. Two of the schools were in hospitals for the mentally handicapped. In addition, the project team worked closely with a number of other schools for particular purposes; these included all the ESN(S) schools in Clwyd, and two schools in the Lancashire area. For a full list of participating schools see page 392.

The work of the project sprang largely from four teacher workshops which were established in different areas. These consisted of groups of teachers, one from each ESN(S) school, who met regularly (on average once a month but often more frequently) to develop work agreed between its members and the project team. We were fortunate in being able to build on the foundations of a working party that had been set up at the Manchester Teachers' Centre, and had designed and carried out its own survey of the language abilities of about three hundred Manchester children in ESN(S) schools and a number of other special schools.[2] We adapted their questionnaire for the wider survey reported in Chapter I, and then continued to work with this group in evaluating the commercially available language programmes (see Chapter IX). This working party is still in operation, and works closely with staff of the Hester Adrian Research Centre. Three working parties were set up by the project team. The Chester group worked on the development of vocabulary tests (Chapter VI); the Hartford group had a particular interest in the most severely handicapped children, and developed the Communication Behaviour Rating Schedule (see Chapter VII). The work of the Cheadle group led to work on questioning, described in Chapter VIII.

The working parties were kept informed of each others' work, and reports, minutes and summaries of discussions were freely circulated. The working parties also commented in detail on drafts of the reports prepared by the project team, and later incorporated in this report. Although it was only possible for one teacher from each school to join in a working party, one of her tasks was to provide a working link with other members of staff in her school. In some cases this was done through written or verbal reports, in others it led to the involvement of all members of staff in a particular aspect of the project. For example, the survey of vocabulary knowledge, developed by the Chester working party, was conducted in every class of every school represented. The project team contributed to the design of the study and analysed the results but the survey itself was undertaken by the class teachers.

In addition to the working party meetings, the project team also worked directly and in detail with a number of individual teachers; some of these were members of working parties, others were not.

Before the three-year Schools Council project began in September 1973, Peter Mittler, director of the project, and Ken Leeming, the deputy director, visited all the project schools in order to meet the headteacher and the staff, to explain the aims of the project and to give staff the opportunity to raise any points they wished about the aims and methods of the project. This was a useful exercise because it enabled the team to form a working relationship with staff, and to anticipate any problems or difficulties which might arise. Staff were enthusiastic about the project. Not surprisingly some were a little apprehensive about the prospect of observers and video recorders in their classrooms, though in the event the cameras soon became 'part of the furniture', and were nearly always operated by remote control from outside the classroom. Of course, it is not possible to know the real effect of the presence of observers or cameras on the teachers, but most teachers said that they often forgot they were being observed and, of the teachers who were videotaped, most felt their work had not been changed in any way by the knowledge that their teaching might be being recorded.

THE PROJECT TEAM

We tried to bring together a team with a variety of skills, abilities and backgrounds. Ken Leeming had considerable experience as an educational psychologist and had taken a particular interest in mentally handicapped children in general, and children in 'special care' units in particular. He also had experience of teaching and teacher training. Will Swann came to the project after a degree course in psychology during which he had worked closely with the SSRC language project at the Hester Adrian Research Centre; he also contributed special skills in the area of data analysis. Judith Coupe had several years' experience of teaching ESN(S) children, had developed an interest in language teaching and had been a member of the original Manchester Teachers' Centre working party. Peter Mittler had been doing educational and clinical work with children with language disorders, and since 1969 had been directing research projects on language and communication skills at the Hester Adrian Research Centre. We hope it sounds neither smug nor sentimental to say that we were a happy team and really enjoyed working together.

A guide to this book

The book can be read in a variety of ways. We hope that readers will be stimulated by the more theoretical sections, but they may prefer to concentrate on the more practical chapters illustrating teaching methods and reporting teachers at work. Because we felt it important to go beyond a mere review of research or an account of our own findings, we have tried to provide enough detailed working examples to illustrate 'what really happened'. We have therefore selected a number of transcripts out of several hundred examples of teaching that we have seen or recorded in the hope that these will convey the flavour of teaching and provide concrete illustrations of the methods we describe.

Chapter I describes an extensive survey of the language abilities of all 1400 children in the nineteen project schools. The information collected by teachers provided the starting-point for the four working parties and the foundation for much of the work reported in later chapters.

Chapter II begins with a brief statement of our own working model of language teaching, and offers some definitions and discussion of the terms we use. It then moves into a basic discussion of the aims of education for mentally handicapped children, drawing on statements made both by teachers and parents about how they view these aims. Finally, we contrast what teachers say about their aims with what they actually do, based on a study of five schools.

Chapter III provides detailed examples of how six teachers adapted our working model of language teaching to their own needs, by developing and defining their own objectives. In some ways, this chapter might be regarded as the core of the book. It shows how well and how quickly teachers can modify their teaching to reach the goals they have themselves selected.

Chapter IV is concerned with fundamental questions about the source of the curriculum – what to teach. It presents an overview of some of the main developments in recent years in our knowledge of the nature of language and communication, and then goes on to consider some of the most important landmarks in the child's learning of his own language. It considers the skills which have been identified for children at three stages: those below the one-word stage, those between the one- and two-word stage, and those at a more advanced level. Having identified the nature of these specific skills, a number of suggestions are made about how they might be taught. Finally, the various functions of language are discussed, and the ways in which language can be put to work in thinking, communicating, and in relating to other people.

Chapter V discusses classroom observation, and presents a number of worked examples of one particular observation scheme in action. Most of the examples are of profoundly or multi-handicapped children, and illustrate how careful observations can lead to planned and systematic teaching which produces results even in children with the most severe disabilities.

Chapter VI summarizes the work of a group of teachers whose concern with the question, 'What words do our children really know and understand?', led to the development of a useful vocabulary test, and to a survey of vocabulary knowledge of all the children in six of the project schools. The results of this survey led directly to the development of specific teaching programmes in five schools outside the project area; these are reported in some detail.

Chapter VII consists of two detailed illustrations of children being taught by their teachers to communicate non-verbally. These examples illustrate how even children who seem to have no expressive language at all, and for whom language as a system still has little or no meaning, can nevertheless be put in touch with those around them by being helped to acquire a system of communication which enables them to express choice and to relate to others. The chapter also describes the Communication Behaviour Rating Schedule which can be used to assess a child's communicative ability, even if he does not speak.

Chapter VIII is concerned with children who have developed useful language, but who make much less use of it than they might. A variety of examples illustrate how the teacher can help a child to use what language he has in a fuller and richer way by varying the nature of the questions and demands made on the child. The chapter discusses various strategies for using ordinary classroom situations to ask questions in ways that help children to use longer sentences and a richer variety of language forms.

Chapter IX reviews four of the main commercially available language-teaching schemes. Although only one of these is specifically aimed at mentally handicapped children, the chapter summarizes the experiences of members of one of the project working parties in using the kits in the hope that their work will be of interest to other teachers contemplating their use.

The final chapter offers suggestions for action that might be taken by teachers and others concerned with ESN(S) children, setting these in the context of current developments in special education.

We would be happy to think that teachers might use this book as a working text and as the basis for critical discussions about curriculum development and content in ESN(S) schools. We also hope that it contains ideas and materials which will be seen to extend beyond language and communication, and that some readers may be stimulated to consider their relevance outside mental handicap and special education itself.

References

1. P. BERRY (ed.), *Language and Communication in the Mentally Handicapped*. Edward Arnold, 1976.
2. B. KELLETT, 'An initial survey of the language of ESN(S) children in Manchester: the results of a teachers' workshop', in P. Berry (ed.), *Language and Communication in the Mentally Handicapped*.

I. A survey of language abilities

In a book which concentrates on individual children's abilities and problems, and how teachers can organize their work to meet the individual needs of educationally subnormal (ESN) children, it may seem strange to begin by describing a large-scale general survey of ESN children's language abilities. But although this might appear contradictory, the individual and group approach are complementary in many ways. Teaching programmes are designed for individuals but, to be effective, teaching programmes must be part of a much wider-scale curriculum. The curriculum needs to have an overall structure for teaching applicable to every problem a teacher may face, and the structure adopted must be influenced by the nature of the children concerned. A curriculum also needs a coherent pattern of content. For an individual child's teaching programme the content must depend on detailed knowledge of that child, but it must draw from a general content framework designed to cover the whole spectrum of abilities from children in special care units to children being considered for transfer to schools for the educationally subnormal (moderate) (ESN(M) schools). The survey has greatly influenced both the structure for teaching we have chosen to use, and the suggestions for curriculum content. It has also been an important influence in choosing certain areas to study in more detail.

Structure of the survey

The survey examined a broad spectrum of language skills, subdivided into four important areas:

1 Production: what language does the child produce?
2 Reception: what language does the child understand?
3 Articulation: how clear is the child's speech?
4 Gesture: how does the child use his body to communicate?

A language questionnaire covering these four areas was devised and piloted by a group of teachers in Manchester,[1] and was subsequently used for our survey in 1973. In addition, we selected the English Picture Vocabulary Test.[2] This standardized test has been used extensively with subnormal children, and is basically a measure of the comprehension of single words. It was thought to be useful as a supplementary measure, particularly since it has established performance levels for normal children. Finally, in order to study the relationship between language abilities and the social, clinical and educational characteristics of the children, a personal information questionnaire was designed. All three instruments were administered by the teachers in the nineteen schools involved in the project, for a total of 1381 severely educationally subnormal (ESN(S)) children.

In the course of the survey it became clear that it was serving a number of valuable functions. It reminded teachers of the stages and processes of language development, and it was a useful assessment device sensitizing many teachers to the language and communication abilities of their children – two aspects which together provided a tool that teachers could use to plan programmes for individual children. In certain respects the survey pre-empts in a simplified form the concerns of the rest of this book – namely, the ways in which children may be observed, assessed and taught language and communication skills.

The schools and the children

For our findings to have any generality, the first concern was to ensure that the 1381 children and the nineteen schools used were a representative sample. Using the personal information questionnaire, teachers provided information on each child's social, educational and clinical characteristics from school records. The major headings included date of birth and age, sex, date of entry into school, number of schools previously attended, mental age, IQ and any other results of tests (since November 1970, to eliminate out-of-date information), medical diagnosis and associated disabilities, sessions with specialists (for example, speech therapists), father's occupation, residential care and family size.

The intention was to include every child attending schools for the severely educationally subnormal (ESN(S) schools) in the Cheshire, Manchester and Stockport areas at the time of the survey, including children attending day schools but resident in hostels or group homes, and others in two schools situated in long-stay hospitals for the mentally handicapped. Local government reorganization in April 1974 and other changes led to the inclusion of schools in authorities due to merge with Cheshire. After April 1974 four schools originally in Cheshire went into new authorities, but remained in the

THE SCHOOLS AND THE CHILDREN 11

project. The final selection of nineteen schools was largely based on considerations of geography and convenience, but no schools within the area covered by Cheshire, Manchester and Stockport before April 1974 were omitted.

THE SCHOOLS

The average number of children per school was 74 with a range of 30 to 115. The average class size was 11·1, ranging from 6 to 21 (the latter in a school with two qualified teachers per class). Most classes lay in the range of 7 to 14. In the sixteen schools for which figures were available, the teacher/pupil ratio was 1:8·9, and the nursery and welfare assistants ratio was 1:10. (There is no reason to suppose that the other three schools are atypical in staffing ratio.) The Department of Education and Science statistics show that, for day schools only, the average school size is 65·1 pupils and the overall teacher/pupil ratio 1:10·7.[3]

THE CHILDREN

The sample is broadly comparable with the national ESN(S) school population with respect to age. However, 2- to 4-year-olds are over-represented and 16- to 19-year-olds are under-represented in the sample. The sex ratio of 59·2 per cent boys to 40·8 per cent girls agrees closely with the national figures of 58·1 per cent boys and 41·9 per cent girls. Eighty-one per cent of the children were living at home, 11·2 per cent were in long-stay hospitals and the remaining 7·8 per cent were in other forms of care. Nationally, 17·2 per cent of ESN(S) children are in hospital schools, so this group of children is under-represented in the sample.

Table 1 Distribution of sex in the survey sample ($N=1378$) and the national population[a]

	National ESN(S) population		Sample	
	N	%	N	%
Male	18 942	58·1	816	59·2
Female	13 645	41·9	562	40·8
Total	32 587	100·0	1378	100·0

[a] Department of Education and Science, *Statistics of Education 1974*, Vol. 1: Schools (HMSO, 1975)

The major diagnostic category was, of course, Down's Syndrome (34·3 per cent) although more children (40·2 per cent) were not reported as belonging to any defined clinical group. The percentage of Down's Syndrome children compares closely with a recent figure of 35 per cent[4] (see Appendix A, Table A1). Father's occupation was used to make an estimate of social class, using the Registrar General's classification of occupations.[5] Although criticized, this index of social class is still the most widely used, and was chosen for simplicity and comparability with other results. Despite low returns, the 34·4 per cent of children for whom adequate information was available showed a social class distribution pattern broadly comparable with the national population. A bias in favour of social classes I and II was possibly due to the teachers being more in touch with these parents (see Appendix A, Table A2).

The above information shows the survey sample to be broadly representative of the national population of ESN(S) pupils. Nevertheless, there was not sufficient up-to-date information on mental age and IQ. Only 20·2 per cent of the children had been tested since November 1970, and only 66·2 per cent of these had been tested on the most common test – the Stanford–Binet.[6] This raises a more general problem about the availability of this type of information in schools. Information was often in a highly unsystematic form, records varied vastly within schools and, in addition to the missing information already mentioned, there was no information on, for example, the number of siblings for 13·4 per cent of the children and for 12·7 per cent the child's position in the family was not known. Since the survey, moves have been made to systematize the record-keeping in ESN(S) schools and other special schools, and in the survey area an improved system was introduced in 1975. While our own survey can draw only interim conclusions on the subject, applicable to a few local education authorities, a much larger-scale survey is currently under analysis at the Hester Adrian Research Centre in Manchester University.

The language questionnaire

The questionnaire used sampled abilities at a fairly general level and over a wide spectrum. It was important that it should be clearly understood and easily completed. There were many instructions on the form, and careful verbal explanation was given.

PRODUCTION SCALE

The production scale listed a number of key stages in the development of productive speech and language, but by no means covered all aspects of this general skill. It was not, for example, concerned with the child's ability to make meaning, that is, with the semantic aspect of his language, nor was it concerned with the uses to which language could be put. Its main concern was the form that language takes both before and after the initial appearance of words and grammar. The main question was not 'What does he say?' but 'How does he say it?'

The link between the items and teaching is indirect but relevant. Most of the items are not specific enough to be used as teaching objectives. The production scale can be seen as a framework for a set of teaching objectives but is not in itself a curriculum. The twelve questions in the scale were:

1. Does the child mainly cry, shriek, scream, grunt?
2. Does the child make long vowel-like vocalizations?
3. Does the child make sound and intonation sequences?
4. Does the child make two-syllable babble (mixed vowel and consonants, for example, 'ga-ga', 'ba-ba')?
5. Does the child make babble sequence with intonation?
6. Does the child imitate single words?
7. Does the child produce spontaneous meaningful words (including child's own made up words such as 'ma-ma', 'beep beep' for car)?
8. Does the child imitate phrases (two or more words)?
9. Does the child make spontaneous two-word utterances (for example, 'Ball gone', 'More din din')?
10. Does the child make spontaneous three-word utterances (for example, 'Mummy gone shop')?
11. Does the child use adequate, even if ungrammatical, speech (for example, 'Me go your room', 'Want go back now')?
12. Does the child use grammatical sentences?

The instruction, 'Please tick the items which apply to the child's *present* production', accompanied the scale. The items, shown here in developmental order, were randomly ordered in the questionnaire to ensure all the questions were checked for each child.

RECEPTION SCALE

A child may indicate his understanding of language without uttering a word.

He may simply point, as in the English Picture Vocabulary Test (EPVT) described below, or he may be required to make more complex non-verbal responses. Since the stages of the development of understanding are not directly observable, we adopted a different approach from the production scale. A series of instructions of increasing grammatical complexity were given. Each instruction required the child to do a simple task without any equipment. The items of the scale, in the order they appeared on the questionnaire, were:

1. Does the child respond to sounds (for example, loud noise, banging door)?
2. Does the child respond to teacher's (or parent's) voice?
3. Does the child respond to his own name?
4. Does the child respond to a name other than his own?
5. Show me your hands
6. Lift your leg up
7. Touch both eyes
8. Stand up and put your hands behind your back
9. Put your feet together
10. Go to the door but don't open it
11. Clap your hands, touch your shoes and wave bye-bye
12. Nod your head, touch your knees and fold your arms
13. Touch the back of your chair with the hand that is on the table.

The scale measures understanding at two levels. It tests the child's knowledge of the words used and his understanding of the grammatical structure of the instructions. To accommodate children who would be unlikely to respond to any instruction, the first four questions were inserted, dealing with the initial prerequisites of understanding. (Question 4 was included as a check against question 3. If a child responded to another name, not merely out of curiosity, the tick on question 3 was cancelled.)

As with the production scale, these items could not safely be used as teaching objectives (with the possible exception of the first three) but they demonstrate abilities we may wish the children to acquire. Making demands such as these on a child points up where performance problems may lie. For example, many children pass the one- and two-part instructions but fail the three-part instructions, suggesting the need for a programme designed to teach just that skill. Assessment of this nature is useful in a general placement of the child, but a much more detailed assessment would be needed to find the right point at which to start teaching.

ARTICULATION SCALE

Here we were interested only in the clarity of speech irrespective of what was said. If the child had not begun to speak single words, he was not assessed on this scale. The scale was divided into two parts: first, the clarity of speech was assessed by the teacher; and secondly, the clarity of speech addressed to someone not normally in contact with the child was assessed. The layout of the two parts was identical, giving four levels of clarity of speech, only one of which could be scored in each part. These were:

1 Unintelligible
2 Mostly unintelligible
3 Mostly intelligible
4 Intelligible

Since learning language depends upon gaining responses from other people, a child who cannot make himself understood suffers many handicaps. If his parents and teachers cannot understand him and are unable to respond appropriately, the situation not only induces frustration but also undermines social relationships.

GESTURE SCALE

In *The Psychology of Interpersonal Behaviour*[7] Michael Argyle suggests that we use non-verbal communication for three main purposes: to communicate attitudes and emotions, to support verbal communication and to replace speech. All three must be considered in the subnormal child's communicative abilities, but the third is probably the most important, and work is currently being carried out in a number of places on teaching non-verbal systems of communication to subnormal children. (The project's work in this field is described in Chapter VII.)

We were interested both in the child's use of gesture as a replacement for speech, and in his own individual uses of communicative gesture. The scale consisted of five questions:

1 Does the child use only gesture to communicate without vocalization?
2 Does the child use gesture to augment inadequate speech?
3 Does the child tend to use gesture in situations where he could use speech?
4 Does the child combine only natural use of gesture with adequate language?
5 Is the child's use of gesture: **i** more primitive, for example, pointing; **ii** more sophisticated, for example, mime.

English Picture Vocabulary Test

This standardized test was originally devised for normal children. It is, however, used frequently with subnormal children in research as well as in the applied field. In the survey the pre-school version was used, intended originally for normal children aged 3:0 to 4:11. The test comprises forty items, each one consisting of four simple line-drawings. One of these illustrates a particular word – the 'target' word. The tester says this word in the sentence 'Show me . . .', without any prompts or hints. The child must then point to the picture representing the word. The test takes only a few minutes to administer to each child.

In the past, claims have been made for this test as a measure of general mental ability, or general verbal ability, but later research suggests that English Picture Vocabulary Test (EPVT) results must be interpreted with caution, particularly with subnormal children. All we can say with confidence is that it is a measure of receptive vocabulary.

Organization of survey

The survey was administered between October and December 1973. Class teachers filled in all the forms for each of their own children. In each school a group discussion lasting about half an hour was held with all the staff who would be filling in the forms. The aims of the survey were outlined and discussed, and the various forms mentioned briefly. Following this, each member of staff completing the forms was visited by one member of the project team for a further half-hour, when the detailed administration of the language questionnaire, EPVT and the personal information questionnaire was explained and usually demonstrated. To ensure that this procedure was, as near as possible, the same for all teachers, team members worked from a previously prepared, detailed form stating all the points to be covered. Finally, the teachers were given a summary sheet intended as an aide-mémoire and were asked to contact the project team for further clarification if necessary.

The individual session with teachers

With the language questionnaire each scale and what it attempted to assess was considered, and each question discussed in detail. The major problem mentioned with the production scale related to children described as 'echolalic', or those whose language seemed highly erratic and unsystematic. In these cases we asked for the child to be scored on items most representative of his production at that time. Thus, uncommon constructions could be discounted if the teacher felt that they did not represent the child's usual performance. On the articulation scale, in the assessment of clarity of speech to people not normally in contact with the child, the teacher had two options. She could herself assess how clear the child's speech would be to someone else or she could bring someone else into the classroom (possibly a dinner lady or a visitor) so that the assessment could be direct. The reception scale entailed more explanation and discussion than the others since it was vital that the 'setting conditions' for the nine instructions (**5** to **13**) should be as similar as possible for all children. For all items the instruction could be repeated once if the child made no response the first time. If no response followed this repetition, then the next item should be presented. Items **1** to **4** did not need to be formally tested, except in cases of doubt. The purpose of item **4** was explained and the testing conditions printed opposite – that the name should be called out while the child was engrossed in an activity, with his back turned – were emphasized.

Teachers were asked to attempt items **5** to **13** with every child who passed items **1** to **3**. The importance of avoiding facial, gestural and situational hints, such as eye pointing or slight movements of the hand, was strongly emphasized. Children were not to begin any actions until the complete instruction had been presented. If the child began to respond before the teacher had finished speaking, the teacher was instructed to stop, ask the child to wait, or hold the child's hands, and repeat the full instruction. Every teacher completed this scale with one child during the session.

Depending upon when the initial visit occurred, the schools had between four and seven weeks to complete the forms. These were then collected by one member of the team who visited each class separately to discuss any problems which might have arisen.

Scoring of language questionnaire and EPVT

The usual practice of summing the correct responses to form a total raw score was used with EPVT and with the reception scale. However this could not be done with the production scale or with the gesture scale. The major score on the production scale assumed items in developmental order numbered from **1** to **12**. A child's score was the highest item he was ticked for, irrespective of ticks on items below that. The gesture scale was left unchanged and examined as four separate items. Scores on the articulation

18 SURVEY OF LANGUAGE ABILITIES

scale (both 'teacher' and 'other') were formed by scoring the four categories as follows:

Unintelligible = 1
Mostly unintelligible = 2
Mostly intelligible = 3
Intelligible = 4

The total score for the reception scale was formed by summing the correct responses, with the one exception that if a child was ticked for item **4** (the check item) as well as item **3**, the tick on item **3** was cancelled. With EPVT, if a child failed to start the test or get beyond the three practice items, he was scored as untestable. Raw scores between 8 and 27 can be converted into vocabulary-age scores varying between 3:0 and 4:11. But since using the vocabulary-age score considerably restricts the number of children who can be examined on EPVT (from 908 to 379), most of the analyses use the raw score.

Results of language questionnaire and EPVT

PRODUCTION SCALE

Using the 'highest item' score, the sample falls neatly into three approximately equal groups: 31·4 per cent are scored as using grammatical sentences (item **12**), 33·5 per cent are scored as imitating single words or at a lower level (items **0** to **6**), and 35·0 per cent fall between these two groups (items **7** to **11**). The results are shown in Table 2.

It is encouraging that nearly a third of the children are scored as using grammatical sentences, though this does not necessarily reflect a consistent, well-developed or appropriate grammatical system.

The figures discussed give preliminary estimates of the time and effort that will have to be devoted to developing the various parts of the curriculum. At the lower end there is a third of the entire sample not yet producing single words, and just over a quarter (26·5 per cent) not even imitating words. Moreover, this percentage does not decrease with age. These children will undoubtedly be able to communicate to a certain extent non-verbally and vocally but this result suggests that some of our efforts must be devoted to opening up other communicative media, possibly non-verbal (see Chapter VII). At the other end of the scale, we must not neglect that third of the children who have reached a degree of grammatical competence. It is at this stage that teaching children what to do with language can

Table 2 Frequency distribution of 'highest item' on production scale scores

Score	Frequency	%
0	40	3·0
1	110	8·1
2	69	5·1
3	24	1·8
4	59	4·4
5	56	4·1
6	95	7·0
7	80	5·9
8	61	4·5
9	52	3·8
10	91	6·7
11	191	14·1
12	424	31·4
Total	1352	99·9

begin. Teaching language is clearly much more than teaching an isolated system – we need to teach children to use language for thinking, acting and informing. Chapter VIII explores some of these possibilities.

The amount of variation demonstrated in the children's productive language points to the need to be aware of the effect of other factors in the context of language, and equally to the need to provide a variety of contexts in which a particular objective can be taught. We need to be wary of assuming that if a child can say 'all gone' he can also say 'more drink' or even 'doggie gone'.

RECEPTION SCALE

The figures in Table 3 show that 8·6 per cent of the children failed at the most basic level of understanding – responding in any way to any sound. The percentage who failed to respond to the teacher's voice is only slightly larger, which suggests that if children are responsive to any sounds then they are responsive to voice sounds. On item **3**, 13·7 per cent failed to respond to their own name and, if the check item **4** is taken into account, an additional 9·4 per cent failed to differentiate their own from other names. The remaining items on the scale, on which 30·6 per cent failed to score at all, fall into two groups. Items **5** to **10** constitute a simpler set of instructions without complicated structure or meaning, and were passed by 44·2 to 61·4 per cent of the children. A large gap separates these items from the final three items, which were passed by under 23 per cent of the children.

Table 3 Frequency and percentage passing and failing items on the reception scale

Item	Pass		Fail	
	Frequency	%	Frequency	%
1 Does the child respond to sounds?	1238	91·4	116	8·6
2 Does the child respond to teacher's voice?	1232	91·0	122	9·0
3 Does the child respond to his own name?	1169	86·3	185	13·7
5 Show me your hands	766	56·6	588	43·4
6 Lift your leg up	832	61·4	522	38·6
7 Touch both eyes	677	50·0	677	50·0
8 Put your hands behind your back	616	45·5	738	54·5
9 Put your feet together	599	44·2	755	55·8
10 Go to the door but don't open it	653	48·2	701	51·8
11 Clap your hands, touch your shoes and wave bye-bye	285	21·0	1069	79·0
12 Nod your head, touch your knees and fold your arms	238	17·6	1116	82·4
13 Touch the back of your chair with the hand that is on the table	301	22·2	1053	77·8

Results for the first three items have the clearest implications for the curriculum. Children failing these present considerable teaching difficulties, since it is impossible to gain their attention by calling their names. Programmes designed simply to teach an orienting response to the child's name would certainly pay dividends for this group.

As discussed earlier, this scale cannot be looked on as a set of educational objectives, but ability levels on it indicate that the skills which go to make up adequate performance need to be taught directly. The particular skills necessary for an individual child would be selected by more detailed observation and assessment.

ARTICULATION SCALE

Since a number of children were scored on this scale who scored below the one-word imitation level on the production scale, and a further number who scored above this level on the production scale were not scored for articulation, the figures were adjusted so that the former group were placed in a 'not tested' category and the latter group in a 'missing information' category. The final percentages are shown in Table 4. Of those children at or beyond the one-word imitation level, a fifth were mostly or wholly unintelligible to their teachers, and well over a quarter were mostly or wholly unintelligible to people not normally in contact with them. Care must be taken with these figures, however, as we do not know where the children not tested fall on the scale. Nevertheless the figures suggest that articulation presents a large problem for a sizable proportion of severely mentally handicapped children, and time needs to be devoted to this particular area, one of the more highly developed areas from the teaching point of view.

Table 4 Frequency and percentage distribution of articulation scales (recoded)

Level	Articulation – teacher		Articulation – other	
	Frequency	%	Frequency	%
Unintelligible	77	5·9	136	10·7
Mostly unintelligible	179	13·6	216	17·0
Mostly intelligible	391	29·8	317	25·0
Intelligible	309	23·5	242	19·1
(Not tested)	(358)	(27·2)	(358)	(28·2)
Total	1314	100·0	1269	100·0
Missing	67	–	112	–

GESTURE SCALE

A significant proportion of the children were also not scored on this scale – 34·6 per cent on part I and 33 per cent on part II, so again results need to be interpreted with care. Assuming the group not scored is a random selection of children, the results shown in Table 5 have interesting implications for curriculum development. On the first item, 18·9 per cent were scored as using only gesture to communicate, and these children form the group for whom questions must be raised about extending their non-verbal means of communication rather than trying to institute a new verbal medium. Children scored on this item fall much lower than other children on the production and reception scales.

The 15·1 per cent of children whose teachers judged them to use gesture in preference to language highlight one danger here – that an individual and limited communication system may hinder the development of a much broader and more efficient system such as language, due to the short-term success of the non-verbal system. In many cases it may be easier to support and encourage non-verbal communication than to initiate imperfect attempts at language. Nevertheless, children scored on this item scored significantly higher on the production scale than others.

Table 5 Frequency and percentage scored and not scored on the gesture scale (scoring indicates a positive response)

Part I
(478 (34·6%) not scored on any item)

Item	Not scored Frequency	%	Scored Frequency	%
1 Does the child use only gesture to communicate without vocalization?	732	81·1	171	18·9
2 Does the child use gesture to augment inadequate speech?	594	65·8	309	34·2
3 Does the child tend to use gesture in situations where he could use speech?	767	84·7	136	15·1
4 Does the child combine only natural use of gesture with adequate language?	546	60·5	357	39·5

Part II

Is the child's use of gesture:				
more primitive?	447	33·0	610	45·1
more sophisticated?			296	21·9

ENGLISH PICTURE VOCABULARY TEST

Of the whole sample 29·8 per cent were untestable on this test. This group consists of children physically unable to point and children who do not have the necessary skills to link pictures and words, or make a choice, even though they can point. Of those who scored on the test, 40·2 per cent fell within the age norms (3:0 to 4:11); 30·1 per cent scored below this range (a raw score of less than 8); and 29·8 per cent scored above this age-range (raw score of more than 27). (See Appendix A, Table A3.)

Language abilities and age

One of the major interests of the survey was to examine the relationships between chronological age and the growth of language ability. Since one major aim of education in general is to produce growth in skills and abilities over age, this problem becomes crucial to the development of a curriculum in schools for the ESN(S) child. If a normal adolescent emerges from secondary school aged 16 without being able to read, we think he has not learned or that the educational system has failed. If a child learns to read more rapidly than is expected, we may think he is intelligent and that the educational system has succeeded. But we also know that normal children develop certain skills irrespective of whether they go to school or not: some skills, such as visual perception, develop with a minimum of assistance from other sources; other skills, such as feeding and toileting, involve some degree of help and teaching by adults. The educational system aims to provide skills such as literacy and numeracy which might not otherwise develop.

The problem is much more complicated in the case of mentally handicapped children. In the first place, the physical markers of age are often missing or distorted, so that a 15-year-old may look like an 8-year-old, or may be so restricted in his ability to move or walk that his experiences correspond to those of a much younger child. Severe physical handicap or gross immaturity of size or development may lead to his mental abilities being underestimated, at least in his earliest years, thus depriving him of important learning experiences.

Secondly, neither research nor experience suggests a clear, predictable relationship between the age of the mentally handicapped child and the development of specific skills or abilities. One study[8] suggested that the average level of development and mental age of a group of 14- and 15-year-old school-leavers from the former Junior Training Centres corresponded to the 5- to 6-year-old level for normal children on a variety of tests and measures. But this study could say nothing about the age at which specific skills first appeared in these children. Beyond knowing that the age of a mentally handicapped child is a poor guide to his likely level of language development, we have little precise information about the rate at which language skills develop. It is therefore relevant to ask what level of language a child has reached when he comes to school, what level of language he leaves with, and at what age the various skills develop.

SURVEY OF LANGUAGE ABILITIES

PRODUCTION SCALE

The format of this scale makes it impossible to state precisely when a particular stage was reached, so figures are expressed in terms of the percentage who are at or beyond a certain stage or, conversely, the percentage who have not yet reached a certain stage. Figure 1 shows the percentages at or beyond three crucial stages of productive language development – one-word utterances, two-word utterances and grammatical sentences (items 7, 9 and 12) – broken down into year-groups. In all three cases we find significant increases between ages 3 and 4 followed by a significant increase over two years from 4 to 6. Patterns for the three behaviours then diverge slightly. There is no significant increase in the proportion of children at or beyond the one-word level until the age of 16, and this is completely accounted for by the increase from 15 to 16. Two-word utterances show no significant rise until the age of 11, most of which is explained by the rise between 9 and 11, suggesting little or no growth occurs between 6 and 9. Beyond 11, the proportion at or beyond this level does not increase significantly until 15. The pattern for grammatical sentences is almost identical to that for two-word utterances, with the exception that the plateau from 6 extends to 10 with a significant rise between 10 and 11, but again no significant increase occurs beyond 11 until 15. In general, the closely comparable slopes between 15 and 16 years are suggestive of a general trend towards an increase at this age.

Despite slight differences, figures for the three productive language behaviours are surprisingly similar. It appears that certain ages are associated with considerable growth in these behaviours, while others are not. The 3–6 age-group is marked in all cases by significant increases in percentages reaching a given stage; to a lesser extent the same applies to the 9–11 age-group. The middle years of childhood and the 11–15 age-group reflect very little growth. Particularly alarming is the finding that the proportion of children not yet uttering single words does not progressively diminish between the ages of 6 and 16. Furthermore, none of these skills shows a significant increase between 11 and 15.

Other aspects of the results are highlighted by comparing the percentages of the children at 3 or less and at 16+ who have reached these three landmarks of development. It is encouraging that 37·1 per cent of the youngest age-group (seventy children) were already at or beyond the one-word stage; 21·4 per cent had reached the two-word stage; and even three children (4·3 per cent) were scored as using grammatical sentences. On the other hand, of the forty children aged 16+, 42·5 per cent did not possess the

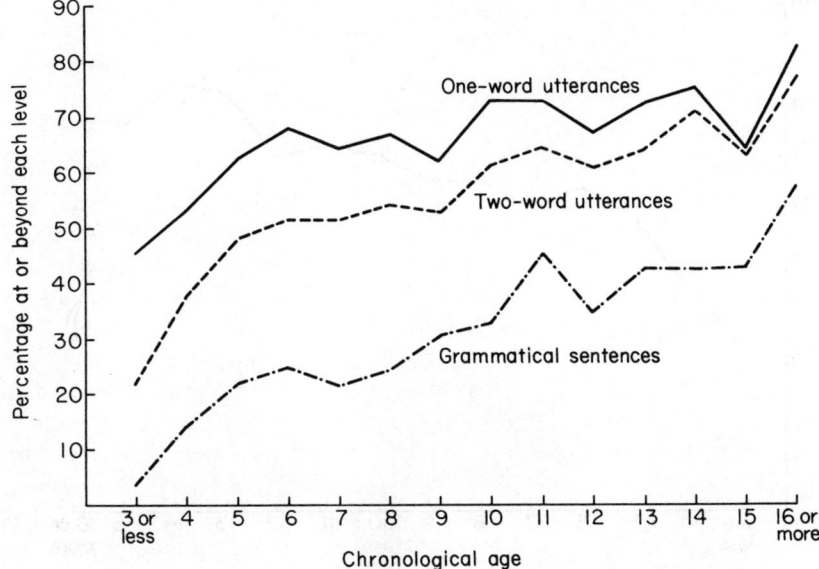

Fig. 1 Three levels of productive language ability by age

ability to use grammatical constructions; 22·4 per cent did not use two-word constructions; and 17·5 per cent were at the pre-one-word stage. Our results suggest that many of this group are leaving school ill-equipped with the language ability needed to cope with a complex environment.

RECEPTION SCALE

Figure 2 shows the growth in average reception-scale score over age. Despite differences in the format of the two scales, the reception scale shows a very similar pattern of growth to the three items of the production scale already discussed: sharp increases from 3 to 6 followed by a plateau through the middle years and, in this case, increasing in the 12–14 age-group. Results for the reception scale are less simple to interpret, since they do not refer directly to major stages of development, but the similarity of the pattern to that of the production scale supports the general trend that has been established.

The data suggest that scores on this scale may be interpreted as follows: if a child scores 5 he passes the first five items and fails the rest; if a child scores 8 he passes the first eight items and fails the final four items, etc. In this

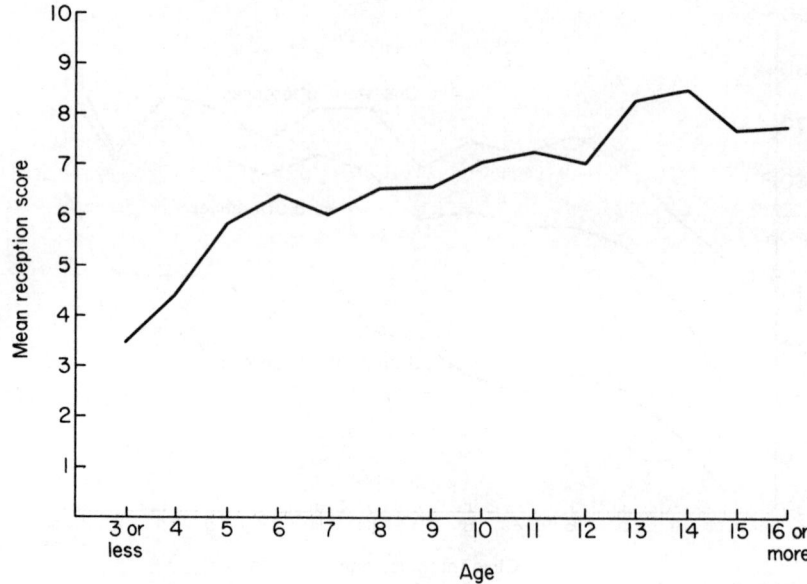

Fig. 2 Mean reception score by age ($N = 1355$)

case, then we can make certain statements about the level of receptive language in certain age-groups with respect to the twelve reception-scale items (omitting the check item **4**). The average number of items passed (out of twelve) rises from 3·5 at age 3 or less to 8·1 at age 16+.

This means that the 'average' 16-year-old can respond appropriately to items **9** and **10** but experiences difficulty with three-part instructions such as items **11** and **12**, and complicated grammatical constructions, such as item **13**.

ENGLISH PICTURE VOCABULARY TEST

Inspection of Figure 3, showing the average EPVT raw score for each age, suggests a much smoother and more gradual progression than that reflected in the production and reception scales. There is a pronounced increase between the ages of 4 and 5, slow but smooth improvement from 6 to 10, followed by a sharper rise to 11. Unlike the production and reception scales the graph shows a plateau from 14 to 16.

The availability of test norms allows the EPVT results to be expressed in terms of vocabulary ages, based on the performance of normal children, though only limited conclusions can be drawn from these figures. In the first place, only 908 of the sample of 1381 were testable on EPVT; secondly, as pointed out earlier, vocabulary age should not be confused with mental age. It can be regarded here only as a measure of the child's ability to respond by attending, scanning the pictures, listening to the test word and pointing to the appropriate picture from a choice of four. Translating *average* raw scores into *average* vocabulary ages, the average vocabulary age for the 16+ group is around 4:7 to 4:8 and that of the 10-year-old group, around 3:8 to 3:9. The average for the 3- to 4-year-olds fall below the test norms. (See Appendix A, Table A3.)

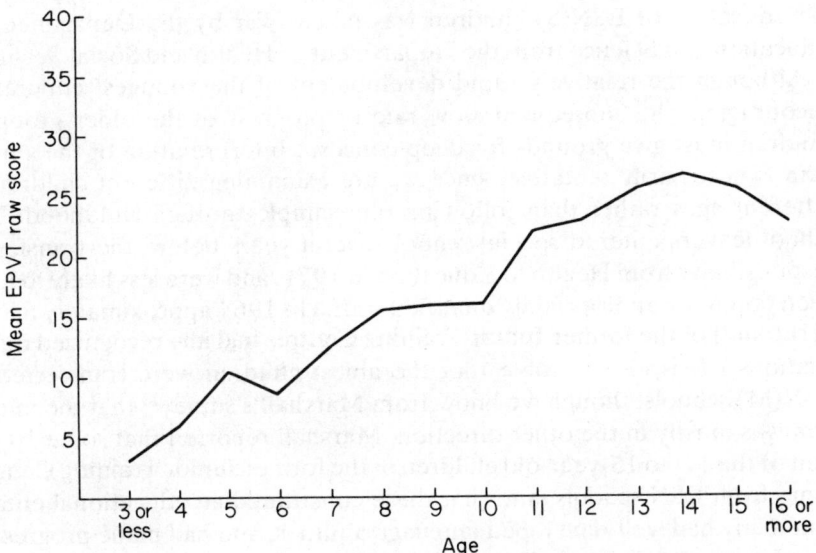

Fig. 3   Mean English Picture Vocabulary Test (EPVT) raw score by age ($N = 908$)

These results reflect grounds for both pessimism and optimism. On the positive side, there is the relatively rapid growth of certain language abilities of children between 3 and 6, though the reasons are largely speculative. It may be due in part to a more active teaching approach by parents of the youngest children compared with parents of older children. Support for such a trend can be found in the work of Cunningham[9] who reported that a small sample of Down's Syndrome babies showed slightly faster rates of growth on the Bayley Mental and Motor Scales[10] than a comparable sample studied by Carr[11] in the mid-1960s. Similar findings to our own have also been reported with a group of 150 mentally handicapped children under 5 years old in the north-west of England.[12] Parental assessment carried out on specially prepared development charts reflected substantial rises in the proportion of children attaining specific skills between the ages of 3 and 5.

Apart from the element of greater parental involvement, children who reach special schools before the age of 5 are possibly those who are relatively competent and therefore likely to make the most progress; similarly, their parents may have pressed more energetically for early admission to special schools. It could also be argued that the youngest children are benefiting most – and at a most important stage of their development – from the many changes introduced into ESN(S) schools since 1971, when responsiblity for the education of ESN(S) children was taken over by the Department of Education and Science from the Department of Health and Social Security.

Although the relatively rapid development of the youngest children is encouraging, the subsequent slow rate of progress of the older group of children must give grounds for deep concern. Interpretation of the survey data is necessarily tentative, since we are examining different children at different ages rather than following one sample through childhood. The school-leavers entered special school several years before the transfer of responsibility from Health to Education in 1971, and were less likely to have been taught by appropriately qualified staff. (In 1964 approximately a third of the staff of the former Junior Training Centres had any recognized qualifications.) It is also possible that the ablest children were transferred to ESN(M) schools, though we know from Marshall's survey[13] that the migration was mostly in the other direction. Marshall reported that some 10 per cent of the 14- to 15-year-old children in the former Junior Training Centres came from ESN schools, and that these constituted an educational elite in that many had well-developed language abilities, and had made progress in learning to read. It is equally possible that due to the difficulties of assessing very young children for placement, the nursery age-group would be more varied in composition until more accurate assessment and placement was possible. This would tend to boost the level of ability of this group relative to older children.

Whatever the explanation that might be advanced, we have no reason to believe that any of these factors is significant enough to affect our basic findings which suggest that the large gains shown by children in the early years of school are not sustained, that the period between the age of 6 and school-leaving is one of extremely slow growth in the language behaviours we have examined, and that the final levels reached by many of the children leaving school at 16+ are low.

Language abilities and identifiable groups

Detailed observation of the individual child is the only adequate answer to finding out about that child and designing learning programmes for him. However, in so far as generalizations can be made about mentally handicapped children, it is useful for the teacher to know about them as a back-up to individual cases. Although the personal information questionnaire gave much information about the variables which may be studied in relation to language, it is important to realize that the establishment of a relationship does not allow causal inferences, nor does it allow an estimate of the direction of effect. For example, evidence presented below shows that children in hospital schools are significantly less able in language than other children. We might conclude that the hospital environment has led to this difference, but this might be false since we do not know whether the children admitted to hospital are a representative group of ESN(S) children. Some have behaviour disorders or have caused so many problems that the parents have felt unable to cope with them at home. Others may be less able in the first place. One must also be aware of the size of the differences between particular groups. With a sample as large as this one it is not difficult to find significant differences. However, it is the *size* of these differences that is most important in assessing any educational implications. A difference of less than one point on a scale hardly suggests that it deserves major consideration.

SEX DIFFERENCES

Results on sex differences (see Appendix A, Table A4) were slightly contradictory. There was a significant difference in favour of boys on EPVT; the average EPVT raw score for boys was 18·6 compared to 16·9 for girls. But there was a significant difference in favour of girls with the production scale, on which the average score for boys was 7·9 and for girls was 8·5; there was no significant difference on the reception scale.

The difference between boys and girls on the production scale is in line with the often held view that normal girls are superior to boys in all aspects of language development. However, this difference should not be exaggerated; girls appear to start talking earlier and to be more fluent in their use of language, but a detailed examination of a large number of language abilities (for example, by Templin[14]) indicates that such differences are rarely statistically significant. In fact the difference in favour of boys on EPVT agrees with the figures reported for the standardization sample of that test, and a number of other findings with various tests of oral comprehension.

Generally, however, the differences between sexes that have emerged from the survey are slight and do not have any obvious educational implications.

DOWN'S SYNDROME

The small numbers in most diagnostic groups meant that the only category we could safely examine is Down's Syndrome, which represents 34·3 per cent of the total (see Appendix A, Table A5). There was a large difference in favour of non-Down's Syndrome children on EPVT, which contrasts with smaller differences in favour of Down's Syndrome children on the production and reception scales. The average EPVT raw scores were 15·8 and 19·3 for Down's Syndrome and non-Down's Syndrome children respectively. For the production scale the figures were (in the same order) 8·8 and 7·8; and for the reception scale 6·6 and 6·1. The difference on EPVT is mitigated by the fact that only 21·2 per cent of Down's Syndrome children were untestable, compared to 54·3 per cent of non-Down's Syndrome children, indicating that the Down's Syndrome children tend to lie less at the extreme of the scale. The contradiction between the scales is therefore less than might at first appear.

The results in part confirm similar studies indicating that Down's Syndrome children tend to be relatively more impaired in language development than other ESN(S) children, but the impairment is far from uniform. It should also be remembered that non-Down's Syndrome children are relatively a more heterogeneous group containing a much wider spread of ability.

RESIDENTIAL CARE

The sample slightly under-represented hospital children compared to the national statistics. The group of children in other forms of care form a much smaller proportion, for whom we have no directly comparable figures. This group is made up of some children permanently in hostels (some of which are attached to schools) or group homes, and some children on a system of 'rotating care'. These children generally spend one week a month in a hostel to relieve their parents.

As expected, the hospital children scored noticeably lower on EPVT and the production and reception scales. However, there were no such differences between children living at home and those permanently in hostels or in other forms of care. Hostel children actually scored higher on EPVT than those living at home. The findings for hospital children are not unexpected, but the lack of difference between hostel children and children living at home is of great interest. Children who can no longer be looked after at home may be initially more severely handicapped, with the result that their language levels are lower. But it has also been shown that a hospital environment is in many ways unfavourable to language development, and more progress is made by children who remain at home.[15] The present results indicate that the scores of children in hostels are similar to those who live at home. We cannot be sure that the selection factor has been removed entirely, since it is possible that hostel children are less handicapped and less disturbed in behaviour than those in hospital. It is likely, too, that the hospital children have been in that environment for longer, on average, than the hostel children. The results suggest that a more detailed examination is needed of differences in environment between hostels and hospitals and also differences in the children being admitted. (See Appendix A, Table A6.)

FAMILY BACKGROUND

Significant differences between children in two-parent families and other children in language abilities were not found with EPVT or the production and reception scales. (See Appendix A, Table A7.) A further breakdown into smaller, more specific groups of children living with adoptive parents, foster parents, one natural parent, etc., again failed to reveal any significant difference. The lack of a difference does not, of course, mean that the parental background of one child should be ignored as a determinant of language ability. Specific situations may produce specific results which would not be revealed in a large-scale survey.

FAMILY SIZE

Our findings on the relationship between language ability and family size contradict all research with normal children, which has established that the larger the number of siblings the child has, the lower his language abilities. Instead, the production and reception scale average scores showed a gradual *rise* from the only child group to the four-sibling group, followed by a lower average for those children with five or more siblings. This overall trend was statistically significant in both cases. The EPVT scores showed a similar trend, but the differences were smaller and not statistically significant. (See Appendix A, Table A8.)

The explanation can only be speculative at this stage. One possibility is that a number of siblings (between one and four) might be beneficial in providing more opportunities for social interaction, but that this benefit would be cancelled out by lack of attention as the number of siblings rose above four. The difference between EPVT and the questionnaire scales is also interesting. The questionnaire scales involve a lot more social interaction than EPVT, and to an extent must measure this aspect of language, whereas EPVT is concerned much more with the cognitive aspects of language development. This distinction is an important one which needs to be understood and accounted for in teaching. A child who uses language well for interacting does not necessarily use it well for thinking or directing behaviour. These problems are discussed in more depth in Chapter IV.

SOCIAL CLASS

The distribution of social class in the children for whom we had information corresponded closely to that found in the normal population, with a minor bias towards social class I and away from social class IV. (See Appendix A, Table A2.) In this respect ESN(S) children differ markedly from ESN(M) children who come predominantly from social classes IV and V, and who tend to be handicapped by adverse environmental conditions, poverty, overcrowding and poor housing, parental unemployment and ill health.

Our results showed no connexion between social class and language ability as measured by the production and reception scales and EPVT. (See Appendix A, Table A9.) This finding is perhaps the most interesting of those reported in this section, since it contrasts so strongly with the results reported on normal children. It supports the argument that ESN(S) children may be generally less responsive to grosser variations in the environment, and that they may not benefit from the advantages of a middle-class home to the extent that normal children appear to do. The absence of a social-class effect on the language development of ESN(S) children suggests that the teacher cannot automatically expect that a child from a middle-class home will do better than a working-class child.

This section has been concerned with the possible relationship between language development and certain more or less objective variables. These are obviously not the main or sole determinants of language development, but some of them have been shown to be of some importance in normal children, and for this reason we judged it valuable to look for similar influences in our sample of mentally handicapped children.

The results yielded averages that inevitably hide large variations within groups; and two groups may have different average scores on a scale, but in practice there will be a great deal of overlap between members of one group and another. Nevertheless the results are useful if they draw attention to marked differences between groups, and also if they fail to demonstrate expected differences. This type of information is useful background information collected on a large number of children, but the teacher must beware of expecting any single child to behave in a way which is typical of his group.

The survey as an assessment technique

The fact that teachers carried out the assessment for the survey reflects a more general trend towards a re-examination of the functions of assessment in education. If assessment is to become part of teaching, the teacher should play a key part. This has rarely been the case, with the result that the educational aspects of assessment have often been secondary to other considerations. For many years, the teaching profession delegated to doctors the task of deciding whether a child was 'educable' or whether he should be excluded from the school system as 'ineducable' (pre-1959) or as 'unsuitable for education in school' (1959–71).

Psychologists too must accept their share of the blame for allowing assessment to become divorced from the aims and objectives of education. While intelligence tests may be of administrative value, they are of little direct use to the teacher in planning a programme suited to the child's specific needs. The conventional intelligence test does not yield enough information about a child's strengths and weaknesses to provide a foundation for the design of a programme of individual teaching. Most psychologists are now well aware of the shortcomings of intelligence tests for handicapped children, and many of them are working hard to devise new and more relevant assessment techniques, such as the British Ability Scales.[16]

More relevant in the present context is the suggestion that psychologists should give up their traditional monopoly of assessment, and that teachers and other practitioners should learn to use certain methods of assessment to a greater extent than they do at present. This is not to deny that the administration and interpretation of psychological tests require training and experience, but there is no reason why teachers should not learn these skills. It is the role of the psychologist to take the initiative to help them to do so. If psychologists could be freed of much of the assessment that only they carry out at present, they would be able to act as consultants and specialists and deploy their limited time more effectively.

It has also been suggested that each special school should include on its staff a specialist teacher trained in the use of assessment procedures. Her task would be to help colleagues to develop and use appropriate methods of assessment and to link these to the design of remedial programmes based on the needs of the individual child. Such 'floating' teachers without a class of their own can be an invaluable resource in the school.

In later chapters we argue that assessment and teaching are two completely interdependent aspects of one process, and that the teacher is in effect assessing whenever she is teaching. Teachers therefore need to acquire skills involved in assessing children in order to plan teaching programmes adequately. Initial assessment might usefully be seen as a process of narrowing down the possible teaching objectives to one suitable one. In this process, instruments such as the language questionnaire provide a valuable starting-point. Having assessed the child's general level of ability on a particular scale, further observations using techniques such as those discussed in Chapter V can lead to pinpointing appropriate teaching objectives.

The survey as a guide to curriculum planning

The main aim in the survey was to gain knowledge about the range and development of language abilities in a large group of mentally handicapped children. In so far as this sample of children is representative, it is useful to generalize to the national population of ESN(S) children. The latest figures from the Department of Education and Science[17] put the total number of ESN(S) children in both day and hospital schools as around 35 000. Using our sample figures of percentages at different stages of productive language ability, we have an estimated 11 000 children (31·4 per cent) using grammatical sentences, and approximately 12 000 (33·5 per cent) not yet producing single words. More interesting are the estimated numbers in these categories in the school-leaving group – those aged 16+ – a total of about 2400. The results suggest that in any one year just over a thousand children (42·5 per cent) reached this age without using grammatical constructions, and over 400 ESN(S) children aged 16+ cannot yet produce single words.

Turning to receptive language, our survey indicates that 3000 children (8·6 per cent) in any year are not yet able to respond to any sound at all and 4800 (13·7 per cent) fail to respond to their own names. With regard to articulation, the survey predicts that nationally, of those children who have reached or passed the stage of producing single words, some 5800 (27·7 per cent) are wholly or mostly unintelligible to their teachers.

In our subsequent work we tried to reflect the whole range of abilities present in the schools. In Chapter V, some techniques are discussed which are especially relevant to profoundly handicapped children, while Chapter VII looks at the problems of teaching non-verbal methods of communication to children low in ability, many of whom are in special-care classes. Chapter VI looks at the teaching of single-word vocabulary; Chapter VIII discusses methods which are appropriate to those children who have already developed some grammatical structure. In none of these cases have we produced a complete curriculum but have simply opened up a number of possibilities.

The survey results suggest that, for many of the children, the educational system is not at present producing steady increments in ability in one of the most important areas of human development. Two possibilities may be put forward to explain this. The first is that the inherent characteristics of mentally handicapped children prevent any efforts at intervention from achieving success. The second is that what happens at present in schools for ESN(S) children is ineffective in bringing about growth.

There are two reasons why the first point is not a valid argument. One is practical, the other more philosophical. In the first place, it has been shown that, given the right conditions and techniques, severely subnormal children learn new behaviours, not just in the field of language, but in many areas. Secondly, arguing that the ESN(S) child's inherent characteristics prevent him from learning is to throw the onus of failure on to the child. If teaching is ineffective, it is the job of teachers and educationists to modify their approaches until it becomes effective.

In many ways the results of the survey should not surprise us, since this project has been one of the first curriculum development projects on this scale for ESN(S) children in western Europe, while normal education has had such studies dating back to ancient Greece. We are not so much advocating our approach to education as the adoption of any approach that is systematic. Teachers have in the past been forced to borrow methods where they could, with the result that most of the teaching that now goes on has little coherent base in theory, nor was it specifically designed to meet the needs of mentally handicapped children.

The aim in the chapters that follow is to lay some foundations on which teachers may build in ways which best meet the needs of their particular children. Each child's needs will be different.

Summary

This chapter gives some of the results of a survey of the language abilities of 1381 pupils attending nineteen schools for severely educationally subnormal children in the Cheshire and Manchester areas. All teachers in the nineteen project schools assessed the children in their class, using a specially devised language questionnaire, as well as a standardized test of receptive vocabulary. In addition, teachers completed a basic information sheet about each child in their class. As far as we know, this is the first large-scale survey of its kind; it is presented here to act as a basis for later discussions about the development of language and communication curricula for mentally handicapped children.

BASIC DATA

1 The average number of children per school was 74, the number of children in each class ranging between 7 and 14. The average teacher/pupil ratio was 1:8·9; and the ratio of nursery and welfare assistants was 1:10. Eighty-one per cent of the children were living at home, 11·2 per cent in long-stay hospitals and 7·8 per cent were in other forms of care. The ratio of boys to girls was 59:41.
2 The biggest single diagnostic category was Down's Syndrome (34·3 per cent); 40·2 per cent of the children were not classified as belonging to any single clinical group.
3 The social class distribution of the children was broadly comparable to the national norms, though this information was available for only one-third of the sample.

LANGUAGE DATA

1 *Language production.* Approximately one-third of the children were rated by their teachers as using fully grammatical sentences, a further third were at or below the level of imitating single words, and the remaining third were intermediate.
2 *Language reception.* About a quarter of the total sample failed to respond reliably when teachers tried to gain their attention by calling their name or by making sounds. Items requiring comprehension of simple instructions were passed by 44·2 to 61·4 per cent of the children; less than a quarter were able to demonstrate comprehension of more complex language instructions.
3 *Articulation.* Of those children who had started to develop speech, 19·5 per cent were unintelligible or mostly unintelligible to their teachers, and 27·7 per cent to people not normally in contact with them.
4 *Gesture.* Just under one-fifth of the children were scored as using only

gesture to communicate and 15·1 per cent as using gesture in preference to language.
5 *English Picture Vocabulary Test (EPVT)*. Of the whole sample 29·8 per cent were untestable on this measure; of the remainder, 40·2 per cent fell within the range of the test norms (corresponding to vocabulary ages between 3:0 and 4:11); 29·8 per cent scored above and 30·1 per cent below this range.

RELATIONSHIP BETWEEN LANGUAGE ABILITIES AND AGE

Comparing the proportion of children rated as reaching specific levels of language ability at each age, the following trends were apparent:

1 The youngest children – that is, those between 3 and 6 years of age – showed marked improvements, in so far as cross-sectional analysis of the data indicated that the proportion of children reaching given stages of development increased significantly during this period.
2 The period following the age of 6 is, however, characterized by very slow development; for example, the proportion of children who have not reached the one-word stage of production does not significantly diminish between 6 and 16.
3 Despite some evidence of a slight spurt just before school-leaving, 42·5 per cent of those aged 16+ could not use grammatical constructions; 22·4 per cent were not yet at the two-word stage, while 17·5 per cent were not yet at the one-word stage of development.
4 Similar trends were apparent in the reception scales: a period of initially rapid development from 3 to 6 years of age, followed by a plateau through the middle years, and some increase between 12 and 14.
5 The EPVT results show a smoother growth curve; nevertheless the average vocabulary age of the 16+ group (4:8) was only 11 months greater than that of the 10-year-olds (3:9).

OTHER GROUP DIFFERENCES

We compared the rated language abilities of various groups and sub-groups, with the following results:

1 There were no conclusive language differences between the sexes.
2 Children with Down's Syndrome on the whole performed at a lower level than other children, but the results are far from conclusive, and must be interpreted with caution.

3 Children in hospital schools performed significantly worse than those living at home or in hostels on all the measures.
4 There was no evidence of any social-class differential in this sample; children from all five social classes were shown as functioning at the same level, in marked contrast to studies of non-handicapped children.
5 Equally unexpected was the finding that children with more than one sibling (up to four) were rated higher than only children.

The significance of these findings for curriculum planning and development is discussed in the final section.

References

1. B. KELLETT, 'An initial survey of the language of ESN(S) children in Manchester: the results of a teachers' workshop', in P. Berry (ed.), *Language and Communication in the Mentally Handicapped*. Edward Arnold, 1976.
2. M. A. BRIMER and T. L. M. DUNN, *English Picture Vocabulary Test* 1. Educational Evaluation Enterprises, Bristol, 1962.
3. Department of Education and Science, *Statistics of Education 1974*, Vol. 1: Schools. HMSO, 1975.
4. J. M. HUGHES, 'The educational needs of the mentally handicapped', *Educational Research*, **17**, 1975, 228–33.
5. Registrar General, *Classification of Occupations and Directory of Occupational Titles*. HMSO, 1966.
6. LEWIS M. TERMAN and MAUD A. MERRILL, *Stanford–Binet Intelligence Scale*, Third Revision Form L–M. NFER Publishing, Windsor, 1960.
7. M. ARGYLE, *The Psychology of Interpersonal Behaviour*. Penguin Books, 1970.
8. A. MARSHALL, *The Abilities and Attainments of Children leaving Junior Training Centres*. National Association for Mental Health, 1967.
9. C. C. CUNNINGHAM, 'Parents as educators and therapists', in C.C. Kiernan and F. P. Woodford (eds), *Behaviour Modification with the Severely Retarded*. Associated Scientific Publishers, 1975.
10. N. BAYLEY, *Manual for the Bayley Scales of Infant Development*. Psychological Corporation, New York, 1969.
11. J. CARR, 'Mental and motor development in young mongol children', *Journal of Mental Deficiency Research*, **14**, 1970, 205–20.

12. D. M. JEFFREE and R. MCCONKEY, *PIP Development Charts*. Hodder & Stoughton Educational, Dunton Green, 1976.
13. MARSHALL, *The Abilities and Attainments of Children leaving Junior Training Centres*.
14. M. C. TEMPLIN, *Certain Language Skills in Children*. Minnesota University Press, Minneapolis, 1957.
15. P. MITTLER, 'Assessment of handicapped children: some common factors', in P. Mittler (ed.), *Psychological Assessment of Mental and Physical Handicaps*. Tavistock Publications, 1974.
16. C. ELLIOTT, D. MURRAY and L. PEARSON, *The British Ability Scales*. NFER Publishing, Windsor, 1979.
17. Department of Education and Science, *Statistics of Education 1976*, Vol. 1: Schools. HMSO, 1977.

II. Aims and the curriculum

A model of the teaching process: some definitions

The assumption that readers share a common understanding about the meaning of the words we use is basic to our discussion. But it is an assumption. Misunderstandings on educational issues have often been traced, not to differences of viewpoint, but to lack of agreement on the terminology used. During the project we noted that words such as 'aims', 'goals', 'purposes', 'objectives' and 'outcomes' were used interchangeably. The words 'methods', 'means', 'techniques', 'procedures', 'mode', and even 'organization' and 'management', were used indiscriminately when discussing how to ensure that children learned what was required by the teacher; and 'assessment' and 'evaluation' were used interchangeably in discussing children's abilities.

As the project was concerned with helping teachers find more effective ways of teaching language and communication, clarity of meaning and consistency of terms was all-important, and a model or framework of the teaching process essential. It was vital, therefore, that meanings were shared and processes and terminology clearly defined. Figure 4 represents a simple model which contains the essentials of the teaching process in a form that explains what takes place in the classroom. The following definitions will help to make the framework clear.

AIMS

To make sense of what we do in the classroom we must be able to relate it to some overall aim. An aim is essentially a general direction for teaching and, by definition, unattainable. It tells us where we want to be, but not how to get there. We might choose as an aim, 'to develop a child's language system so that it is essentially normal.' This statement gives a clear indication of the teaching, though there are many paths leading towards it. However, no one is currently in a position to say exactly what a normal language system is.

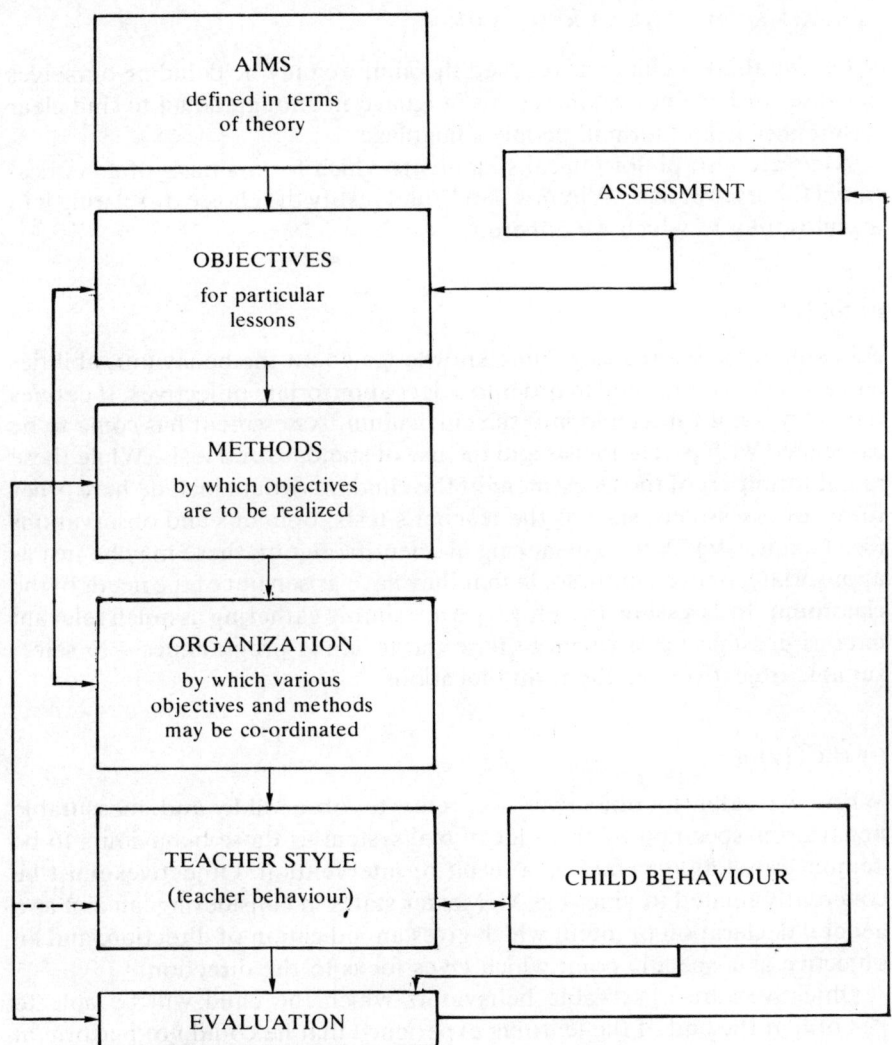

Fig. 4 A teaching model

When we think a child has reached the aim, we may be deluding ourselves because we have not examined his language in enough detail to find clear differences from 'normal' people's language.

Aims are also philosophical statements which form a basis of an educational theory. We ask, 'Why *this* aim?', and justify the choice by relating it to a philosophy to which we adhere.

ASSESSMENT

Assessment is defined as gaining knowledge about the behaviour, abilities and attitudes of the child in order to select appropriate objectives. It defines the entry point for a child into the curriculum. Assessment has come to be associated with psychologists and the use of standardized tests. While these might form part of the assessment of the child, we would include here other forms of assessment such as the teacher's tests, opinions and observations (see Chapter V). Although lacking in scientific rigour, these may be just as appropriate, or even more so, in that they have arisen out of the needs of the classroom. In assessing, therefore, we are simply gathering as much relevant data as possible upon which to base the teaching programmes – to select suitable objectives, methods and locations.

OBJECTIVES

When we refer to objectives we refer to observable and measurable behaviours, specified by the educational system as those behaviours to be demonstrated *by the child* as a result of intervention. Objectives must be coherently related to aims – as McMaster states in considering 'an aim as a general declaration of intent which gives an indication of direction, and an objective as a specific point which gives focus to the direction.'[1]

Objectives are observable behaviours which the child will be able to perform at the end of the learning experience that he could not perform at the beginning. In framing an objective it is useful to begin with, 'The child will (at the end of the teaching) be able to . . .', thus emphasizing what the child will be able to do at the end of the teaching that he could not do before. Objectives are clear, precise, observable and measurable behaviours, that make it possible to evaluate the effectiveness of the child's learning.

For those who find it difficult to decide whether a statement is an aim or an objective, we recommend Mager's 'Hey Dad Test'.[2] Simply add the statement in question to the end of: 'Hey Dad let me show you how I can . . .' If the result is absurd, the statement is broad enough to be an abstraction rather than a performance (objective). For example, 'Hey Dad, let me show you how I can *internalize my growing awareness*'! Contrast this with, 'Hey Dad, let me show you how I can draw a man.' Obviously, the first is a broad aim statement and the second an objective.

Which of the following are aims and which objectives?
    Develop the child's road sense
    Get on a number 44 bus
    Help the child to understand historical perspective
    Paint a picture of a cat
    Enable the child to think logically
    Develop the child's sense of humour
    Make a wooden model of a boat.

METHODS

Methods are the prepared means by which the objectives are to be achieved. They include the order of presentation of the teaching content, the teacher's decision whether to present the lesson orally or in written form on the blackboard, and what form the teaching objectives should be – oral, written or in other graphic form. A method is not the behaviour the teacher performs in the classroom but a planned general strategy, or set of principles for achieving an objective. The use of positive reinforcement in a behaviour modification framework would come under the method section of the framework.

ORGANIZATION

It is the teacher's classroom organization which leads to the co-ordination of the different objectives, methods and resources for different children or groups of children. This includes the use and allocation of time, space and personnel, and involves the establishment of priorities. The possibilities in classroom organization are considerably increased where classroom assistants are available, and with imaginative use of audio-visual equipment, individuals and small groups can function independently of the teacher. The amount of time saved through deliberate planning for individual and small-group learning can be enormous.

TEACHER STYLE

This includes personal mannerisms, attitudes and values which manifest themselves in behaviour characteristic of the teacher, impinge directly on the children in the classroom, and lead to and control child behaviour. What does the personality and attitude of the teacher bring to the teaching? Does she bring liveliness, warmth and friendliness and an infectious enthusiasm that engages the children in the work? Has she a quieter style of presentation, a more relaxed and easy manner of speech, which nevertheless involves the children totally in the activity? Is the teacher one who naturally and frequently reinforces the children's learning or is this important aspect of teaching dependent on mood or whim?

Investigation of a small number of teachers seems to indicate that, given the same teaching objectives, materials and methods, differences in teacher style can transform the two pieces of teaching totally (see Chapters III and VI).

CHILD BEHAVIOUR

By child behaviour we mean all those responses produced by the child – whether oral, written, or gesture. It is impossible to evaluate the effectiveness of teaching methods unless the child's total range of behaviours is also taken into consideration.

EVALUATION

This is the measurement of the quantitative and qualitative discrepancy between the child's behaviour as observed and the child's behaviour as specified by objectives. If there is a discrepancy, then modification of the objectives, methods, organization or techniques is necessary.

Aims and education: the teachers

The charge is frequently levelled at teachers that they are unclear about the aims of their work. Ashton et al.[3] suggest that teachers are mainly concerned with the 'here and now', the 'what' and 'how' of teaching, and state that teachers 'admit to giving little, if any, conscious consideration of what they are aiming at'. Although it would be wrong to decide that teachers are aimless, they find it difficult to make statements about teaching in terms of aims – possibly because they are 'neither required nor encouraged to formulate them.' Simpson[4] comments upon what he regards as an absence of aims in the training centre world, and Hughes[5] notes that although teachers have aims, a drastic reappraisal is called for and priorities need to be examined.

Our own observations of teachers in the classroom led us at first to think that the teacher's approach to the curriculum was conceived at the activity level, and that few thought in terms of a philosophy of education from which aims and teaching content could be derived. There seemed to be a total acceptance by teachers of the activities on the timetable rather than questioning why they did what they did and what it achieved for the children. But looking at class and school timetables it was evident that there was purpose and that a considerable amount of thought had been given to the planning. We attempted to find out exactly how teachers conceived the work they were doing. Having watched the teacher at work in the classroom, she would be asked the reasons for her choice of activity, why that activity rather than another, and its purpose.

One major issue which arose from our talks with teachers concerned the question of whether educational aims are universal, applying to all children, normal or handicapped. At the beginning teachers put forward the view that aims would be different for handicapped and normal children. The very nature of many of the handicaps, physical, intellectual or sensory, altered one's expectations to such a degree that it was unrealistic, even ludicrous, to have the same aims for handicapped as for non-handicapped children. Discussions were interesting in that focusing on the nature of the handicap and then determining aims tended to produce a hierarchical system of educational expectations for different groups of children. It was plain that thinking of this kind could lead to an elitist doctrine of education which deliberately aimed to foster these differences by providing a different form of education. Teachers agreed that all children should be educated in such a way that they would move towards, for example, complete social, physical and emotional development. Obviously it was realistic to expect differences in the speed at which children would move along each continuum and in their final levels of performance. Teachers who at first appeared to be arguing for different aims for different groups of children, were simply making the point that specific handicaps interfered in varying degrees with the individual child's ability to move towards these aims. There was general agreement that the *aims of education should be the same for all children, irrespective of ability or disability and would apply to all ages and stages of development.* As the Department of Education and Science pamphlet 60 concludes:

the inclusion of mentally handicapped children within the education system implies broadly common aims for all children, young or old, normal or handicapped. The same hopes of developing an individual able to operate as efficiently as possible within his environment, to contribute as well as he can to the community and to show appropriate concern and consideration in his relationships with others, might be held for all children. The extent to which these or other aims may be realised is determined by the responsiveness of the child to learning experiences and the skill with which they are devised.[6]

The teachers outlined the fundamental aims which should guide their teaching. Statements made by teachers, and also by parents, were collected in the course of informal discussions and are presented here as a stimulus to discussion rather than as a formal piece of research on attitudes. A preliminary study of these comments showed that 131 separate aims had been formulated. Most of these fell naturally into certain categories as follows:

General: aims which could apply to any of the specific areas below, but which cannot be categorized under 'independence' or 'norm reference'.
Independence: direct reference or implying ability to look after self in non-specific way – for example, 'take care of self', but not 'cook for self'.
Norm reference: direct references or comments indicating aim is for person to be normal or average as opposed to abnormal, handicapped or below average. References to *specific* skills go to appropriate category.
Social: direct references or comments implying interaction/relationship with other adults/children:
   a Immediate relations – familial ('Mum', 'Dad', 'Uncle Fred'); familial-parental (references to *having* family, being married, domesticated); non-familial (friends, workmates)
   b Wider relations – non-specific references, but implying relationships with other human beings ('sociable', 'friendly', 'good citizen')
   c Moral – direct references to moral behaviours ('honesty', 'sincerity', 'truthful', 'moral').
Emotional: implying a general state of mind, for example, 'enjoy life', 'happy', but not 'loving' or 'well adjusted' which imply social relationships.
Spiritual: direct references to spiritual, religious, Christian, etc., aims.
Intellectual/academic: direct references to comments on cognitive skills, ability to think in a convergent or divergent manner, select or choose.
Communication: direct reference to verbal and non-verbal ways of conveying ideas to others.
Work: references to work, occupation or earning a living.
Skills: reference to specific skills or activities, not related to either future 'employment/job', 'leisure activities' or 'physical categories'.

Physical: direct references to physical state, for example, 'healthy', 'mobile', 'ambulant', particular physical skills, or hygiene.
Leisure: references to need to entertain, amuse self, hobbies and leisure pursuits.
Aesthetic: reference to artistic aims, subjects, accomplishments.
Sexual: direct references to individual's sexual life unrelated to familial-parental role.

SOCIAL AIMS

Over 29 per cent of the aim statements fell within this category. Teachers stressed the wider, more general, social aims, suggesting the need to relate to people, the 'building up of social relationships', 'acquisition of socially acceptable manners' and the 'importance of promoting social integration'. While over 15 per cent of teachers' aims were stated in the wider context, less than half as many (6·1 per cent) were concerned with the closer social ties (familial and non-familial), 4·6 per cent involving close, though non-familial, relationships. This is not surprising. The teacher will tend to see her

Table 6 Comparison of teachers' and parents' aims (rank order and percentage of aim statements)

TEACHERS Rank order	%	PARENTS Rank order	%
1 General	19·1	5	8·9
2 Wider social relations	15·3	1	19·8
3 Intellectual/academic	10·7	4	9·9
4 Emotional	9·9	2	18·8
5 Social: moral	8·4	11	1·0
5 Independence	8·4	3	15·8
7 Physical	5·3	10	2·0
8 Social: outside family	4·6	11	1·0
8 Communication	4·6	9	3·0
10 Work	3·8	6	5·9
11 Skills	3·1	14	–
12 Social: family	1·5	6	5·9
12 Leisure	1·5	14	–
12 Aesthetic	1·5	11	1·0
12 Environmental	1·5	14	–
16 Spiritual	0·8	14	–
16 Sexual	0·8	14	–
18 Norms	–	8	5·0

role in terms of broadening the child's social skills and competence beyond the family, helping the child to relate to a changing and ever widening range of social situations and experiences. Only two statements referred to the need to prepare for parenthood or marriage. Teachers were also aware of the moral aspects of education, 8·4 per cent of their aims statements relating to this issue. They wished for children to become adults with compassion for those less fortunate than themselves; responsible people who respected the rights and property of others; adults who practised self-restraint, conformed to the established moral code of the community, who worked hard and persevered at tasks they took up.

GENERAL AIMS

While social statements dominated the hierarchy of teachers' aims, a large percentage (19·1 per cent) fell within the 'general' category. Teachers were concerned that children should 'reach their potential', develop their 'awareness' and be able to make choices in their daily living. They would aim to develop 'as full a person as possible', encouraging children to develop in every direction according to their 'appropriate needs'. Such 'education for living' would aim at producing an 'improved quality of life', the 'complete man', with varied interests and capabilities. In these statements teachers voiced their concern that education should not be on a narrow front relating only to the acquisition of academic and intellectual skills but should be life-related.

INTELLECTUAL/ACADEMIC AIMS

It might be expected that teachers, traditionally so concerned with the intellectual and academic aspects of education, would place these at the apex of the aims hierarchy. However, in this study such predictions would be wide of the mark, as only some 10 per cent of the statements related to intellectual/academic aims. Teachers were not only anxious to foster the child's ability to learn but also to think critically and imaginatively and develop his ability to cope with and adapt to the demands of a new situation. Additionally they made the point that the ability to select, take decisions and make choices is basic to the intellectual development of the individual.

EMOTIONAL AIMS

Entirely consonant with the teachers' emphasis on social aims was their concern about the child's emotional development. They not only aimed at an adult able to behave in society in a socially acceptable manner, but also for the individual to bring emotional stability into these social interactions. They looked toward the development of an adult who was both happy in his relationships with the outside world and 'happy within himself'. Teachers were aware that stability and happiness are partly dependent on the individual's self-confidence.

INDEPENDENCE

One of the major functions of any teaching, or education system, is increasingly to develop the individual's ability to look after himself and his own needs. As the child grows he gradually begins to take over, one by one, the functions at first performed by those close to him. Teachers stressed the need of the children to become more independent and to be given the opportunity to develop their individuality. They should be able to look after themselves and 'direct their own lives' becoming as 'self-reliant' as possible. A number of teachers indicated that *total* independence or self-reliance was not possible for anyone – we are all dependent on other members of society to a varying degree, and total independence, even if possible, would cut the individual off from society at large. The child should be as self-reliant or independent as possible, given that a degree of reliance on others is necessary and desirable.

This view of independence linked closely with the teachers' social, intellectual and academic aims – they wished their pupils to be able eventually to think for themselves and make their own decisions about matters that affected them closely. There were close links too with the emotional aims for the child, as any movement towards independence of thought and action must be intimately tied in with a person's feelings of self-confidence and individual security.

PHYSICAL AIMS

Some teachers gave general aims for developing the child's physical abilities; others specified the development of the child's mobility, gross and fine motor movements and the bodily co-ordinations; and others put the acquisition of good habits of health, hygiene, eating and toileting high on the list of aims.

WORK AIMS

A small number of teachers (just under 4 per cent) produced aims directly related to the occupation of a future adult. A few thought that 'education for work' or for 'a career' was important, but it was not clear whether this meant teaching children an occupation while at school, or ensuring that some skills (unspecified) were acquired by the children which would be of direct benefit to them in relation to work. It was clearly important to these teachers to aim to give all adults the ability to earn a living, and that there should be job satisfaction.

COMMUNICATION

We found it somewhat curious that teachers rated this particular aim so low. Communication in one form or another is undoubtedly necessary, and it is difficult to conceive of, for example, the social and intellectual development of an individual without taking communication into consideration. Hughes[7] notes that responses from a sample of seventy-eight headteachers indicated that 'social competence' and 'improved school facilities' were considered to have a greater priority than 'language development' in the schools. Only 28 per cent of his sample regarded language as the major priority area. However, he states that a sample of parents of mentally handicapped children recognized language as one of the major areas. It is also worth noting that teachers talked of communication rather than language, indicating perhaps that they did not wish their statements to be interpreted in the narrow sense of expressive language only.

SKILLS

A few of the teachers' statements (3·1 per cent) were concerned with aims to educate the individual in specific skills useful in adult life. One teacher's response suggested that all adults should acquire the skills of 'cookery to survive'. Other responses stressed the self-help skills – they wished to ensure that the children could feed and dress themselves, and see to their own toileting needs.

Aims and education: the parents

The educational process concerns both parents and teachers, and any discussion of the aims of education would be one-sided unless parental viewpoints were represented. Mitchell[8] has recognized the importance of the parental contribution emphasizing the view of parents of handicapped children as being goal-directed, active and generally successful teachers of children. 'They must not be viewed as passive recipients of advice, but as skilled participants in the education of their children, actively involved and accurately informed about all aspects of their children's education.' Accordingly the views of fifty parents were sought in a series of discussion groups. Each of the parents had at least one mentally handicapped child attending a day special school; many had normal children as well.

Parents were asked to state, as briefly as possible, what they considered to be the aims and purposes of education – what kind of adults they would wish to produce and what education should do for their children. Thirty-one lists of aims statements were obtained. In some cases a child's parents combined their statements to produce a single set of aims. No attempt was made to select a representative sample of parents and therefore we cannot claim that comments obtained reflect in any way the views of a total cross-section of parents of mentally handicapped children.

SOCIAL AIMS

The table shows a clear hierarchy of aims so far as parents are concerned, greater emphasis being given to social aims than to any other category (27·7 per cent). Parents stressed the need to bring up the child in such a way that he would be sensitive, able to get on with, and be socially acceptable to, others. It was interesting that parents placed greater emphasis upon these wider social aims than on the closer relationships of the family or intimate friends. Possibly parents feel that children already have experience of closer familial relationships and it is in wider relationships that the child needs to gain more experience if he is to be accepted by those outside the immediate family orbit. This emphasis on the wider social issues may stem from a recognition that the component skills which form and maintain social poise, confidence and acceptability do not occur spontaneously and can only be acquired within the appropriate social settings. Parents of handicapped children may be conscious that acceptance by society will depend upon the frequency with which the mentally handicapped person comes into contact with society at large, as well as the extent to which the individual can be 'useful to the community' and 'helpful to his fellow men'.

A small percentage of aims concerning closer familial relationships (5·9 per cent) suggested that parents wished to see their children happily married, enjoying family life and having children of their own, while maintaining happy kinship ties.

Although one direct reference was made to a clear moral aim – 'honesty' – parental aims tended to *imply* concern for moral issues, rather than stating them directly.

EMOTIONAL AIMS

About 20 per cent of the total number of statements related to the emotional adjustment of the individual. Parents wanted their children to grow up to be happy, stable adults, contented and secure individuals who enjoyed life and brought a confidence and a sense of humour to living. It is worth noting that above all emotional states 'happiness' was selected by the greatest number of parents.

INDEPENDENCE

Parents placed a high premium on independence – 15·8 per cent of the aims fell within this category. Depending upon the nature and severity of the handicap, parents inevitably saw their children as more dependent, needing greater time and attention from them, than those with no such disabilities. Unlike other categories where identical aims were formulated in a variety of ways, in this case the words 'independence' or 'independent' were used in fifteen out of sixteen aim statements. This would seem to reflect the very real depth of feeling and concern and preoccupation for parents who see their children becoming progressively more dependent upon society as they grow older. 'What's going to happen when we're no longer here to look after them?' is the question asked repeatedly of professionals who work with the mentally handicapped and their parents.

INTELLECTUAL/ACADEMIC AIMS

Parents apparently placed greater emphasis upon aims relating to social and emotional areas and independence than to the intellectual and academic areas. Apart from skills such as reading, parents were anxious that their children should grow up able to think for themselves, and hence able to make decisions. Independence, or autonomy, is what they were aiming at for their children – a thinking person able to assess a situation and take appropriate action.

GENERAL AIMS

Parents producing general aims stressed the need for *all-round* development of the child, aiming at his total development, enabling him to be more generally 'aware' and 'understanding' and 'able' to cope with life. Parents' responses echoed those from teachers, stating the need for children to achieve their 'potential'.

WORK AIMS

It is hardly surprising that parents were concerned with their children's future employment prospects. Almost 6 per cent of the responses related to this, statements being couched in general terms, for example, 'being able to work' or 'able to follow a career'.

COMMUNICATION

Few parents produced responses which fell within this category; again, we consider this surprising, particularly in view of the importance that parents gave to the social aims of education. Possibly in stating the importance of social interaction, language and communication aims are implicit in the parents' social aims statements.

INTELLECTUAL/ACADEMIC AIMS

Parents gave similar emphasis to the intellectual and general aims for children. While they were anxious that each person should be able to think for himself and make rational, intelligent decisions, they were equally conscious that intellectual and academic aims are only part of the child's development.

It would seem, then, that the social education of the child is the parents' prime concern – bringing up the child in such a way that he will be able to relate to others in different social situations and have sufficient skill, poise and confidence to be accepted by others. The parents' statements suggest that we should aim to produce happy, emotionally stable people able to exercise a measure of independence or autonomy. It is interesting that independence was not seen as a negative, non-relating to or withdrawal from society, but as something positive in terms of standing on one's own feet, learning how to do things for oneself, and not allowing the individual to impose himself by being unnecessarily dependent.

A study of the curricula of five schools

Our investigation showed that teachers in our sample did consider the aims and purposes of education to be important and that they had thought about the issues involved. Our next step was to see the extent to which teachers' aims matched the existing curricula in the schools concerned. Five schools were asked to supply details of their curriculum, copies of the school and class timetables and any schemes of work and syllabuses. We anticipated that we would receive materials which would briefly explain the aims of the work with the mentally handicapped child in such a way as to place the rest of the curriculum within some form of theoretical framework. Again, we thought that alongside this statement of aims would come a series of statements formulating the areas of the curriculum which teachers were to develop.

Perhaps the most obvious finding was the similarity of the curriculum contents. These were broken down into a number of areas – physical education, movement, games, art, music, play, the three 'R's, cookery, drama, etc. – the familiar spread of curriculum content found in most primary and special schools. Physical education activities ranged from the formal use of gymnastic apparatus through team games, swimming, hiking and horse-riding to more informal activities involving fine motor and eye–hand co-ordination related to spontaneous play, eating and music and movement. Toileting and washing skills were seen as part of the wider programme of physical education. Skills in the three 'R's appeared to develop slowly throughout the schools with a growing emphasis only with the top intermediate and senior pupils. The prerequisite skills (attending, looking, matching and discriminating, and sorting) were taught with the lower age-ranges. Language teaching was mainly approached incidentally, through stimulating situations using story, puppetry, finger rhymes, free play, etc., although two schools did use language kits and one referred to a school-devised language curriculum. In all the schools 'play' or 'free play' appeared on the timetable with pupils of all ages. With seniors this tended to be some form of physical education or a free choice of activity; with younger children there was a wide spectrum of activities, from the imaginative play of the Wendy House or dressing up, to the motor skills involved in making a wooden toy or playing on the slide.

Looking at the school and individual class timetables, 'preparatory' or routine activities in the daily timetable is a notable common feature. By 'preparatory' is meant activities aimed at getting the children ready for some normal daily activity or routine. 'Getting ready for' the first activity, midmorning break, lunch- or dinner-time, or going home, were noted, with the emphasis on 'self-help' skills – toileting, washing, dressing, feeding. These activities were explicitly stated as part of the curriculum. There seemed to be a total agreement about their importance as part of the schools' socialization programme. At the top junior and senior levels preparatory activities were no longer within the daily programme, presumably because by the age of 12 or 13 pupils were able to complete these routine tasks for themselves.

All the schools took children of all age levels out into the environment. Shopping, visits to parks and playgrounds, travelling by bus and train to the airport, zoo, theatre and fire station, were all found. Outside activities were seen as a necessary part of the curriculum to enable the children to 'widen their horizons' and 'have experience of an ever-widening number of situations'.

Another common feature was a block allocation of time labelled 'language', 'speech and language' or 'language extension', which covered materials and activities thought to stimulate the children's language abilities. Activities ranged from blowing and sucking for the more handicapped children, to story, puppets, singing, nursery rhymes, finger play, and matching games, and in the upper age-range included television, cookery, reading, writing and number work.

Reading the curricula reinforced the view that teachers tend to see the curriculum as a series of activities at various levels of complexity which will develop the children's language. Only in one school was there any suggestion that language and communication have many facets, and that programmes other than talking to, or getting the children to talk, are required. There was the implicit suggestion that 'language and speech' need a great deal of stimulation but the stimulation was seen in terms of activities, not in terms of the effect of the activity on one area of language or another. It was recognized that some form of structure or systematic teaching programme was necessary or useful. Two schools were using the *Peabody* and *Jim's People* language kits.[9]

In one school the material presented suggested that the curriculum was envisaged as the sum total of activities/subjects on the timetable. Here the headteacher allocated broad blocks of time and teachers were expected to work with the children within these general outlines. Curricula from the other schools showed an appreciation that both curriculum and content must have purpose. However, only two gave an overall purpose for education: **a** to educate the child to his full potential; and **b** to prepare a child for life. But, as Ashton[10] points out, it may be wrong to conclude that, because the school curriculum consists of a number of stated activities, aims do not exist, and our own investigations would support this view.

In none of the schools was there a written curriculum which could be handed to members of staff, amended and kept up to date. None of the schools' curricula contained an overall statement of the programme of work to which contents could be related. It seemed to be common practice for the headteacher to lay down the main headings within which the teachers would work, and to allocate broad blocks of time. It was the teachers' task to determine content and method within this framework.

SOCIAL AIMS

From our discussions with teachers about aims, we noted that they regarded the social aims of education as of prime importance. However, the timetables suggest a contradiction between content and aims. Only three schools referred to social aims: one indicated that 'free activity' leads children to share and wait their turn; one mentioned 'team games' and 'co-operative table games' as part of the learning development programme; and a third referred to 'the ability to join in a group'. It appears strange that teachers laid such stress on the social aims of education yet said so little of putting them into practice. These are skills which teachers can teach and children can learn. Why should the 'social' content of the work be omitted from the curriculum? It may be that social skills acquired in this way are mainly non-verbal and specific to the school (and later the Adult Training Centre) situation. Hughes'[11] findings partly support this. He concludes that socialization outside the school is particularly poor. He finds that despite social training in school 'none of the youngest was able to make minor purchases and only 14 per cent of the 8- to 11-year-old group and 37 per cent of the remaining older children could do so.' It would not be true to suggest that the children do not come into contact with the outside world during school hours – quite the reverse. Patently a policy of taking the children out into the world was common to all five schools. However, it is questionable whether there was progressive development from the necessarily teacher-escorted situation to the final group or individual journey by bus or shopping expedition.

INTELLECTUAL/ACADEMIC AIMS

In our discussion of teacher aims, we noted that most statements related to intellectual aspects – the ability of children to think for themselves and to make choices – and few statements related to formal academic aims of reading, writing and number. In this case curriculum content reinforced the aim statements. The learning development activities, beginning with simple concept development and going on to sorting and matching by shape, colour and size, were nicely calculated to develop the individual's ability to search, select and then act upon the decision. Creative activities, play, physical education and language and communication also had the choice element built into them. Potentially, choice and selection were catered for in classroom activities, but the extent of planned progression was uncertain. Ideally, home economics, visits outside the school, meals in and out of school, shopping and the adult-related activities involved in later life, should place an increasing burden of decision-making on the children in preparation for adulthood. This demands an outward-looking teaching policy and a conscious effort to plan and build into these activities realistic decision-making. Hughes' comments[12] on children's lack of ability to carry out these real-life activities may suggest that teachers hold back from planning this kind of work. Nesbit,[13] in her study of twenty-nine schools, notes teachers' opinions that decision-making tended to be related mainly to free activities. In only nine schools were children allowed to go out of school on their own and thus make their own decisions in the outside world.

Pre-number and number was specifically mentioned in all five schools and, apart from the reference to sorting and matching activities noted above, three schools referred to shopping activities. Two mentioned development of one-to-one correspondence and another ordination. It is surprising that Hughes reports so few children being able to make even minor purchases at shops when, according to the curriculum content, all children are exposed from the infant class upwards to number teaching. The fact that only one school referred to the teaching of money may be important, suggesting a preoccupation with an overall *activity*, for example 'shopping', while failing to develop adequately the component skills – *a preoccupation with the aim at the expense of the objective*.

EMOTIONAL AIMS

Both parents and teachers were concerned about the emotional development of children, parents placing it second and teachers fourth. Despite this, however, only one school mentioned it and a careful check of the curriculum content of the five schools revealed no content relating to emotional development. Presumably while its importance was recognized, teachers considered it was impossible to formulate specific content and method and, like social development, it could only occur spontaneously.

Is it possible to formulate content and method leading towards the child's better emotional adjustment? Perhaps if we define some broad principles, for example: self-confidence, feelings of adequacy, enjoyment of activities, delight and satisfaction from exercising skills old and new, a happy rewarding classroom, etc., it becomes possible to define the emotional content of the curriculum.

INDEPENDENCE

We noted that teachers and parents were concerned with enabling the child to develop into an individual able to think for himself, make his own decisions and act upon them. Some teachers were aware that we should not be trying to produce a totally independent adult, lacking social empathy and involvement. In this respect we should, more correctly, refer to the 'autonomous' rather than the 'independent' person. All the schools set out deliberately to develop self-help skills (eating, mobility, dressing, toileting, washing), to provide a background of classroom and extra-classroom situations in which the children could develop conceptually, and constantly to provide the opportunity to select and make decisions. Teachers, moreover, attempted to generalize the learning by planning frequent contact with the outside world in a wide variety of situations. Unquestionably the organization and curriculum content provided the potential opportunity to develop the children's autonomy. Interestingly enough, not one of the schools mentioned this important aspect of their work in the brief notes accompanying the timetables, neither were there any comments on how we should attempt to move progressively towards the autonomous person.

If neither parents nor teachers have sufficient confidence in their teaching/training programmes, are mentally handicapped children ever going to learn to become independent enough, for example, to go about the neighbourhood unaccompanied? Is it really the task of the Adult Training Centre to develop this measure of autonomy or are the children capable of learning tasks of this sort at a much earlier age? Naturally these are difficult questions for both parents and teachers. We suggest that the prerequisite skills can be isolated and can be taught effectively. Teacher willingness must obviously depend on parental wishes and support. However, it can be argued that the teacher stands in loco parentis to the child and is entitled to act as any reasonable parent would act. Whether it is reasonable to expect a mentally handicapped child to move independently about the neighbourhood naturally depends upon the child and on the kind of teaching, its thoroughness and effectiveness preceding the new activity. It would seem entirely reasonable to devise situations and activities which, as the child moves through the school, allow him to become capable of greater independence of action.

Such programmes should be home and school programmes conceived co-operatively and with mutual support and feedback. As the professional in the parent–teacher partnership, it is the teacher's task to develop a progression of situations and experience which moves systematically towards the eventual goal of, for example, unaccompanied journeys by bus. Programmes of this kind should be conceived in the long term – from when the child enters school – and the individual stages or intermediate goals stated, achieved and practised to a required standard. Careful planning and systematic teaching are essential if the results are to be effective and mutual trust between parents and teachers established. Parent–teacher co-operation, important at all times, is particularly essential in this area.

PHYSICAL AIMS

Despite the fact that only 5·3 per cent of teachers' aim statements directly related to this area, teachers did consider the physical education of their children to be important. Reference to physiotherapy, physical education in the hall and playground, use of large and small apparatus, walking, hiking adventure weekends, etc., pointed to a deliberate policy of widening the range of physical activities, skills and experiences. Physical activity of some kind was timetabled on average at least once a day. Obviously, self-help activities, creative play and free activity sessions involve large components of physical skills, and teachers clearly considered such activities to be part of the children's physical development.

WORK AIMS

The whole range of activities and experiences in which the children engage in school must contribute to the individual's eventual ability to work in adult life. But neither curriculum notes nor timetables concerned themselves with future occupation or work, and no statements were made about prerequisites for the children leaving school and stepping into adult life. It is surprising that the problems relating to the transfer of senior pupils to adult provision were apparently not considered important enough to be noted, though preliminary visits to Adult Training Centres during the pupils' final year in school were favoured and took place regularly. Nesbit[14] notes that twenty-one out of her twenty-nine schools had established visits by pupils to the Adult Training Centres in order to allow the children to accustom themselves to the work environment.

COMMUNICATION

All the schools set out to foster and develop the children's language and communication abilities, using informal situations such as story, news-time, drama and, more formally, through talk, discussion sessions and lessons in the three 'R's. Speech therapy was available for a number of children. Three schools mentioned listening and comprehension, recognizing the importance of developing the children's receptive language. However, the curricular contents suggested that perhaps teachers gave greatest emphasis to productive language. This was not unexpected in view of the acknowledged difficulty of mentally handicapped children with expressive language, and the teachers' aims to develop the children's social skills. (Chapter I amply demonstrated how productive language poses problems for both teacher and child.)

Apart from direct language teaching, there were many curricular activities which would enable the children to generalize linguistic skills in a wide range of contexts. None of the schools referred to the teaching of non-verbal communication. This was disturbing as 17·5 per cent of senior purpils leave school without any means of communication at all (see Chapter I). Since this survey was conducted, however, there has been an upsurge of interest in the teaching of non-verbal communication. This issue is discussed in greater depth in Chapter VII. It is worth speculating why two schools should use commercial language kits. What is it that kits have to offer which teachers, through existing curriculum content, cannot? This important issue is dealt with in Chapter IX.

LEISURE

In the main, children in these schools were given time by their teachers to follow up activities which interested them. Play, free choice or free activity time was made available almost daily, though when pupils reached the senior classes in three of these schools, the 'free choice' element had been dropped. This follows the pattern noted by Hughes[15] who found only 5 per cent of the time devoted to free choice or free play activities in senior classes, whereas nursery children were allocated 41 per cent.

Autonomy

The aim statements of parents and teachers suggested that they would wish their children to grow up into adults who were capable of independent thought and action, and who recognized that in our society interdependence was essential. For this reason we suggested substituting 'autonomous' for the word 'independent'.

How realistic is it to talk about autonomy for the mentally handicapped? Surely a mentally handicapped child must be regarded as being more restricted and less autonomous than a normal person? Is it reasonable to expect the mentally handicapped child to reach a level of intellectual skill or cognitive functioning to which only the most able can aspire? Such children have: **a** a limited range of intellectual skills; **b** a lack of physical skills which may limit them to the extent that they may not be able to walk, crawl or even move; **c** communication abilities so limited that they are unable to put across even the simplest of messages to others; **d** a lack of communication skills which limits interaction and the development of social skills. So how can the concept of autonomy help?

We could also ask how autonomous is the normal person – hemmed in by physical, social, moral, political and judicial restrictions. The difference between the normal and the handicapped person is one of degree. We would suggest that regarding autonomy as an ultimate aim under which all others are subsumed has advantages when looking at the curriculum.

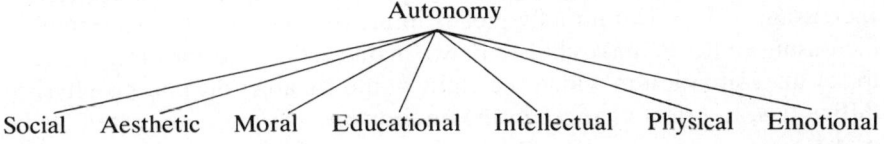

Under each of these sub-aims further long-term aims could be identified. As an example, consider the aim, 'to develop the child's physical abilities'.

PHYSICAL AUTONOMY

Ashton, et al.,[16] identified a number of aims for the physical development of a child. For example, 'precise and economic body control for ordinary physical activities including tools and equipment'; the child should know how to play a variety of games; should have a range of manual skills; should be mobile in water, etc. Given that *some* objectives within these aims could be attained and the child is able to move about the environment generally, their attainment makes it possible for the child to achieve greater physical autonomy. Thinking in terms of various aspects of autonomy helps to get round one of the teachers' most difficult problems in the education of the mentally handicapped, namely selecting the most appropriate area of content to teach. Usually, after outlining relative strengths and weaknesses by the use of tests, the teacher selects tasks developmentally one step further on the normative scale. In this way she hopes gradually to take the child nearer the norm in as many areas of development as possible. Unfortunately, this approach tends to suggest that there is only one road to achieve the desired goal – that of following the normal development pattern.

Consider the problems of a quadriplegic mentally handicapped child. How can the concept of physical autonomy help him? Clearly such a child is going to be physically restricted from birth. As he grows he is unable to learn the many physical skills that the normal child will acquire. Furthermore, he is deprived of the variety in sensory input and output – of action and reaction to changes in the environment. Such a child will inevitably lack some of the basic experiences of normal children. Although it is possible to compensate for some of these deficiencies by allocating one person to be responsible for constantly moving the child's position and stimulating him, this is impracticable. Moreover, it leaves out one of the major features of cognitive development – that the individual himself should be the agent of change gaining greater control over the movements brought about, that he should learn to control the environment. If the child's position changes are to be imposed from without, cognitive development will obviously be restricted. Increasing self-control initially means improved self-direction and implies increasing ability to make choices between one action and another. We need to set up a situation in which the child would be able, despite his physical difficulties, to effect changes in the environment to a greater extent as he grows.

If our aim is physical autonomy and it cannot be achieved by helping the child to walk, then we should ask what other means are open to us to facilitate mobility. Obviously some form of prosthetic device (temporary or permanent) is necessary, such as a walking aid or wheelchair. But is the device introduced because it is a means of moving the child about easily, or is it seen as a means of enabling the teacher to help the child achieve educational objectives which otherwise he could not attain? Of course, it is sensible to provide a wheelchair to achieve easier mobility, but this is only part of the picture. The provision of this or any similar device should *enable the user to move nearer to the attainment of previously specified objectives*. An electric wheelchair might be appropriate for one child, whose hand and arm control are severely limited but who could, with the right type of programme, be helped towards finger/hand control sufficient to manipulate the controls of an electric wheelchair. For such a child it now becomes possible to *develop choice* – to move or stay in the same place; select one position as against another; choose one route as opposed to another; to go with others or remain on his own. The child capable of propelling an ordinary wheelchair has similar choices. The provision of equipment of this kind, therefore, can have profound repercussions, not only on the physical development of the child, but also on the social, intellectual and emotional development. Mobility offers the opportunity to decide what one wants to see, touch, listen to, take part in and experience generally. With this facility the possibility of *the child effecting changes in the environment* is enormously increased.

Adopting autonomy as the ultimate aim not only gives direction to the various sub-aims, but also gives a reference point against which to check the relevance of the work we are doing with any particular child or group of children. We can repeatedly ask the question, 'In what way does this action or activity make the child physically, socially or intellectually autonomous?' With even the most handicapped children, it is possible to define curriculum content, and hence learning objectives, by questioning what is meant by, for instance, educational, social, or even moral autonomy with reference to a particular child.

MORAL AUTONOMY

Morality can be viewed as the instrument of society by which it regulates the behaviour of individuals and groups. Initially the demands made on the individual are external to him, the rules therefore appearing to be imposed by authority. Later on, as the child grows, he comes to see the validity of restraints of one kind or another and accepts them. Piaget[17] notes the development of moral autonomy, following an earlier stage during which rules were thought to be imposed from outside. Both Piaget and Frankena[18] suggest one of the vital elements in the process is the child's ability to *choose* between alternatives. Wilson[19] underlines the importance of learning to make judgements between alternatives, and Peters[20] suggests that the ability to reason, and therefore make choices, lies at the heart of morality.

Developing 'choice' programmes need not present difficulties. The opportunities presented in and out of school are many. Alongside this aspect of education could also be developed systematic teaching of those moral values which society would consider essential, for example, honesty, truthfulness, responsibility, persistence, industriousness, conscientiousness, sincerity. The use of story and everyday life situations and personal example are valuable here.

AESTHETIC AUTONOMY

It may be assumed that the range of creative activities presented in school should not only lead to some mastery of craft and technique, but also to awareness, feeling for and appreciation of shape and form, words, sound and movement, etc. Additionally, the individual ought to be able to express and communicate these ideas and feelings to others. The aesthetic development of the individual, therefore, is deeply rooted in his ability to select and make choices between one item and another. The type and quality of his choices will depend upon the cultural environment and the quality of his experience. They will also depend on the kind of teaching to which he has been exposed.

If the approach has been to present aesthetic experiences in terms of adult values of good and bad, with no opportunity for the child to react personally, the end-product may be considerably different from an approach which stems from the child's own reactions. One will tend to restrict and stereotype possible choices and reactions, while the other will stimulate and progressively enlarge the individual's range of responses and hence his autonomy.

Even in the aesthetic field cognitive demands based on choice situations are being made of the children. The greater the aesthetic autonomy of the individual, the more generalized are his intellectual abilities and the greater his ability to think for himself.

We have suggested that it is helpful to develop curriculum content/teaching programmes by considering the individual and his ability to act autonomously, and three areas of the curriculum have been examined. It would be possible to consider other curricula aims in the same way. When this is done the 'choice' factor emerges in all areas. This is important for it suggests the need to have choice in mind when planning the curriculum. Moreover, it is encouraging since it indicates that one can plan and work in one area and immediately see the relationship with all other aspects of the curriculum. Above all it suggests another way of approaching and determining curriculum content by asking the teacher to question whether a planned or existing curricular activity adds to or leads towards the individual's eventual autonomy.

Summary

This chapter presents a working model of teaching, and defines and illustrates its basic elements, including aims, assessment, objectives, methods, organization, teacher style, child behaviour and evaluation. It then presents a summary of teachers' aims for the education of mentally handicapped children, based on discussions in teachers' workshops and elsewhere. These aims tend to be expressed in very general terms, and to make frequent reference to the child 'reaching potential', and developing as 'fully as possible'. Strong emphasis is also placed on different kinds of 'social aims'.

Similar discussions were held with some fifty parents who were explicitly asked their views on the aims and purposes of education for their mentally handicapped children. Teachers and parents tended to have similar priorities, particularly regarding social aims, though there were also marked differences. Communication was not given a very high priority by either group.

We then report on a small study of the curriculum of five schools in which we tried to establish how far the aims corresponded to practice, using information supplied by members of the working party. There was little relationship between teachers' aims and the work of the schools. None of the schools supplied a statement of general aims or of content areas through which aims could be realized. Curriculum was interpreted primarily in terms of the timetable, and consisted largely of a list of activities. The chapter ends with a brief discussion of the notion of autonomy as an aim of education, and gives a few examples of its relevance to the education of the mentally handicapped.

References

1. J. MCMASTER, *Towards an Educational Theory for the Mentally Handicapped*. Edward Arnold, 1973.
2. R. F. MAGER, *Goal Analysis*. Fearon, Belmont, California, 1972.
3. P. ASHTON, P. KNEEN and F. DAVIES, *Aims into Practice in the Primary School: a Guide for Teachers* (Schools Council Aims of Primary and Nursery Education Project). Hodder & Stoughton Educational, Dunton Green, 1975.
4. P. F. SIMPSON, 'Training centres – a challenge', *Special Education*, **56**, 1967, 34–8.
5. J. M. HUGHES, 'The educational needs of the mentally handicapped', *Educational Research*, **17**, 1975, 228–33.

6. Department of Education and Science, *Educating Mentally Handicapped Children*. Education Pamphlet 60. HMSO, 1975.
7. HUGHES, 'The educational needs of the mentally handicapped'.
8. D. R. MITCHELL, 'Parent–child interaction', in P. Berry (ed.), *Language and Communication in the Mentally Handicapped*. Edward Arnold, 1976.
9. L. DUNN, J. O. SMITH and K. HORTON, *Peabody Language Development Kit*. NFER Publishing, Windsor, 1968. B. THOMAS, S. GASKIN and P. HERRIOT, *Jim's People*. Hart-Davis Educational, St Albans, 1973, rev. edn, 1977 (available from Learning Development Aids, Wisbech, Cambridgeshire).
10. ASHTON, KNEEN and DAVIES, *Aims into Practice in the Primary School*.
11. HUGHES, 'The educational needs of the mentally handicapped'.
12. HUGHES, 'The educational needs of the mentally handicapped'.
13. M. NESBIT, 'The final year in the special school', in R. J. Kedney and E. Whelan (eds), *The Education of Mentally Handicapped Young Adults*. Bolton College of Education (Technical), 1976.
14. NESBIT, 'The final year in the special school'.
15. HUGHES, 'The educational needs of the mentally handicapped'.
16. ASHTON, KNEEN and DAVIES, *Aims into Practice in the Primary School*.
17. J. PIAGET, *The Moral Judgement of the Child*, trans. M. Gabain, Routledge & Kegan Paul, 1932.
18. W. K. FRANKENA, *Three Historical Philosophies of Education: Aristotle, Kant, Dewey*. Scott, Foresman, Glenview, Illinois, 1965.
19. J. WILSON, *Introduction to Moral Education*. Penguin Books, 1968.
20. R. S. PETERS, *Ethics and Education*. Allen & Unwin, 1970.

III. Defining teaching objectives: a study of six teachers

This chapter develops the discussion of the teaching model introduced in Chapter II, to see what it means in classroom terms to use an objectives approach. Here we are concerned with the procedures involved rather than the content of the teaching which is taken up in later chapters. The illustrations and examples used are exclusively from the area of language and communication, but the principles apply with equal force to other areas of the curriculum for mentally handicapped children.

For a long time, both in normal and special education, there has been a great emphasis on the importance of stimulation: children should be provided with a rich, exciting, diverse environment in which movement, colour, form, action and people surround the child and provide him with the experience he needs to develop his intellect and emotions. This emphasis has done a great deal to alleviate the lot of many deprived, disadvantaged and institutionalized children, and today most institutions for children and schools provide interesting, stimulating environments. But for the mentally handicapped this is only part of the story. We are fast learning that just to put things into a child is not enough; we need also to get things out: the quality of the response we demand of the child is as important as the quality of stimulation we provide. Teaching is a business of changing and inducing behaviour; if we did not intend to do this, we would not bother with education. Behaviour means children not just seeing, hearing and feeling things but *doing* things. This is the position from which we start – that education is based upon getting children to behave, to act, in ways that they have not done before.

At first reading this may seem to contrast starkly with much of the writings of most educators, who write of 'knowledge', 'belief' and 'attitude', and who argue that education is a process of expanding these in certain directions. So it is: the underlying aim of most of the programmes we discuss is to expand children's knowledge of language. But it is also true that the only means each of us has of knowing what others know is to ask them to do things (at least until the advent of thought transference); and so the only means a teacher has of finding out whether or not her children are acquiring new knowledge is to find out if they have acquired new behaviours. Similarly, since we have no direct access to the circuits of the brain, the only way we can hope to change children, and know we have succeeded, is to change their behaviour. This is the basis for the use of an objectives approach to the curriculum.

The intervention study

The teaching model was put into practice in an intervention study with six teachers. Here we were interested in seeing the problems and difficulties in implementing the teaching model and in investigating how readily teachers could change their approach, their reactions and what the consequences were for the children during the lessons. Naturally enough, our ideas were as much developed by this study as those of the teachers, so what emerged is not a quantitative evaluation of the approach, but a careful analysis of the various elements, and many useful ideas on methods and organization.

Teachers were selected so that the children included in the study provided a spread of ages ranging from nursery to senior levels. The organization and conditions in the schools and the teachers' ways of working varied, and the six teachers included one who worked full-time on language work with individual children, and one who tended to work mainly with the whole class, while the other four varied the size of their groups according to the activities.

The teachers were asked to teach three lessons, all of which were videotaped. The first lesson was completely in their own hands; we asked only that they choose a group to work with, and teach a lesson in the area of language and communication. After this lesson, the teachers were interviewed by a member of the project team who had not seen the lesson. The interview covered the aims and objectives of the lesson, the methods and organization, the teacher's evaluation of the lesson and what changes she would make if doing it again. Teachers also gave the team their written lesson plans.

Between the first and second lessons, the teachers met together with the team for a full day, when the teaching model and in particular the assessment, aims, objectives and methods sections were discussed in detail, and sample lessons drawn up based on the model. Teachers were then asked to redraft their original language lessons in terms of the teaching model with emphasis upon pre-specified objectives and criteria for success. They were given two to three weeks to do this and then individually met the team and saw the videotape of the first lesson. This was discussed, and the final redrafted plan was then taught as the second lesson, which again was videotaped for comparison.

Although teachers were free to select any subject for the third lesson, they all chose language. This last part of the study was introduced to see what problems teachers, without support from the project team this time, would have in preparing and teaching a lesson planned on the objectives model. Again, the teachers were interviewed immediately after the lesson by a team member who had not seen the lesson.

Planning lessons

OBJECTIVES

Notes for the first lessons showed that only one teacher had come some way to distinguishing between aims and the objectives of a lesson; in five cases what the teacher expected the child to do was stated in terms of aims:

1   To reinforce work done during the last two-and-a-half weeks in teaching the words 'house', 'mummy', 'daddy', 'hello'
2   The development of oral language skills
3   Language teaching of body parts
4   To extend D's language from short phrase answers into full grammatical sentences
5   The whole point is to help the pupils put into words what they perceive
6   To develop the use of 'and' as a linking word for sentences in a descriptive situation.

Only **6** comes near to being specific enough to be an objective. In **1** we do not know whether the teacher was thinking of receptive or productive language. Example **2** reveals only that productive language would be involved. In example **3**, what body parts are to be involved? What are children going to do with the words? Are they going to point to the body parts when asked, or say the words? These three examples are entirely suitable as aims, but as objectives they give no guidance at all as to what the teacher would be trying to get the children to do. From example **4** we might be forgiven for thinking that the teacher, in one short session, intended to teach children who use two- or three-word phrases to produce grammatical structure. This cannot really be what the teacher meant to accomplish in the time. Similarly, example 5 is obviously a wide-ranging aim and could not possibly be achieved within the space of one lesson. These examples are broad directions to teaching which need to be narrowed down to a limited number of specific, observable behaviours so that they provide a precise guide to the teacher in the classroom.

This narrowing down is well illustrated by comparing the lesson plans for the first and second lessons of one of the teachers:

Teacher A
Lesson 1–aim: language teaching of body parts.

Lesson 2–objectives:
1   Production of body-part vocabulary:
    head and eyes – recapitulation
    chest
    tummy
    toes   new words
    feet
    thumb

2   A second objective will be the association of specified object with *some* of the body parts, for example:
    hat – head
    glasses – eyes
    vest – chest
    sock – feet.

In her first lesson teacher A does not distinguish between aims and objectives. The first statement is an aim giving a general indication of the content area to be included in the lesson – body-part language. But it fails to tell us what aspects of language (concept, reception, production) are to be developed and what the children will be able to accomplish at the end. With the second lesson, however, the teacher states clearly that it is productive language related to specific body parts which is going to result from the lesson. Moreover, a second objective is identified – the naming of objects, other than body parts, which are associated with each of the specified body parts. At the same time, the lesson has been brought within manageable limits, and only nine words are to be covered.

Another teacher's lesson plans illustrate the same process of refining and stating objectives in behavioural terms.

Teacher B
Lesson 1 – aim (objectives): to reinforce work done during the last two-and-a-half weeks in teaching the words, 'house', 'mummy', 'daddy', 'hello'.

Lesson 2 – objectives: comprehension of 'mummy' and 'daddy'; children will select mummy/daddy dolls when asked to 'Take/give me mummy/daddy' when both dolls are available.

As with teacher A, the first lesson is stated in terms of an aim and although we know that four words only are to be involved, there is no information as to what the children are to do. Notes for the second lesson leave the reader in no doubt as to what is expected from the children. The teacher has decided that the children need practice at the receptive stage and this will be given through a simple discrimination activity.

Of course, specifying objectives is not a guarantee of successful teaching: there are many pitfalls between lesson plan and lesson. But if things do go wrong, there is a chance of seeing more precisely where it happened, simply because the plan is more precise.

Having narrowed down the aim and specified objectives, it becomes much easier to see what form assessment of the children should take. Assessment consists of trying out the objective against the child. Teacher B would assess her children by finding out whether or not they can do what the objective prescribes. Can the children select mummy/daddy . . . ? We immediately learn something about the children and discover whether or not the objective is appropriate. If the children pass, then the objective is too simple and would need to be changed in order to take the children to a further level. Unfortunately, the converse is not the case. If the child fails the assessment, it does not mean that the objective is appropriate, since children could fail for many reasons. In this case, perhaps it is not that they did not understand the specific word, but that they cannot select objects, or are not attending to the teacher, or do not understand the instruction. These prerequisite skills need to be present as well before we can be sure that the objective is appropriate. This is a child-centred approach, not in the sense of letting the child do what he wants, but of matching objectives to the children, rather than forcing children into an inappropriate programme.

One of the drawbacks often felt to be part of detailed programming is that it becomes piecemeal: objectives spring out of nowhere and lead nowhere. This is not necessary at all, but it does emphasize the need constantly to bear in mind how the objectives selected relate to aims. Each objective needs to be related to previous and consequent objectives which together form a programme, and individual programmes have to be conceived within the context of the total curriculum of the school. For each objective we need to determine both what skills are necessary prerequisites and what the behaviour being taught is itself a prerequisite for. The answer to both these points depends upon the curriculum content involved. (Chapter IV deals with issues of content.)

A fairly common reaction to planning with objectives is the following: 'If I plan in such detail, my lessons will become stereotyped and boring, and I may well become less sensitive to the children since I will be concentrating on specific objectives.' Loss of spontaneity would obviously be a major criticism of the approach, but it seldom works out in practice. Neither the project team nor the teachers involved sensed any noticeable loss of interest in the lessons among the children – often the reverse. Clearly, if the child is to learn what the teacher has decided is important, then it is necessary to stick to the programme. However, this does not mean that a lead from the child cannot be noted and followed up later. The question is one of priorities. If the teacher feels that every time a child initiates a side issue this has priority, the original selection of objectives might be questioned. 'Following the children' like this is much more difficult than it would appear, since it involves almost instantaneous mental objective writing – a far more difficult process than pre-planned objectives.

Even if pre-planned objectives do not lead to any loss of spontaneity or fun, how easy is it to deal with areas of the curriculum other than language, particularly those concerned with social and emotional development? We can approach these aims from two different angles. All programmes, no matter what their content area, can be multi-dimensional, capable of achieving several objectives at the same time. All programmes should build up a child's feeling of adequacy, self-confidence, enjoyment and satisfaction from success. That children should learn to enjoy the company of others can be planned for and achieved very often in secondary objectives during the same lesson.

But the challenge of promoting a child's social and emotional development need not be left to the side-effects of success in programmes developing cognitive skills. Objectives can, with some care, be developed even in this difficult area. The following are some of the behaviours which form part of social and emotional relationships with others:

Listening to sounds
Making eye contact
Reacting and grasping
Smiling
Laughing
Cuddling
Kissing.

This list only illustrates that it is possible to specify objectives for social/emotional development. Complete programmes would need much more detailed consideration.

There are many gains to set against the problems and drawbacks of the objectives approach. Despite the difficulties in planning, objectives are much easier to implement; there is no room for doubt or floundering, and so the value of every minute of teaching is maximized. There is much less chance, if the objectives are appropriate, of confusing the children, and much more chance of there being a clear and observable growth in the children's abilities. This in turn provides much needed reinforcement for the teacher who can see her efforts being successful. If you begin with only a vague idea of what to teach, you can have only a vague idea of whether you have succeeded. Furthermore, other adults involved with the child, especially the parents, will know exactly what is going on, and so can more readily collaborate with and extend the teaching outside the classroom.

METHODS

How the objectives are to be achieved is a question of method. Teacher B begins the method section of her first lesson plan as follows:

Group the children on a semicircle of chairs facing a model of the house made from a cardboard box which will be covered by a blanket. Endeavour to gain their interest as to what is hiding under the cover. Remove the cover and see if any of the children supply the word 'house'. Praise anyone who does. Supply the word if there is no response. Repeat the word several times. Encourage children to repeat the word.

Ask the children, 'I wonder if anyone lives in the house?' Encourage individual children to knock at the door. When several children have done this, produce the peg doll to represent mummy giving her name at the same time. Show the doll to each of the children in turn repeating, 'It's mummy'. Encourage them to repeat her name.

Suggest we say 'hello' to her and encourage each of the children to do this. Put figure of mummy on one side and suggest children knock at the door again. Produce figure of daddy, giving his name when doing so. Show the figure to each of the children to emphasize his name. Suggest children say 'hello' to daddy.

There is evidence of planning, and progression is built in. The teacher is going to use the element of surprise to stimulate the children's interest, and suspense too is built in. If the children fail to produce the required words, she is going to prompt, followed by imitation; she has already planned to use reinforcement if correct responses occur. However, note that she is going to 'endeavour to gain their interest', 'encourage children to repeat the word', 'suggest children knock at the door', and so on. How are these things to be done? What happens if they fail? Words like 'encourage', 'endeavour' and 'suggest' give no real evidence as to precisely what the teacher is to do in order to get the children to do things. The particular strategy adopted depends on the level of the children being taught. As we shall see later, the differences between physical prompting, imitation and questioning are extremely significant, and yet all of these are forms of 'suggesting' or 'encouraging'. Looking at the same teacher's second plan, we can see exactly what is to be done during the lesson.

Pre-sessions
1   Short play session with each child to get the children used to the new situation.
    Use known object (Michael – plastic apple; Elizabeth – car, etc.)
    Put object on table. Say, 'Take that . . .' Reward or prompt.
    Say, 'Give me the . . .' Reward or prompt. Continue as necessary until the child takes and gives without prompt.
2   Short play session to get the children used to the wooden spoon.

Stage 1
Take out mummy doll. Say, 'What's this?' Reward or prompt. When child holds mummy doll, say, 'Give me mummy.' Reward or prompt.
Repeat until both instructions are obeyed without prompting, one after the other.

Stage 2
Take out wooden spoon. Put down beside mummy doll.
Say, 'Take mummy.' Reward or prompt.
Say, 'Give me mummy.' Reward or prompt.
Change positions of objects on the table and repeat the instructions above.
If prompts are unsuccessful, remove the wooden spoon and go back to Stage 1.
Repeat this stage until both instructions are obeyed consecutively twice.

The teacher realized that there is a need for what she terms 'pre-sessions' during which the children are given the chance to adjust to the new situation. She is no longer 'hoping' or 'endeavouring' to reach the objectives but sets out specifically how the objectives are to be achieved. Again she plans to reinforce correct responses at the moment of success. Now that she has specified the method to be used, two levels are evident. First of all, she will ask a question of the child, and then if that fails, and only if it fails, she will use imitation. Later on she will return to asking the question, so the children are freed from direct imitative control. The process of progressive simplification would be unlikely to occur unless it had been planned for by stating the method in full. In addition, it now becomes much easier to evaluate the different strategies, and note down for the future the kinds of response they evoke from the children.

Teacher C in her first lesson with a class of senior children intends to get them to talk about a visit to a cafe the previous day.

Plan – follow-up of Monday's outing (cafe visit to buy a drink)
(On Friday mornings we have class 'cafe', children bringing in 3p from home and buying coffee made with their milk and whatever they have made in cookery the day before. This was first real cafe visit.)
Equipment – series of pictures showing stages of activity; also picture of mother baking in the kitchen.
1   Introduce topic – 'Where did we go yesterday?'
2   Try to get children to describe all the happenings using questioning – 'What came next?', 'Before and after'.
Order
Park minibus
Into shop (which one?)
Up escalator
Into cafe
Find table and seat
Go to counter
Pick up tray
Choose a drink
Ask lady for what you want
Pay – do you remember how much?
Carry tray back to table
Drink up
Did you take coat off? Why?
Back down in lift
What else did we see in shop?
Back to school.
3   'I'll show you pictures now.' Show children activity pictures – let them talk spontaneously about them.
4   Ask, 'Which one is first?', 'Next one?', etc., 'Last one'.
5   Ask, 'Shall we have cafe in the classroom this week?', 'What day?', 'What day is outing day?', 'What day is cooking day?', 'What shall we make?' Ideas from the children; ask if they know how to make what they suggest.
6   Show picture of mother in the kitchen (if the children are still fresh). Name things in the kitchen – compare with domestic room.
    Remind them of an enjoyable outing.
Comment: hope to get the children talking rather than listening.

As it stands this is a formidable task in a short session, particularly since, despite the children's good comprehension, the teacher has selected children who are 'not the most talkative in the class'. In about twenty minutes, she is hoping to introduce six time concepts, and over fourteen words relating to the visit; sequence ideas; get the children to use general descriptive language; and do several other things as well. Clearly the session has far too many objectives in it, with no chance of giving more than a cursory few minutes to each. There are also many points at which the method is not clear. Although some of the questions she will use are specified, it is not clear when they are to be applied, and she will have to use a number of other questions, for example, to get the children to describe the pictures adequately. A second problem is that she has not said what will happen in the event of a failure. Will she ask another child? Use imitation?

In the second lesson these difficulties were solved by concentrating on fewer objectives and using a more precise questioning approach which builds in contingencies in the event of failure. As it turned out the objectives changed quite substantially because the teacher felt on seeing the lesson that the complex time concepts she was trying to teach were well in advance of her children's abilities.

Minibus sequence
Teacher places picture of each child and minibus readily at hand.
1 Present picture of child A.
   'Who's this?' Child names picture (for example, 'John').
   'Good.'
   Picture of child A only to be presented to children B, C, D and not to child A or we may have difficulties with pronouns.
   Picture of child B – present to children A, C and D.
   'Who's this?' – child names.
   'Good.'
   Picture of child C – present to children A, B and D.
   Repeat as above.
   Picture of child D – present to children A, B and C.
   Repeat as above.
2 Picture of minibus
   'What's this?' Child – 'Minibus.'
   'Good.'
   Repeat with rest of group.
3 Place first child's picture in minibus (for example, John).
   Show first child.
   'Who's this?' Child – 'John.'
   'Good.'
   'Where is John?' Child – 'John is in the minibus.'
   'Good.'
   If child fails, take out picture and repeat from 3.
   If child fails again, teacher models answer – 'John is in the minibus.'

'Tell me.' Child – 'John is in the minibus.'
'Good.'
'Who's in the minibus?' Child – 'John is in the minibus.'
'Good, tell me.' Child – 'John is in the minibus.'
'Yes, he's in the minibus. Good.'
'Tell me about the picture.'

In this lesson the teacher avoided the problems encountered previously with time concepts and sequencing, opting for sentence production using three prepositional phrases. She avoids the difficulty of introducing pronouns by ensuring that no child produces a sentence about his own picture. A simple procedure is introduced in the 'minibus' teaching sequence which, if the child fails to understand the demands of the task, teaches him precisely what is required. (Chapter VIII explores this method in some depth.) So, in this lesson plan the method is precise. The teaching content and materials are stated in sequence, the reinforcement noted and the method plans for initial lack of comprehension or failure.

The great contribution of behaviour modification has been to develop and refine methods of teaching generally applicable where objectives are expressed in behavioural terms. A great deal is now known about the techniques of shaping, reinforcement, fading and imitation and their effectiveness, and much of this knowledge can be used in the classroom in a variety of ways. (See *Teaching Special Children* edited by Haring and Schiefelbusch and *Helping the Retarded* by Perkins and others.)[1] Throughout this book we have made use of such techniques where appropriate, although the precision with which we specify how they are to be used is not as rigorous as many behavioural programmes used by research workers.

ORGANIZATION

Classrooms often appear, both to teachers and visitors, as places of constant pressures and few resources to meet them. Time is short, children are constantly making demands, materials are never sufficient to meet requirements, and more help would not come amiss. In the middle of all this, how is one to begin to use detailed programmes with all the children equitably? Are there dangers in spreading resources too thin so no one gains? How is one to take decisions of priority?

A question of time

Using objectives in detailed programmes is not an all-or-none business.

There is no reason why specific programmes cannot be written for only limited areas of the curriculum if that is all the teacher feels there is time for. With practice, objective writing becomes steadily easier; often general principles emerge that make it fairly easy to design new programmes. As this facility develops it becomes easier to extend the approach.

It is often a salutary exercise to do some detailed future planning: to say, over the course of a year or so, what you expect the children to be able to do. Naturally this sort of prediction can only grow out of informed estimates of how long it takes to reach individual objectives, and again it is worth setting deadlines for these to avoid either slowing down because of other demands or taking an unnecessarily long time. Of course, deadlines can always be modified if they become patently unrealistic. The most important advantage of setting deadlines, and so actively allocating time, is that there is some basis on which to see whether all children are getting the amount of attention they need. Priorities cannot be decided in this way, but it is possible to check whether the priorities are working out in practice.

The length of individual lessons will depend upon the abilities of the children. Short lessons are generally preferable, but children often produce surprises. We have found that where carefully structured lessons are used, children's ability to concentrate often exceeds all expectation, and may last up to forty minutes. This is not, of course, a recommendation for such timing to be used in general. The optimum time between lessons is equally a matter of the needs of individual children, but it is important that large gaps between lessons are avoided otherwise the routine may be lost and forgetting takes its toll of learning.

Personnel

Collaboration between teacher and assistants is generally very close and fruitful, but what role should the classroom assistant take? Is she to be a child minder, a teacher, or a general helper to relieve the teacher from routine duties?

There is much to be gained by using classroom assistants as a teaching resource. Indeed they cannot avoid taking this role with language teaching, since everything said to a child can have a potential effect on his development. Apart from the obvious way in which assistants act as teachers in individual or group programmes, it is often very useful to have someone who can act as a stooge or model for the child to observe. (In Chapter IV programmes are described where the assistant takes the role of the child first of all, so the child can more readily see what is required of him.)

In a class of ten or more children, varying in ability, children may also be able to act as teachers to each other, in paired activities through which objectives can be achieved for both 'teacher' and child. This strategy is especially useful in group games like lotto, where one child can be the caller, learning to direct and control others and to adopt a particular social role.

Working with groups

Group teaching does not mean all children have to be working on the same objective. Language provides many opportunities to work with different children at different levels of ability on related objectives. Teacher D worked with a group of seven senior pupils, containing two of very limited ability (ambulant special care), two who were just able to produce two-word utterances, and three capable of producing whole sentences. She evolved a method capable of achieving the following objectives with these three sub-groups: **a** production of single words, either subject or verb; **b** production of subject and verb; and **c** production of a complete sentence including a 'because' clause. The lesson took the form of children miming things that the teacher whispered to them.

Example: 'Drinking' – Linda mimes.
Get whole class to guess at mime first. Response required: 'Drinking'.
Group 1
Ask one child, 'What's Linda doing?' Response required: 'Drinking'.
If fails, ask other child.
If other child fails, ask Group 2, then go back to child in Group 1, and repeat, 'What's Linda doing?'
Ask other child, 'Who's drinking?' Response required: 'Linda'.
If fails, ask other child or Group 2 as above, then go back to Group 1.
Group 2
Ask each child in turn, 'Tell me the whole sentence.' Response required: 'Linda is drinking', 'Linda drinking', depending on child's ability.
If child omits subject, ask, 'Who's drinking?', and give answer if necessary. Then say, 'Tell me the whole sentence.' If child omits verb, ask, 'What's Linda doing?', and give answer if necessary. Then, 'Tell me the whole sentence.'
Ensure each child gives both subject and verb.
Group 3
Select one child per mime. Ask child, 'Why is Linda drinking?' Response required: 'Because she's thirsty'.
If child omits 'because', say, 'Yes, *because* she's thirsty. Why is Linda drinking?' Accept any appropriate reason. If no reason or a wrong reason is given, ask another

child in the same way. If no child can supply reason, give them the reason, then return to original child and ask, 'Why is Linda drinking?' Only move on when child gives correct response, 'Because she's thirsty'. Then say, 'Tell me the whole sentence.' Response required: 'Linda is drinking because she is thirsty.'
If the child fails, ask questions depending on response.

Part of sentence omitted	Question
Subject (Linda)	Who is drinking?
Verb (drinking)	What's Linda doing?
Because clause	Why is Linda drinking?

If child still fails, supply the missing parts of the sentence and repeat, 'Tell me the whole sentence.'

Here the teacher manages to integrate different objectives appropriate to different children in one lesson; she also uses the more able children to provide responses which are incorrect or omitted by less able children, thus giving the more able groups practice. However, the plan also ensures that once the response has been given by the more able group, she then returns to the less able children to get the response from them.

Another approach to integrate objectives is to put children in different communicative roles – as initiator and responder, or teacher and learner, or controller and controlled. We have already mentioned how lotto games adapt well for such objectives, which can also be tied to teaching production and comprehension of words to different children. For example, one child might have an array of objects and the other child ask for one of them. Of course this would have to be done under close supervision.

These examples illustrate some of the possible ways of spreading resources to achieve more objectives with more children in a shorter space of time. It is worth stressing just how little time children actually have in which to be taught. At the very most, children are available for direct teaching in the school four hours a day. In practice, the maximum is more like three hours, that is, only one-eighth of the day for only five days a week. With so much to do, and so little time to do it, advance planning of resources and time is vital.

Implementing the plan

Turning a lesson plan into a lesson is by no means a simple task, for it involves the teacher in keeping a very close watch not only on the children, but also on herself, monitoring her own behaviour to ensure that it matches up with the desired pattern of the lesson. In what follows, we discuss in very general terms some strategies teachers can adopt.

Take a fairly short and straightforward extract from one of the second lessons:

Teacher Collette, what's this? (Touches head.)
Collette Head.
Teacher Good girl. Sandra, what's this? (Touches head.)
Sandra Head.
Teacher Your head, good girl. You are clever, aren't you? I wonder what I can put on my head. Let's see. Let's see. Keith, which one would I put on my head?
Keith That one.
Teacher Right, put it on. What is it?
Keith A hat.
Teacher A hat and where are you going to put it? On your . . .
Keith Head.
Teacher Good boy. Do you want to see yourself? (Picks up mirror.) There doesn't he look smart? You look like a farmer. Yes, put it down then. Put it down then. Dawn, which one would you put on your head?
Dawn A hat.
Teacher A hat, good girl. Oh Dawn looks nice, doesn't she? There you are. Very smart. OK, thank you.

How can this extract be usefully described, so that the teacher could analyse her own behaviour and assess it against a lesson plan? In fact, nearly all the behaviour in this extract can be described by classifying it under four headings. First of all, the teacher makes a large number of *demands*, such as: 'What's this?' and 'Where are you going to put it?' In all, this extract contains six demands; it also contains some things that look like demands, but are not, for example: 'You are clever, aren't you?' and 'Do you want to see yourself?' On the surface, these appear to be demands because they seem to invite responses from the children; however, closer examination shows that the teacher does not intend them in this way at all. In the first case, she is concerned to reward the child for a correct response, and whether or not Sandra replied 'Yes' would have been unimportant. In the second case, the teacher was not really interested in whether Keith wished to see himself or not, since at the same time she was picking up a mirror and handing it to him. This is not to say that these pieces of language could never be demands. In other lessons they might form a central part of the teaching and the teacher might be genuinely interested in the responses.

These examples show that what counts as a demand is not only a matter of form but also a matter of *function*. Not all pieces of language in imperative or interrogative forms are demands, and some declaratives *are* demands. These relationships between the form of language and its functions are subtle and complex, and it is easy to be misled. The central question in identifying a demand is: does this piece of language expect a response from the child? Demands made during teaching are generally unusual in that they expect responses which are well known to the teacher. So when the teacher asks, 'Collette, what's this?', the function of the demand is not to gain information but to get the child to do something.

The second category is *feedback*. This covers utterances such as 'Good girl' and 'Your head, good girl. You are clever, aren't you?' All such utterances provide the child with information about his performance. Some of these only tell the child that whatever he did was correct; some repeat the correct response. Of course, feedback is not always positive – this category also covers utterances which tell the child he has made a mistake. Equally, feedback does not always come through language. Hand-clapping, edible reinforcers, hugging, and so on, serve the same purpose of letting the child know how he has done.

The third category is the *demonstration/prompt*. This covers cases where, rather than demanding a response from the child, the teacher provides all or part of the response required, so the child can imitate or do it himself. The extract above contains no examples of this, but behaviours covered by this category might range from providing a verbal response for the child to imitate to physically moving the child's hands into the position for a sign.

The last category, the *response*, has already been mentioned. This is simply what the child does following demands and demonstration/prompts.

Clearly, this list of four categories is not exhaustive; a number of behaviours in the extract do not belong in any of these groups: 'I wonder what I can put on my head? Let's see' and 'There you are'. If these pieces of teacher language have a function at all, it is probably something to do with keeping the conversation going or maintaining a relaxed atmosphere. They are not directly concerned with implementing a lesson plan. Occasionally, such language seems to dominate a conversation and hamper the teaching; at other times a lesson may seem dry because everything said is related to the current objectives. In general, we found that the six teachers on this study reduced this type of language between the first and second lessons quite considerably.

DEMANDS – 'LET HIM KNOW WHAT HE HAS GOT TO DO'

Having discussed briefly the four categories of behaviour, how do they relate to the lesson plan? What we demand of a child must match exactly the objectives we set for him; there is no point in saying, 'What's that?' to a child if we are interested in comprehension. If the plan is specific enough, then the central demands will already be written out, and confusions of this kind will not arise. It is nevertheless a useful exercise for the teacher to record herself, or get someone to observe her, and discover how many of the demands she made of the children were specifically related to the lesson objectives. In most lessons there will be a period at the start of the lesson in which demands for attention and demands establishing control predominate, and throughout the lesson such demands will crop up when necessary, but generally speaking the fewer that *are* necessary, the better for all concerned. If the teacher finds herself continually having to regain a child's attention, then she may decide the lesson is inappropriate, or that some work specifically on attention is needed.

Let us now look at an extract from the first lesson of teacher D:

Teacher Yes, that's the black dog. What is he doing? Have a look. What is he doing? The black dog, what is he doing? What is the black dog doing? Pardon, I can't tell what you're saying. What is the black dog doing? Tell the class because they can't hear you. Right, big voice, what is the black dog doing? Tell Angela and Richard over there. Pardon?

Angela (Responses inaudible.)

Teacher Can't hear, can't hear you Angela, can't hear you. Come on big voice. What is the black dog doing? Can you tell Mrs F——? What is he doing? Paddling, yes. Yes, paddling. Let's ask Wayne. Wayne, where's the black dog Wayne? What is the black dog doing?

Wayne Playing ball.

Teacher Playing ball, good, yes. He's paddling as well. You're right Jean-Anne and he's playing with the ball. Is that necessary Linda?

Linda No.

Teacher Oh, well don't do it then if it's not necessary. Well don't. Right, we're going to get Linda to do one now. Right, Linda, Linda is anyone swimming in the picture?

Linda That girl there.

Teacher You think she's swimming do you? How many are swimming? How many are swimming? How many's that? Do you think one is swimming? Well now, I'll ask you in a minute. You think she's swimming? Oh she isn't. Well I only want those that are swimming.

Notice, first of all, how much of the time the teacher takes up, compared with the children. This long extract has only four verbal responses from a group of seven children, but a great deal of teacher talk. Most of this consists of two types of demand: first, a great deal of control demands, many of which are concerned with getting Angela to speak up, and secondly, a great deal of repetition. Very few demands in this long extract actually function as useful

84 DEFINING TEACHING OBJECTIVES

teaching; only two bring forth clear verbal responses from the children: 'What is the black dog doing?' and 'Linda, is anyone swimming in the picture?' Another point in the extract may have produced a non-verbal response, although only a nod: 'Do you think this one is swimming?'

Contrast this extract with one from teacher D's second lesson which combines a firmer control of the situation with fewer demands for control needed, with a much larger number of objective-related demands which bring forth responses.

Jean-Anne   Hands.
Teacher   Hands, what was he doing with his hands? Are you watching Jean-Anne? No, she's not watching Trevor.
Trevor   You're not watching me.
Teacher   Watch Trevor.
Jean-Anne   Putting his clothes on.
Teacher   Putting his clothes on, yes. Who is putting his clothes on?
Jean-Anne   Trevor.
Teacher   Trevor, well let's see what Linda thinks.
Linda   Putting his buttons on.
Teacher   Putting his buttons on. Angela what is Trevor doing?
Angela   Getting dressed.
Teacher   Getting dressed. Right.
Mark   Trevor is putting his coat on. He wants to get dressed.
Teacher   That's good Mark. Now then, Peter.
Peter   Trevor wants to put his shirt on.
Teacher   Why does he want to put his shirt on?
Peter   Because he wants to.
Teacher   Because he wants to, well . . .
Peter   Because he wants to get dressed and look tidy.
Teacher   Yes. What do, what do you think Richard? You'll have to shout because there's a lot of noise from next door.
Richard   Trevor is putting his shirt on.

Summarizing, the crucial questions that can be asked about the demands in any lesson are:

1. How many demands are made?
2. To whom are they directed?
3. Do the demands match up to the objectives?
4. How many demands are not directly related to the objectives?

These four questions can form the basis for a critical look at teaching, by using an observer or a tape recorder to record one's own behaviour in lessons.

RESPONSES – 'LET HIM DO IT'

The extract from teacher D's first lesson illustrates the futility of continued repetition of demands that get no response. If there is no response made to a demand, there is usually a good reason. Momentary loss of attention may be the answer, but it may also be that the child simply cannot respond: what he has been asked to do exceeds his abilities. The same point applies to a response that only partly fulfils the requirements of the demand; the issue is one of *match* or *mismatch* between the demand and response. If there is a mismatch, then the demand may well need to be simplified or the objective may need to be replaced. Some changes can be made in the lesson, others will involve replanning. One particular form of simplification technique – the use of the demonstration/prompt – is discussed below. An excellent discussion of others is given by Marion Blank in her *Teaching Learning in the Preschool*.[2] The wrong responses a child offers are as important as the correct responses, because they provide clues to the next move in the lesson.

FEEDBACK – 'LET HIM KNOW HOW HE DID'

Since teaching involves getting children to do new things, they are not themselves likely to know if what they offered was what the teacher wanted, so it is vital that the teacher tells the child if he got it right. This is feedback, or positive reinforcement. This general rule does not always apply. In learning some physical skills, a response from the child may lead to some clear result, for example, fitting a piece in a hole of a form-board. In this case, the child himself can see if there is a gap between what he is doing and the correct response. With language teaching, it is very often impossible for the child to see that gap or to see when there is no gap, hence the need to tell the child when he begins to narrow the gap.

Feedback needs to be clearly related *for the child* to the response concerned, so it needs to follow on immediately. There is little point in taking a child right through a long chain of responses and then saying 'Well, some of that was right', or a similar piece of global feedback, because he cannot then have any idea which parts were right and which wrong. For each separate response, if the demand and response match, positive feedback can follow. With a mismatch, one can possibly reward a child for those parts of the response that were correct, and then issue a modified demand for those parts that were missing or incorrect. For example:

Teacher Pick up the ball and put it in the box. (Child picks up ball.)
Fine John, you picked it up. Now put it in the box.

DEMONSTRATION/PROMPT – 'SHOW HIM HOW TO DO IT, IF NECESSARY'

Imagine this sequence had continued and the child had failed to put it in the box. There seems no other alternative demand possible, and so the response must be demonstrated. Once a demonstration has taken place and the child has responded, it is important to return to the original demand and link the response to that, otherwise there is a danger of the child staying at an imitative level. Occasionally it may be necessary to go beyond a demonstration and physically prompt the child to a response. In the example above this should not be necessary since the need for physical prompting would suggest a level of ability below that suitable for such complex demands. Again, when prompting is needed, if the prompt is not gradually withdrawn, the child may get stuck at that low level.

TEACHING SEQUENCES

There is one sequence of these categories that ideally should form the basis for most lessons: demand–response–feedback. One might say that teaching advances in circles, the basis for which is this demand–response–feedback loop, illustrated in Figure 5. The demand is followed by a response from the child. Next the teacher asks: 'Does this response fully match the response I demanded?' If the answer is 'Yes', then she can provide feedback and go on to the next demand. If the answer is 'No', the teacher optionally provides feedback for those parts of the response which do match the demand, and then simplifies the demand. If simplification is not possible, she gives a demonstration of the response or a prompt. Finally she returns to the child for a response. So the teaching pattern goes on in demand–response–feedback loops moving through the lesson, the teacher simplifying when necessary, and extending the demand when appropriate.

This is teaching described at its most abstract, for there are still many questions unanswered. How can demands be simplified? What demands can I reasonably make of a child? Am I in danger of overloading the child with too many demands? The answers to all such questions depend on both a knowledge of the content of the specific curriculum area and on a detailed understanding of the child.

Teacher F's method section of her second lesson plan provides an example of the demand–response–feedback loop incorporated at the planning stage. Working with a ten-year-old child she requires him to answer demands with specific forms of sentence:

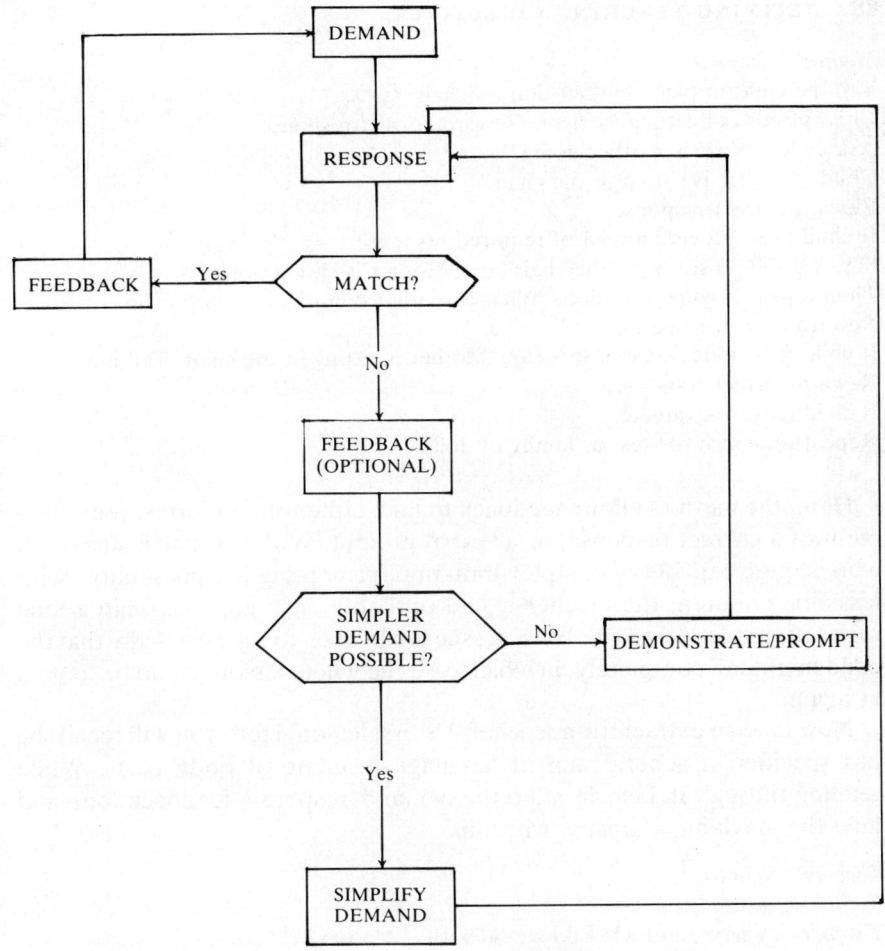

Fig. 5 Demand–response–feedback sequence

88   DEFINING TEACHING OBJECTIVES

Method – Stage 3
Tell the child to place mother doll on chair.
Child places doll sitting in chair. Reward correct response.
Ask child, 'What is mother doing?'
Child: 'Mother is sitting in the chair.'
Reward correct response.
If child fails, provide model of required response.
Say, 'Mother is sitting in the chair', or, 'Mother is sitting down.'
Then repeat original question, 'What is mother doing?'
Reward correct response.
If child fails, model response – say, 'Mother is sitting in the chair. Tell me.'
Reward correct response.
If child fails, re-evaluate.
Repeat sequence for rest of family of dolls.

Here, the method allows feedback to take either of two forms: reinforcement of a correct response, or a verbal prompt. With this particular child, who is quite capable of complex imitation, prompting is a possibility. With less able children, the teacher would probably have gone through a long series of simpler demands. Even so, she is still open to the possibility that the child might fail completely, in which case the whole lesson would be looked at again.

Now take an extract from teacher A's first lesson. Here you will recall she has specified a general aim of language teaching of body parts. While reading through it, bear in mind the demand–response–feedback loop and how the teaching compares with this.

Teacher   What is it?
Keith   A nose.
Teacher   A nose, and what do we do with our noses?
Dawn   Sniff.
Teacher   Yes, we sniff, what else do we do with our noses? What do we use our noses for? To smell with don't we? I wonder if I've got anything that smells in my little box? Let's have a look. Do you think that might smell? Let's have a look and see what it is, Lisa, shall we? What's that? Some perfume. Shall we take the top off and see if it smells? Then we can use our noses to smell it with. You smell. Do you want to smell, Tracy? No, your nose, a bit higher up. That's it. Does it smell? Does it not smell very nice? Does it smell nice or horrible?
Group   Horrible.
Teacher   Horrible, you don't like my perfume?

Here, the teacher not only presents demands and feedback, but most of the responses as well. From all this extract, there are only three

EVALUATING AND MODIFYING THE PLAN 89

demand–response–feedback loops, that is, only three occasions when the children have a chance to find out if they are learning anything. In the second lesson, with a clearly defined method, the children offer productive language and the demand–response–feedback loop is maintained throughout. The children are allowed to take part and achieve the teacher's objectives, and the teacher has a measure of each child's responses. An extract from the second lesson was given at the beginning of this section (page 81).

Evaluating and modifying the plan

A certain amount of evaluation and change in the light of children's responses can go on during the lesson, in simplifying demands when there is a mismatch between demand and response. However, the bulk of this process has to happen after the lesson, when the teacher, armed with records of the lesson, and the original plan, can decide what changes, if any, need to be made.

RECORD KEEPING

Adequate and accurate evaluation is impossible without detailed record keeping. The teacher cannot possibly keep track of children's responses without keeping notes made either during or immediately after the lesson. We should be careful here to separate record keeping in this sense from observations, the subject of Chapter V.

Observations are intended to provide information in, initially at least, a fairly non-specific way. This information helps to build up a picture of the child unconstrained by particular objectives, so that suitable programmes can be devised. Record keeping for evaluation purposes is a much more limited and precise affair: at its simplest, it need consist only of a series of ticks and crosses which represent responses which match or fail to match the lesson objectives. Progress can be charted either during the lesson, perhaps using a chart marked into pass/fail columns for each child, or alternatively, after the lesson when each child is given a test with a fixed number of demands, in which no actual teaching takes place. The advantage of the latter approach is that there is less danger of over-estimating the child's achievements, since the cues the teacher offers are much more carefully controlled.

MODIFYING THE PLAN

At every point in the teaching model something can go wrong, but we concentrate here on objectives, method and organization. Aims are of a different order: they may be wrong but it is not likely that the outcomes of specific lessons would tell you this. Teacher style is such an individual matter that it is impossible to offer suggestions which apply in general. For the remainder:

Objectives

1   They may be too difficult, too large a step from present abilities
2   Specific prerequisite skills may be missing.

Method

1   A method may have been used which relied on the presence of a skill, such as sustained attention, which was not present
2   The situation or materials may have been unfamiliar
3   The reinforcer was ineffective
4   Prompts may not have been faded out.

Organization

1   Too large a group
2   Social conflict in the group
3   Group not homogeneous enough in abilities
4   Not enough time allowed
5   Too much time allowed.

This is only a selection of possible problems; there are many others. By observing what is going on in the demand–response–feedback loop, a teacher should probably spot the difficulties. The first area to check where teaching programmes fail is the objectives; these often prove to be either unrealistically demanding or over-simple.

Teacher A, discussing the results of her second lesson, evaluated the lesson in this way:

Objectives

1   All the children produced the words correctly to the required criteria of these successful responses.
2   Recapitulation of 'head' and 'eyes' was quick and easy and it was not necessary to use the failure sequence with any of the children.
3   Although the children correctly produced the words 'chest' and 'tummy', it was obvious that three of them did not differentiate these body parts physically.

Further work will be necessary at the concept/labelling stage rather than production.
4   The words 'feet' and 'toes' were correctly produced but again confusion existed between the actual body parts. As with 'chest' and 'tummy' further work will be needed to discriminate between the two.
5   'Thumb' was correctly produced by all the children and no confusion was noted between 'thumb' and 'fingers', although shortage of time curtailed the lesson at this point. We will need to check discrimination of 'fingers' and 'thumb' later.

The interesting point which arises from these comments is that the teacher had picked up these points while teaching; because the objectives were clear, discrepancies stood out.

Children
The size of the group (four) was manageable and the abilities of the children fairly evenly matched although P is slightly quicker than the rest of the group. Next session it should be possible for him to take over some of the teaching role initiating the responses for the other children.

Method
1   The children were asked to show or say the body parts in turn. All children therefore reached the criteria of three successful responses. Because P was slightly quicker than the other children it was necessary to avoid asking him first each time. This worked particularly well.
2   The associated objects were selected easily by all children.
3   Recapitulation of the words (built into the method) proved to be successful and not at all difficult to arrange.

Time
The amount of time allowed (just over twenty minutes) was sufficient for the children's attention abilities but not quite enough to conclude the word 'thumb' without rushing. In retrospect this should have been left out and dealt with at a later session.

Reinforcement
This was planned to occur after every response from the children, although on several occasions it was never given.

This chapter has outlined the implications for classroom teaching of an objectives approach, but it leaves the content of the curriculum quite untouched. The remaining chapters take up this challenge and try to turn the teaching framework into specific teaching programmes.

Perhaps the final word in this chapter should go to one of the six teachers who took part in the intervention study, who felt positively about the approach and said so in the final interview:

It made me realize that I was trying to achieve too much and was in fact achieving very little. So it has made me think more about every lesson that I plan and made each lesson simpler, and I feel that both I and the children have got more out of the lesson – either in an individual or a group situation.

I think my own particular language is more direct, I don't gabble on quite so much, I wait for the children to speak more ... I want to hear them say it on their own whereas before I never paid sufficient attention to this. I tend to address individuals within the group but, using this teaching model, I have found that I can have the same lesson but have it in degrees of difficulty and still keep the attention of all the group. It doesn't really matter what lesson it is, whether it's a number lesson or pre-reading lesson or whatever. I found that having these objectives (and knowing which children I'm going to be with) has definitely improved my teaching.

References

1. N. HARING and R. L. SCHIEFELBUSCH (eds), *Teaching Special Children*. McGraw-Hill, 1976. E. A. PERKINS, P. D. TAYLOR and A. C. M. CAPIE, *Helping the Retarded: a Systematic Behavioural Approach*. Institute of Mental Subnormality, Kidderminster, 1976.
2. M. BLANK, *Teaching Learning in the Preschool*. Merrill, Columbus, Ohio, 1973.

Note. Part of the intervention study is shown in 'Setting language objectives', one of three published videotapes made by the project. (See note on page viii.)

IV. Curriculum content: sources, concepts and objectives

This chapter sets out both to provide a guide to teachers through the complex area of the development of language and communication skills, and to build a content framework for a language and communication curriculum. To define objectives for language and communication we need to know how language and communication develop normally – the composite skills, the order in which these develop, how they relate to each other and to other aspects of the child's growth. However, this knowledge is of little value to the teacher unless it has direct relevance to the education of mentally handicapped children, and leads to a realistic framework of objectives.

The development of language and communication is far too complex and extensive for us to cover the field in detail. Major trends can be picked out, but we cannot hope to represent the controversies, disputes and conditions attached to various findings. The approach adopted here cannot be definitive, since some of the basic assumptions underlying this work are still very much in debate, and knowledge about language and communication is growing rapidly.

A framework rather than a complete curriculum is provided for two reasons. First, we are still a long way from an exact knowledge of the development of language and communication skills either in normal or in mentally handicapped children; secondly, the precise objectives selected by a teacher depend as much on the characteristics and abilities of the child as they do on the curriculum framework. We have concentrated on areas which have received least attention in the past. There is less emphasis on the development of phonological and articulatory skills, and the acquisition of more complex language skills, since a number of useful curriculum 'packages' are available at this level (some are reviewed in Chapter IX). Our emphasis lies in the initial stages of language development, particularly from the first communications we might expect a normal baby to make, through to early phrases and word combinations.

Sources for a curriculum framework

The education of the severely mentally handicapped is, in one sense, at a fortunate stage in its development. There are as yet no established 'schools of thought' or approaches to the curriculum exclusive to the field. Consequently, people are open to ideas and suggestions from any source which may prove helpful, whether it is psychology or education, whether the ideas derive from classroom practice or not, or whether or not they need adaptation. The first steps towards a curriculum for language and communication are bound to be a combination of many different and supposedly contradictory ideas from many different sources.

RESEARCH TRENDS IN LANGUAGE AND COMMUNICATION DEVELOPMENT

To make some sense of the growth of this work and its implications for teaching language to mentally handicapped children, we need to go back to the late 1950s. In 1957 two major books were published which appeared to represent completely conflicting accounts of the nature of language – B. F. Skinner's *Verbal Behaviour*[1] and Noam Chomsky's *Syntactic Structures*.[2] These accounts seemed to conflict both psychologically and in basic philosophy; and it is curious that recent psychological studies on teaching language to retarded children have used aspects of both.

The aspect of Skinner's work which is most important to teachers is the idea that language may be taught. If language is a system of learned responses to stimuli, it is in principle possible to control the stimuli and conditions under which learning takes place, and to intervene in the learning process. This fundamental idea has led to many achievements in teaching language to different groups of handicapped children.

In contrast, Chomsky argues as a linguist that language is not primarily a learned system, but that the child is born with a set of built-in language structures, and that language learning involves tuning these structures in to the language of the culture into which he is born. The emphasis on language as a set of structures led psychologists to think about the child's developing language as a set of structures which obeyed their own rules. The emphasis shifted from thinking about child language as an imperfect version of adult language, to seeing it as a progression of different sets of rules which were increasingly accurate approximations to adult language. This idea is important to the teacher of mentally handicapped children because it breaks the development of language down into a series of interrelated, ordered steps. The implication is that what can be defined can be taught.

Much of the credit for this early work must go to the American psychologist Roger Brown and his associates, who were among the first people to write grammars which described children's early language at different stages.[3] Many other people also carried out important studies.[4] See Brown's *A First Language* for a useful overview.[5]

These ideas centred almost exclusively on the child's acquisition of *syntax*; very little indeed was discovered about the development of *meaning* – the relationships between the sounds the child makes and the things they signify. Interest in this aspect began in earnest with an important study by Lois Bloom,[6] which focused on the *context* in which the child's utterances were made. She discovered, perhaps not surprisingly, that a child could mean different things by the same utterance depending on the context. The two-word utterance 'Mummy sock', when Mummy was putting the child's sock on, could indicate an 'agent–object' meaning (refering to the person doing something and the object affected), but if the child was picking up a sock, the same utterance would indicate possession. The syntax of the child's developing system can often mask important differences in meaning. Since this study, research into the meaning or semantic aspects of child language has grown apace. Other significant figures in this work have been Bowerman,[7] Schlesinger[8] and again Brown[9] who reinterpreted much of his original information in terms of meanings. Bowerman showed that a very limited range of meanings was necessary to account for the first utterances of children in four different languages. (Table 7 (page 129) lists these common types of meaning.)

The basic principles of this research have already been applied to teaching retarded children, and it forms one of the bases for the curriculum framework. Three general implications for teaching emerge:

1 We need to help children to express meanings
2 We need to make a clear distinction between meaning and form
3 To try to teach grammar in isolation is not likely to be very successful.

Obviously, a child cannot mean anything which he cannot somehow represent, so the discovery of what a child can and does mean is intimately tied up with the development of his thought processes. Piaget[10] had for a long time argued that language was only part of the more general symbolic ability, and that cognition preceded language. Recent research has tended to support this view. Cromer[11] makes it clear that there are arguments both for believing that language precedes cognition and that cognition precedes language and concludes that: 'We are able to understand and productively use particular linguistic structures only when our cognitive abilities enable us to do so. Our cognitive ability at different stages of development makes certain meanings available for expression. But in addition we must also possess certain specific linguistic capabilities in order to come to express these meanings in language.'

Clearly, if we are to teach a mentally handicapped child a new meaning, we must ensure that he has the prerequisite cognitive abilities before we attempt to teach any purely linguistic behaviour. The other important implication is that we must be careful in our interpretations of a child's meaning. This is best demonstrated by the work of Margaret Donaldson and her associates[12] and in the USA by Eve Clark[13] and many others. These researchers have found that a normal pre-school-age child's understanding of words such as 'more' and 'less', and prepositions such as 'in', 'on' and 'under', etc., differs systematically from the way adults understand them. Recent work has also shown how much the context in which the child is tested can affect his understanding. Such processes are much more complicated than we might wish, and it is clearly important that teachers do not presume anything about a child's language abilities without careful assessment.

The most recent research has emphasized neither form nor meaning but what children can do with language. Tied up with this has been a growth of interest in pre-linguistic communication and the transition from non-language communication to language. Bruner,[14] Halliday[15] and Trevarthan[16] are among the significant figures. This work is important to teachers of the mentally handicapped because by illuminating the very early patterns of non-speech communication, especially between mother and child, it is unique in pointing the way for teaching pre-linguistic, profoundly handicapped children.

Halliday's work is based on an extended study of one child, Nigel, from 9 to 24 months, in which he showed how Nigel used pre-speech sounds to achieve various ends, which Halliday classified into six basic types. The most important for us are:

1 Instrumental function – communication for satisfying needs
2 Regulatory function – involved with controlling other people
3 Interactional function – concerned with communicating to get on with people.

Halliday's work has demonstrated the fundamental point that the child does not have to possess language to be able to make meaning.

The research described by Bruner places an equal emphasis on the growth of communicative competence rather than the development of form or meaning as such, and also on the role of interaction between mother and child. Particularly interesting is his demonstration of the importance of 'joint action patterns' between mother and infant and the way in which both mother and child come to focus attention and action on the same object through non-speech means. For if both can share the same point of attention or action, the mother can interpret the child's early actions and sounds, and the baby can note the effects of his behaviour and modify it or not, depending on the effect it has achieved. If for mother we read teacher, then this takes on great significance for teaching profoundly handicapped children who are just beginning to communicate. If the teacher is aware of how important her interpretations of the child's behaviour are, she can engineer situations in which consistent responses to the child's behaviour can be made, and thus begin to give the child communicative effectiveness.

This discussion of psychological sources for the curriculum has been extremely brief and we have omitted many important studies, but it will be clear how much research has to offer the teacher as a basis for a language and communication curriculum.

RESEARCH IN TEACHING LANGUAGE TO THE MENTALLY HANDICAPPED

Most studies designed to teach language to retarded children have been based on the principles of operant psychology. The emphasis so far has been on method rather than content. Their achievement is in demonstrating that language behaviour can be controlled by subsequent reinforcement. These behaviourally based studies are given excellent reviews by Garcia and De Haven,[17] Yule and Berger[18] and Snyder, Lovitt and Smith.[19] This work initially emphasized limited aspects of syntax such as the plural ending, but successful attempts have also been made to teach functional aspects of language, such as asking questions and talking about current events. These programmes owe little to the work on language development described above, although more recent work by behaviourally oriented psychologists suggests an increasing willingness to take account of this work.[20] Nevertheless this research has been of great value in illustrating the details of successful method, and in showing that it is possible to teach retarded children 'generative' use of language. For example, in one study[21] three retarded people were taught to use 'is' and 'are' in one set of sentences; it was then found that they spontaneously and appropriately used 'is' and 'are' in sentences they had never been taught.

One series of operant studies has been notable for its use of knowledge about language development, and for a much greater emphasis on a content framework. W. A. and D. D. Bricker have drawn on Piagetian studies and some of the work discussed in the previous section, to produce a 'mini-curriculum' which takes children from very simple motor imitation through to actor–action–object sentences.[22] This research is significant in that it uses a cumulative approach to language teaching and pays attention to prerequisite skills. In particular, their programme has used a progression from pre-linguistic concepts, through understanding to the production of a word. This sequence forms the basis for much of the framework presented here and in Chapter VI.

Two studies have directly applied some of the more recent research on language development, particularly the work of Bloom[23] and Brown.[24] Miller and Yoder[25] stress the importance of knowledge about language development as a basis for teaching programmes and outline four basic principles which we use later. MacDonald and others[26] used a similar approach to language teaching, based on meaning, with six pre-school-age Down's Syndrome children and achieved considerable success, both in increasing the number of two- and three-word utterances and in expanding the range of meanings available to the children.

There are, therefore, already some successful attempts to apply recent language development research with an emphasis on meaning, to teaching severely mentally handicapped children, which should encourage teachers in general to adapt such approaches to their own mentally handicapped pupils.

One other source of ideas deserves mention. David Premack[27] has carried out pioneering research into teaching 'visual' language to chimpanzees – to a famous one (Sarah) in particular. Premack avoids vocal/articulatory difficulties by using various plastic chips as symbols to attach to specific meanings. He succeeded with comparative ease and speed in teaching Sarah simple sentences involving giving different objects to different people, and later taught much more complex structures such as 'if . . . then' sentences and 'same/different'. Premack's work is useful for teachers of mentally handicapped children in three respects: he uses a functional approach in first teaching Sarah to demand rather than describe, using strong motivations to communicate to great effect; the programme emphasizes the importance of the non-verbal concept prior to teaching the linguistic form; and it teaches normal linguistic meanings using a non-English and non-vocal form. These

SOURCES FOR A CURRICULUM FRAMEWORK   99

points will be expanded and used in developing the curriculum framework.

EDUCATIONAL APPROACHES

Until recently there were very few curricula for teaching language and communication to ESN(S) children. Indeed very little is available of a general nature. McMaster[28] produced a useful summary of the basis for a curriculum, and a number of practical guidelines are presented by Stevens[29] and by the Department of Education and Science in *Educating Mentally Handicapped Children* (Education Pamphlet 60).[30] At the time of the project only one set of published curriculum materials for teaching language specifically to severely subnormal children was available – *Jim's People*[31] (reviewed in Chapter IX). Since then more have appeared, such as Bill Gillham's *First Words* (Allen & Unwin, 1979). For other educational sources we can turn to normal pre-school and infant education, particularly education concerned with culturally disadvantaged children. Published language programmes for this group are already used in schools for the severely subnormal, but all these assume a considerable amount of linguistic and conceptual ability. This is one of the main problems in applying programmes such as *Distar*[32] and the *Peabody Language Development Kit*[33] to severely subnormal children (see Chapter IX). However, these programmes are extremely useful in developing a language curriculum at the higher ability levels, since *they provide a ready-made breakdown of language skills at this stage*, which can be adapted to co-ordinate with earlier stages in the curriculum.

A number of developments concentrate on the dialogue between teacher and pre-school child and the ways in which teachers may control this to foster communication skills. Joan Tough[34] has produced a series of guides for teachers of normal pre-school children, which examine methods of assessing children's language skills, and building on these observations to increase the child's skill in using language. She is concerned primarily with the functions language can perform in helping the child to report and interpret events, to project beyond the immediate situation and to reason logically. Again it would not be possible to adapt many of the suggested teaching strategies wholesale, but the principles of this approach may prove invaluable as a source of methods for helping severely subnormal children to generalize and use existing language skills.

Marion Blank[35] has developed a comparable approach to teaching preschool children through teacher–child dialogue which equally has implications for severely subnormal children. She is concerned with helping the child towards abstract logical thought. Language is both a part of this process, and also the means by which it is taught. By concentrating on the wrong response to a demand from the teacher, Marion Blank illustrates a variety of 'simplification techniques' available to the teacher to make the crucial concepts in a lesson clearer to the child. The most significant features of Marion Blank's approach are that it illustrates the complexities of language learning and concept formation, the ways in which the teacher may sensitize herself to the precise capabilities and limitations of the child, and the large variety of teaching strategies available to extend children's capabilities at the normal pre-school level.

The selection of these two approaches is made primarily because they both suggest precise teaching strategies for achieving specific objectives, but there are of course many other approaches in the pre-school field. These are briefly examined in a general review by Parry and Archer.[36]

THE ENVIRONMENT BEYOND THE SCHOOL — DEMAND AND COMPETENCE

A knowledge of the demands that the normal environment makes on normal adults contributes to the curriculum in two ways. It can make us aware of skills which might otherwise be overlooked. For example, in shopping there are many requirements for successful performance: the ability to understand and respond to a wide range of questions; the ability to describe objects accurately; the dexterity to select coins from a handful of change; number skills; the social skills of being polite and responsive to general conversation, and many other aspects of normal competence. In a similar way, any common situation can be analysed to arrive at a list of necessary component sub-skills, and these can be inserted into the curriculum at the appropriate stage. An awareness of environmental demands also helps us to decide on priorities. A close study of the kinds of situations which normal adults experience will help us to separate those skills and abilities which are essential from those which are optional.

The communication process

If we are to teach language and communication skills effectively, we need to have some basic idea about the nature of the processes involved; we also need to have some knowledge of the stages of language development so that we can take children through a carefully ordered series of small steps aiming towards a mature language system. Normal adults are generally highly skilled and competent users of language, but are largely unaware of the nature of this behaviour. They communicate, using many complex rules to do so, but leave it to specialists to find out about those rules – they simply use them.

THE IMPORTANCE OF COMMUNICATION

Our existence depends on communication, since we are all to an extent reliant on other people for survival. Our food, warmth, shelter and our ability to develop into adults involves co-operation with and reliance on others. Every little gesture or sound says something about the person who produced it. We quickly learn to let others know our emotional state, our needs, desires, curiosity, interest, etc., and to recognize these signals and messages coming from others. But communication is too important to humans and other animals to be left solely to learning; we are born with a considerable number of 'wired-in' programmes to communicate.

It is difficult to conceive of any situation in which survival is possible without some form of communication, no matter how primitive. It might be said that a person in a complete coma does not communicate, and in the sense that he does not actively send out messages this might be true. But the only way he can survive is through the skill of others in providing artificial channels to allow communication. Doctors will connect such a patient to instruments to monitor basic bodily functions, and by virtue of this 'communication' they are able to sustain the patient's life.

To refer to a child as 'non-communicating' is in all but the most exceptional circumstances a contradiction in terms. Communication is part of living and learning. No matter how severely handicapped the child may be, he needs to be helped to communicate; otherwise he cannot learn to care for himself, to develop thought processes, establish a stable emotional life or develop all other aspects of human competence.

THE NATURE OF COMMUNICATION

Communication, being an exchange of information, implies that at least two people are involved – the speaker and a hearer. (Or, since we are equally concerned with non-verbal communication, the 'transmitter' and a 'receiver'.) Since communication involves sending and receiving messages, we must be prepared to teach both production and reception, speaking and listening. The relative emphasis on the two processes varies in the curriculum outlined below, depending on the stage of development. At the earliest stages, we rely directly on teaching productive communication, partly because of the extreme difficulty in teaching comprehension at this stage, but also because our knowledge of receptive processes is at present so limited. Later, as the child's communication system begins to approximate to an adult system, comprehension can be taught before production (as in the detailed programmes in Chapter VI.)

Sending and receiving information involves something to communicate about, and something to communicate with. There is no information in a message unless it has some content; the content of the message is the most fundamental component of communication – *meaning*. But we also need something to communicate with – meaning must have a *medium* with which to be communicated. From this medium we draw a set of individual *symbols* which represent meanings. The medium of language is the set of speech sounds we produce. In standardized non-verbal systems of communication, the medium is a limited number of fine movements of the hands and arms. It is important to realize that there is nothing sacred about sound as a medium for communication. Although we are predisposed by evolution to use sounds, the sound patterns we use are essentially arbitrary, and we could equally successfully, in the initial stages of communication development, use *any* medium available to convey the meanings we are teaching.

With a set of symbols representing a set of meanings we can do quite a lot, but it is still a long way short of a sophisticated system like language. With a one-to-one relationship between meaning and symbol, we could say we were hungry, or refer to individual objects, or describe them, but if we wished to express something as simple as 'Pick up your spoon', we would equally need one symbol to convey this meaning. Obviously this system would become unusable since we would constantly need new symbols to convey minute differences in meaning. Language and similar systems overcome this problem by introducing *structure*. The structure of language is usually called grammar or, more correctly, syntax. We use a limited set of symbols, but have a set of rules which define the ways in which we can combine these to form particular meanings. The number of ways in which we can combine symbols is to all intents and purposes infinite, and this is why language is such a powerful system. So meaning is not only conveyed by individual symbols; it is also conveyed by the way in which symbols are put together. Unless we are teaching individual symbols we must be concerned with structure, and if we are to extend a child's capacity to make meaning we must be directly involved in teaching structures.

Finally, there is always a *purpose* underlying messages we send. We do things with communication, so teachers must be prepared to teach children how to use the patterns of language and communication they have learnt for various purposes.

Communication, then, involves meaning, medium, structure and function, and effective teaching must be concerned with all these aspects.

MEANING

Imagine ourselves faced with a displaced Martian intent on learning our language. One word he hears is 'dog', and it becomes clear he wishes to know the meaning of 'dog'. We have no other way of teaching him this word than by showing him a dog, or a picture of a dog, which we do and with which he seems satisfied. Later we are dismayed to find him pointing to cats, cows and sheep and saying 'dog', although he does not use 'dog' to refer to birds or humans. Our teaching obviously went astray, and the Martian has learnt a meaning different from ours. He refers to all four-legged animals as 'dog'. We extend our language programme and tell him the names of cats, cows, sheep and other four-legged animals. This, however, leads to even more confusion, and it seems impossible to teach him different labels for different four-legged animals. We call in a psychologist who sets up a discrimination learning experiment to see if this Martian can differentiate dogs and cats even without words. The outcome is that he does not discriminate between any four-legged animals at all. As far as he is concerned, they are the same thing.

Meaning is not simply a connexion between a symbol and an object in the environment, or some other topic, it is rather *a connexion between a symbol and a representation of the environment*. The reason our programme for the Martian failed was because we assumed his representation of reality was the same as ours. When we thought we were teaching him that 'dog' meant dog, we in fact taught him that 'dog' was a symbol that represented his own category 'animal with four legs'. When this was followed by an attempt to teach him the correct labels for other animals, it failed because he had no separate conception of these animals. It might be possible to teach him to construct separate cognitive categories for each animal non-verbally, and then attach labels to them.

Teaching meaning to a mentally handicapped child is thus a two-stage process. He must first have a consistent mental representation of the aspect of reality we wish him to convey, and only then can we teach him the symbol to stand for this representation. When we talk about 'cognitive prerequisites' we refer to the first stage of this process. This applies as much at the beginning of language as it does at later stages.

To take a very early example: child A may make two distinct cries, one when he is alone and needs changing, another when he sees strangers. Child B makes two similar sounds in the same situations but does not use either consistently in either situation. For child A we have clear evidence that he distinguishes discomfort and fear, that he has some consistent mental representation of these two states, and that he has attached different symbols to indicate them. Child B offers us no evidence that he has developed either of the two stages, although we cannot judge whether he has differentiated them but simply not attached symbols. If efforts to teach two different sounds succeeded, we would have grounds for believing that he had the necessary distinction. If they failed, we might question this assumption.

As a later example, take a programme to teach the word 'bottle'. The cognitive prerequisites for this meaning are that children should be able to sort bottles and non-bottles, and know something about the distinctive functions of bottles – that they hold water, that they can be poured from, etc. A child at the start of the programme may only mouth, bang and shake bottles, so the first objective would be to teach him to use them appropriately, possibly with water play. Following this we could teach him to sort bottles from very distinct objects, increasing the variety of bottles until we were sure that he had a consistent non-verbal representation of 'bottle'. Only then can we introduce the word 'bottle' (or a non-verbal equivalent) and thus allow the child to make the meaning.

Meaning is only useful if it is communicated – a meaning communicated is a meaning shared. In the anecdote about the Martian the symbol was shared between Martian and human, but not the same meaning. Of course, the opposite is equally possible. We share with the French the same meaning of 'pencil', for example, but not the same symbol. Communication when symbols are not shared is generally unsuccessful; communication when meaning is not shared may be partly successful, but will often lead to confusion.

In general, we will wish to teach meanings shared by most people, but it may be that the symbols we wish to use are not generally shared. Because we are teaching a child to communicate with others it is vital that we specify *who can be communicated with*. If we teach a new meaning we must make certain people aware of what the child has learnt, for communication depends as much on the child making the meaning as on an adult being sensitive to that meaning. Similarly, if we use unconventional symbols, 'important others' must know what meanings these are conveying. Obviously, the most important people in a child's life are his parents, and we must co-operate with them fully and let them know exactly what the child is learning. Parental co-operation is crucial in language and communication, because we are teaching skills that must be used outside the teaching context if teaching is to succeed. Many other groups of people need to be considered: other teachers in the school, regular visitors such as speech therapists, ward staff in hospitals and, not least, other children. These groups form part of the social context which sustains communication and in which communication must develop.

Two major points bear directly on teaching meaning. First, the link between symbol and representation must be *consistent*. If a child uses two symbols in connexion with the same situation, and selects between the two almost at random, he cannot communicate. However, we may well have to accept less than complete consistency initially. After all, communication between adults is full of slips, false starts and misinterpretations, so it would be expecting a great deal of a severely subnormal child to make no mistakes. We need to accept a certain amount of error. It is only as a programme progresses through a series of carefully planned steps in which increasing demands for accuracy are made on the child that we will progressively diminish that error to an acceptable level.

The second point is obvious on the surface, but it leads to two major teaching principles. We do not have direct access to the child's cognitive representation of the environment. Therefore, we must interpret from his behaviour to find out about the kinds of meaning he is making. This process of interpretation is rather like carrying out a small experiment. We make an assumption about the way a child is dealing with the environment, design a situation that will test this assumption, then try it out. An example may make the point clearer: we want to teach a child shape words, so in order to discover how he deals with shape we ask him to sort some squares, circles and triangles into three piles (making no mention of the actual words). He sorts the circles correctly but fails to sort the squares and triangles, mixing them up in both piles. This assessment-cum-experiment gives a clear indication of that child's representation of shape, and consequently the sort of programme needed to teach shape meanings.

This is referred to as intervention observation (see Chapter V), but there are other situations in which we could simply observe naturally occurring behaviours. For example, suppose we wished to teach a child an 'agent' meaning – the meaning which refers to a person carrying out an action. The most important cognitive prerequisite is that the child should be able to conceive of other people as independent sources of events. (There is an early stage in development when this conception may not exist.) In normal everyday observations of the child we would look for evidence that he has reached this stage. For example, if something he wanted was out of reach and he pushed someone else's hand towards it, this would be evidence enough, or if an adult rolled a ball to the child and he gave it back to her to repeat the activity. We can, of course, engineer situations like this as intervention observation. In fact the last behaviour is one item in a specially designed assessment technique.[37]

So, by careful manipulation of the physical and social environment, and by observing the child's reactions to it, we can discover something about what the child is capable of meaning. This manipulation forms the core of teaching meaning as well as assessment. For teaching purposes both symbol and representation must be 'set up' by the teacher, by careful shaping and reinforcement of the child's behaviour, and by manipulating the physical and social context to create the necessary representation. To return to the last example, assuming we have clear evidence that the child can conceive of people as independent originators of action, then we must design a teaching situation. Let us further assume we have decided to use the sound 'teh-teh' to refer to the teacher as agent, since we have already observed that sound. We now have to organize the context to create a representation of the teacher as agent. A pleasant situation like tickling the child's tummy might suffice. The teacher could tickle the child, withdraw her hand, and then model the sound. When the child made the sound, the teacher would tickle him. Repetition of this context, and fading the model might lead to the child independently using the sound as a symbol for the agent meaning with reference to his teacher. Parallel programmes could be developed for teaching symbols for other agents, particularly his mother. This brief example is only one possible way of manipulating the physical and social context to produce a consistent link between symbol and cognitive representation.

MEDIUM

We say 'thank you'; the French say *'merci'*; the Italians say *'grazie'*. There are as many different ways of saying 'thank you' as there are languages in the world. But we can say 'thank you' with a hug or a smile, or in many verbal forms – 'thank you so much', 'ta', 'thanks' or even 'I don't know how to thank you'! The medium or form we use to convey a meaning is essentially arbitrary. There is nothing in the sound pattern of 'thank you' that has anything to do with being thankful. It derives all its meaning from the consistent link with a certain emotional state or social context. Because the sound system is arbitrary, it is possible to replace it with other media, notably non-verbal gestures, or to begin a communication programme using some medium other than sound. The increasing predominance of non-verbal gestural systems such as the Paget–Gorman Sign System (see Chapter VII) should not lead us to ignore other media, particularly the use of objects as in the work of Premack discussed earlier.[38] However, it is vital to remember the question: 'Who can be communicated with?' There is little point in giving a child a special medium of communication unless the people with whom he normally interacts are conversant with it. Even more difficult might be the case of a child transferring between institutions or schools in which different systems are used.

The importance of a standardized communication medium grows as the child grows in communicative competence. In the very early stages, children are often limited in the people they interact with and personal systems normally develop in the first year of life. However, pre-linguistic personal systems soon give way to the socialized standard system of language. The progression is similar with severely subnormal children. Personalized media for communication should be seen as a stepping stone to a standardized medium; only when we are sure that language cannot develop, generally for physiological reasons, can we accept a personalized system as fixed. The great advantage of non-sound media, however, is that they sidestep severe articulatory defects, and thereby enable the child to communicate meaning.

The social context is only one factor in deciding which medium to adopt. Perhaps more important is the set of sounds or gestures available to the child. Obviously, we stand more chance of success if we make use of a child's available sounds and gestures than if we try to teach him new meaning and a new form at the same time. It is crucial that the teacher is aware of the sounds and gestures (albeit non-communicative) a child can produce which may be used in communication. Detailed observation of sounds and movements produced is necessary, and the specialist skills of a speech therapist may be of value in elucidating exactly the sorts of sounds produced and those which will cause fewest problems in teaching meaning. There are many well developed methods for aiding sound production. New sounds not observed can, of course, be taught and inconsistent or inaccurate sounds corrected. But it must be borne in mind that teaching sounds in isolation is only a prerequisite (although often a necessity) to teaching communication.

STRUCTURE

We know immediately the difference in meaning between 'The dog is running', and 'Is the dog running?', although they contain identical elements.

The differences are carried entirely by the structure. Most meanings involve combinations of symbols; thus we sometimes have to teach a new structure in order to teach a new meaning. On the other hand, alternative structures often convey identical meanings. Compare 'My doggie' with 'This is my doggie' or 'No more ball' with 'Get rid of that ball'. Given contexts which allow interpretation of the earlier utterances, the meaning of these two pairs does not differ, yet the structure does. So we can often teach new and essentially adult meanings without having to teach new structures. The important difference between the earlier and later structures lies in the context. A sentence such as 'Get rid of that ball' does not need a context to be understood by the reader. But 'No more ball' could mean 'The ball has gone' or even 'Where's the ball?' The development of structures helps the child towards a more flexible and context-free system of communication.

In one sense, then, structure and meaning are interdependent – we can convey many meanings only given certain structures. In another sense they are independent – we can convey the same meaning with a wide variety of structures. Both aspects are important in selecting language objectives, but the second should perhaps be stressed since it implies that it is not necessary to use the adult structure to teach a particular meaning. Indeed we may impose too much on the child if we expect him to learn a new meaning and a new structure at the same time.

As we have seen, structure acts in one way as a medium for meaning. It is convenient for subsequent discussion to combine medium and 'structure as a medium' under one heading which we shall call 'form'. From now on we will concentrate on meaning and form, remembering that these two terms mean 'meaning plus structure as meaning' and 'medium plus structure as medium'.

FUNCTION

In teaching meaning, medium and structure we give a child the means to do things with the communication system, but we do not teach him what to do with it. Philosophers of language have been very interested in this aspect of language – indeed one of the most influential works is called *How To Do Things With Words*[39] – and they have provided useful classifications of types of 'speech act' or language function. Searle,[40] for example, has recently classified functions into five groups:

1   Expressives – expressing feelings and emotions
2   Directives – to get things done

3   Representatives – 'how things are'
4   Commissives – committing the speaker to do something
5   Declarations – a change occurs merely by speaking.

The first, the expressive, is probably available to the most profoundly handicapped children. The second is perhaps the most fundamental use of language. The third becomes increasingly important as the child grows older when more demands are made on him to describe and classify the environment. The last two functions are much more advanced, and it would be interesting to know how often they are used by subnormal people. Commissives, for example, 'I promise to be good' or 'I'll do it soon', could obviously be important to the child in coping with his environment. Declarations generally involve the speaker in holding some authority over others, but this is not inconceivable in a highly developed educational programme aimed at autonomy – for example, a child as leader of a game saying, 'You're not playing any more.'

The types of use to which language is put represent one aspect of language function; the other, equally important, is the variety of situations in which language may be used. In this sense, function is similar to the common meaning of generalization. It is important not to assume that because a child can use language in a tightly defined teaching situation he can use it elsewhere. Most teaching situations involve a very limited number of stimuli and an equally limited number of responses, all intended to achieve one limited objective. But out of the classroom there is a multitude of competing stimuli and demands which easily overwhelm and confuse the child. A programme to teach a particular skill must include stages intended to expand the context in which that skill is applied. The programming here needs to be as careful as in the initial teaching.

RELATING COMPONENTS

The four components of communication are all closely interrelated. Two major principles show how the teacher can use their interrelationship to greatest effect.

First, we can teach one component at a time. New meanings can be taught using existing forms, and new forms can be taught using existing meanings. Similarly, new functions can be taught using existing meanings and forms, and new meanings and forms can be taught using existing functions. There is no need to overload a child by, for example, expecting him to learn the plural meaning at the same time as learning the adult form '-s'. If he can already combine two words, we can use this structure with a word such as 'more' to give 'more X'. Once this meaning is established, we can begin to teach the adult form.

Secondly, the word 'readiness' need not exist in the curriculum. If a child is not ready to communicate at one level then he must be ready to communicate at a more basic level. There will nearly always be some representation of reality to which we can attach a symbol, and thus allow the child to communicate. At the same time we may be teaching the child prerequisites for the next meaning we wish him to communicate. Our first concern must be to give the child some sort of communication, or to extend his communication, so that he can begin to control others and make demands on his environment.

The curriculum framework – introductory note

The framework is divided into three stages of development for convenience only. The stages often overlap heavily, and one child may be working on programmes drawn from two of these stages at the same time, particularly if he is at a prerequisite level on one. Another point to remember is that 'word' is again only a convenient term and should be read as 'word or its non-verbal equivalent'.

Concepts which form the basis for a group of objectives are given, followed by a definition and examples, then by general comments on teaching approaches. Details of method are not provided since we are concerned here with the curriculum content rather than with how to teach it. Consequently, example programmes are not given in such detail as to be used as they stand – they would generally require several sessions to complete, and many crucial details, for example the criteria for the objectives, are omitted.

Stage I. Children at or below the one-word level

Information for cognitive prerequisites at this stage is largely drawn from a knowledge of the sensorimotor period of development (normally between 0 and around 24 months). Because there is no structure to language until symbols are combined we are mainly dealing here with meaning and medium, which are generally in a one-to-one correspondence.

Meanings

For convenience meanings are divided into four groups: expressive, demand, relational and substantive.

1 *Expressive meanings* are among the very earliest communications a child makes. Often more reflexive than intentional, they include cries and other non-speech sounds which signal bodily or primitive emotional states to other people. The fact that they are not intentional does not mean they have no role to play. They are the first meanings by which the child interacts with and begins to control his environment, and they form the basis for subsequent communication. Most common among this group are *pleasure, hunger, fear,* and *discomfort*.

2 *The demand*. Although many things a child does make demands on the environment and the people around him, this function/meaning is sufficiently important to be treated separately. This is the earliest form of Halliday's instrumental or regulatory functions, and at this stage function and meaning correspond. The *demand* is vital as a separate entity both because it is the basis for the growth of these functions, and because it acts as a general operator in connexion with objects or people in the environment and is one of the most 'generalizable' and generalized early meanings.

3 *Relational meanings* relate together various aspects of the environment or of the child's feelings, perceptions and actions. Relational meanings can signal relations between individual words, but only when the child has learnt some basic structures. At this stage these meanings are one of the bases for that structure and rely partly on the utterance and partly on the context. The most important are *recurrence, disappearance, rejection* and *existence*.

4 *Substantive meanings* form the building blocks for subsequent structures and relational meanings. Rather than relating two aspects together, they refer to single aspects of the environment. Some have already been referred to, such as *agent, action* and *object*. Others might be classified as relational or substantive such as *possession* and *location*.

1   EXPRESSIVE MEANINGS

Expressive meanings are generally possessed by even the most profoundly handicapped children. There are very few children who will not indicate *discomfort* by crying, or *pleasure* by smiling and gurgling. Nevertheless we cannot exclude the possibility of children below this level; and these meanings can be extended and used to develop the basis for communicative functions.

Pleasure

The term serves to indicate a generally satisfied state in a familiar context, often communicated by a smile, or pleasant gurgling sounds. As important as the forms of the child's communication is the relationship between what the teacher and the child do. These pleasurable settings are ideal for developing the earliest forms of interaction.

Some recent research has shown that in this sort of situation, mothers and normal infants respond to each other in a non-random way – that is they show the beginnings of 'conversation'.[41] Sequences of mother vocalizing followed by child vocalizing were observed; and the research implies that at this very early stage we should maximize the chances of this type of interaction occurring. There are many classroom situations in which this could occur. The crucial feature is that the child should be calm and apparently contented. A sensitive teacher usually tunes in quickly to situations pleasurable to the child.

The problem is to help the child to express *pleasure* and then use *pleasure* to develop 'proto-conversation'. A child in pleasurable situations will often simply be quiet, and in that sense he will communicate since at other times he cries. A more severe problem is the child who does not differentiate between patently pleasant and unpleasant situations. The apparently simple sequence of selecting a pleasurable and calm situation, finding an appropriate reinforcer, eliciting the behaviour from the child, and then reinforcing it, masks some of the most difficult problems in teaching profoundly handicapped children. Much of the teaching has to be guesswork initially. We do not know what is a reinforcer until we find one that works. Similarly, eliciting the desired behaviour from the child may be a case of simply waiting until it occurs, if it proves impossible to get the child to imitate general sound patterns, and even then there is no guarantee that this behaviour can be brought under control of reinforcers. The first steps are always the hardest. Nevertheless, procedures like these can be successful in getting the child to produce a variety of sounds in a pleasurable situation. (A detailed example is given in Chapter V.) A brief summary of a programme that might be used is as follows:

Objective
The child will produce any sounds (other than crying sounds) in a pleasurable calm situation.

Method
a   Select, on the basis of past observations, a situation which is calm and pleasurable. The following features may be important in this selection:
Child's position
Teacher's position
Physical contact between child and teacher
Noise and lighting level
Presence of other adults or children
Presence of objects
b   Select an appropriate reinforcer. The child may be reinforced by many things: food, drink, visual stimuli, auditory stimuli, tactile stimuli, etc.
c   Talk quietly to the child, in order to produce a flow of sounds he can imitate, stopping regularly. (There is, of course, no guarantee that a child of this level responds.)
d   Watch and listen carefully for sounds from the child. Reinforce immediately both by responding with your own vocalization and by using the reinforcer.
e   Repeat procedure over several sessions, gradually withdrawing the reinforcer by reinforcing progressively fewer responses but only after the required criterion of number of vocalizations has been reached.
f   Generalize this procedure to other settings.

The development of 'early conversation' can be taught using essentially the same method as in this example. However, the emphasis here will be much more on the interdependence of teacher and child vocalizations than on simply reinforcing the child's vocalization. A non-verbal response such as a smile could equally be used in this sort of programme. It may also be useful to have a third person observing the teacher and child and counting the criterial behaviours and whether they follow each other in a non-random way, since the teacher will be very heavily concentrating on her own and the child's behaviour.

At this early stage, meanings taught are so general that it is easy to think that a child is expressing a meaning when he is simply producing sounds. But sounds are to the child part of a general state of being and at this level meaning and form are not clearly separated. This *pleasure* situation can also be used specifically for form rather than meaning, as we discuss later.

In teaching at this level we are not yet in a position to make direct demands on the child; this depends on setting up the best possible context to encourage the behaviour we wish to produce.

Discomfort, displeasure, distress

These other expressive meanings may include a wide variety of bodily states such as hunger, thirst, skin irritation, or pain from teeth – states generally signalled by cries, which in normal circumstances are extraordinarily powerful communications. The trouble a human adult will take in order to calm a baby is remarkable. It is very rare that a child is too handicapped to cry; and in such cases it is difficult to prescribe any set procedures for teaching. When a child does cry, we at least have something to work on. Research by Bell and Ainsworth[42] points the way to possible teaching programmes although, as with *pleasure*, we are responding to the child and setting up conditions, rather than making demands on him. Bell and Ainsworth found that, with normal mother/infant pairs, the consistency and promptness of the mother's response was closely associated with the reduction in the baby's crying, and with growth in non-crying communications. The earlier patterns of crying were expressive and not directed to any one person, but later crying changed in that it was directed specifically to the mother and so could become a type of *demand*.

This research suggests that the teacher can best make use of crying in children by being immediately responsive to the child, although the findings do not necessarily generalize to ESN(S) children. Such a procedure is only meaningful when crying is an early expressive communication and not a later tantrum behaviour.

2 THE DEMAND

The *demand* is a relational meaning, relating some aspect of the environment to the child's desires. It is important because it allows the child to begin to control others. Pointing is a particularly valuable form for a *demand* because it makes quite explicit what is required. Sound forms are also possible, though they can only signal that the child demands something, not the object of the *demand*. But they have the advantage of drawing the attention of people not near the child which pointing cannot do. Obviously using both verbal and non-verbal forms would be a great step forward.

The *demand* can be taught by using the strong motivations the child already has, whether for food, cuddling or a particular toy. The general principle of this teaching situation is to make some desirable event depend for its occurrence on the child's *demand*. If we found a toy the child was particularly fond of, we could hold it in view but out of reach, then model the form we wished the child to produce, say a long 'wa' sound. When the child makes this sound we immediately give him the toy. In this way the child learns that he can have an effect on other people. See Chapter VII for details of a programme using a pointing response. Here is an example programme using a vocal form and a feeding situation:

Objective
The child will use a 'wa' form to demand food.

Prerequisites
We assume that the child has already been observed to produce this sound and that we can gain his attention for long enough to teach him during feeding.

Method
a   Teacher and child sit together where child can see both teacher and food
b   Teacher gives one spoonful of food to child to ensure child's attention and desire to eat
c   Teacher holds spoonful of food close to child, but out of reach of mouth and hands, and models sound
d   Listen for *any sound* and respond by giving food to the child
e   Establish this first phase until the child consistently produces a sound in order to receive the food
f   Now listen for sounds which approximate to the sound required and feed only following these
g   Gradually fade responses to non-'wa' sounds and demand increasingly fine approximation to the required sound.

Extensions
This basic format could be extended to different situations, to get the child to demand toys, drink, cuddling, etc. Each new situation may require equally detailed programming.

As with expressive meanings, we cannot be sure exactly what meaning the child is developing. In the initial sequence in the example, we may be teaching him something like the meaning 'food' and not a generalized *demand*, and may only cause confusion when generalizing to other situations. To avoid such problems, watch closely how the child uses the form outside the teaching situation – does he use it spontaneously to demand other things? One of the advantages of using a pointing response is that it is unambiguously general.

3   RELATIONAL MEANINGS

These meanings are among the first identifiable words a normal child learns. All of them lay the foundation for later development, and a child will have considerable difficulties with a number of more advanced structures and meanings if he has not acquired these.

Recurrence

A child will often shout 'mu-mu', furiously demanding the repetition of an event. *Recurrence* can also be signalled in less obvious ways. We have observed one profoundly handicapped child push a plastic sofa towards an assistant, making it quite clear that he wanted a repetition of a previous play sequence with the object. At the same time he made sounds suspiciously like an 'm'. This observation leads to the obvious way to teach *recurrence*. We can make repetition of a game contingent upon a particular form, say, 'more'. Another possible teaching context is feeding.

Objective
The child will say 'more' or an acceptable approximation to request a repetition of a game (for example, throwing a ball into his lap).

Prerequisites
We assume that the child has been observed to make some form of non-verbal request for repetition, even if by a general excitement and bodily movement.

Method
a   Play the game a number of times to arouse the child's interest and attention, until it is clear the child wishes for repetition
b   Hold the ball ready, and model the word 'more'
c   Listen for any approximation to 'more' and throw the ball immediately
d   Repeat to establish the approximation
e   Demand successively fine approximations until an acceptable form is achieved.

Extensions
Once a consistent 'more' is achieved, it can be used in other games with other people. Under supervision, it might even be possible to teach two children this meaning and help them to use it in a game between themselves.

Recurrence is equally important as a description or comment. When *recurrence* is a request, the reinforcement of the desired behaviour is the fulfilment of the request, but a separate 'extrinsic' reinforcer is needed for comment situations. The general principles here are: a set up a situation which indicates *recurrence*; b model the form we wish the child to produce; c reinforce the behaviour when it occurs.

Objective
The child will say 'more' to describe a situation in which two objects appear successively.

Method
a   Choose two familiar objects such as toys which are identical to each other
b   Ensure the child is attending and hold one object up so the child can clearly see it

1. MEANINGS

c   Bring the other object into the child's field of vision and model 'more'
d   Reinforce any approximation to 'more'
e   Establish consistency of response but ensure that the child only says 'more' when the second object appears
f   Fade the prompt out, again ensuring the child refers to the appropriate feature of the context – the repetition.

Disappearance

The most common form this meaning takes in normal children is, of course, 'gone' or variations of this. As with *recurrence*, we can teach this meaning either as a request or as a description. Unlike *recurrence, disappearance* in these two situations may mean slightly different things. More common as a comment, it might be re-stated as 'X was here, but now has gone'. The teaching strategy is essentially the same: select an appropriate and clear context which contains the meaning, model the form, reinforce the child's response, then slowly withdraw the prompt.

Objective
The child will use 'gone', or an acceptable approximation, to indicate the disappearance of an object.

Method
a   Choose a familiar object, hold it in front of the child, then hide it behind a screen
b   Repeat this game to establish a routine, familiar context
c   Now model the word 'gone' immediately after the object has disappeared
d   Reinforce any approximation to 'gone'
e   Establish and improve the approximation to 'gone'
f   Withdraw the prompt, ensuring that the child only says 'gone' after the object has disappeared.

As with the other programmes, *disappearance* can be extended to other objects in different games. If both *recurrence* and *disappearance* have been established we can demand both meanings at an appropriate stage of the game – 'gone' when the object has disappeared and 'more' to make it reappear, giving the child practice at using two meanings within one teaching session.

As a request, *disappearance* could be re-phrased as 'Make it go away'. Rather than referring to the context in the example above, it anticipates it, and it is preferable to give it a separate name.

Rejection

In teaching *rejection* we can use the same sort of context as in the previous example, but the child is required to use the meaning before the object disappears. An equally good setting would be 'peek-a-boo' or a game with a jack-in-the-box. Possible verbal forms could be 'away' or 'no'. *Rejection* could be extended to cover situations in which the child wishes something undesirable to go away, although the strong motivation here might be expected to lead to spontaneous use.

Existence

This might seem less important, but it forms the basis for much subsequent language. As with other single-word relational meanings, it depends on both language and context. Additionally, *existence* often has non-verbal accompanying behaviour, particularly pointing. It is used to signal the appearance or existence of some part of the environment and forms part of the basis of the ability to refer to things. Its common forms in normal language development include 'there' and 'oh!' and variations of these. The non-verbal pointing response of the *demand* is also a form of *existence* meaning.

Existence is used primarily as a comment, but can subsequently be associated with a demand for someone's attention to a particular object. Although it is a precursor to some substantive meanings discussed below, this does not necessarily imply it must be taught. This is one step in the normal sequence which could be omitted. Its advantages are that it is a general operator and like the *demand* can be used to refer to any object, whether the name is known or not.

The methods used to teach the *existence* meaning are basically the same as we have outlined for other relational meanings. A possible sequence might be the following:

Objective
The child will say 'there' in response to the appearance of the object. (Pointing to it at the same time.)

Method
a   Select a familiar object and hide it behind a screen in front of the child
b   Make the object appear and repeat the routine once or twice
c   When the object appears point and model 'there'
d   Reinforce pointing and any approximation to 'there'
e   Establish and fade out the prompt.

4 SUBSTANTIVE MEANINGS

Whereas single-word relational meanings depend on the context for full understanding of what the child is saying, substantive meanings do not necessarily, since they contain a one-to-one correspondence between the word and what the word stands for.

Agent

This is the meaning which contains the people in the child's environment. We have grouped two distinct meanings together under this heading. *Agent* refers to people as a source of action, whether intended, ongoing or past, and *vocative* refers to the child's calling for the presence of people. The teaching process is the same for both.

The child must learn to refer to himself as well as other people as *agents*, and teaching must take this into account. As with most other meanings, *agent* meanings can act both as requests and as comments. Both functions need to be mastered but the request is probably more useful initially. Clearly the more frequent *agent* forms are 'Mummy', 'Daddy' and 'me', and their idiosyncratic variations. The choice of form to signal 'teacher' is a personal one, provided the child is capable of producing that form.

We have already encountered various situations which could be used to teach the *agent* meaning as a request. A game in which both teacher and child perform an action can be used to teach both other and self as *agent*.

Objective 1
The child will say the teacher's name (for example 'Ann') to request her to do something.

Method
a Select a familiar, fast and enjoyable toy such as a jack-in-a-box
b Demonstrate the game to establish attention and the routine
c Model 'Ann' (point to self) and demonstrate the toy
d When the child makes an approximation of 'Ann', demonstrate the toy
e Establish the response and fade the prompt.

Objective 2
The child will say an assistant's name (for example 'Liz') to request her to do something.

Method
Exactly as above, but this time the assistant demonstrates the toy and the teacher is a passive observer.

Objective 3
The child will say the correct name depending on who is holding the toy.

Method
As above, but this time swop the toy at random between assistant and teacher. If the

child makes a mistake then hand the toy to the person who was named and she should demonstrate it.

Objective 4
The child will choose one person to demonstrate the toy.

Method
This time, put the toy on the floor between the two adults, and whoever the child names picks up and demonstrates the toy.

The same sort of programme could be used to teach self as agent. If this play situation proves not to motivate the child enough, it could be replaced by feeding, in which the child must name the person who provides the food.

Action

This group of meanings contains the beginning of the child's use of verbs, translating the way the child and others affect the environment through action into language. Again we can use similar methods for teaching *action* as a request or as a comment. Early on, some *action* meanings are redundant since the context makes the action required clear. For example, the games described above could be used to teach 'give' but it is unnecessary since giving is the only possible action. A number of actions need to be possible, so the child can control or describe selectively. A game in which the teacher and child could hit a ball on the ground or throw it might be one possibility:

Objective
The child will say 'hit' or an acceptable approximation to request the teacher to hit a ball on the ground.

Method
a   Hit the ball on the ground once or twice saying 'hit' at the same time, to gain the child's attention.
b   Let the child hit the ball, again model 'hit' while he performs the action.
c   Hold the ball ready to hit and model 'hit'. Perform the action as soon as the child makes any approximation to 'hit', and give verbal reinforcement.
d   Shape up the accuracy of this word.

Extensions
Use this word with different objects and different games.

Once the *action* meaning is established, the child can learn a whole series of *action* meanings which represent things which can be done with objects.

Object

This group of meanings is self-explanatory. We will normally teach the

I. MEANINGS 121

names of those objects which the child uses regularly: toys, food, important features of the classroom, toilet, etc. It is important to remember that we are teaching the names of *present* objects at this stage, not objects which cannot be seen.

Object meanings refer to objects not only by labelling, but also by distinguishing them from other objects, or categories of objects. Consequently, when we teach a name we must make it clear to the child that this name not only belongs with one object, but that it also belongs to no other. This can only be achieved by teaching two or more labels together, as in the following example which teaches *object* meanings as comments.

Objective
The child will say 'ball' and 'car' on presentation of the appropriate object.

Method
a   Hold up the ball only and model 'ball'
b   Reinforce the child for approximations to 'ball'
c   Establish the response
d   Repeat **a** to **c** with 'car'
e   Place the ball and the car in front of the child. Lift up each object in turn and require him to label them. Continue to reinforce correct responses.

As with *agent* and *action* meanings, *object* meanings can be extended by teaching the same words as requests and gradually building up a vocabulary of objects familiar to the child.

TEACHING COMPREHENSION

So far we have concentrated on productive language, to give emphasis at this stage to the active controlling functions of language, and to establish communication as a useful skill for the child. But control by language is only possible by other people responding through comprehension. We cannot be sure of the exact relationship between production and comprehension at this stage. There is a vast discrepancy between the type of language used by the child and adult language, so children are not normally subjected to input which is the same as their language. We cannot assume that the child gives the same meaning to other people's language that he gives to his own. Nevertheless in the language teaching procedures we have used, we can be reasonably sure that the child will understand in the language of others most of what he produces himself.

The major difficulty in teaching comprehension at such an early stage is in selecting which response to accept as indicating understanding. Pointing is often unsuitable since it is a passive response. The child's motivations can be used to much more effect in play situations, in which the child is active, and responding to language in order to control the environment in particular ways. Again it must be remembered that a child cannot be expected to learn the label for an action he does not perform or for an object for which he has no clear representation.

We can illustrate teaching procedures for comprehension by taking a relational meaning – *recurrence* – using the form 'more' and two substantive meanings – *agent* (with the child as agent) and *action*. The comprehension and production situations are very similar and we are as likely to get a productive response from the child as a comprehension response.

Recurrence

Comprehension teaching involves the teacher asking the child to cause the repetition. The following example deals with *recurrence* in relation to objects:

Objective
The child will respond to the instruction 'more' by taking another object from a tray.

Method
a   Show a tray of various objects to the child, take one out and place it in front of him
b   Take another object out and say 'more'
c   Put the objects back in the tray, give the tray to the child and take one object out
d   Say 'more' and physically prompt the child to take another object out
e   Repeat **d** but gradually withdraw the physical prompt, until the child is taking an object out of the tray in response to 'more'
f   Give two consecutive 'more' instructions, then gradually increase the number of responses required.

Note. The objects should not be labelled, since this programme teaches *recurrence* not *object* meanings.

Agent

It may be simpler to teach a child to comprehend his own name before he produces it, using the following type of programme, which teaches two children together:

Objective
The child will perform an action (opening a jack-in-the-box in this example) when the teacher says his name.

Method
a   Establish the game by opening the toy once or twice and having each child open it
b   Model each child's name as he opens it
c   Place the toy in front of and between the children and say one name – allow only that child to open the toy
d   Reinforce correct responses as well.

Action

By making only minor modifications to the example programme to teach *action* above, we can produce a suitable comprehension programme:

Objective
The child will hit and push a toy when told to do so by the teacher.

Method
a   Establish a hitting routine by both teacher hitting and prompting child to hit, modelling the word 'hit' when he does
b   Say 'hit' (when the child is not hitting) and prompt him to hit
c   Reinforce correct responses until response is established
d   Repeat **a** to **c** with 'push'
e   Combine 'hit' and 'push' gradually until child obeys both instructions appropriately.

These examples show it is relatively simple to convert a production programme into a comprehension programme and vice versa. Later it becomes much easier to teach comprehension first, especially as we begin to teach adult forms to children. But in the first stages, the teacher must decide which approach is best for her own circumstances with her own children. Subsequent sections contain both comprehension and production example programmes.

PREREQUISITES TO SINGLE-WORD MEANING

At the very early stage of expressive meaning there is little that can be done to ensure the necessary prerequisites since we are dealing with internal experiences. If the child has some outward sign of this experience then he has made the meaning. There is no intermediate stage between cognitive representation and meaning. Relational and substantive meanings deal with the child's representation of the external world, so we can look for behaviour which demonstrates the child's level. We can gain information both in unstructured situations and by setting up specific situations to assess particular behaviours.

Agent

Obviously it is unrealistic to teach an *agent* meaning to a child who is at the stage of development when he does not conceive of other people as sources of action. There are many situations in which to observe children's behaviours demonstrating this ability. Repetitive games which depend on another person activating a toy are one possibility. If the child hands back the toy to the teacher, or pushes her hand towards it then we have a clear indication that he recognizes his teacher as a source of action.

Action

Play situations offer the best opportunities to watch how the child acts on his environment. Given a variety of toys, does the child do the same thing with all of them, or are the actions differentiated according to the particular toy? We must ensure that a child performs an action consistently before we teach that meaning. There is obviously little point in teaching a child the word 'run' if he cannot run, but there are more subtle problems than this. These observations have a bearing on the specific *action* meanings taught first. Regularly observed, familiar actions might include: eat, drink, pull, push, throw, drop, sit, stand, hit. The meanings selected must depend on the individual child and what he is observed to do, but care must be taken not to attribute unwarranted *action* meanings to children. For example, we observe children 'playing' but they may be going through a series of discrete actions which bear little relationship to one another, and to teach a meaning such as 'play' could be anticipating later developments.

Object

Again, we cannot expect a child to make any *object* meaning unless he has a consistent representation of that object. Until around 15 to 18 months, the normal child does not develop the notion that objects have an independent existence. In the very earliest stages of development objects only exist for the child when they are in one place and in view. When they disappear, they also cease to exist.

The development of the object concept is very complex, but the teacher can set up simple situations which will test a child's ability:

1   Using an attractive object, move it across the child's visual field. Does he follow it accurately? When it stops does he continue to follow it as if it still moved?
2   Hide the object under a cloth leaving it partly uncovered. Does he retrieve it?
3   Hide the object completely behind the cloth. Does he retrieve it?
4   Hide the object in your hand, put it under the cloth and then move it to another cloth still covered by your hand. Can he retrieve it?

If the child can find an object after successive invisible displacements as in the last situation, then he has a well developed general object concept. There are many intermediate stages between these four situations. One very useful assessment devised by Uzgiris and Hunt[43] gives eighteen items in a scale which measures development of the object concept. Such detailed assessment is time consuming but might be carried out with the help of an educational psychologist.

Relational meanings

The same prerequisites apply to relational as to substantive meanings. Teaching *recurrence* implies a stable object concept as much as the actual *object* or *action* meaning. If taught as a request, *recurrence* possibly requires all three prerequisite skills. Requests involve another person doing something as an *agent*, a consistent representation of the *action* to be repeated, and quite possibly of the *object* which reappears.

It is impossible to be exact about the cognitive prerequisites for first meanings, because of the current lack of knowledge on the subject, and because much depends on the individual case. While we emphasize the importance of prerequisites, it is just as important not to delay teaching meaning unnecessarily. Speedy and efficient teaching rests on detailed observations of what the child does in relation to people and objects, and the use of his existing repertoire of behaviour to build the beginnings of a communication system. Only in exceptional circumstances will it be impossible to find some communication to teach.

Teaching the medium for communication

The success of a teaching programme can be dramatically affected by the selection of one particular medium. A child may possess all the cognitive prerequisites for a meaning, and yet not learn to express it because of problems in producing the required form. The major concern is to minimize these problems by selecting a form which he can already produce. How can this be achieved?

First, we can listen carefully to the child and record which sounds he produces normally. Clear, consistent sounds can be selected for teaching a meaning or for work aimed at modifying and improving just these sounds. Similarly, careful record-keeping of a child's motor abilities will produce a list of behaviours which might be used, and a list of limitations which are just as important in selecting a set of non-verbal symbols for the child to learn.

Secondly, forms can be taught in their own right. Morehead and Morehead[44] provide a very useful, if somewhat difficult, discussion of the applications of the Piagetian theory for these problems, centring around the use of imitation and play. Piaget distinguishes three major stages in the growth of the symbolic function:

1 *The signal*. At the earliest level, the child makes no differentiation between form and content in his behaviour. This is exemplified by expressive meanings in which the form (for example, a cry) can only occur when the experience it signals occurs.
2 *The symbol*. When the child learns that a form can be separated from its context, both in time and in space, he has made a vital step forward. Symbols are forms which bear some resemblance, either physical or functional, to their content. Piaget sees symbols as a transitional stage from representation by action to fully developed internal representation. Symbols are therefore limited in that they cannot be combined internally to form new meanings.
3 *The sign*. Finally, when the child uses an arbitrary form to express an internal representation and can combine this form with others to create new meanings, the form will become a true sign.

These three levels should not be confused with words and actions. Words can be both symbols and signs, as can actions in certain circumstances. We can help a child towards the use of symbols by using imitation and symbolic play procedures.

IMITATION

In imitating an action or sound, a child makes his behaviour stand for someone else's behaviour; thus imitation is one path towards the general use of symbols. The Uzgiris and Hunt[45] assessment contains a scale on vocal and gestural imitation which gives clear guidelines as to the steps through which a child must be taken:

I. TEACHING THE MEDIUM FOR COMMUNICATION

Vocal imitation

1. Differentiating of cooing from crying
2. Responds non-specifically (with mouth movement, smiles, etc.) to familiar sounds
3. Vocalizes similar sounds in response to familiar sounds (that is those the child can produce)
4. Vocalizes, but not the same sound, in response to familiar sound patterns
5. Imitates the familiar sound patterns vocalized by the examiner
6. Vocalizes sounds similar to the unfamiliar ones vocalized by the examiner by gradual approximations
7. Imitates unfamiliar sound patterns vocalized by the examiner
8. Imitates familiar words
9. Imitates new words by gradual approximations
10. Imitates new words directly
11. Imitates practically all new words.

These eleven steps are sufficiently detailed to be treated as a set of objectives for developing vocal imitation. If a child is at step **3**, the programme devised would concentrate on shaping up the accuracy of the imitation of a familiar sound, then expanding this to other sounds and then gradually introducing sounds which the child does not already produce, thus moving through step **4** and on to step **5**. The important features of this progression are:

1. Moving from the familiar to the unfamiliar
2. Moving from sounds to sound patterns to words
3. Increasing the accuracy of imitation.

Gestural imitation

1. Makes some movement in response to the examiner, but does not imitate familiar motor (action) schemas
2. Imitates familiar motor schemas performed by the examiner
3. Imitates complex actions after gradual approximations
4. Imitates complex actions directly
5. Imitates unfamiliar visible gestures directly
6. Imitates unfamiliar invisible gestures (that is, the examiner stops gesturing before the child starts) by gradual approximations
7. Imitates unfamiliar invisible gestures directly
8. Deferred imitation of actions is reported.

Again, these eight steps can be treated as the basis for a motor imitation programme, the important features of which are:

1 Moving from familiar simple actions to familiar complex actions to unfamiliar actions
2 Moving from visible to invisible actions
3 Moving from immediate to delayed imitation.

Imitation programmes achieve two goals. They are a useful medium to develop the 'conversational' mode of communication, since what the child does depends on the teacher's behaviour and vice versa. They also teach forms which can then be fitted into the main stream of the curriculum and used to express meanings. They can be returned to periodically when it is necessary to develop a new form – they should not be seen as a stage which must be passed through before any meanings can be taught. Certainly one can begin to use vocal forms to teach meaning at least from step 5 in the vocal imitation sequence above.

PLAY

The child develops symbols in imitation by adjusting his behaviour to match his environment. In play, he develops symbols by adjusting the environment to match his behaviour. The child learns to substitute one object, action or event for another and thereby demonstrates mastery of symbols. Such common situations as pushing a block of wood round making car noises, or shooting with a finger illustrate symbolic play.

In the development of communication symbolic play can be used as a method of developing a general symbolic ability, rather than developing specific forms. Teaching would involve noting the object the child played with, then pairing the real object with a chosen substitute and demonstrating the similarities of appearance and function. Once the child used the substitute, the original could be withdrawn. Many other games are possible contexts for this type of programme – 'Let's pretend' games are the most obvious choice. (See D. Jeffree, R. McConkey and S. Hewson, *Let Me Play*, Souvenir Press, 1977.)

Using the Stage I curriculum – an example

Now that the major components of the Stage I curriculum have been described, we can see how it can be applied to a hypothetical child, whom we shall name Paul.

Table 7 Stage I. At or below one-word level

Key concept	Cognitive prerequisites	Subsequent developments
Expressive meanings		All communication
Demand	Others recognized as independent agents	Agent + object Demand + object
Recurrence	Others recognized as independent agents. Stable object concept?	Recurrence + object Recurrence + action
Disappearance	Stable object concept?	Disappearance + object
Rejection	Stable object concept?	Rejection + object Rejection + action
Existence	Stable object concept?	Existence + object
Agent	Others recognized as independent agents	Agent + action Action + object Agent + object Locative Possession Instrumental Attributes
Action	Generalized action schemas	
Object	Stable object concept (unless object is highly familiar and frequently present). Recognition of object concerned as a distinct category	

Paul is aged 3, physically active and easy to get on with. An extended period of observation yields the following:

1. He screams and shouts when forced to do something he does not want to do
2. He pushes people and objects away when he wants to get rid of them
3. When shown a sweet which is then hidden behind the teacher's hand, he pushes her hand away to obtain the sweet

4 He plays repetitive games with his teacher and is especially fond of being tickled; he anticipates this by giggling just before the teacher tickles him
5 He holds and plays with a variety of objects among which are a toy car, a ball, a picture book, a plastic cup and a doll
6 He has been observed to push, pull, open, shut, hit and rock these objects, plus a variety of other actions
7 He makes quite a number of sounds in a non-systematic babble: most vowels, and a number of consonants, including 'p', 't', 'k', 'm' and 'g'
8 He responds to his own name
9 He is very fond of chocolate.

These observations indicate that Paul is already using certain meanings, notably *rejection* and *pleasure*, in a non-verbal manner, and that he has the beginnings of language comprehension. It is also clear that he has acquired many of the cognitive prerequisites for Stage I meanings: he performs a variety of well-defined actions on various objects, he has developed a long way towards a stable object concept, and there is evidence from **4** above that he conceives of his teacher as an independent source of action.

From a large number of possible approaches, we decide upon the following meanings and forms as the initial programme, giving him a vocabulary of ten words:

Meanings		*Forms*
Recurrence		More
Disappearance		Gone
Agent:	teacher	Ba-ba (for Barbara)
Action:	push	Pu(sh)
	bang	Bang
	open	Open
Object:	car	Car
	ball	Ball
	cup	Cup
	book	Book

1 *Recurrence*. To teach this, we use Paul's favourite tickling game. We begin by carrying out the normal game to establish a routine, then we delay the tickle and model 'more'. As soon as Paul approximates the 'm' sound, he is tickled. Once 'more' is established, it can be taught in other settings, especially at dinnertime.

2 *Disappearance*. 'Gone' is taught to Paul as a request, using a glove puppet. The teacher puts the puppet on, plays with Paul and hides it once or twice to gain his interest. Then she models 'gone': 'Paul say "gone" ' when the puppet disappears, and reinforces any hint of a 'g' by giving him a small piece of chocolate.

3 *Agent*. From the many ways of teaching a name, we could use the classroom assistant to point to the teacher and model her name, 'Barbara', then say, 'Where's Barbara?' or 'Find Barbara' and prompt the child to go to the teacher. By reinforcing correct responses and fading out the physical prompt, Paul learns to understand 'Barbara' and we can then set about teaching him to produce the name, and to use it to control his teacher's actions.

4 *Action*. We use similar methods to teach the three *action* words, moving from comprehension to production. We present Paul with a variety of objects and bang them and prompt him to bang them. Then the word is introduced followed by a prompt to bang and finally the prompt is withdrawn so that Paul is banging in response only to that word. Once one word is established, the others can be taught and finally we must go through the important stage of alternating between words, so that we give a series of instructions to bang, open and push in any order. Production of these words is taught using standard imitation and reinforcement methods, remembering that we can teach *action* as a request or comment.

5 *Object*. Finally, *object* meanings require careful prerequisite checking and, if necessary, teaching these prerequisites. Paul could, for example, be given a wide variety of balls to play with so he learns the characteristics they have in common. He could also be put through sorting and matching programmes involving discrimination between balls and other objects. Given that he has a well-developed representation of 'ball', normal comprehension and production programmes can follow on.

After Paul has learnt these ten words he is ready to learn more single words, but more significantly he is ready to learn to combine words and to say 'More car', 'Ball gone', 'Open book' and 'Baba push'. These are the meanings with which the second stage of the curriculum framework is concerned.

Stage II. From one to two words

The great step forward at this stage is the development of structure. The central aim is to teach the child to combine meanings taught in Stage I to express new and more specific meanings. There are three major groups of two-word meanings:

1 *Relational + substantive*. By combining a relational with a substantive meaning, the child learns to be more specific about the part of the environment he is talking about. For example, in Stage I a child learns to say 'more' and the context specifies what is to recur. By combining 'more' with an *object* such as 'More ball', he learns to specify the *recurrence* and the *object* of the *recurrence* in his language.

2 *Substantive + substantive*. Linking two substantive meanings in a particular structure allows the child to use a combination of simple statements together to make new meanings. These could not express new meaning by themselves but achieve this in combination within a more complex structure.

3 *New types of words* can be introduced and combined with previously learnt substantive meanings. Particularly important here are prepositions, adjectives and adverbs.

1 Extending relational meanings

Teaching the child to combine the relational with a substantive meaning, helps him to be more specific and less dependent on help and context to make himself understood. Suppose a child has been taught to say 'more' and 'din-din' as separate Stage I meanings. The child can be taught to combine these by the following programme. The methods used are basically the same as in Stage I, except that higher level demands are made of the child.

Objective
The child will say 'More din-din', or an acceptable approximation, to request another piece of food.

Prerequisites
The child has already learnt to say 'more' and 'din-din' in appropriate contexts in Stage I.

Method
a   Show the food to the child and have him label it 'din-din'
b   Give the child a piece of food and offer him another
c   Have him say 'more' to get the next piece of food
d   Repeat **a** to **c** as necessary to establish consistency
e   Hold up piece of food and model 'More din-din'
f   Give the child the food as soon as he imitates 'More din-din', verbally or by indication
g   Establish the response under imitation then fade the imitative prompt.

Programmes to teach *recurrence + object* can readily be extended by helping the child combine a variety of *object* meanings with 'more'. The teacher should also be careful to listen for combinations which have not been taught, showing that the child has developed a generalized *recurrence + object* meaning.

The second example programme for this group combines *disappearance* and *object*, but here the child is taught to comment instead of request.

Objective
The child will say 'Ball gone' when the teacher hides a ball.

Prerequisites
The child has already learnt to say 'ball' and 'gone' in appropriate contexts in Stage I.

Method
a Show the child the ball and have him label it 'ball'
b Hide it and have the child say 'gone'
c Repeat **a** and **b** as necessary to establish consistency
d Show the ball then hide it and model 'Ball gone'; do not ask for response before the twofold process is complete
e Reinforce any approximation to the combination immediately
f Establish the response 'Ball gone' then fade the imitative prompt.

By combining the relational and substantive meanings taught in Stage I, the child's communicative potential can be improved dramatically, forming an extensive list of types of meaning:

Meaning	*Example*
Demand + object	Want drink
Recurrence + object	More din-din
Recurrence + action	More hit
Agent + recurrence	Mummy more
Disappearance + object	Ball gone
Rejection + object	Away ball
Rejection + action	No hit
Existence + object	'Uh ball

2 Combining substantive meanings

In this group of meanings the child learns to express new meanings by virtue of the structure of two-word utterances. These meanings can also initially be approached through comprehension much more readily than the first group of meanings.

Combining *agent*, *action* and *object*, three-word combinations are formed:

agent + action; agent + object; action + object. In the following programme, which teaches comprehension, we ensure the child learns to respond to both parts of the instruction 'Hit the ball' (*action + object*) by allowing him the opportunity to hit two objects.

Objective
The child will hit a ball and a drum when given an instruction to do so.

Prerequisites
The child has already learnt to understand 'ball', 'drum' and 'hit'.

Method
a   Put the ball only in front of the child and say 'Hit the ball'
b   Reinforce correct responses, and repeat until established
c   Remove the ball and repeat **a** and **b** with the drum
d   Put both objects in front of the child and say 'Hit the ball'
e   Reinforce only correct responses. Ignore incorrect responses.

A programme like this would be followed by the productive use of 'Hit ball' and 'Hit drum' and extension to other actions and objects.

Three significant types of meaning in this group involve slight changes in single-word meanings as well as a new combination: these are *possession, instrumental* and *location*.

Possession specifies the possessor (a person) and the possessed (an object). Stage I teaches the child to talk about people only as *agents*, but in this meaning they assume a different role as possessors. The next example teaches comprehension of *possession*. Note that the instruction used is longer than two words but the child is only expected to understand the crucial elements.

Objective
The child will touch the teacher's and assistant's shoes when given the instruction 'Where's X's shoes?'

Prerequisites
The child has learnt the individual *agent* meanings and 'shoes' in Stage I.

Method
a   Stand or sit in front of the child so your shoes are visible and within reach
b   Have the child point to your shoes on the instruction 'shoes'
c   Give the instruction 'Where's (name)'s shoes?' and reinforce correct responses
d   Repeat **a** to **c** with another person
e   Repeat **a** to **c** with both people present and alternate the instructions between the two people.

This programme can be extended by teaching the child to point to different objects possessed by one person, or by introducing production of an utterance such as 'Anne shoes'.

Instrumental meanings express an action and the object used to perform that action. Objects take on a slightly different role as *instrument* in utterances such as 'Hit it *with a hammer*'. Teaching procedures are very closely related to the example programme for *possession*. The child is provided with something to hit and two objects to hit with and taught to respond to 'Hit it with the X'. Later, productive use of this meaning with a form such as 'Hit hammer' can be used.

Location combines one substantive meaning as an object and one as a position, as in the utterance 'Ball chair'. This type of utterance precedes the use of more complex forms specifying the exact relationship between the object and the position using prepositions, but prepositions can be introduced at this stage as the next section suggests.

It will be clear by now that language and equivalent non-verbal communication systems are already becoming alarmingly complicated. It is impossible to illustrate all possible combinations of two substantive meanings, but the following list summarizes the major types which may be taught:

Meaning	*Example*
Agent + object	Anne spoon
Agent + action	Anne hit
Action + object	Hit ball
Action + action	Hit shake
Object + object	Ball car
Possession	Anne shoe
Instrumental	Hit hammer
Location	Ball chair

3 New meanings

At Stage II we can begin to introduce words which qualify (adjectives and adverbs), and words which specify time and space relationships (prepositions). The cognitive prerequisites for the first two groups of meanings are largely ensured by Stage I programmes, but this group introduces new concepts which demand that we check the child's non-verbal ability to cope with the specific meanings we aim to teach.

One of the more useful *attributes* to teach is size, represented by the words 'big' and 'little' or their non-verbal equivalents. Before a child can attach these labels to abstract concepts he must be able to differentiate objects according to size. The first stage will be non-verbal sorting of, say, big and little balls, and other methods of teaching the child non-verbally. Once the non-verbal concept is established, comprehension and then production of utterances such as 'big' can be introduced. This concept–comprehension–production sequence has already been outlined. The following programme teaches an adverb *attribute* and combines with an *action*.

Objective 1
The child will run slowly and quickly by imitating the teacher.

Method
Use PE to demonstrate the difference (non-verbally) between slowly and quickly. Have the child run quickly and slowly, with physical prompts at first if necessary and then possibly using music of different tempi.

Objective 2
The child will run slowly or quickly in response to verbal instructions.

Method
a   Model running quickly and have the child imitate this
b   Say 'Run quickly' and model running quickly – have the child imitate
c   Fade out the physical prompt so that the child is running quickly in response only to the instruction
d   Repeat **a** to **c** for 'slowly'.

Objective 3
The child will say 'Run quickly' to describe another person performing that action.

Method
a   One person runs quickly so the child can see
b   Model 'Run quickly' – have the child imitate it
c   Establish the imitation, and progressively withdraw the verbal prompt so that the child describes the action directly.

(All the example programmes in this chapter are greatly abridged. Chapter VI provides similar programmes in detail.)

The second set of new words in this group are prepositions. Words such as 'in', 'under', 'on' are all very powerful tools with which to express meanings, as they are applicable to many situations. Concepts involving *location* can usefully be approached by combining *object* words, but this only describes where an object is, and not the relationships the objects bear to each other. (See Chapter VI and Appendix D for detailed programmes to teach prepositions, particularly 'near to' and 'far away'.)

Words or meanings

In Stage I we discussed words which refer to people under *agent* meanings.

This is the most important use of these words, but we use words for people in many ways:

1 'John handed the baby to Mary.' This sentence uses words for people to make three different meanings. 'John' is the *agent* of the action, 'baby' is the *object* of the action, and 'Mary' is the *recipient*.
2 'John, I think Mary feels ill.' In this sentence 'John' is used as a *vocative* meaning and 'Mary' is the *experiencer* of a state.
3 'That is John's ball.' This sentence has 'John' as a *possessor*. There are, therefore, at least six ways of using one word referring to a person, which express six different meanings.

This also applies to words which refer to objects. Words for objects can be used for at least the following five meanings:

1 Agent: '*John* hit the ball'
2 Object: 'John hit the *ball*'
3 Instrument: 'John hit it with a *bat*'
4 Possession: 'It was Mary's *bat*'
5 Location: 'He hit it into the *house*'

or all together: The *ball* which *John* hit with Mary's *bat* rolled into the *house*.
            ↑   ↑   ↑   ↑
      object   agent   instrument   location
                              possessed

The last sentence shows that words can not only convey different meanings at different times, but also indicate several meanings at the same time. Such daunting complexities make it much more convenient to talk of words rather than meanings at later stages.

At Stage I, we must be highly specific about what meanings a child can make with particular forms, but as the child learns a more flexible system, we can shift our attention to teaching words. It is still important to remember the different meanings involved – at no time can we guarantee a child will use a word in all its possible meanings. Careful observation is necessary to find out how a child is making use of the words he is taught.

Forms at Stage II

The choice of a form for a meaning in Stage I depends on what the child is capable of producing, and the need for standardized forms is not vital. So long as the most important people in a child's life – parents and teachers and others with whom he is constantly in touch – can interpret his communications, we can be content at that level of development. During Stage II, however, children begin to expand their horizons. Communication with strange adults and with other children becomes much more feasible. We need to give careful attention to the forms being used and the degree to which other people will understand them.

There are two paths to solving these difficulties, neither of which is simple. First, we can ensure that most adults in contact with the child understand his idiosyncratic forms. If a non-verbal communication system is introduced in a hospital school, it is obviously vital that hospital staff outside the school should be conversant with the system. For a child living at home, this approach relies completely on the degree of co-operation between staff and parents. It is not unreasonable for neighbours and local shopkeepers to learn a few of the child's more frequently used non-verbal signs, but it is well beyond the scope of the teacher to teach them. This job of extending a child's communicative horizon must be the prime responsibility of the parents.

An alternative is the use of two different systems to combine meanings. The child can call someone's attention vocally and then point to the object of interest. This is what another child, Ian, described in Chapter VII, does. Ian was originally taught to point to an object he wanted. Although this is a powerful sign, it is limited to controlling people already attending to him. By shouting and then pointing, Ian could begin to control people at some distance, combining *vocative* and *demand* meanings using a vocal form and signing.

Combining verbal and non-verbal forms might be very useful for a child heavily limited by articulation difficulties. One particularly useful strategy might be the use of vocal forms for relational meanings such as 'more' and signs to indicate *object* meanings. Because relational meanings apply to many different settings, the child would use his limited vocal potential to the full and constantly be reinforced for exercising this ability. At the same time he would not be limited by articulatory difficulties, since signs would be used to represent substantive meanings. Stage II combines the vocal and non-vocal forms using each medium as much as possible.

Much of what was said in Stage I about teaching form on its own continues to apply in Stage II. Careful use of observations, imitation and shaping procedures will lead to an increasingly large 'pool' of sounds or gestures which can be selected from for meanings.

Prerequisites for Stage II

There are behaviours which are necessary precursors to the new skills to be taught – this is the sense in which we have used 'prerequisite' earlier in the chapter. And there are behaviours which are necessary for the successful use of teaching methods, but which do not contribute to the curricular content.

1 CONTENT PREREQUISITES

The introduction of new types of words and new meanings at this stage adds a new set of prerequisites which form the 'concept' stage in the programmes developed in Chapter VI. This sort of prerequisite has been discussed in the example given above (page 136), but it is worth emphasizing the general principles. We are dealing with abstractions when we teach prepositions and adjectives. There is no 'on' or 'big' – they are generalized aspects of the environment which we are able to represent. Furthermore, words such as 'big' are defined only by reference to their opposites. Nothing is big unless something else is small, and vice versa. We know that normal children do not suddenly understand these abstract words as adults do. It takes a considerable time during the pre-school years, when a child passes through several stages, varying his interpretation of these words. These issues are currently being debated by psychologists.

There are at least three approaches to teaching the non-verbal concept underlying these abstract words.

1 *Sorting*. The child is presented with a jumble of objects which differ in certain attributes and is asked to put them into a number of piles.
2 *Matching*. The teacher holds up an example, say, of a colour, and the child has to find the same colour from a number of colours.
3 *Functional use*. While we can use sorting and matching to teach words like 'in' and 'on', perhaps a more viable approach is to emphasize these concepts by having the child use them non-verbally to put things under and on things, to get under tables, and sit on tables, etc. Success with such programmes does not, however, guarantee success at the communication level.

At Stage II, we can also expect increasingly diverse materials to be used as stimuli, varying in familiarity, present or non-present, and objects or pictures of objects. We must not hinder progress by selecting material out of step with the child's abilities. The question most often raised is: 'Does the child understand the connexions between pictures and objects?' The answer comes in two stages. First, the child must know about an object in some way before he can use pictures of it. The second stage involves the translation from objects to pictures. Most teaching programmes at this stage use stimuli which are present in the teaching context. At some stage we must teach children to refer to objects which are not present, particularly when teaching the demanding, controlling functions of language. This 'indirect reference' in language depends on a fully mature object concept (see Stage I), and on using material which the child has used recently.

2 METHOD PREREQUISITES

Teaching programmes are very often defeated not because of the content of the programme, but because of peripheral problems – for example, the child does not attend to one stimulus for long enough, he has a hearing loss of some sort, he is reluctant to imitate, etc. Often there is waste of time and effort because such problems have not been tackled.

For example, if a child's hands are constantly moving around, it is unrealistic to teach non-verbal forms of communication. The first part of a programme for such a child would involve establishing some base-line resting position for the hands. Similarly, if a child does not look at an object, there is no way to teach its name efficiently – we must ensure his attention to the object for a minimum time before beginning the communication programme.

Generalizing Stage II objectives

There are three clear ways in which we can talk about generalization:

1   The generalized use of a meaning type. If, for example, we teach 'more' and a number of *object* meanings in Stage I, and then teach 'More ball' in Stage II, we cannot claim the child has a generalized conception of *recurrence + object* until he can spontaneously combine 'more' with other *object* meanings.
2   Generalization to other situations. If a child is taught in a quiet room with only child and teacher present, can he then use that meaning with other people, in other rooms, at different times, etc?
3   Generalization to other functions. If a meaning is taught as a request, can the child use it as a comment, or vice versa?

1 THE GENERALIZED USE OF MEANING TYPES

We cannot directly teach this but we can set up the best possible conditions for its development, and watch very carefully for spontaneous new utterances. In Stage II we attempt to teach a child *rules* for combining meanings.

II. GENERALIZING OBJECTIVES 141

It would be optimism indeed to expect a child to use the rule after only one or two examples, so our programmes must teach a *series* of examples using different single-word meanings. We must make it clear that the examples have something in common, by teaching them one after each other, and by recapping on previous objectives just before teaching a new example. We can also give the child opportunities to use the rule in new ways with different single-word meanings by providing *probes*. A probe for generalized use of *recurrence + object* might be as follows:

Previous objectives
The child has reached criterion on the production of 'More ball', 'More teddy' and 'More din-din'. He has also learnt the word 'drink' in Stage I.

Probe
1   Hold the drink up to the child. Have him label it, then give him a drink.
2   Take the drink beyond arm's reach and hold it up ready. *Do not prompt.*
3   Does he spontaneously produce 'More drink'?

Failure simply means that more direct teaching of the meaning concerned will be necessary.

2 SITUATIONAL GENERALIZATION

The cardinal principle here is: assume nothing about a child's ability to use language in different contexts until you have observed it. Generalizations that are not observed must be taught. Essentially, this type of programme is concerned with modifying three aspects of the environment in which language is used:

a   People: who is communicated with?
b   Place: where does the communication take place?
c   Time: when does it occur?

Take the following list of generalizations planned for a Stage II objective:

Previous objectives
The child has already learnt 'Hit ball' as a request in a one-to-one situation in a small, undistracting room.

Generalizations
1   Use of 'Hit ball' in the same room with a large number of distracting objects
2   Use of 'Hit ball' in the same room with another adult
3   Use of 'Hit ball' in the same room with a child
4   Use in the classroom with the teacher
5   Use in the classroom with another adult

142   CURRICULUM CONTENT

6   Use in the classroom with a child
7   Use in the playground with the teacher, another adult and children.

This is a very detailed list – a degree of detail which is not often necessary – but it shows the possibilities which may need to be considered.

3   FUNCTIONAL GENERALIZATION

The principles which apply to this aspect of the generalization problem are much the same irrespective of level of language ability, and we devote a separate section to this later in the chapter.

Using the Stage II curriculum – an example

We return to our hypothetical child, Paul, somewhat older now, having passed through Stage I, but not without difficulty. Nevertheless, he has reached all the objectives set for him in Stage I and is now ready to learn one or two combinations of meanings. In Stage I Paul was taught four *action* meanings and four *object* meanings in addition to his teacher's name as *agent*, *recurrence* and *disappearance*.

As we progress up the developmental scale, the number of possible objectives expands vastly. Keeping within the scope of available resources, the following Stage II objectives are selected for Paul:

	Meanings	*Forms*
1	Recurrence + object	More ball
		More cup
2	Disappearance + object	Ball gone
		Cup gone
		Book gone
3	Agent + action	Ba-ba push
		Ba-ba bang
		Ba-ba open
4	Action + object	Push car
		Bang car
		Bang cup
		Open book

1 + 2   RECURRENCE + OBJECT AND DISAPPEARANCE + OBJECT

Using the same methods as in Stage I, we play with the ball, have Paul label

Table 8 Stage II. From one to two words

Key concept	Prerequisites	Subsequent developments
Demand + object	Demand, object	Functional control of others
Recurrence + action	Recurrence, action	Plurals, number/quantity words
Recurrence + object	Recurrence, object	
Agent + recurrence	Agent, recurrence	
Disappearance + object	Disappearance, object	Negatives
Rejection + object	Rejection, object	
Rejection + action	Rejection, action	
Existence + object	Existence, object	'Deixis' – demonstrative pronouns; articles, identity statements
Agent + object	Agent, action, object	Subject–verb–object sentences
Agent + action		
Action + object		
Action + action	Action	Plurals, conjunctions
Object + object	Object	
Possession	Agent, action	Possessives
Instrumental	Action, object	Instrumentals, adverbial phrases
Location	Object	Prepositions
Attributes	Object	Adjectives, adverbs, Comparatives, superlatives, Same/different
	Degree of non-verbal representation of concept	
Prepositions	Object	Prepositions
	Degree of non-verbal representation of concept	

it, then hide it. Paul should say 'gone'. This is followed by the teacher modelling the two-word combination 'Ball gone'. Any approximation to the two words is reinforced immediately. Spontaneous use of 'more' can be used in the same teaching sequence. If this occurs, then the teacher models 'More ball' and reinforces any approximation to the combination by making the ball appear. Depending upon Paul's reaction to the situation, the two combinations can be taught separately or together at first.

3 AGENT + ACTION

In Stage I, Paul learnt to produce both these meanings individually. This meaning cannot be taught receptively, except with picture material, and photographs of the teacher doing things are probably rare. Consequently, we teach Paul to use this meaning to direct his teacher to do something. An assistant directs the teacher in Paul's presence then models the phrase. Any approximation should lead to the teacher carrying out the action as directed.

4 ACTION + OBJECT

This group of meanings can be successfully taught to Paul using comprehension first, even though he may have productive use of the individual words. To ensure he is responding to the instructions appropriately, he is given the opportunity to make mistakes so that, for example, the car, book and cup are available following the instruction 'Push the car'. Following successful comprehension, Paul is then taught to produce these combinations.

This very small number of individual meanings is only a beginning. Paul's teacher will watch and listen very carefully for the generalized use of the meanings in everyday activities, and will certainly teach many more combinations. The fact that Paul has reached Stage II with some meanings does not imply he has finished with Stage I. Normal adults never stop learning new single words, so there is no reason why a mentally handicapped child should.

Stage III. Extending meaning and structure

Having taken a child through Stages I and II he should be able to provide a variety of one- and two-word utterances or their non-verbal equivalents. He will have developed a wide range of meanings classified under various headings, and may have developed generalized meanings. In Stage II he has learnt that the way meanings are put together into structures can also carry meaning. We have been able to keep track up to Stage II of his overall growth in language and communicative ability, but he is now on the threshold of an explosion of language which means that most of his ability will go unnoticed and unrecorded. Our job in Stage III is to select and teach the most important aspects of language, and to be much more concerned with teaching *rules* to the child which he can use to generate new language outside the teaching context.

When children begin to tie more than two words together in their language, the currently available commercial language programmes become more viable. (Four of these are reviewed in Chapter IX. These programmes are very much geared towards the development of more complex meanings and structures.)

Because there is no limit to the ways in which we can combine various structures and meanings, we have selected just a few of the crucial skills which form the building blocks of complex sentences. Many others have been omitted but it should not be too difficult to apply the principles to other areas of language.

Basic teaching strategies – Stage III

A central principle of teaching at this stage is that we expand on what the child can already do by increasing our demands for adult constructions and forms. A child will continue to communicate at a certain level as long as that type of communication is adequate. When it becomes clear to a child that his behaviour is inadequate, we can expect development to occur. As with Stages I and II, we create this sort of situation by using a child's strong motivation and making increased demands on him. If a child has learned in Stage II to say 'Hit ball', he will continue to use that utterance until we demand more complete and adult-like language. He has only to add one small word – 'the' – which is a minor step to take.

It is clear that as a child moves towards adult-like structure and form, the number of meanings he can make grows vastly. Increasingly, we are forced to teach structure in order to teach meaning – particularly when a child learns to express the relationships, not between words, but between groups of words. Take the following sentence:

> If John throws the ball, then I will catch it.

The sentence contains two clauses which have their own meaning and structure, but they are also linked together in a particular way using the words 'if . . . then'. These words link clauses, not individual words. Not only are the words important, but their positions are vital to the meaning.

With the move towards adult structure, the relationships between comprehension and production are also simplified; in most cases the groups of objectives discussed below can be approached in the standard concept–comprehension–production sequence. However, certain highly abstract words will still present problems at the comprehension level. For example, the meaning of 'because' is so complicated and abstract that a child would probably have to try it out productively to observe the effects of using it, before he could grasp its complete meaning.

It may happen that the word order in the Stage II form is incompatible with the adult structure. A child might have learnt 'Gone ball', and if we wish to teach him in Stage III to say 'The ball has gone', we might need a transitional programme to turn 'Gone ball' into 'Ball gone'. This difficulty should only occur, of course, in Stage II utterances which combine relational and substantive meanings.

Aspects of the Stage III curriculum

The discussion here is divided into three sections, for convenience rather than to suggest a sequence for teaching: the building blocks of clauses, simple clauses, complex sentences.

1 THE BUILDING BLOCKS OF CLAUSES

Plurals

Table 8 shows how Stage II has laid the groundwork for the development of adult pluralization, by teaching *recurrence + object* and *object + object*. The differences between these meanings and the adult plural is subtle, and implies an added check at the cognitive level. Adult plurals distinguish 'one' and 'more than one' – a distinction which does not necessarily exist in Stage II and therefore should be checked and possibly taught using sorting procedures. The child might be required to sort pictures of single objects and groups of objects.

There is more than one way to signal the plural in English. Even the '-s' ending is three different sounds: ca*ts*, do*gs*, fish*es*. We can also say: 'many cats', 'lots of cats', 'several cats', etc. To begin with, children may experience difficulty with the '-s' ending since the sounds are very short, and it may be necessary to use words like 'lots of' as an initial verbal prompt. Confusion between the three sounds is much less important, but can be remedied later if necessary.

A basic programme to teach plurals, first as comprehension, might look like the following:

Objective 1
The child will point to a collection of objects in response to 'Show me lots of Xs', and to one object in response to 'Show me one X'.
Method
a   Put a collection of objects in front of the child. Say, 'Show me lots of Xs'.
b   Reward correct responses and repeat a few times.
c   Remove the collection, and put one object in front of the child. Say, 'Show me one X'.
d   Reward correct responses and repeat a few times.

III. ASPECTS OF STAGE III CURRICULUM

e   Put both one object and a collection of objects in front of the child. Present the plural instruction.
f   Reward correct responses. Prompt if necessary at first.
g   Repeat **a** to **f** with different objects until response is established.

Objective 2
The child will point to a collection of objects in response to 'Show me Xs', and to one object in response to 'Show me X'.

Method
As above, but this time emphasize the plural ending.

Objective 3
The child will imitate 'Xs'.

Method
a   Run through the method for objective 2
b   After a correct response to 'Show me Xs' ask the child to 'Say Xs'
c   Reward approximations to the '-s' ending
d   Repeat and establish.

Objective 4
The child will say 'Xs' in response to 'What are these'?

Method
a   Present the child with a collection of objects and label them 'Xs'.
b   Say, 'What are these?' Reward correct responses or provide imitative prompt.
c   Repeat, gradually withdrawing the prompt.

Possessives

Since the basic meaning has been developed in Stage II, our job in Stage III is to add the possessive ending '-'s' to the possessor. This is a fairly easy programme in which we simply make higher demands on the child for the required ending. However, unless a child is capable of producing an 's' on the end of a word there is little point in trying to teach it as the plural or possessive ending. In this case, a separate programme to teach just this form could be introduced.

    Not all possessive constructions are of this type – from casual observation, one might think the child is more likely to learn the irregular possessive pronouns, 'my', 'mine', before the structurally simpler forms. Possessive pronouns are useful words to learn – possibly more so than simple personal pronouns such as 'I', 'he', etc. Take the following possible programme, using a mealtime situation:

Objective
The child will respond correctly to the instructions, 'Eat yours' and 'Eat mine'.

Method
a   Teacher and child sit at the dinner table each with their own plates of food.
b   Point to each plate in turn and say, 'mine' and 'yours'.
c   Say, 'Eat mine' and prompt the child to take a spoonful. Praise correct responses.
d   Repeat c with 'Eat yours'. Establish both instructions individually, and withdraw the prompts.
e   Alternate the instructions.

Negatives

Rejection and *disappearance* in Stages I and II form the conceptual and linguistic foundations for teaching negatives, which comprise a very large and diverse group of objectives. The most common approach to teaching negatives is with materials depicting objects and actions, with the teacher asking: 'Is this a bus?' or 'Show me the man who is not running', etc. Listening to normal classroom conversations, children are much more likely to come across negatives in sentences such as 'Don't do that' and 'No, it's not in there'. If possible, teaching negatives should be geared to the way a child is likely to use them. Negative meaning can be attached to many aspects of language, including objects, actions, people, location and attributes. In teaching negatives in relation to objects, one possibility is a competitive game in which the teacher works with a small group, as in the following example:

Objective
The child will give a different object to the teacher following the instruction, 'It's not an X'.

Method
a   Each child is given the same two objects.
b   The game is established by a series of instructions like 'It's the X'. Children who succeed are rewarded, those failing are prompted until each child is performing consistently.
c   The teacher now says, 'It's *not* the X', and rewards correct responses.
d   Repetition of the instruction, imitation and prompting should lead to correct responses.

If this seems too difficult, it could be taught individually at first, or by using another adult as an errorless stooge.

Similar situations can be devised for teaching negatives in relation to verbs, adjectives, etc. It is better to use methods which have relevance to the child and do not seem artificial. Instructions such as 'Don't run' in PE are better than 'Show me the one who is not running' using picture materials. The former is commonly used and structurally simple; in the latter, the negative is swallowed up in an unusual and complicated sentence.

Verb tense

It is very hard to find out about the children's understanding of time. *Action* meanings in Stages I and II have been in the present tense, but this does not imply they are conceptually bound to the present. Many of the meanings involve implicit reference to the past and future. 'Ball gone' describes a present state by reference to the past. 'More ball' anticipates a future event, although describing a present desire. Thus children use time in their language at an early stage, giving us something to build on. Later children will talk about the past and future without necessarily altering the verbs they use. We can gain knowledge of children's comprehension of the temporal aspects of language by asking questions such as 'What did you have for dinner today?' and 'What are you going to do next?' Appropriate responses suggest that the child has established some of the prerequisite skills for learning verb tense.

Suppose a child replies to the first question with correct facts but immature syntax: 'Eat chips and peas'. This response indicates a programme based on imitation in which the teacher would provide the correct model – 'ate' – and reward for approximations. More immediate situations could easily be devised: a picture lotto game could be used to teach 'I won', or a miming game to teach children to describe bodily actions in the past. Exactly the same ideas apply to teaching the future tense. The principles of such situations may be summarized as:

1 Find an event in the past or future which children already refer to in some way
2 Teach the syntactic tense marker for the verb.

Avoid situations which involve complicated inferences by the children. One might, for example, show the child a model of a car teetering on the edge of a cliff, and expect him to describe it as 'The car is going to fall', but this kind of method assumes the child perceives the situation as we do. Why should he? It is also not the sort of event the child is likely to encounter in his everyday life, and generalization problems may result.

It is desirable to keep tense as simple as possible initially but important that the eventual complexities are not ignored. There are many ways of indicating the past and future in language, each having a slightly different connotation, and we can express relationships between events by linking clauses, using words such as 'before' and 'after'. The first problem is to get children to mark tense in their communication, and then we may begin to expand the variety of ways of indicating time.

Pronouns

The cognitive prerequisites for pronouns are established if the child differentiates between males, females and objects, and between one and more than one. The paradox of teaching pronouns is that we teach them when they are not necessary to the meaning of the communication. We can make the meaning of a sentence depend on a pronoun but a rather unusual sentence results. If we teach 'you', we might begin by getting the child to respond correctly to 'You do it'. But he will probably know perfectly well from the context what is expected, and the instruction 'Do it' would probably be just as effective. For the sake of teaching, we could just say 'you' but that would be very strange. Again, we might teach 'me' and 'him' in a game in which the child had to throw a ball to the teacher (me) and to another child (him). 'Give it to me' is simple and real enough, but we would never say 'Give it to him' without previously saying who he is or without pointing at 'him', and in both these cases we do not know whether the child is responding to the pronoun or to something else. Teaching production of pronouns is less problematical than comprehension. One possible approach is to demand answers to questions such as 'What's John doing?', which involves pronouns, such as 'He is running'.

We often miss pronouns in the child's normal use of language. Observations of dialogue between children might well reveal a number of uses, particularly in sequences such as: 'Bet you can't, 'Bet I can', etc.

Other building blocks

The four aspects discussed represent a few of the elements which go to make up clauses. Many others have been discussed in Stages I and II. Among the elements not discussed are articles, demonstrative pronouns, number words such as few, many and some, and superordinate category names (for example, 'animal'). (Many of these are dealt with in the language kits reviewed in Chapter IX.)

2 SIMPLE SINGLE CLAUSES

Subject–verb–object clauses as requests and comments

Meanings referring to objects, people and actions can be taught as basic subject–verb–object (SVO) constructions, beginning with simple three-word utterances and gradually combining them to form more complex versions. We can also teach this construction in various *modalities* which relate closely to the functions of language already discussed. The three basic modalities are: declarative ('The boy hit the ball'), imperative ('Hit the ball') and interrogative ('Did the boy hit the ball?').

Much of our language is built from SVO clauses in various forms, so one might look on this as the central group of objectives for Stage III. Having taught the word combinations of *agent + action*, *action + object* and *agent + object*, it is relatively simple to teach the basic *agent + action + object* meaning as a request (that is, in the imperative modality) and as a comment (in the declarative). Rather than accept an utterance like 'Hit ball', we increase the demands on the child and expect 'Boy hit ball'. At this stage, before the child inserts the ending and 'function words', the imperative and declarative have the same form. It is much more important at this stage to get the child to express the basic meaning of an utterance, perfectly conveyed by 'Boy hit ball' than to insist on syntactic perfection as in 'The boy is hitting the ball'. Articles and verb endings can be added as 'building blocks' later. A sequence of objectives leading to an adult SVO clause might be as follows:

1 'Boy hit ball' – basic structure which communicates meaning adequately
2 'Boy hitting ball' – present continuous ending added
3 'Boy is hitting ball' – auxiliary verb added
4 'The boy is hitting the ball' – definite article added to form the complete construction.

Once the basic SVO clause has been taught using an *agent + action + object* meaning, different meanings can be fitted into the same syntactic structure. The sentence, 'John likes sweets' describes an *experiencer + state* meaning, but has the same structure as 'John hits the ball'. The complexities of meaning at this stage, therefore, make it easier to base the curriculum on groups of syntactic objectives, and to expand the types of meaning that may be communicated within them. The number of different examples of SVO clauses that can be taught depends only on previously learnt words and the opportunities for communication in the classroom. As in Stage II, probes become very important in checking whether or not the child has a generalized use of a construction.

Turning simple clauses into questions

To ask a question, we can either turn a sentence around to ask a 'yes/no' question like 'Is this a ball?', or we can use a rising intonation, without changing sentence structure, or we can use a particular set of words to form 'wh—— questions' – what, who, whose, where, when, etc. Each of these words asks for a particular sort of information. The 'who' asked about may be the subject or object of a sentence. Some question words have different meanings depending on the sentence they occur in: 'What's that?', 'What's he doing?', 'What's that for?', 'What's the time?'. Each of these questions asks for different information, but uses the same word. In devising objectives to teach children to ask questions, a major consideration must be the type of information which the question seeks. A basic list of question types might include the following:

1 Agent of action – who's doing it?
2 Action – what's he doing?
3 Object of action – what's he hitting?
4 Identity of person – who's that?
5 Identity of object – what's that?
6 Possession – whose is this?; who's got an X?
7 Location – where's X?
8 Time – when are we going?

In all likelihood, Stage II teaching methods have used questions such as 'What's that?', and the child must be able to understand if he responds correctly. If a child did not originally understand the question he probably will learn it as a by-product of the teaching method, since it involves asking the question, modelling the answer, and rewarding correct imitations. In this way a child learns that certain questions expect certain sorts of answers. The same approach can be adopted to teach comprehension of questions directly, as in the following example:

Objective
The child will answer, 'On the table', or an acceptable approximation, in response to 'Where's the ball?'.

Prerequisites
The child has already learnt the individual words required in the answer as a Stage II *location* meaning.

Method
a   Place a ball on the table in front of the child.
b   Say, 'Where's the ball?' If no response occurs model, 'On the table. You say it.'
c   Reward any approximations such as 'table'.
d   Repeat **a** to **c**, fading the imitative prompt, until the child answers directly.

Of course, this is only the first part of a programme to teach comprehension of 'where' questions. Generalized understanding would require a variety of different situations.

Teaching productive use of questions requires situations in which there is a real need for the child to get the information. It also requires that the answer should be immediately forthcoming. One possible way of teaching use of 'who' questions arose out of observing a child alleged to use very little language put in charge of a lotto game. Once given control of the situation, 'Who's got . . .?' questions poured forth as she held up pictures and asked, 'Who's got a gate?', 'Who's got a ship?', etc. This situation is easily converted into direct teaching by ensuring that all other participants in the game will respond correctly, and by making the child to be taught the caller. The initial stages might involve the child only calling out the name of the picture, and once this is established, the teacher could model the question form, and reward correct approximations.

Adding building blocks to the basic clause

It is at this stage that matters begin to get complicated beyond our ability to describe language, so we can only hint at the possibilities for teaching. Take the following sentence:

John's dogs are playing with a ball in the street on a Sunday afternoon.

This is one clause which builds on a subject–verb construction (dogs are playing), by combining possessives (John's), instrumental (with a ball), location (in the street), and time (on a Sunday afternoon). Each of these components has its own structure. A full description of such a sentence is a lengthy and detailed process, and yet we would wish children eventually to be able to produce sentences of comparable complexity. How do we arrive at such an aim?

Clearly, there is no room to expand in detail on the groups of objectives as in Stages I and II, but we can provide basic guidelines. The most important principle is: one element at a time. Once a child has learnt to say 'Throw the ball' or an approximation such as 'Throw ball', and has moved on to Stage

III, then we can teach 'Throw *me* the ball' – adding the indirect object to the sentence. Next, we might add a qualifier such as size, as in 'Throw the big ball', and then combine these two elements into 'Throw me the big ball'.

Secondly, build up a variety of short sentences, rather than a limited number of long sentences. Most sentences spoken to children are fairly short and generally involve a very few elements at a time. Similarly, children can do a great deal with fairly simple sentences. The demands of the environment come into play in controlling objectives here. It is very rare that anyone needs to use such a complicated sentence as the example above in everyday life.

Finally, help the child to be fluent at combining elements both in comprehension and production, by selecting objectives involving elements in combination with each other. For example, a locative phrase, 'In the cupboard', could be taught in combination with simple, single subject–verb constructions – 'The ball is in the cupboard'. Then it might be combined with the plural subject – 'The knives are in the cupboard'; with present-tense verbs – 'John is hiding in the cupboard', etc. So, we are not merely teaching a locative phrase, but also fitting it into a wide variety of short sentence frames.

3 COMPLEX SENTENCES

All the clauses examined so far have stood alone, but language also combines clauses in many ways to form complex sentences which are generally classified into two groups:

1. Those with co-ordinate clauses, connected by conjunctions such as 'and', 'but', 'or'
2. Those with subordinate clauses, connected by linking words such as 'since', 'because', 'when', etc.

Conjunctions are nearly always found in language programmes at some stage, and are certainly most important. Successful teaching depends on an understanding of the many ways in which words like 'and' can be used:

> *John and Mary* are tall – linking nouns
> John is *tall and thin* – linking adjectives
> John is *kicking and screaming* – linking verbs
> *John is hot and Mary is cold* – linking clauses.

A complete programme to teach the use of 'and' would begin simply with three-words constructions such as 'ball and book'. Comprehension of this phrase might be taught using pictures of various people and the instruction, 'Give me the ball and the book'. Similarly, combinations of verbs, adjectives and adverbs could be taught in this simple manner, before moving on to fitting conjunctions into sentences, and then to teaching conjunctions as links between clauses. It should be said that children will probably already use 'and' in their language in various ways which only detailed observations will reveal.

Another group of complex sentences are those expressing cause and effect, most frequently with 'if . . . then' and 'because'. 'If . . . then' constructions predict what will take place as in 'If I hit her, she will cry', whereas 'because' constructions give reasons, as in 'She cried because I hit her'. These sentence patterns can be taught by using a combination of production and comprehension in which we ask the question using the information in one clause, for example, 'Why is she crying?'. The child must comprehend the question, and at the same time produce the answer, 'Because he hit her'. The process can be simplified by initially not demanding the word 'because', and concentrating on the meaning of the question and answer and the links between them, as in the following example series of objectives:

1   The child will reply to the question 'What's happening in the picture?' by describing the picture as 'He is hitting her' and 'She's crying', or approximations to these
2   The child will reply to the question 'Why is she crying?' with 'He is hitting her' or an acceptable approximation
3   The child will reply to the question 'Why is she crying?' with 'Because he is hitting her'
4   The child will reply to the question 'Why is she crying?' with 'She is crying because he is hitting her'.

It should be emphasized that programmes teaching causality in language can begin at a much earlier stage than this example suggests, particularly if the child's productive language lags considerably behind his comprehension. The basic meaning of the sentence can be communicated by a child who is only putting three words together, for example, 'Hit 'cos cry', although this utterance is limited to a very specific context if it is to be understood by others.

Language in use

Although we have made meaning the central theme of the curriculum framework, it should be clear that no one can make a meaning without using it at the same time. For the purposes of the curriculum framework, language functions can be classified as follows:

1. Language for controlling others
2. Language for social interaction
3. Language for imagination
4. Language for inquiry and discovery
5. Language for expressing emotions and feelings
6. Language for describing the world
7. 'Language for language'.

Each of these groups involves both production and comprehension. They form the basis for the development of a series of teaching situations, but many also occur naturally in the course of teaching meanings.

1 LANGUAGE FOR CONTROLLING OTHERS

We have emphasized this function most strongly at Stage I. We are fundamentally concerned with helping the child to affect his environment – to realize that what he does matters. This is achieved by making appropriate demands upon the child, and by being responsive to his directions. We need not let the child have his own way all the time, but unless he makes demands upon the people around him, he will remain very restricted.

The fundamental aspects of this function are established in many profoundly handicapped children (see Chapter VII). Beyond that low level, we must constantly ensure that the child can use any new skill he is taught for this purpose. How can we manipulate the situation to force the child to do this? Basically, the child must be put in an *initiating role*. He could hand out bottles of milk; be a shopkeeper or a lotto caller; lead a 'Simon Says' game – in fact, within limits, children could be put into most roles the teacher normally fulfils, to teach them to use language to control others.

The comprehension of this function – being controlled – can be given less priority since so much of the child's time is spent in this role. It is important not to confuse situations in which the child does not understand the meaning of a piece of language, with those where he does not realize the language is intended to make him do something. The two are hard to distinguish, but we can minimize the difficulties by making instructions to the child direct, such as 'Pick it up', rather than indirect, such as 'Would you like to pick it up?' Under normal conditions, a child's non-response to an indirect instruction would probably lead to a simplification of the language, and various non-verbal prompts until the child responded adequately. Observing the child's response to instructions in various forms reveals a lot about his ability to decode the speaker's intention.

2 LANGUAGE FOR SOCIAL INTERACTION

We often use language, not to control people, but simply to establish and maintain social contacts. Many aspects of this function are not necessary in the classroom, where the social context is so well established that the child can avoid the use of language to get along with other people if he chooses. Teaching the function requires situations which demand language for social interaction. Even a child with very limited one- or two-word utterances can develop basic conversational strategies, both as responder and initiator, in which the primary purpose is simply to get on with other people. Using language for this function can probably take an incidental place in the curriculum, but specific programmes could be written to teach the use of conversational devices such as 'thank you'. Indeed, this is one aspect of language with which parents and teachers are often most concerned.

3 LANGUAGE FOR IMAGINATION

Opportunities abound in the classroom for imaginative use of language, which develop from earlier symbolic play programmes – playing houses, playing doctors, racing 'cars'. A child who has developed a wide range of Stage II meanings plays with the doll in a Wendy house. We accept the child's fantasy situation and ask 'Who's that?' and 'What's she doing?' in a planned sequence aimed at eliciting certain specific meanings. Such situations form the beginnings of creative uses of language. Later, when the child has learnt to use various meanings and structures in simple imaginative ways which describe his symbolic play, we can introduce story-telling, describing pictures, guessing at the functions of strange objects, and all the other well-known bases for creative language.

4 LANGUAGE FOR INQUIRY AND DISCOVERY

This function involves controlling other people to gain information which the speaker does not possess. In teaching this function, we are trying to make the child his own teacher. This is a skill normal children develop early with a stream of 'What's that?' and similar questions. However, it may be an aspect of language use which is lacking in mentally handicapped children. The acquisition of this function depends on placing the child in a controlling, initiating role, in which he needs certain information. Responsiveness to his language is also vital. The basic structure for this function is of course the question, and much of the discussion on questions in Stage III of the curriculum framework applies directly to teaching this function. An alternative approach is the use of a stooge (another adult) as a model for the desired behaviour. The stooge would ask the teacher the desired question to which a correct response would be given, and then the child would be told to ask. This type of programme depends, of course, on the child's understanding that objects have names, and on experience of having been taught these names before. Other more naturalistic situations could be devised using the same approach in which, for example, the child might be required to ask where something was.

5 LANGUAGE FOR EXPRESSING EMOTIONS AND FEELINGS

There is rarely any problem at a basic level in teaching this function, since expressive meanings are nearly always present. Mobilizing more sophisticated language for this function may require teaching programmes, but these are not particularly distinct from any other. The use of words such as 'want' and 'like' grows out of Stage I meanings; very often children acquire these words without teaching. The main concern is to expand limited utterances into more complex adult-like sentences, and to move from comprehension to production. When it is necesary to teach these words from scratch, one approach is to use a story involving a character (possibly a puppet) who, for example, eats jelly and therefore likes it. The child would be told: 'John eats jelly'; 'John likes jelly'; 'What does John like?' etc. This would be inadequate on its own to teach comprehension of 'like' as we understand it, but it represents the beginning of a more extended programme.

6 LANGUAGE FOR DESCRIBING THE WORLD

Whenever a meaning is taught as a comment it is fulfilling part of this function. In the past this function has tended to dominate approaches to language teaching, to the exclusion of others. Nevertheless, it is one of the most significant aspects of our use of language.

7 'LANGUAGE FOR LANGUAGE'

Various aspects of our language are concerned with communicating about communication. We may ask for clarification of an utterance: 'Did you say ball?'; or about the appropriateness of a response to an instruction: 'Do you want this one?'; or we may acknowledge that someone has spoken, providing feedback to the speaker that we are tuned in and listening. These three aspects can be conveyed by both verbal and non-verbal forms – we can acknowledge a speaker by nodding or by saying 'yes' – and they involve comprehension and production. The curriculum package, *Jim's People*, recognizes the importance of feedback and teaches facial expression, but rather than teaching the appropriate use of facial expressions in communication, it draws attention to it as an aspect of communication conveying certain meanings in isolation from use.

All three skills are vital for smooth interaction, but it is difficult to imagine concise practicable methods of teaching them. Since they perhaps have a lower priority than other skills, they might best be left to opportunism in exploiting situations as they arise, in which the teacher could identify the need for, say, clarification seeking, model it and have the child imitate.

Conclusions

We have tried in this chapter to show how the use and application of knowledge and ideas from various areas can contribute to the basis of a language curriculum. All considerations, however, must eventually give way to the basic aims of the curriculum which must determine and justify what is taught.

The central question in deciding upon the content of the curriculum must be: *what is the most efficient and effective way to lead the child towards communication which will allow him to become an autonomous person?* Everything discussed above lies within the frame of reference of this question, and the choice of specific objectives from a framework must be made with this in mind. Given a child's particular characteristics and abilities, what is the optimal approach towards autonomy? The answer involves the selection of the particular meanings and forms to be taught, determined by what the child can already do, and by the social and material context in which the child is to function. If a child is very heavily handicapped in articulation, communicative autonomy can perhaps best be reached through the use of non-verbal forms. If a child's life consists of hospital wards and classrooms, there is little point in teaching him about objects he will never experience. There is, however, great benefit in teaching him how to gain other people's attention, or how to ask for food.

It will be clear now that this chapter can logically only present a framework for a curriculum and not a complete curriculum. On the basis of this framework, teachers and educators should be able to select, adapt and develop programmes, matching objectives to the individual child.

References
1. B. F. SKINNER, *Verbal Behaviour*. Methuen, 1957.
2. N. CHOMSKY, *Syntactic Structures*. Mouton, The Hague, 1957.
3. R. BROWN, *A First Language: the Early Stages*. Allen & Unwin, 1973; Penguin Books, Harmondsworth, 1976. D. MCNEILL, *The Acquisition of Language: the study of Developmental Psycholinguistics*. Harper & Row, 1970.
4. M. D. S. BRAINE, 'The ontogeny of English phrase structure: the first phase', *Language*, **39**, 1963, 1–13. S. M. ERVIN, 'Imitation and structural change in children's language', in E. H. Lenneberg (ed.), *New Directions in the Study of Language*. MIT Press, 1964.
5. BROWN, *A First Language: the Early Stages*.
6. L. BLOOM, *Language Development: Form and Function in Emerging Grammars*. MIT Press, 1970.
7. M. BOWERMAN, *Early Syntactic Development: a Cross-linguistic Study with Special Reference to Finnish*. Cambridge University Press, 1973.
8. I. M. SCHLESINGER, 'Production of utterances and language acquisition', in D. I. Slobin (ed.), *The Ontogenesis of Grammar*. Academic Press, 1971.
9. BROWN, *A First Language: the Early Stages*.
10. J. PIAGET, 'Piaget's theory' in P. H. Mussen (ed.), *Carmichael's Manual of Child Psychology*, Vol. 1. John Wiley, New York, 1970. J. PIAGET and B. INHELDER, *The Psychology of the Child*. Routledge & Kegan Paul, 1969.
11. R. CROMER, 'The development of language and cognition: the cognition hypothesis', in B. M. Foss (ed.), *New Perspectives in Child Development*, Penguin Books, 1974.
12. M. DONALDSON and R. WALES, 'On the acquisition of some relational terms', in J. R. Hayes (ed.), *Cognition and the Development of Language*. John Wiley, New York, 1970.
13. E. V. CLARK, 'What's in a word? On the child's acquisition of semantics in his first language', in T. E. Moore (ed.), *Cognitive Development and the Acquisition of Language*. Academic Press, New York, 1973.
14. J. S. BRUNER, 'The ontogenesis of speech acts', *Journal of Child Language*, **2**, 1975, 1–19.

15. M. A. K. HALLIDAY, *Learning How to Mean – Explorations in the Development of Language*. Edward Arnold, 1975.
16. C. TREVARTHAN, 'Descriptive analysis of infant communicative behaviour', in H. R. Schaffer (ed.), *Studies in Mother–Infant Interaction*. Academic Press, 1977.
17. E. E. GARCIA and E. D. DEHAVEN, 'Use of operant techniques in the establishment and generalization of language: a review and analysis', *American Journal of Mental Deficiency*, **79**, 1974, 169–78.
18. W. YULE and M. BERGER, 'Communication, language and behaviour modification', in C. C. Kiernan and F. P. Woodford (eds), *Behaviour Modification and the Severely Retarded*. Associated Scientific Publishers, 1975.
19. L. K. SNYDER, T. C. LOVITT and J. O. SMITH, 'Language training for the severely retarded: five years of behaviour analysis research', *Exceptional Children*, **42**, 1975, 7–16.
20. D. GUESS, W. SAILOR and D. BAER, 'To teach language to retarded children', in R. L. Schiefelbusch and L. Lloyd (eds), *Language Perspectives – Acquisition, Retardation and Intervention*. University Park Press, Baltimore, 1974.
21. J. R. LUTZKER and J. A. SHERMAN, 'Producing generative sentence usage by imitation and reinforcement procedures', *Journal of Applied Behaviour Analysis*, **7**, 1974, 447–60.
22. W. A. BRICKER and D. D. BRICKER, 'A program of language training for the severely language handicapped child', *Exceptional Children*, **37**, 1970, 101–111. 'Behaviour modification programmes', in P. Mittler (ed.), *Assessment for Learning in the Mentally Handicapped*. Churchill Livingstone, Edinburgh, 1973. 'An early language training strategy', in Schiefelbusch and Lloyd (eds), *Language Perspectives – Acquisition, Retardation and Intervention*.
23. BLOOM, *Language Development: Form and Function in Emerging Grammars*.
24. BROWN, *A First Language: the Early Stages*.
25. J. F. MILLER and D. E. YODER, 'An ontogenetic language training strategy for retarded children', in Schiefelbusch and Lloyd (eds), *Language Perspectives – Acquisition, Retardation and Intervention*.
26. J. D. MacDONALD, J. P. BLOTT, H. GORDON, B. SPIEGEL and M. HARHMANN, 'An experimental parent-assisted treatment program for pre-school language-delayed children', *Journal of Speech and Hearing Disorders*, **39**, 1974, 395–415.

27. D. PREMACK, 'A functional analysis of language', *Journal of Experimental Analysis of Behaviour*, **14**, 1970, 107–25. D. PREMACK and A. PREMACK, 'Teaching visual language to apes and language deficient persons', in Schiefelbusch and Lloyd (eds), *Language Perspectives – Acquisition, Retardation and Intervention*.
28. J. MCMASTER, *Towards an Educational Theory for the Mentally Handicapped*. Edward Arnold, 1973.
29. M. STEVENS, *The Educational and Social Needs of Children with Severe Handicap*. Edward Arnold, 2nd edn, 1976.
30. Department of Education and Science, *Educating Mentally Handicapped Children*. Education Pamphlet 60. HMSO, 1975.
31. B. THOMAS, S. GASKIN and P. HERRIOT, *Jim's People*. Hart-Davis Educational, St Albans, 1973, rev. edn. 1977 (available from Learning Development Aids, Wisbech, Cambridgeshire).
32. SIEGFRIED ENGELMANN and JEAN OSBORN, *Distar Language*. Science Research Associates, Henley-on-Thames, 1969.
33. L. DUNN, J. O. SMITH and K. HORTON, *Peabody Language Development Kit*. NFER Publishing, Windsor, 1968.
34. J. TOUGH, *Listening to Children Talking: a Guide to the Appraisal of Children's Use of Language*. (Schools Council Communication Skills in Early Childhood Project.) Ward Lock Educational, 1976.
35. M. BLANK, *Teaching Learning in the Preschool*. Merrill, Columbus, Ohio, 1973.
36. M. PARRY and H. ARCHER, *Pre-School Education*. Schools Council Research Studies. Macmillan Education, 1974.
37. I. UZGIRIS and J. MCV. HUNT, *Assessment in Infancy: Ordinal Scales of Psychological Development*. University of Illinois Press, Urbana, Illinois, 1975.
38. PREMACK and PREMACK, 'Teaching visual language to apes and language deficient persons'.
39. J. L. AUSTIN, *How to Do Things With Words*. Clarendon Press, Oxford, 1962.
40. J. SEARLE, 'A classification of illocutionary acts', *Language in Society*, **5**, 1976, 1–23.
41. TREVARTHAN, 'Descriptive analysis of infant communicative behaviour'. M. LEWIS and R. FREEDLE, 'Mother–infant dyads: the cradle of meaning', in P. Pliner (ed.), *Communication and Affect*. John Wiley, New York, 1973.
42. S. M. BELL and M. D. S. AINSWORTH, 'Infant crying and maternal responsiveness', *Child Development*, **43**, 1972, 1171–90.

43. UZGIRIS AND HUNT, *Assessment in Infancy: Ordinal Scales of Psychological Development*.
44. D. M. MOREHEAD and A. MOREHEAD, 'From signal to sign: a Piagetian view of thought and language during the first two years', in Schiefelbusch and Lloyd (eds), *Language Perspectives – Acquisition, Retardation and Intervention*.
45. UZGIRIS and HUNT, *Assessment in Infancy: Ordinal Scales of Psychological Development*.

V. Observational methods

Assessment and evaluation are at the heart of systematic teaching. In this chapter we are particularly concerned with methods which can be used by the classroom teacher. A simple framework is outlined for different levels of observation and the approach illustrated by detailed examples. The examples are not limited to language teaching, but illustrate the approach through a wide range of behaviours.

The problem of assessing the child and building up a profile of his strengths and weaknesses is made more difficult by the fact that there are few tests capable of giving detailed and relevant information. Published tests, checklists and developmental scales can provide an initial profile in a comparatively short time, and should indicate areas of competence, but these are not always sufficiently detailed.

To provide the teacher with accurate information in order to design effective teaching programmes may take the teacher or psychologist a number of sessions, particularly where the child is hyperactive, physically handicapped or simply unco-operative. Standard tests or checklists form a major part of the assessment procedure, but no device for gathering information of this kind is completely adequate for a large number of profoundly handicapped children who may present a wide range of individual difficulties – physical, emotional or intellectual. Existing tests help the teacher to locate and identify specific behaviours, but offer little help with other important aspects: the *context* in which the behaviour (or lack of it) occurs, and the *sequence of events* of which the behaviour forms a part – for example, social and emotional factors.

Assessment techniques are not totally objective. They call upon the investigator to see and note what the child is doing and, at the same time, to make a judgement, to interpret what the child does or says based upon an existing knowledge of his previous behaviour. The following items are taken from a number of published tests and illustrate the difficulties for both the person who constructs the 'objective' test and the user. Can we really know whether the child:

Enjoys bath
Visually *recognizes* mother
Listens to conversations
Likes pushing a pram about
Enjoys vigorous, straight scribble
Knows strangers from friends.

How does the observer ensure complete objectivity with the following:

Table manners are *acceptable*
Gobbles food
Other *unacceptable* habits
Cannot be taken out (write down *why not*)
Can take a guest out to a meal *adequately*
Can, but does not, help in simple domestic jobs (*state why*)
Has *some idea* of a balanced diet
Will sit on potty/toilet seat *willingly* for a few minutes
Dries hands *adequately* without much assistance
Expression shows *awareness*.

The observer has to judge the meaning of words such as 'adequate', 'knows', 'enjoys', 'listens', and interpret what is, or is not, 'acceptable'. Sometimes test or checklist items are so subjective they are meaningless unless qualified in relation to a specific context. For example, 'expression shows awareness' – what does this really mean? As educators we are concerned with the total child, not just those aspects of his life which can be demonstrated in terms of clearly defined pieces of behaviour. The teacher will always have to make judgements about what she sees, and interpret the child's intentions.

It is not simply a matter of discovering areas in which the child lacks skill and then devising learning situations to remedy this. With many children the more immediate problem may be the unlearning of unwanted behaviours for which no tests are appropriate. It is not a question of test versus observation but of each complementing the other.

Children who are profoundly handicapped, and appear to show few behaviours, present a problem in that superficial observation provides little information on which to build educational programmes. Many special-care children have multiple handicaps, and the appropriate selection in teaching content, analysis, and above all presentation and reward, becomes very difficult. The teacher may have to attempt to forecast the child's future development and take this into account when planning. With a physically handicapped ESN(S) child it may be more realistic at one stage to provide a wheelchair so that he achieves immediate mobility rather than attempting to do this only by trying to get him to walk or crawl.

Levels of observation

Observation may be conveniently regarded as falling into three broad categories:
>   General observation
>   Specific observation
>   Intervention/observation.

GENERAL OBSERVATION

In general observation the observer remains at a distance from the child, noting how the total classroom setting impinges on the child and the child on the classroom. Do other children or adults make contact with the child? Does the child react to the banging of a door or to changes in light intensity? How do teachers/other children respond to his crying, to his banging on the floor, to his aggression, or slight movements of head or hand? These observations should build up a general picture of the interrelationships of the child and his surroundings and raise questions and hypotheses about the child's abilities and functioning.

Most teachers already observe and note a great deal of general information in a daily or weekly diary. The extent to which this results in further questioning of the child's behaviour or formulating hypotheses is, however, uncertain.

SPECIFIC OBSERVATION

Specific observation results from a closer proximity to the child, without actual physical contact. It calls for the observation of finer details impossible to pick up at a distance or when looking at the child in total context – for example, the direction of head turning, eye, hand and leg movements. Which hand does the child use to pick up small toys? Is it hand grasping or does it involve finger and thumb opposition? When the door bangs how does the child respond? What are the actual body movements he produces? What are the actual sounds he makes? Does he make these when adults/children are near him? What do adults say or do to him? Some form of observation sheet, which the teacher has only to mark with a tick or a cross, reduces the problem of recording.

INTERVENTION OBSERVATION

Intervention observation follows naturally from the general and specific but is more experimental in intent. It involves asking questions such as 'What happens if and when?' and makes predictions that a child will react in certain ways to a given stimulus or approach. For example, with one visually handicapped child we may note that there are a number of movements which appear to be part of a visual searching strategy – an important hypothesis to test out. Apart from the fact that careful observations may reveal previously unnoticed behaviour, the information may be checked systematically, to gain more understanding of the actual behaviour and lead to more effective teaching programmes.

At the intervention level simple situations may be devised to test out hypotheses. For example, noting that on some occasions the child's hands are tightly closed while on others they will open and relax spontaneously might suggest that grasping activity could be appropriate. The teacher could then devise simple activities to see whether this is feasible – attempting to obtain the hand-grasp in a number of situations, using objects of varied sizes and textures. These are not formal test situations but investigatory 'look and see' procedures. With this kind of intervention, ideas about the child's functioning can be checked and revised and tentative programmes to aid the child's development drawn up.

A framework for observation – a worked example

It is useful to see how this model can be applied in the classroom. The following example is about a fictitious child whom we will call Johnny.

GENERAL OBSERVATION

If we want to know whether a child has sounds, whether these sounds have communication value or potential, and whether they can be increased in frequency and complexity, we begin with general observation of the child in the classroom. Does Johnny make sounds at all? What kinds of sounds are they? Do they seem to follow specific events in the environment? Observations may reveal that Johnny makes sounds when the teacher:

>Is near him
>Interacts with the child
>Uses an object or materials with the child

Touches him
Is in eye contact, etc.

SPECIFIC OBSERVATION

These observations would suggest that the teacher might then begin finer, more specific, observations on the following:

Activity
Objects and materials
Proximity of the teacher
Child's posture
Teacher's posture
Head levels
Orientation
The sounds made.

It would then be possible to draw up a preliminary observation form (Figure 6) with which the teacher could observe the child over short periods, noting

EVENT		
ACTIVITY		
OBJECTS AND MATERIALS		
SOUNDS		

Fig. 6 Preliminary observation form

whether sounds occurred, their frequency and the conditions noted in the observation schedule. Initially perhaps only a limited number of variables might be followed up – for example, activity, objects and materials, sounds the child produces. It is useful to leave some part of the observation sheet blank for writing in notes on the child's behaviour. The *sequence* of observation should be noted, hence the heading 'Event', indicating the number of the observation session.

As familiarity with recording is gained, a larger number of variables can be added. The behaviour may appear to be affected by the time of day, or the proximity of the teacher/adult. The observation form could then look like the form in Figure 7. A great number of different aspects of context can be

EVENT			
ACTIVITY			
OBJECTS AND MATERIALS			
TIME OF DAY			
PROXIMITY	WITHIN ARM'S LENGTH		
	BEYOND ARM'S LENGTH		
SOUNDS			

Fig. 7 More detailed observation form

included (see Figure 8), but the fewer the variables, the easier it is to record. Over a period a number of these would be seen to be relevant to Johnny's sound production, while others were not. New items can be added to the observation schedule and checked out. It is thus flexible and capable of development. The teacher can check those aspects of the context which are more frequently connected with sound production. Obviously this approach also applies to behaviours other than sound production, and can also be used with behaviours one would like to get rid of.

INTERVENTION OBSERVATION

Armed with the knowledge that sound production is more probable in some situations than in others, tentative (experimental) situations can be devised. For instance, the teacher might want to:

>Increase the output of all sounds
>Increase the output of specific sounds
>Encourage one sound so as to eventually produce another
>Increase the sequencing of sounds
>Generally make sound production a situation in which a child can have fun and obtain satisfaction and rewards.

It is possible to do this with the knowledge that some sounds are likely to be produced when you:

>Touch him
>Gaze into his eyes
>Sit him on your knee
>Hold him tightly
>Play with his fingers.

We also know that different sounds can be produced depending on whether:

>You touch him
>You play peek-a-boo
>He is lying on his back on the floor.

We know this from the carefully recorded specific observations. Parents may also provide a great deal of general observation which can be looked at during the second stage, so helping programme development.

Situations developed and tried out at the intervention level need to be carefully monitored and evaluated. Difficulties often develop because aspects of the context are not considered important enough to be included.

EVENT				
ACTIVITY				
OBJECTS AND MATERIALS				
HEAD LEVELS	SAME				
	DIFFERENT				
ORIENTATION	SAME DIRECTION				
	OPPOSITE DIRECTION				
	IN BETWEEN				
OTHER PERSON'S POSITION	BEHIND				
	FRONT				
	SIDE — RIGHT				
	SIDE — LEFT				
CHILD POSTURE	STAND				
	SIT				
	KNEEL				
	PRONE				
	SUPINE				
PROXIMITY	WITHIN ARM'S LENGTH				
	BEYOND ARM'S LENGTH				
SOUNDS				

Fig. 8 Observation form with many more context variables

The activity then needs to be modified to take account of what, in the light of new information, are considered to be the more relevant variables. This is an inevitable part of the whole process. A teacher adopting this approach will be in a much better position not only to know the child but to state his needs with greater certainty, and be able to help him develop specified behaviours.

Do we have the time?

The question arises as to whether the teacher can afford to spend time on regular observation periods. Clearly, prolonged periods of observation are impossible in the hurly-burly of a normal day, nor is there sufficient time afterwards for a detailed analysis of several hours of information gathering. It is feasible, however, to set aside, on a regular basis, a few minutes per day – perhaps five or ten minutes – aimed at following up observation data or ideas from previous teaching situations, on which further information is needed for suitable teaching situations to be devised.

Allocating a few minutes, one can observe a child in different activities throughout the day and note reactions to the same activity on a number of occasions to see whether the behaviour is consistent. Much useful information can be acquired incidentally – for example, 'He seems to make sounds when other children are noisy' or 'He won't play with the beads if anyone is near him'. Observations of this kind may indicate much more than that the child is 'aware of others'. With children who are both physically and mentally handicapped the teacher's observation that the child seems to act differently in one situation from another may be extremely important. This kind of observation need not take much time but demands regularity and consistency of recording.

A chance observation by a teacher that a very distractable child looked at an unusual wind-up toy for a few seconds led to a highly successful progamme for increasing the child's attention to selected objects. The teacher's initial observation was recorded, and checked by further observation in two ways:

> Presenting the child with a wide selection of toys and noting the behaviour in this more structured situation
> Observing the child in free play and noting the length of time of involvement with objects/activities.

The initial periods of observation were extremely short as the child's recorded attention span lay in the region of one to five seconds. At the beginning, the wind-up toy elicited attention duration of forty-five seconds. As observation periods were so short, it was possible to monitor the child's attention several times a day. A stopwatch enabled very accurate information to be obtained which made successful planning easier.

Long periods of observation are not necessary or desirable save in exceptional circumstances. Moreover, problems which really need prolonged observations are possibly best dealt with by the psychologist in conjunction with the teacher rather than by the teacher on her own.

Courses for intending teachers of the mentally handicapped have always emphasized observation and the necessity for keeping careful records.[1] The notebook filled in at the end of the day can be an extremely useful aid for focusing teachers' attention on important points, though there are a number of important limitations. If comments are written at the end of the school day or even at the end of the week, observations become isolated pieces of behaviour, perhaps somewhat inaccurate because of the time lag between observation and note-taking. Furthermore, the behaviour reported is rarely seen as part of a sequence of behaviours. Finally, *the most vital information for helping the child may be contained in the behaviour immediately preceeding or following the observed behaviour*. Unless we know its setting within the sequence, the behaviour itself may provide little information except to say that it occurred. The most vital questions would seem to be: 'When did it happen?', 'What went before?', 'What came after?', leading to the final question, 'How do I get it to happen again?'

Using the approach in the classroom: three examples

The practical use of such an approach is best shown by describing children to whom it has been applied.

Ruth

Ruth was a 5-year-old, severely spastic, quadriplegic child subject to *petit mal* attacks. When first seen, she lay in a small cot for some of the day, and was occasionally taken out to lie on the floor or be propped up with pillows. There was little or no head control; in a sitting position her head mostly dropped forward, although occasionally she would lift it spontaneously. The problem for the teacher (new to the school and to profoundly handicapped children) was what could be done with a child with so many problems? The classroom was small, contained twelve children and several pieces of large apparatus, so space was limited. A full-time assistant was available.

GENERAL OBSERVATION

General observation revealed quite an extensive repertoire of behaviours from Ruth, some already known to the teacher, others not.

Child posture

For most of the day Ruth would be lying down in the cot or on the floor or occasionally in a sitting or semi-sitting position, with her head and back propped up with pillows so that it was possible for her to observe what was going on around her. In the sitting position her lack of head control made this very difficult. Occasionally she would lift her head for a few seconds, probably to be able to observe what was going on. Sometimes the teacher or her assistant would place Ruth on her knee and play with her, as one would with a small baby.

Visual behaviour

Visual regard occurred in all four posture situations noted above. However, head and eye movements occurred with greater frequency when Ruth was:

1 In the semi-sitting position
2 Lying on her back (cot or floor)
3 On teacher's knee.

They appeared to a lesser extent in the sitting position. Head lifting could only be noted in the true sitting position.

Sounds

Ruth made a number of sounds, and these often occurred in sequences of two or three syllables. It was noted that the sounds occurred most frequently when:

1   Lying on her back in a cot looking at an object placed on the side of the cot
2   In a semi-sitting posture when she was in a position to see what was going on around her

3   The teacher or her assistant moved within her vision (lying or in a semi-sitting posture)
4   Teacher or assistant spoke (occasionally)
5   Being or about to be changed or fed
6   On teacher's or assistant's knee and eye contact established.

It was noted, though not consistently, that the sound of children's voices, their touch or even presence (when Ruth could see them) seemed to stop sound production although looking behaviour was probably stimulated.

Arm, hand and finger movements

Although bodily movements were minimal, the teacher was anxious that Ruth should be able to hold objects and acquire reaching behaviour, no matter how crude. However, her arms were limited to a slight amount of lateral and vertical movement and her hands tightly clenched; objects pushed into her fingers were rejected.

Reactions to teacher and assistant

Ruth was aware of both teacher and assistant as they moved, whether she was in the sitting or lying position. She responded vocally when the teacher or her assistant played with her and what appeared to be a smile reaction appeared on several occasions, although this could equally have been a reaction to internal stimuli.

Reaction to children

Ruth seemed aware of children and reacted differentially to children and adults. She went quiet when she saw or heard other children but would appear to watch their movements.

Reaction to objects

Ruth reacted to objects placed on the cot side or in front of her gaze in a semi-sitting position by apparently looking at them. With larger objects (painting), slight hand movements also accompanied the eye searching. Occasionally, sounds would occur while the searching behaviour was going on.

These extracts from the original notes present only a part of Ruth's behavioural repertoire but they illustrate the low level of development and the difficulties faced by the teacher in attempting to help her. They suggest that her behaviour is subject to environmental influence and that there are a number of behaviours which, if investigated in greater detail, could yield information useful in planning programmes for her. Consideration of the general data suggested that the following variables should be followed up:

Event	Number of adults in room
Date	Number of children in room
Time	Number of adults known to child
Activity	Other person's position
Objects/materials	Child posture
Position of child	Proximity
Room temperature	Distractions
Child temperature	Sounds made by child.
Physical contact	

SPECIFIC OBSERVATION

An observation form was drawn up and the teacher and classroom assistant asked to spend a few minutes each day observing the child with these variables in mind. ('Room temperature' was added to the list several days after the original proforma was drawn up.) The teacher and her assistant decided they would observe Ruth for two to three minutes immediately after she had been placed in a new situation (that is, moved from cot to semi-sitting posture, while being changed or just after she had been changed), so that data could be collected in a variety of situations. In addition to the context sheet, behaviour notes were also made.

Information which emerged from this fairly detailed observation schedule suggested that the following factors were relevant and important:

1 Time of day (she was sleepy after dinner and after medication)
2 Type of activity affected the sound output
3 Physical contact
4 Number of adults in room
5 Number of children in the room
6 Other person's position
7 Child posture
8 Proximity
9 Distractions – easily distracted by sudden sounds (startle response)

10 Results were inconsistent with regard to objects and materials
11 Results were also inconsistent for position of the child – for example, near the window
12 Ruth tended to produce more sounds (number of utterances):
    a   between 10.30 and 11.30 in the morning
    b   in a semi-sitting posture/on teacher's knee
    c   when in physical contact
    d   in close proximity to the adult
    e   when directly facing the adult (in apparent eye contact)
    f   during some activities on the part of the teacher, particularly singing, physical contact games like 'round and round the garden', 'touch your nose', 'touch your mouth'
13 It was also noted that looking behaviour occurred more frequently:
    a   between 10.30 and 11.30 in the morning
    b   in a semi-sitting posture
    c   in physical contact or in close proximity to adult
    d   in close proximity to other children
    e   when other person directly in front and facing Ruth
    f   when movement going on – that is, child or adult whom she could see
    g   when distractions occurred – led to head turning
    h   with varying objects and materials
14 Arm, hand and finger movements. While the behaviour notes picked up only a few of these movements, it was interesting to note that these occurred:
    a   between 10.30 and 11.30 in the morning, and 2.30 and 3.30 in the afternoon
    b   in a semi-sitting position or lying down
    c   in physical contact situations with adult
    d   in close proximity to adult
    e   in close proximity to children (children in full view of Ruth)
    f   when distractions occurred – loud sound resulting perhaps in startle response
    g   when object in Ruth's view and close to her – that is, within arm's length.

INTERVENTION OBSERVATION

These data raised a number of questions about the child's abilities, and it was necessary to test them. As the teacher intended to check them systematically, it meant that she was in a position to put some structure into Ruth's day.

The actual school time available for the teacher in the normal day is about five hours – about 300 minutes – and this *theoretically* means that each of the twelve children could receive about 25 minutes personal attention. Again theoretically, adult attention time could be almost doubled if the teacher assistant's time was taken into consideration. The teacher, therefore, could plan a daily timetable of activities for Ruth. Time was also allocated to intervention programmes aimed at gathering information on Ruth in the following situations:

1. Lying in the cot with selected objects placed on the cot side
2. Semi-sitting position (so that head was almost erect), with teacher in front facing her, manipulating objects/plaything
3. On teacher's knee playing games.

If the same routine was adhered to in each of these situations the context variables on the proforma sheet would always be the same. The only information the teacher needed to gather during the session was the frequency of the behaviour, its position within the sequence of behaviours, and the child's responses.

Sound production

The teacher's aims were:

1. To see whether it was possible to stimulate Ruth to increase the number of sounds made
2. To reinforce sound sequencing
3. To reinforce specific sounds arising from **1** which could be 'shaped' over a period of time into specific sounds.

The extract from the context coding sheets (Figure 9) illustrates the variables originally thought to be significant for Ruth's sound production. It also indicates how her sound output could be increased by altering the conditions from lying in the cot to semi-sitting position and by introducing a child–teacher interactive situation. With observation in this form it is possible, over a period of time, to look back and determine with some degree of precision the kinds of sound production *potential* of one group of context variables as opposed to another.

The following short extract from the teacher's observation notes for session 1 with Ruth in the semi-sitting position shows how, in the early data-gathering stage, relevant information quickly accrues.

		LYING IN COT	SEMI-SITTING POSITION
EVENT		3	7
DATE			
TIME		11.00am	11.15am
ACTIVITY		Looking at picture	Peek-a-boo game
OBJECTS/MATERIALS		Picture on cot side	Child's painting
POSITION OF CHILD		Cot near window	Near 'activity' table
ROOM TEMPERATURE	COLD		
	NORMAL	X	X
	HOT		
CHILD TEMPERATURE	COLD		
	NORMAL	X	X
	HOT		
PHYSICAL CONTACT			
NO. OF ADULTS IN ROOM		2	2
NO. OF CHILDREN IN ROOM		10	9
NO. OF ADULTS KNOWN TO CHILD		2	2
OTHER PERSON'S POSITION	BEHIND		
	FRONT		X
	SIDE RIGHT		
	SIDE LEFT		
CHILD POSTURE	LYING		
	SITTING		
	SEMI-SITTING		X
	PRONE		
	SUPINE	X	
PROXIMITY	WITHIN ARMS'S REACH		X
	BEYOND ARM'S REACH	X	
DISTRACTIONS		Children's loud voices	Children at table banging
SOUNDS MADE BY CHILD		'er' (crowing) 'ab' 'ah' (10 sounds only)	Chuckling, laughing, 'ah', 'ababa', 'awah'. (Almost continuous sound production)

Fig. 9 Observation form: Ruth – sound production

Ruth in semi-sitting position. Peek-a-boo game (with teacher) hiding behind picture. Ruth smiled(?) and began to babble. Peek-a-boo game several times with similar reaction. Ruth quiet when returned to floor and no one with her but looked at puppet placed to her right-hand side. Five-minute session.

These notes revealed that in the first session in the semi-sitting position, the materials chosen could elicit some vocalization and that there seemed also to be a potential social situation developing.

Hand grasping

The objective here was to see whether Ruth could learn to grasp simple objects and hold them for increasing periods of time. The programme was planned to include the following conditions:

1   Insertion of teacher's thumb or fingers into Ruth's fingers, teacher's hand closed over Ruth's
2   Insertion of a 9cm × 1½cm dowel rod into Ruth's fingers:
    a   with teacher's hand closed over child's hand
    b   without teacher's hand closed over child's.

These two activities to be carried out in three different contextual situations: lying in a cot; in the semi-sitting position; and sitting on teacher's knee.

When Ruth was lying in the cot or on the floor, it was also possible to introduce lifting her arms to the extent that her shoulders and head were raised from the supporting surface. Repeated on a number of occasions throughout the five-minute session, it was possible to give Ruth an opportunity to begin developing or increasing head support.

As the context situations were defined, recording was confined purely to observations of behaviour. In condition **1** notes referred to whether finger or thumb was used, the number of times inserted into child's grasp, plus reference to any other significant behaviours – sound, hand, arm or leg movements, etc. In condition **2** observations included whether teacher's hand closed on the child's hand holding the rod, the number of times inserted, the number of times the rod was rejected, the length of time held in the child's grasp (the teacher had to assess without using a stop-watch). These teacher interventions were carried out over a period of five weeks with the following results.

Sound production programme

Sitting on teacher's knee, Ruth could be made to produce a sustained babble with smiling reactions. Moreover, the teacher thought that sustained looking behaviour (eye contact) improved over the five-week period. Working with Ruth in the semi-sitting position produced a flow of utterances and it was also noted that some objects helped. The peek-a-boo game (for example hiding behind the picture), tended to produce sounds when the teacher was in view but little or no sound when the teacher was hidden, though eye-searching behaviour did occur. Sound production when Ruth was lying in the cot with objects fastened to the side could be stimulated to some extent by varying the objects – picture, toy, etc. Utterances were not only fewer but in the teacher's opinion were muted, and at no time was any sustained babbling observed. Information also indicated that there was an optimum length of time for the continuation of these activities: sound production began to fall off after about four minutes, but the one-minute period did not allow her to settle. There appeared to be both a 'warm-up' and a 'satiation' effect operating.

Hand grasping programme

At the beginning Ruth tended to display a withdrawal reaction to the teacher's finger, both hands jerking away although perhaps only one hand was touched. She quickly accepted the physical contact, however, and after only a few sessions her hands could be held and manipulated without this happening.

With the dowel rod, Ruth initially reacted by finger withdrawal, as noted above. The dowel rod would gradually be rejected, the fingers moving upwards letting the dowel rod fall out. This rejection never came about because the fingers were deliberately opened. When the teacher held Ruth's hand in which the rod was enclosed there did not appear to be any withdrawal reaction. She, therefore, adopted the policy of placing the rod into Ruth's hand, holding Ruth's hand in hers and then slackening her grasp and finally taking her hand away. When Ruth's fingers began to reject, the teacher once again closed her hand over Ruth's.

A second technique using the dowel rod was also adopted. The rod was inserted under Ruth's fingers and as she gradually attempted to withdraw them the rod was rotated in the direction of the withdrawal movement. With another child (Sarah) this had been noted to produce an opposite reaction, a tightening of the fingers. With Ruth this did not appear to work; her fingers opened slightly and allowed the rod to fall out. Referring back to notes taken during the work with Sarah, an important contextual variable had been overlooked. Sarah had been studied in the summer during particularly hot weather. The programmes with Ruth had been started during the spring term when the weather was cold. The important point was that Sarah's hands had been warm and clammy, whereas Ruth's were cold, dry and the skin slippery, hence the rod tended to slip out of the fingers. When this was realized, Ruth's hands were washed in warm water and then dried and the procedure begun again. The result this time was as expected – as the fingers moved upwards to reject the rod it was rotated in the same direction and the fingers immediately grasped. By altering the direction of rotation it was possible to get Ruth to tighten or release her grip. After a five-week period Ruth could maintain hold of a number of objects – the dowel, a small wooden block and a small bendy toy – for periods in excess of half an hour.

The teacher and assistant were convinced now that Ruth was capable of acquiring some basic skills. They felt she could be taught to increase the number of utterances by carefully selecting the situation and selecting appropriate objects and materials. They were equally convinced that there was a need for recording base-line data prior to carrying out the programme so that any differences in behaviour could be noted after the programme had been running for some time. They were confident that hand/finger behaviours could be acquired and that programmes could be drawn up for this work.

The teacher's initial fears that time spent observing Ruth would not be productive were dispelled. Fears that collection of the required data on context and behaviour would be impossible were shown to be unfounded. The actual time spent collecting behaviour samples amounted to, on average, about ten minutes a day.

Peter

Peter was a well-built, 10-year-old boy whose expressive language was limited to two sounds produced by the intake of breath. Although unable to walk, he could pull himself along the floor and was capable of bearing his own weight. The teachers would take him for a short walk down the corridor supporting him by the arms. Attempts were made to get him to use the walking frame into which he was strapped, although he greatly resented this. The physiotherapist was giving some attention each day to his right ankle which was weaker than the left. The problem posed to the staff was how they could get Peter to walk.

GENERAL OBSERVATIONS

The following points seemed to be important:

1. Peter appeared to enjoy walking supported on the teacher's arm.
2. He disliked the walking frame intensely:
   a. being put into it
   b. being strapped in
   c. moving or walking with it.
3. He seemed to be unhappy when the physiotherapist manipulated his right ankle each day – kicked and became generally aggressive, tried to move away and had to be restrained. He was generally unco-operative in this situation.
4. Peter could not be induced to use the support of the parallel bars by going between them.
5. Although his movements were somewhat slow, he was an active child, into cupboards and boxes, constantly pushing other children over and aggressive with them.
6. In moving about the floor his left leg actively did the pushing.
7. The problem of getting Peter to walk appeared to be related to motivation rather than to physical incapacity.

SPECIFIC OBSERVATIONS

A simple checklist indicating frequencies of behaviours together with space for behavioural notes indicated the following:

1. Peter continually showed enjoyment when being walked by the teacher. This happened in situations where the teacher was perhaps taking bottles of milk into another classroom.
2. On no occasion was he noted to show any kind of enjoyment of physical manipulation of his right ankle.
3. The walking frame (now with a bell on it) seemed to produce conflicting responses. It was noted that he:
   a. liked to pull himself up on his feet and on occasion actually get into the frame
   b. enjoyed ringing the bell
   c. when strapped in, squirmed round repeatedly in order to unfasten the belts and get out of the frame
   d. was reluctant to use the frame although he co-operated at a

minimal level when taken into the hall or the corridor where there was greater space available.

4   Under no circumstances could he be induced to go between the parallel bars though on two occasions he was noted to move along the outside voluntarily. The hypothesis that Peter's lack of ability to walk was more a question of motivation was not fully confirmed when careful note was taken of his ability to balance – this was poorly developed. However, the negative behaviour noted regarding the walking frame and the parallel bars was still felt to be a good indicator of poor motivation.

5   Observations of his hand movements and preferences indicated that he was right-handed.

6   Peter seemed to enjoy his food – lunchtime meal, biscuits, sweets.

INTERVENTION OBSERVATIONS

It was decided to develop Peter's walking by:

1   Giving him practice throughout the day by leaning on the teacher's arm.
2   Ensuring regular walking practice using the parallel bars as support both around and between them.
3   By the use of the walking frame.

So far as **1** was concerned, this only meant ensuring that the teacher or assistant took the trouble to walk with him to other classrooms throughout the school a number of times a day. With **2** and **3**, however, the problem was how to make him want to do it. Initially a simple reward was used (Smarties) which would be given only when the behaviour occurred.

Parallel bars

This particular programme proved much easier to carry out than forecast. Peter enjoyed his daily sweets and these became dependent on him pulling himself up to a standing position using the bars and moving along the outside, eventually round the bars. Getting him to move between the bars also proved less difficult than anticipated. The teacher moved between the bars herself and Peter's first movement towards her was immediately reinforced with a Smartie. Only two Smarties were used to get him through the whole length of the bars on the first occasion – five feet. By the end of the first week he was moving round and between the bars without the use of food reinforcement at all, smiling and enjoying the activity, whereas up to that point he had firmly resisted attempts to use the apparatus.

Walking frame

The walking frame provided a similar situation to the parallel bars. Smartie reinforcement was again used when Peter pulled himself up by the frame and when he actually got into the frame. No attempt was made to strap him in. On the first occasion that Peter moved into the frame himself, he attempted to ring the cycle bell which had been placed on the left-hand side. This was difficult for Peter who was right-handed and caused him to lose his balance. The bell was immediately changed over to the right-hand side. To smiles from Peter and encouragement of the teachers, Peter began to ring it, and this he did repeatedly. While this was going on, a slight push by the teacher to the walking frame caused Peter to begin to move forward. And to further encouragement he moved the frame out of the room, down the corridor, into the hall and back into the classroom – a task which he completed with ease. From this point onwards no more Smarties were used, the intrinsic reward offered by the frame and the bell proved sufficient. Peter did not need to be persuaded or coaxed into the frame but went spontaneously.

Detailed notes after the second week were quite superfluous. However, more general notes were made on his progress and the comments recorded in the fifth week are worth quoting:

Having been in the frame for some time moving round the classroom and in the corridor, Peter returned to the classroom and slid out of the frame on to the floor. He began to move across the classroom towards a doll's pram, pulled himself up with one hand on the handle and another on the wall, steadied himself, wheeled the pram across the room, through the door and, in negotiating a 90° left turn, fell heavily. However, he pulled himself up and continued along the corridor and once again fell at a corridor intersection. At this point, an adult wheelchair was obtained – a heavier and more stable object – another child was placed inside it and Peter continued to push him around the corridors and the school hall with lots of staff encouragement for the remainder of the morning.

In attempting to evaluate what had been achieved with Peter in a short space of time, clearly one would wish to stress that it was possible to predict that Peter could be induced to *want* to walk. The notes, both general and detailed, yielded enough information to indicate this as well as the possible means of achieving it. The work carried out was based on knowledge of Peter's behaviour and an insight into his motivation. However, this could not be achieved without a fresh look at the child by the teacher and her assistant. It was the extra information obtained by the use of a structured observation approach which revealed the possibilities for Peter. The information was there to be found if only one looked.

Linda

Linda, an 8-year-old, hyperactive, Down's Syndrome child, had spent all her life in subnormality hospitals, homes for the mentally handicapped or boarded out in local authority homes. In 1975 she was placed in a residential home which has a small LEA special unit attached to it.

The teacher in charge found Linda a difficult child, aggressive with other children, hyperactive, her behaviour unpredictable. The teacher began to set aside short intervals of time to gather more general information about her. The observations noted below show how, with the minimal investment of time, useful information can be obtained.

Behaviour on 18 September 1975

- 9.30 Sitting on floor kicking the door.
- 10.00 Stacking beakers with classroom assistant. When assistant moved away to cope with another child Linda climbed on top of Chris in his wheelchair and had to be quickly taken off.
- 10.30 Looking at picture book with teacher and trying hard to repeat certain words e.g. 'please', 'ta', 'clap'.
- 11.00 Joining in with group, singing nursery rhymes; fascinated by own hand movements. 'Peacock' sounds emitted at regular intervals.
- 11.30 Lunch – attacked Jill twice – pulled her hair and then pushed her on to the floor. Weird sound patterns.
- 12.30 Played on the climbing frame; she has no fear of heights and needs constant supervision to ensure her safety.
- 1.00 Played with new wooden toy for about half a minute and then threw it away.
- 2.00 Water play. Played with others for the first time and did not grab all the containers, even when she was splashed by Jill. Water play continued for about five minutes, then she removed her protective clothing and asked to return to the classroom.
- 2.30 Climbed on top of the apparatus in the classroom and then listened to the tape recorder.
- 2.45 Taken to the Home for tea where she tried to grab Robert's drink from him as soon as she had drunk her own.
- 2.50 Taken to the playroom where she lay on the floor and wrapped a blanket round herself. Jumped up and fought with James – tears followed.

While these notes demonstrated that Linda could be aggressive, other interesting behaviours were highlighted. Despite the fact that Linda was hyperactive and said to have a short attention span, from 2.0 pm she played for five minutes *with* other children. When she climbed on top of Chris in the wheelchair, she did not attack him at all. The teacher and assistant, however, were well used to Linda's aggression and constantly alive to the problem of her directing it at Chris and hence normally quick to defend him.

SPECIFIC OBSERVATION

The opportunity to observe Linda more closely came about when three of the members of the group were absent from the Unit because of illness. The main target of Linda's aggression, Jill, was missing from the Unit. Linda sat down at the table, played with the bricks quite happily for two minutes, then darted from her chair towards Chris. Usually a member of the Unit staff would have stopped her before she reached Chris's wheelchair but this time we allowed her to go right up to him and, instead of pulling his hair as we had anticipated, she carefully picked up a toy from the floor and handed it to him. We encouraged this behaviour by giving her a big hug and saying, 'Good girl, Linda.' We have all tried to reinforce this better social behaviour on every occasion since and have found that previously we had been reprimanding Linda when she was only trying to help, e.g. when she started moving chairs around we were angry, but since we have allowed her more freedom she frequently arranges the chairs in a semicircle ready for the TV session in the afternoon. At teatime Linda arranges the chairs in a row along one wall of the dining-room, and now comes for her reward when she has finished her task. We had anticipated trouble when Jill returned to the Unit, but so far none has been forthcoming. Linda is happiest in a one-to-one situation, but this is only possible for about thirty minutes of the day. We keep Linda occupied by allowing her to 'help' in the classroom (e.g. by putting toys away in the cupboard, picking up papers, placing the drinking mugs on the tray), and now find that her behaviour is far more reasonable. She will still attack others when she is frustrated, but these occasions have become very infrequent in comparison with her previous behaviour.

The teacher and Unit staff came to the conclusion (hypothesis), as a result of more detailed observation, that they had misunderstood Linda's intentions in relation to Chris. As a result, they decided to observe her more closely, reinforce appropriate behaviour and delay taking action until her actions were clearly noted to be aggressive. The staff reappraised their whole attitude to Linda's intentions. As a result Linda quickly became more co-operative in a wide variety of situations. This is interesting in that it was as a direct result of the teacher being asked to observe a child by the project team, given only minimum help regarding the approach to the observation model. It is also worth noting that in the hurly-burly of the classroom the intervention observation stage developed into the actual treatment stage.

These examples show that observing children carefully and systematically in the classroom, and then looking critically at the resulting data, pays off.

Evidence obtained from running courses on observation methods indicates that results can be quite impressive even when the course is short.

It is possible to carry out similar work with parents or with untrained adults working in residential homes, often with minimal guidance. Changes in behaviour can be effected, even with major behavioural problems.

Using the approach outside the classroom – two examples

Working with a mother

As a baby Diane had appeared to be fairly normal, if somewhat slow, particularly in relating to others. By the age of 2 she was a problem child, capable of screaming continuously for long periods until hoarse. The parents sought medical help and were told it was just a developmental problem and that Diane would 'grow out of' the screaming behaviour. The child was seen at three-monthly intervals and later at six-monthly intervals by the paediatrician.

At the age of 10 Diane still screamed and was very difficult. She had been to several schools for normal children and a number of units for special children. A mixture of home tuition in the morning and normal school in the afternoon was tried, but after eighteen months the problems persisted. Her behaviour was always disruptive and eventually teachers and headteachers would complain and Diane would be moved on. Despite the record of behaviour difficulties, Diane acquired a reading age of about $7\frac{1}{2}$ years and when tested by the educational psychologist her mental age would place her at the ESN moderate rather then ESN severe level. Her speech was poor and almost unintelligible to anyone not acquainted with her, and both parents were concerned that she had a hearing loss, although this could not be demonstrated as it was difficult to get Diane to co-operate in the test session. It was rarely possible for her mother to take her out to the shops without Diane screaming and causing a disturbance. Her mother had often been rounded on by members of the public for not controlling such a 'naughty girl'. Life was difficult at home and at school. The mother was on the verge of a nervous breakdown and under medical care.

What could be done with a child with such a long-standing history of difficult behaviour which so far no one had succeeded in tackling, let alone correcting? It seemed in this case that home rather than school ought to be the prime focus of attention at the beginning. Data collection at home usually means that the mother is the only one who can obtain information regularly. Additionally, it means that this approach to behaviour change is put to a severe test. The mother had to learn to observe Diane's behaviours, and to be able to observe with some detachment what was going on in an emotionally loaded situation.

GENERAL OBSERVATION

The mother was asked to keep a daily diary of the main events in Diane's day. This is not such an impossible task as it sounds. The contents of the diary were discussed with Diane's mother once a week and a picture of the difficulties for all the family, including Diane, quickly emerged. Moreover, other unexpected material came to light. Screaming proved to be only one of a hierarchy of problems of which this was perhaps the most spectacular and immediately disturbing. A whole spectrum of bizarre, eccentric, and blatant 'attention-getting' behaviours came to light. No previous references had been made to these problems and no information was available from the teacher's, doctor's or psychologist's notes. While collecting this information, two questions were kept in mind:

Where/when does Diane display the behaviour?
Where/when does Diane not display the behaviour?

After only two weekly sessions with the mother, a number of factors were emerging highly relevant to the screaming behaviour and to other deviant behaviours in general. Furthermore, the data was already throwing into relief aspects of better adjustment of which mention had never been made to anyone. Out of these emerged information which suggested likely activities and situations which might be used to reinforce appropriate behaviours once programmes had been developed.

Of the behaviours noted in the first phase of observation, some of the most important were:

1 Screaming (sustained and short bursts)
2 Spitting
3 Ritualistic behaviours of many kinds
4 Phobic behaviours – about buttons, white coats, lights, shops
5 Poor sleep
6 Eating problems
7 Head banging
8 Vomiting

9 Violent tempers
10 Dislike of physical contact
11 Poor speech
12 Aggressive behaviour towards other children.

On the positive/constructive side:

1 Liked to read (reading age about $7\frac{1}{2}$)
2 Liked collecting pictures
3 Liked collecting plastic soldiers
4 Enjoyed simple cooking
5 Reacted well if told she 'looks a pretty girl'
6 Liked chocolate
7 Liked cutting out pictures
8 On occasion liked doing things with mother.

In the second phase of observation, the following were looked at in greater detail:

1 Screaming
2 Relationship with mother
3 Effect of firm control by mother on screaming behaviours
4 Reinforcers.

A list of what appeared to be critical factors relating to context was drawn up and a suitable observation form designed (Figure 10). In all future discussions with Diane's mother her notes and comments were examined with these factors in mind.

SPECIFIC OBSERVATION

Screaming

The major trends observable were:

1 Screaming behaviour was shown not only to be related to activity but also to adults and location, to the difficulties inherent in the situation or activity, and even the day of the week
2 Diane produced more screams at the weekend when in contact for a longer time with her family
3 There appeared to be three types of screaming behaviour:
    a   a high pitched, sustained screaming at full power capable of going on with short breaks for long periods

EVENT					
DATE					
TIME					
MEAL					
ACTIVITY	CHILD				
	ADULT				
OBJECTS/MATERIALS					
PHYSICAL CONTACT					
LOCATION	HOME	BEDROOM	CHILD		
			PARENTS		
		KITCHEN			
		OTHER ROOM			
	SHOPS				
	BUS				
	SCHOOL				
	OTHER				
PERSONS PRESENT	MOTHER				
	FATHER				
	SIBLING				
	OTHERS				
PROXIMITY	WITHIN ARM'S LENGTH				
	BEYOND ARM'S LENGTH				
CONTROL	FIRM	EFFECTIVE			
		NOT EFFECTIVE			
	NOT FIRM	EFFECTIVE			
		NOT EFFECTIVE			
SCREAMS	MAJOR				
	MINOR				

Fig. 10 Observation form: Diane – screaming behaviour

b a scream of short duration arising within the context of an activity, possibly as a reaction to frustration when she could not complete the task
   c a form of emasculated scream which turned into a grunt; this again occurred during an activity in which she was obviously absorbed but not frustrated by an inability to complete or carry out the task – this seemed to be a true habitual behaviour
4 Screaming occurred in bed at night but rarely in the morning when she woke up
5 Screaming occurred in the presence of any member of the family
6 Screaming occurred in the presence of any adult
7 Screaming occurred in any location – home, shops, school, grandparents' house, on holiday, etc.
8 Fewer screams were noted when she was engaged in cookery (grunts rather than screams here)
9 Screams at mealtimes
10 There were more screams when mother was on her own with Diane than when both parents were present (father was a shift worker).

Relationship with mother

The details of family life, the interactions between members of the family and their relationship to screaming behaviour were partially explored and a number of what looked to be important dimensions were identified:

1 Diane had never been an affectionate child and had never liked to be hugged, kissed, etc., by mother
2 The diary revealed few occasions on which Diane received any physical affectionate handling from mother
3 No occasion on which Diane approached mother for physical comfort or affection was noted
4 Mother, according to her notes, appeared to spend most of her time admonishing or setting limits to Diane's behaviour
5 A few references were noted which showed mother was alive to the value of praise – during cooking, reading and cutting out pictures
6 Diane used almost every interaction to dominate mother or other members of the family
7 Diane was able to manipulate relationships with her younger brother (aged 7) so as to get him into trouble with mother

8   In the first few sessions one behaviour was noted which seemed out of character – on several occasions in the first three weeks Diane woke around 6.45 in the morning and came, of her own volition, into mother's bed. The younger brother did the same and cuddled up to mother – Diane remained aloof.

Reinforcers

It was necessary to discover any situations or activities when the mother was led to praise Diane. Because of the problems these were few, but there were some:

1   Diane enjoyed simple cooking and usually gained a great deal of praise from mother for her efforts. The kitchen, therefore, was a positive location for Diane where her relationship with mother was at its best.
2   Diane enjoyed reading, and it was noted that the time after the tea dishes had been washed and put away produced fewer screams and a greater number of praise responses to Diane for her reading.
3   Mother was concerned about Diane's lack of fine motor co-ordination and encouraged her in cutting pictures out and pasting them in a book. This became a favourite activity with Diane.
4   Verbal praise from father paid dividends in terms of increased conformity.
5   Verbal punishment had a variable effect and quite possibly tended to reinforce undesirable behaviour.
6   Physical punishment was used on occasion in the household, although few references to this were made in the mother's notes. Such treatment would stop the screaming or other anti-social behaviour immediately but within minutes it would recur.
7   There appeared to be no relationship between time of day and the effectiveness of reinforcers.

The mass of data yielded by specific observation led to a number of hypotheses on which programmes could be based and carried out with some hope of success. The most relevant involved building up a more normal and affectionate mother–child relationship.

INTERVENTION OBSERVATION PROGRAMME

General and specific observation of Diane's behaviour had revealed the following:

1. An unending clash of wills between child and mother
2. Diane could usually be triumphant in situations of this kind by resorting to screaming, spitting, vomiting, etc. – behaviours which would occur in any location, at home, in school, or out shopping.

On the positive side:

1. Mother had the incentive to try to get rid of these behaviours
2. Diane enjoyed reading and cooking and mother tended to praise her in these situations
3. Diane also reacted to simple personal praise such as, 'You look a pretty girl today'
4. She liked chocolate
5. On occasions she enjoyed performing activities of various kinds with mother
6. She would come into mother's bed in the morning
7. Diane had a simple sense of humour.

On the basis of this and other information the following programmes all relating to physical contact situations were set up.

1. Mother was asked gradually to shape up Diane's behaviour until, on the occasions when she came into mother's bed in the morning, Diane could be cuddled and kissed by mother.
2. In the cookery and reading situations mother was asked to increase the amount of verbal praise and physical contact with Diane. Mother would give verbal praise as usual, at the same time giving Diane an affectionate pat or hug.
3. Mother was asked to read *regularly* when Diane went to bed and to ensure that a goodnight kiss was accompanied by a big hug.
4. In the mornings when Diane was about to go to school, a kiss accompanied by a big hug was given and on return home a similar reaction on mother's part was called for.

The response to this approach was interesting. Previously the number of screams per day or week was uncountable. After the programme commenced things began to alter. Figure 11 shows how Diane's screaming rapidly began to diminish although fluctuations did occur.

Programmes were tried out in an attempt to build up physical contact with mother and child and this developed rapidly after the sixteenth week. Diane was, by this time, coming into mother's bed, the frequency of kissing behaviour had been increased, and the mother was reporting that Diane was becoming more affectionate with the father and grandparents also.

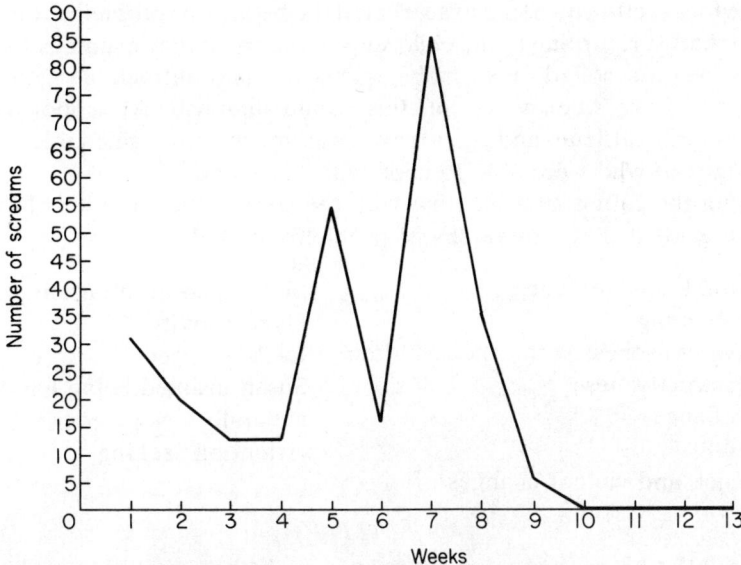

Fig. 11 Frequency of screams at home over twelve weeks

Diane's difficult behaviours were tackled intensively over a period of twelve months with the result that screaming disappeared. Right from the beginning of the programme the school had been kept fully informed about Diane's progress at home. At the age of 12 Diane had to be transferred to another school and screaming recurred although not with the same intensity and frequency. After some time and with firm handling in the school situation it again disappeared.

Working with staff in a residential home

Susan was referred to the project as a naughty, aggressive, defiant little girl who at school was placed in the ambulant special-care class. When first seen by a member of the team she was aged $9\frac{1}{2}$. At school and the children's home she was described as disruptive, of variable and inconsistent mood, destructive with books and doubly incontinent. She had no speech. The initial picture was of a difficult child who presented physical, emotional and management problems.

Susan had been in the care of the local authority for some years and although living in a children's home during the week, returned home on most weekends. Differences in styles of management between the family and the local authority home exacerbated the behaviour problems considerably so that on returning to the children's home on Sunday evenings she was usually wet or soiled, invariably aggressive and intractable generally although, as the week wore on, this would diminish. At school Susan, although still difficult and aggressive, was much more amenable to the teaching staff who were able to cope with her moods.

During the course of a meeting with the staff at the children's home it became evident that a hierarchy of problems existed:

Double incontinence	Short span of attention
Screaming	Hyperactivity
Aggressiveness with other children	Lack of speech
Destructiveness	Susan disliked being handled
Defiance	generally
Biting	Attention seeking.
Quick and violent changes of mood	

Originally the project team thought it might be possible to tackle the difficulties by developing the child's ability to communicate, but the staff of the residential home were adamant that the double incontinence and screaming behaviour had priority for them. It was agreed, therefore, to tackle the most pressing problem of double incontinence, and as the child improved only then perhaps to deal with the screaming. The staff were asked to keep a daily diary and to gather as much information as possible of events relating to toileting. General observation data were gathered within the course of two months, and revealed the following pattern:

1 Lifted from bed at 7 a.m., usually wet and immediately placed on potty. Sometimes she used it. She would then be washed and dressed in preparation for breakfast. Often, however, she was already wet before she went in for the meal.
2 After breakfast again placed on the pot which on occasions she did use. (There was a tendency to keep her on the potty or commode for long periods to make sure that she would use it.) The usual pattern at this time was for her not to use the pot but to wet or soil herself a few minutes after leaving it, irrespective of the length of time sitting on the pot.
3 After toileting and washing she would be fully dressed for school but made to sit on the commode until the school bus came, as 'accidents' were frequent just before leaving.

4 On returning from school on the school bus (frequently wet) Susan was *placed* on the potty. Occasionally she obliged.
5 She was again placed on the potty or commode before teatime.
6 After tea she was placed on the potty and then played until suppertime. She was checked at intervals of about 30 to 45 minutes between teatime and bedtime, frequent wetting and soiling occurring, most often just after she had been checked.
7 At bedtime she was again placed on the commode before having a bath but would often soil in the bath.
8 Time of day did not appear to be a relevant factor in wetting or soiling behaviour.

A number of other interesting points were also noted:

9 Susan could be requested to put out the cutlery on the table at mealtimes and she enjoyed doing it.
10 *Occasionally* she would respond with a smile if, having used the potty or commode, a member of staff said 'Good girl' and gave her a kiss or hug. Often, however, hugging or kissing was rejected by her pushing the person away or on occasions biting.
11 On three occasions Susan was noted spontaneously to approach a member of staff (matron) and want to be hugged and kissed.

Out of this mass of information a number of points are worth noting:

1 Susan *could* be co-operative in some situations – for example, when *asked* to set out the cutlery
2 She spent a great deal of her life supervised sitting on the commode or potty when the other children were active; this demanded a tremendous amount of adult supervision
3 She was invariably *placed* on the commode or potty and rarely *told* to go, and never went spontaneously
4 Being kissed and hugged was *on occasions* acceptable to Susan
5 Sometimes members of staff would hug or kiss her when she had used the potty
6 On some occasions when kissed and hugged she would smile with obvious pleasure, kiss or even hug the adult
7 Toileting was not a pleasurable activity normally
8 Because of staff shortages toileting was always carried out under pressure and in a hurry.

The information suggested that too much emphasis was being placed on toileting and the whole situation was fraught with emotion for the staff and Susan. Moroever, if Susan was consistently *placed* on the potty she would never gain autonomy in this respect and learn to cope herself.

SPECIFIC OBSERVATION

The following factors appeared to be worth looking at in greater detail:

1   Time of day
2   Demands made of Susan – whether placed on potty, told to go on potty, or spontaneously used potty
3   Results of use of potty
4   Reinforcement given by adult
5   Positive responses from Susan *to* adults.

A simple form was drawn up (Figure 12). Each time Susan went on the potty the member of staff supervising was responsible for noting the above points, and signed at the bottom of the column. It was recognized that staff might be stimulated to use the specific data collection as a treatment programme – consistently reinforcing with a hug or a kiss when Susan used the potty; but while from a data-gathering exercise this would confound observation and treatment data, the aim of the work was to reduce the child's problems *not* simply to collect data to a particular pattern.

INTERVENTION OBSERVATION

As anticipated, intervention, observation and treatment were run concurrently. This is obviously possible where appropriate general and detailed information has been collected and the hypotheses formulated are accurate. With the introduction of the proforma, the staff immediately began to reinforce Susan for using the potty and, as a matter of course, instead of placing her began to ask or tell her. The effect of doing this can be seen in Figure 13. After the eighth week Susan began to respond well to being asked to use the potty, and by the thirteenth week she rarely needed to be placed on the potty. The fourteenth week showed that reinforcement of the desired behaviour – being told to use the potty and successfully doing so – was effective. Only twice in that week did she have to be placed on the potty. However, the staff were beginning to increase the frequency of Susan's use of the potty, albeit successfully, which was the very opposite of our long-term objective – successful use of the toilet, perhaps three or four times a day. Without recording this information, important data would have gone

DATE		
TIME OF DAY	AM	
	PM	
SITUATION	Placed on potty	
	Told and goes on potty	
	Spontaneously goes on potty	
RESULTS	Uses potty 'U' 'F' or 'UF' *	
REINFORCEMENT	Hugged by adult	
POSITIVE RESPONSES TO ADULTS	Smiles at	
	Kisses	
	Hugs	
	Others – specify	

Note: U=urine; F=faeces

Fig. 12 Observation form: Susan

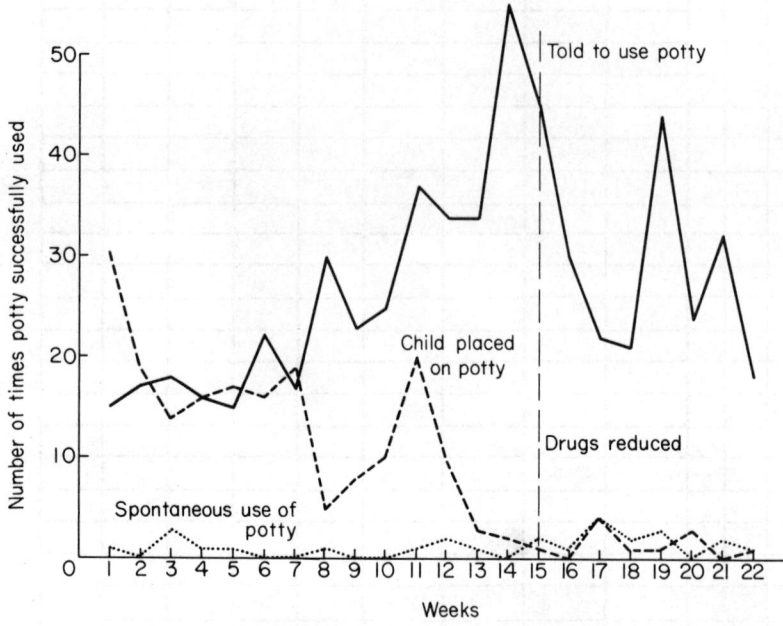

Fig. 13 Susan – use of potty

unnoticed, which emphasizes the need to record observations systematically.

From the fourteenth week onwards Susan was told to go to the potty about every one-and-a-half hours instead of at half-hour to three-quarters of an hour intervals. The effect of this can be seen from the graph. Despite the fact that the interval between toileting had been (on average) doubled, no increase in the number of times Susan had to be *placed* on the potty occurred. She had learned the desired behaviour. The frequency of spontaneous and successful use of the toilet did not increase. However, this would be the next objective.

SCREAMING BEHAVIOUR

Up to the tenth week, the staff collected information on screaming, which was noted to occur generally when groups of children were playing inside the house supervised by only one adult. It was apparently related (hypothesis) to situations in which Susan could not obtain the undivided attention of an adult. It was also noted that when matron on one occasion placed her outside the room for a few minutes the screaming quickly died down. A 'time out' policy was therefore adopted. Each time Susan screamed she was immediately *placed* outside the room and left there until the screaming subsided. Figure 14 demonstrates the effectiveness of this approach which was put into effect from the tenth week. Within five weeks the problem had subsided so that occasional screams occurred when Susan became particularly frustrated. There may still be occasions when there will be an increase in the screaming behaviour for one reason or another.

Summary

We have suggested that general observation should precede specific observation in the classroom. This is nothing new – much of our teaching is based upon the principle of moving from the general to the particular. Nor is there anything new in setting up hypotheses about children and their behaviour, and trying out tentative ideas – that is, intervening. We have tried to reinforce the view that observing children is not only useful but vitally necessary if we are to be effective in teaching.

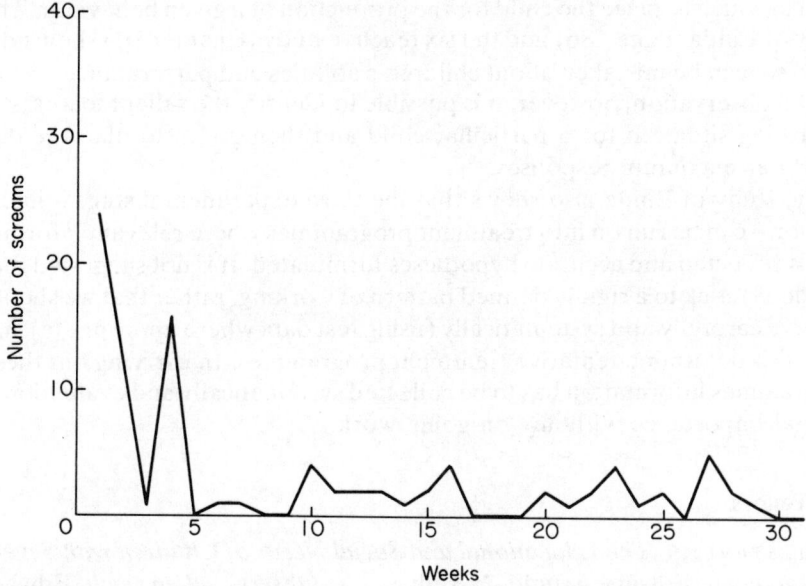

Fig. 14 Susan – number of screams per week

We have pointed out the limitations of checklists and tests as methods of gathering information on children and have suggested that by looking at children in the classroom it is possible to gather vital information which will enable teaching to be more effective. The formal tests and checklists based on developmental scales are complementary to the more flexible observation data-gathering. Indeed, they are inseparable as the tester/observer must look at the child's behaviour and interpret it if it is to be of any practical use to the teacher or parent.

Observation periods need not be lengthy. In the examples, short coding sheets were used to note frequencies of behaviour, although in one case a simple diary technique was used which proved perfectly adequate, though the material was later coded onto observation sheets. The number of items on the coding sheets can be varied according to the problems. With one child the sheet may need only to include the child's behaviour and the activity within which it occurs – for example, the sounds the child makes during different activities. Collected for a number of days over a range of activities even simple observations like this can provide material about the usefulness of one teaching situation as against another. When other data such as time of day, physical contact with teacher, are added, the usefulness of the material is increased and it becomes possible to specify the best situation/environment in which to place the child for the production of a given behaviour. The study of Linda (page 186) and the six teacher study (Chapter III) show how easily we can be mistaken about children's abilities and performances. With careful observation, however, it is possible to identify the salient features of a learning situation for a particular child and then go on to plan the day aiming at maximum responses.

The study of Linda also shows that the third experimental stage – intervention – can be run on into treatment programmes where relevant information is collected and accurate hypotheses formulated. It is not suggested that we should stick to a rigidly defined pattern of working, rather that we should observe carefully and systematically (using test data where appropriate) and from this determine tentative treatment programmes. In carrying out these programmes information has to be collected systematically and evaluation is of vital importance with any on-going work.

References

1. M. STEVENS, *The Educational and Social Needs of Children with Severe Handicap*. Edward Arnold, 2nd edn, 1976. *Observe – then teach*. Edward Arnold, 2nd edn, 1978.

VI. Teaching vocabulary

How many of the words we expect children to know are really understood? More importantly, what can we do when we find gaps in children's knowledge of specific groups of words?

Results of the English Picture Vocabulary Test[1] in the language survey outlined in Chapter I demonstrated the inability of many pupils to understand large areas of vocabulary, and led us to question just how much children understand teachers. While we gained valuable data from the survey about vocabulary which children did not understand, it gave very little information about words they could understand. To develop teaching methods, it was necessary to devise tests for areas of vocabulary which teachers thought their children should know. Discussions with teachers led us to design a series of vocabulary tests in the following areas:

> Body parts   Clothes
> Colour   Transport
> Spatial   General environment
> Movement   People
> Personal objects House
> Objects of the home Furniture.

The tests were devised in close collaboration with colleagues on the Chester teachers' workshops, and developed in six schools, covering 230 children of varying ages and levels of ability. The tests all follow a fairly standard format which is described later. This involves asking the children to show the teacher, by pointing at or otherwise indicating, the item required. For example, in the test of transport words, the item testing comprehension of 'car' consisted of four pictures of different types of vehicles, one of which was a car. Children were tested individually by their own teacher.

Although we were very careful to standardize the conditions of administration of the tests, so that the results reported came from closely comparable situations, care should be taken in interpreting the results. First of all, in no sense should the results be taken as normative. If, for example, we found that 83 per cent of our group of children understood the word 'car', this does not mean this is a standard for a class or school to work towards. The purpose of the results is to give a general picture of the strengths and weaknesses as a lead-in to teaching vocabulary. Secondly, a note on the presentation of the results: tables present words in order of difficulty, measured by per cent passing, but this should not be interpreted as being a developmental order of acquisition. Of course even if it were, this would not mean that teaching should automatically follow this order.

The teaching programmes detailed later are based on teaching models already described and are intended primarily as examples. It is the underlying principles we wish to emphasize here, so that teachers may use them in formulating their own work to meet their specific needs.

Tests of common nouns

Most areas tested were concerned with common objects and these nouns were known by most of the children. Results of the 'transport' test (Table 9) show that 'car' was understood by a greater number of children than any other transport noun (82·8 per cent), and even the most difficult word, 'van', was known by 70·3 per cent. For the teacher, though, it shows that even the vocabulary *she expected the children to know* was not understood by groups, varying between 17 per cent and 30 per cent of the total.

Table 9 Transport test – percentage passing each item ($N=242$)

ITEM	PASS	
	N	%
Car	192	82·8
Bus	188	81·0
Boat	187	80·6
Train	180	77·6
Bike	178	76·7
Lorry	168	72·4
Van	163	70·3

Results from the 'objects of the home' test (Table 10) again suggested that concrete nouns were known, and this area too seems to pose relatively few problems.

Table 10 Objects of the home test – percentage passing each item in order of difficulty ($N=244$)

ITEM	PASS N	%
Spoon	202	82·8
Telephone	198	82·8
Bottle	195	80·9
Knife	194	80·8
Cup	195	79·9
Fork	193	79·4
Plate	193	79·4
Mirror	191	78·3
Pillow	189	77·5
Pan	181	75·1
Radio	183	75·0
Glass	181	74·2
Iron	178	73·3
Tea towel	176	73·0
Teapot	177	72·8
Lid	175	71·7
Table cloth	173	71·2
Sugar bowl	171	71·0
Tray	165	68·8
Kettle	163	66·8
Plug	162	67·2
Dish cloth	162	66·7
Milk jug	158	65·0
Saucer	158	64·8
Beaker	154	63·1

From the 'people' test (Table 11) we were surprised to discover that 'boy' was known by fewer children than any of the other words, especially as other words included 'nurse', 'fireman' and 'policeman'.

Analysis of the 'general environment' test (Table 12) presented satisfactory results. 'Cat' was known by most of the children and at the other end of the scale 'building' was understood by only 63·9 per cent.

As one would predict, vocabulary concerned with everyday items of clothing (Table 13) was understood by most children, although variations occurred. 'Shoes' and 'socks' were understood by most, and 'hat' and 'coat' were next in order of difficulty.

Table 11 People test – percentage passing each item ($N=228$)

ITEM	PASS N	%
Baby	177	77·6
Footballer	173	76·2
Girl	162	71·1
Lady	159	69·7
Man	158	69·3
Nurse	157	68·9
Policeman	157	68·9
Dustbinman	156	68·4
Fireman	151	66·2
Boy	148	64·9

Table 12 General environment test – percentage passing each item ($N=230$)

ITEM	PASS N	%
Cat	188	82·5
Dog	186	80·9
Shop	172	74·8
Telephone box	172	74·8
Church	168	73·0
Post box	167	72·6
Traffic lights	164	71·3
Wall	157	68·3
Zebra crossing	148	64·3
Building	147	63·9

Note. Between 20 and 22 children were untestable.

Table 13 Clothing test – percentage passing each item (N=230)

ITEM	PASS N	%
Shoes	191	83·0
Socks	188	81·7
Hat	183	80·5
Coat	180	79·3
Trousers	178	77·4
Dress	172	75·8
Cardigan	182	75·5
Vest	172	74·8
Shirt	164	71·3
Anorak	161	70·0
Tie	160	69·6
Tights	165	68·5
Underpants	157	68·3
Skirt	162	67·2
Cap	145	63·0
Blouse	133	55·2

BODY-PART VOCABULARY

Body features are not objects seen in isolation; they merge into other body areas and become parts of other bodily features. No lines separate them physically – for example, toe from foot, face from head, chest from tummy. For many body parts there is an obvious observable function, whereas for others there is not – for example, contrast 'hand' and 'chest'. Perhaps this helps to explain why parts such as 'hand', 'eye', 'nose', 'fingers', 'ears', and 'tongue' are well known in comparison to less clearly defined parts such as 'chin', 'shoulder', 'eyelash', 'chest' and 'cheeks'. The more distinguishable and easily observable features were known by most children.

As the test results show (Table 14) most of this vocabulary was known by at least 70 per cent of the children. An age analysis (see Table 15) indicates that the easier words show little developmental progression after the age of 7, and that there is little consistent increase in percentages understanding the harder items over the years.

Those body parts broadly associated with some outstanding feature proved more difficult. For instance, 'eyes' was known by 90·6 per cent but 'eyelash' and 'eyebrow' by only 52·9 per cent and 47·8 per cent respectively.

Table 14 Body-parts test – percentage passing each item ($N=210$)

ITEM	PASS %	ITEM	PASS %
Hand	91·8	Tummy	76·7
Eyes	90·6	Lips	75·5
Hair	90·5	Knees	75·2
Nose	89·0	Bottom	74·9
Head	87·6	Back	74·3
Teeth	87·2	Neck	70·6
Fingers	86·9	Nails	70·0
Ears	85·7	Thumb	68·9
Legs	84·8	Chin	67·1
Tongue	84·5	Elbow	58·7
Mouth	84·4	Shoulders	57·9
Face	84·2	Eyelashes	52·9
Feet	84·0	Eyebrows	47·8
Arm	82·1	Chest	47·6
Toes	80·5	Cheeks	43·5

Table 15 Percentage passing the easiest item (hand), the middle item (toes) and the hardest item (cheeks) in each age-group

Age	Hand ($N=212$)	Toes ($N=210$)	Cheeks ($N=210$)
6 years and under	75·3	56·4	19·3
7 years	100·0	80·0	40·0
8 years	90·0	90·0	35·0
9 years	92·3	69·2	46·0
10 years	96·0	92·0	28·0
11 years	95·5	77·3	54·5
12 years	96·0	84·0	60·0
13 years	100·0	95·0	50·0
14 years	93·3	100·0	73·3
Over 14 years	93·8	86·6	71·4

Similarly, 'hand' was understood by 91·8 per cent, 'fingers' by 86·9 per cent, 'nails' by 70 per cent and 'thumb' by 68·9 per cent. It is interesting that 'head' was understood by a greater number of children than 'face', although the percentage difference is very small.

Body parts such as 'thumb' and 'chin' are among the least well known in spite of being used frequently in rhymes and stories. The action song 'Tommy Thumb', for instance, is commonly used yet only 68·9 per cent understood what a thumb is. The phrase 'chinny, chin, chin' may be familiar to the reader as part of a familiar story, but to 32·9 per cent of the children in our sample the word 'chin' was not familiar.

It may be argued that normal children derive much pleasure from saying something over and over, without necessarily understanding the meaning of the words. The sound may be much more important than the meaning. Whether, and to what extent, these principles apply to children with severe language and learning problems is a question that must be left to teachers to decide. All we wish to stress here is that normal children are often not only much more advanced in language development when they reach the stage of enjoying nursery rhymes involving nonsense words, but their rate of language growth is also much faster. We are not claiming that such nursery rhymes are dangerous and to be avoided – merely enjoining caution in their use, and in making assumptions about the extent to which they are either meaningful to the child or contribute actively to his language development.

A test of verbs – movement

The movement section of the vocabulary tests was the only one designed to investigate children's understanding of verbs. Movement vocabulary was selected because of its frequent use especially in games, PE, movement and dance. The results (Table 16) show that at least half the children were familiar with nineteen out of twenty-three words. The verbs more frequently used were known by a larger percentage of the children. 'Sit down', the easiest item, was known by 89·2 per cent while over 80 per cent of the sample responded appropriately to 'stand up', 'stop', 'jump', 'run', 'turn', and 'walk'. At the other extreme 60 per cent to 75 per cent failed to respond appropriately to 'skip', 'crawl', 'curl up' and 'walk sideways'. Excluding these last four items, however, the results showed a similar pattern to those obtained from the noun tests.

Table 16 Movement test – percentage passing each item in order of difficulty

Item	Percentage passing	Item	Percentage passing
Sit down	89·2	Fall down	66·8
Stand up	88·7	Roll over	63·8
Stop	83·8	Walk slowly	61·3
Jump	83·2	Walk quickly	60·9
Run	82·6	Hop	57·4
Turn round	82·4	Stretch out	55·3
Walk	80·8	Walk backwards	54·8
Lie down	79·0	Skip	40·8
Clap	78·8	Crawl	36·6
Stamp your feet	72·3	Curl up	24·8
Bend down	71·6	Walk sideways	24·7
Kick	69·8		

Spatial test results

Spatial vocabulary, as expected, presented greater difficulties for the children than the verbs or common nouns (see Table 17). Most words were know by less than 70 per cent and the results highlight an area where both teaching and learning have proved somewhat difficult. Clearly spatial vocabulary presents greater problems since it involves abstract relationships and not simple concrete objects or movement-related words. It is worth emphasizing that, as with the other tests, spatial vocabulary was selected as an area which teachers expected children to know.

Although over 70 per cent of children understood the concepts 'down', 'out', 'in', 'off', 'inside', and 'on', this left a further twenty-two items, eleven of which were known by less than 50 per cent of the pupils. This contrasts markedly with the other areas where, on average, 60 per cent to 70 per cent of the children understood the items, and further reinforces the view that the abstract areas require much more careful consideration.

There was only a marginal trend towards the older children understanding more than the younger ones. The easiest item 'out', was known by 80 per cent of all age-groups, apart from the 15-year-olds and those of 5 years and under. For these the figures were 76·9 per cent and 73·9 per cent respectively. This pattern also applies to words of middle-order difficulty (for example 'thin') and what would appear to be the most difficult word, 'back'.

Table 17 Spatial test – percentage passing each item in order of difficulty

Item	Percentage passing	Item	Percentage passing
Down	88·6	Top	56·6
Out	85·8	Long	56·0
In	82·8	Near	51·3
Off	81·4	Middle	45·8
Inside	78·4	Bottom	42·2
On	71·1	Under	40·0
Empty	69·0	Far away	37·8
Big	66·7	Side	37·1
Full	66·4	Low	31·4
High	64·3	Behind	28·4
Fat	63·6	Corner	26·7
Little	62·2	Front	23·9
Short	60·2	Between	23·1
Thin	58·2	Back	22·2

Summary of results

On the whole, the vocabulary selected by teachers was known by about 70 per cent of the children. This is gratifying in so far as the English Picture Vocabulary Test had presented more negative findings. However, almost a third of the children tested failed on words which teachers expected them to know.

The spatial test, as expected, showed that children have difficulties with abstract concepts and words; movement and body-part vocabulary proved more difficult than teachers had expected. The data from these tests offers some guidance to teachers in identifying the capabilities of their pupils in terms of vocabulary. It remains for us to question whether the vocabulary involved a true selection of essential and important areas. For example, we felt that words of quantity or time, although difficult, are important. 'Quantity' would have enabled us to check children's understanding of functional vocabulary such as 'more' or 'less' or 'another one'. In retrospect we might question the need to study the children's understanding of colour. This is an area which is perhaps less functional than others, and emphasized to the detriment of other attributes such as size and shape. Apart from traffic-lights, it is very difficult to think of cases where colour is an *essential* part of a situation. Perhaps too some consideration should have been given to the concept of 'weight'.

Designing vocabulary tests

In an area as complicated as language it is as easy to make the mistake of teaching the child something he can do already as it is to attempt to teach well beyond his current capabilities. The only sure way to avoid this problem is to use careful assessment procedures before teaching.

Observation is as important in teaching vocabulary as it is in working with behaviour problems. Careful records need to be kept of the vocabulary used and understood by children in everyday settings, noting how it is used and how it is related to the context in which it is spoken. But observation is only one way of assessing vocabulary. It is equally important to test children's understanding in more controlled situations. Normally the context in which we talk is full of clues as to the meaning of words. One of the purposes of controlled test situations is to eliminate non-verbal clues, attempting also to reduce the demands of the context to the point where only a limited number of options are open to the child but not to the point where only one action or behaviour is possible. The child must have some alternative course of action by which he can demonstrate that he does not understand the teacher's demand.

This section is intended as notes of guidance for teachers who wish to develop vocabulary or other language-assessment tests suited to the needs of their own children. It draws heavily on the work of teachers involved in the project, but the vocabulary tests presented are not the outcome of a scientific exercise in test construction and administration. Results are merely illustrative, and should not be taken as representing 'norms' for mentally handicapped children. However, individual teachers, or preferably groups of teachers meeting in workshops, can usefully conduct a small survey of the language abilities of their own pupils.

The tests we have devised and the principles on which they are based are concerned only with the understanding of vocabulary, not with its use in the child's expressive language.

Although generally we must first comprehend before we can produce a word, understanding does not imply the ability to produce. The programmes described later make this point clear by separating the teaching sequence into stages: concept, reception, production. Some words will be used productively without understanding them. Wheldall[2] gives an amusing example concerning his son who, at the age of two, referred to all his books as 'my psychology books'. With some words, perhaps those implying causality or relationships (for example, 'because'), it is difficult to see how children can learn their full meaning except by trying them out and being told by adults when they are using them inappropriately. Children will always understand something by a word but not necessarily the adult meaning.

All these points need to be borne in mind when designing vocabulary tests. For convenience test design can be separated into three main stages: selecting the vocabulary to be tested, devising the test, and specifying the details of administration. This leads to a form of assessment referred to as 'criterion-referenced testing'. Tests of this type judge a child's ability in relation to a specific criterion: the child can or cannot produce a stated behaviour – here the child either does or does not respond correctly to a given instruction. It is important to make the distinction between this form of test and the kind referred to as 'standardized' or 'normative'. Standardized tests, which include most of the common intelligence tests, judge the child's ability in relation to the whole population of children in his age group. A test can be both criterion-referenced and normative; the EPVT, for example, has elements of both, as do developmental charts such as the Parental Involvement Project Charts.[3]

SELECTION OF VOCABULARY: WHICH WORDS?

It would be difficult, if not impossible, to examine a group of children to see whether they have knowledge of every word we expect them to know. To establish some priorities, a core vocabulary, for the classroom and the environment beyond the school, must be selected. The words selected fell into four groups, as outlined in the previous section, requiring different assessment procedures: concrete nouns, body-part words, verbs of movement, and abstract words relating to spatial relationships and colour.

Some words were omitted because of the problems they caused in assessment and teaching. The difficulty with such words as 'beauty' or 'nasty', or even words such as 'nice' or 'think', is that no two adults are likely to agree on their precise meaning, since each involves subjective judgement. 'Yesterday' and 'month' present problems which need specialized, individual solutions. Our concern here is to present general principles which apply to a wide range of areas of vocabulary. Many words were excluded simply on the grounds of time. But teachers can compile their own lists of words which they feel are important and apply to these the assessment and teaching principles described.

Another selection problem worth mentioning is plurality of labelling – for example, 'settee', 'couch', 'sofa'. Variations can arise from colloquial usage, or occasionally perhaps from differences between American and British usage. Care is needed to avoid confusion of alternative meanings of words in the testing and teaching sessions. For example, is the 'top' of a box the lid or the area at the top? What is the difference between the 'front' of an object and 'in front of' an object?

While there are problems, the selection of vocabulary is mostly straightforward. Defining the priority of one group of words over another must be left to the teacher's own needs and judgement.

DEVISING THE TESTS

It might seem obvious to say that before we test a child's comprehension of a word we must know what the word means. Most concrete words present no difficulties but more abstract words often mean many things and have many different usages, or their meaning is only relative. How big is 'big'? Or can something be 'on', 'under' and 'in between' at the same time? Words such as these are partly defined by their context. Something four centimetres high is big compared with something two centimetres high, and if you decide they are both small, then one is still bigger than the other! These are verbal games for adults, but present major conceptual learning hurdles for children. To overcome them we must be aware of the complex meaning of such words, and able to assess which elements of meaning the child has and does not have. For example, let us examine the word 'front'. For this purpose, we will split the development of the word into three stages. First, the child learns to understand 'front' in relation to his own body – he can specify what is in front of himself and what is not. Next, he learns that objects also have fronts and that things can be in front of other objects. This stage is further broken down into objects that possess obvious fronts, such as a television, and those objects that have no fixed front. At a more advanced stage, children will learn that something can be behind one object and in front of something else at the same time. Separate assessments can be devised for each stage and thus a clear indication be given of where to begin teaching. A possible assessment sequence might look like this:

1   Hand the child an object and ask him to put it 'in front' or 'behind'
2   Lay down a number of 'fronted' objects, such as a toy television and cars, and ask him to put an object 'in front' or 'behind' these
3   Repeat 2, but use objects without distinct fronts, such as cubes and spheres
4   Arrange a number of objects in a line with spaces in between and ask the child to put something 'in front' of X and 'behind' Y.

This sequence could be extended using different objects to be placed and varying objects in the arrangement. The child's responses will give a clear idea of what the word selected means to the child. Stages **1** and **2**, therefore, are concerned with analysing the meaning of a word and devising ways of testing the alternative meanings.

But even with a fuller analysis it is still easy to be mistaken about a child's ability. One item in a carefully designed standardized test illustrates the pitfalls. In vocabulary comprehension scale B of the Reynell Language Development Scale,[4] the instructions 'Put the spoon in the cup' and 'Put the doll on the chair' occur. Looking at these items in isolation, one might think that the words 'in' and 'on' had been tested but, as the test manual points out, they are only designed to *test the child's ability to relate two verbal concepts*. The non-verbal context of the instruction provides clues which make the words 'in' and 'on' all but redundant. The same response would probably have been obtained just by saying 'Spoon cup' or 'Doll chair'. To test 'on' we would have to devise a test which allows the child more than one obvious alternative in order to find out whether he fully understands the word – we must allow the child the opportunity to make incorrect responses.

In the project's spatial vocabulary test 'on' was tested by using a plain square box and a brick. The child was given the brick and asked to 'Put it on the box'. He had many possible response options open to him. If he made the correct response, we could therefore be reasonably sure that he understood the word 'on'.

THE WORDING OF THE INSTRUCTIONS

Instructions are required which do not confuse the child but provide him with adequate information. For most words, 'Show me . . .' is an effective and simple means of gaining a response. However, this is only appropriate in situations where a child is asked to perform an action or select a particular object. It would not be a suitable way of testing all verbs and spatial words – for instance, 'Show me in between' would, in most contexts, be a confusing instruction. A more effective way of wording a demand such as this might be to position two objects a distance apart and give the child a third object, asking him to 'put it in between'.

The spatial vocabulary test was the only one which included alternative instructions to 'Show me . . . '. These included:

'Put it . . . '
'Where's the . . . '

and for the individual words 'low' and 'off':

'Hold it low'
'Take it off'.

OBJECTS AND MATERIALS TO BE USED

Selection and presentation of materials is crucial. When testing 'clothes' vocabulary, for instance, selection of materials could involve real clothes, doll's clothes, or pictures of clothes. In the 'clothes' test it would have been possible to dress a child in the items and use him as a model. However, we envisaged numerous problems if the child concerned offered cues to the child being tested. Pictures could have been used, but difficulties would have arisen if each item was not clearly illustrated. In this particular test we selected a large rag doll which was dressed in the appropriate attire.

THE MEANS OF PRESENTATION

When testing vocabulary, certain associated words will almost certainly be involved, which give clues to the correct response if presented together. A child may always *know* a 'saucer' if it is accompanied by a 'cup'. The mere context of their being presented together, combined with the fact that the child knows 'cup', would most likely aid the chance of a successful response. But this does not necessarily imply that the child knows or understands that the object in question is a 'saucer'.

Care needs to be exercised to ensure that associated or connected words are not tested together. If two open boxes are presented, one full and the other empty, little information would be gained if we first asked: 'Show me the box that is full', and immediately followed on by asking, 'Show me the box that is empty'.

Presentation needs to be carefully controlled, especially in tests which involve the selection of one item from a choice of objects. These situations potentially allow chance responses to be correct. An analysis of the English Picture Vocabulary Test results (discussed in Chapter I) provides evidence that when in doubt the tendency is for the children to point to the two items in the lower half of the page, and inevitably some of these guessed responses are correct. It is not possible to eliminate responses of this type.

The test of 'colour' words could have been designed with a minimal number of colour cards: to test six colours we could have placed a set of six cards on the table in front of the child with the instruction, 'Show me . . .' By adopting this procedure, with every successful selection the number of options diminishes and correct guessing becomes easier. This arrangement might help the child in another way. Faced with four colours, three of which he knows, he could correctly select the unknown colour by exclusion of the three known colours. Again, this would result in a 'correct' response and lost information to the tester. With this particular test a procedure was devised which enabled us to allow for chance responses. We produced a range of colour cards and organized the combinations in such a way that each colour was presented and tested on four different occasions. To pass on a particular colour, a child was required to obtain a total score of three out of four correct responses.

Presentation becomes complicated when a range of objects or pictures is required from which the child is to select. Replacing tested objects with new ones should not allow the child to predict that the newly presented object is the one to which the teacher is going to require him to respond. An extract from the 'objects of the home' test illustrates how this can be organized:

To begin, place sugar bowl, tray, plate and plug on the table. As each item is tested, replace it with a new object as directed. Teacher asks:
'Show me plate'.
Child responds and teacher replaces plate with knife.
Teacher asks:
'Show me tray'.
Child responds and teacher replaces tray with bottle.
Teacher asks:
'Show me sugar bowl'.

SPECIFYING THE DETAILS OF TEST ADMINISTRATION

Any test will involve the teacher in giving instructions and these will vary depending on the type of vocabulary being tested. There will, however, be certain administrative instructions common to all the tests, consisting mainly of procedural details for the teacher to give a uniformity in the way the tests are presented. Because the project tests were designed for over two hundred children and arranged so that the results could be successfully analysed, uniformity of test administration was essential.

There were a number of issues which, for the purpose of our own work, were considered to be important and it was essential that they should be made clear. The problem of whether a child is to be coded as testable/untestable is a case in point. Our instructions on this and other points were as follows:

a All children are to be tested *unless* physically incapable of making a response. As we see it, very few children should be untestable in this way. Although most tests require a hand-pointing response, it would be quite acceptable with certain children to seek an alternative response such as eye pointing. In most tests we allow for practice items to be used with those children who do not understand the requirements of the situation. With some children it may be necessary actually to teach them how to respond, i.e. to point. This question of whether a child is testable or not must not be confused with situations where the child just does not know any of the responses. For instance, a young nursery child may fail to respond correctly because he may not have the attention span, the ability to point or be able to understand the instruction – this means that the child fails to score on that item, not that he is untestable.

b   Non-verbal cues of any sort are to be avoided. Most 'natural' situations where an adult is working with a child will involve a great deal of non-verbal communication. The adult will combine hand movement with speech and thus emphasize certain meanings. When issuing instructions, eye pointing is quite a common occurrence. For example, the teacher might ask the child to 'bring me the doll' and at the same time look towards the doll. Also a common form of communication is facial expression. If a child does what is asked of him the adult will normally register pleasure, or if a child fails to respond the adult will often offer cues by means of his facial expression. In a test situation, however, we must be careful about these non-verbal cues. The very nature of the test is to find out what the child can or cannot do, and this can only be done without assistance from another person. It is essential therefore, that the adult is consciously aware of this point in order to refrain from offering vital cues.

c   Correct responses are *not* to be rewarded. During a test it is obvious that a child will be required to offer responses. Some of these responses will be correct and some of them may be incorrect. Most children will be used to responding to the type of instructions used in the test, and at the same time they will be used to receiving immediate feedback to their responses, so that normally the correct response will be rewarded by the teacher. Care must be taken to ensure that the child is not given praise for appropriate responses. In the first place, this situation could very easily upset the child, especially if he receives information that few responses are correct. Secondly, the child could easily attempt responses in order to please the teacher. We do not advocate that the teacher should offer no verbal feedback as this would make most children somewhat uneasy. We suggest that after each response, irrespective of whether it is right or wrong, the teacher provides some form of neutral feedback such as 'OK' or 'fine'. There are a number of additional points which are important in the case of our own specific tests and which will be relevant in most general test situations.

d   Each child is to be tested individually and no children should be near enough to watch or listen to the test situation. This will not only ensure that the child being tested is offered no vital cues, but will also prevent other children from becoming familiar with the instructions, materials and order of presentation.

e   The test instructions and materials are to be presented in the order specified. [In

DESIGNING VOCABULARY TESTS 219

each case, the order in which the words were to be tested had to be carefully controlled and this was to be the final order of presentation.]

f A common occurrence is the situation where a child fails to respond or responds inappropriately. This can arise due to any one of a number of reasons and it is therefore helpful if one considers the following points:

i Gaining the child's attention – if, when the instruction was given, the child was not paying attention, it is quite possible that he will not have heard the instruction. It is essential that attention is gained *before* the instruction is given, and when necessary this can be done by saying 'look' or by calling the child's name.

ii Make sure that the child understands the instruction. Sometimes, because a child fails to respond or responds inappropriately, it may mean that he did not understand what he was expected to do. He may understand the word but not know how to 'show' or to 'give' as the case may be. Where there is doubt, we recommend that the teacher teaches these responses in a separate session.

Where a child fails to respond or responds inappropriately it is advisable to score him as failing the item. Otherwise, if the instruction is repeated, the child may feel he has to make some response and hence may guess. This situation often leads to a correct response being given by chance. If a teacher feels that the instruction should be repeated, it is essential first to consider the fact that repetition may help the child and aid his chances of success.

DESIGNING TESTS: AN EXERCISE

Many teachers feel that the vocabulary connected with play and pastimes is important. How can we check whether the child understands this vocabulary?

Selecting the vocabulary

To find out whether pupils understand the vocabulary they are expected to know, a test will be needed involving the selection of familiar objects and experiences. We are not attempting to trick the children; we wish to know what they understand. For instance, a Meccano set would probably mean very little to a nursery child, whereas a teddy bear or a ball might. How might we design tests to suit a nursery child and a senior pupil?

For the young child a selection of toys might be most realistic; for a teenager, a slightly more sophisticated vocabulary connected with sports and hobbies. For the purpose of this exercise the final selection of vocabulary is:

Nursery age	*Senior age*
Teddy	Football
Ball	Cricket
Car	Tennis
Doll	Running
Gun	Swimming

Devising the tests

For all test instructions, the child will need to have certain prerequisite skills – for example, pointing to indicate one object from a selection of objects or being able to respond appropriately to a verbal demand such as 'Show me'. Obviously, the type of instruction selected depends very much on the children involved. The following notes outline some of the main points to be considered when designing tests of vocabulary to suit specific children.

1. In devising an order of presentation, the consecutive presentation of any two items might need to be avoided; and it might be advisable to test some words more than once, if one wishes to avoid chance responses.
2. Exact instructions need to be specified. With senior pupils, and most nursery children, a verbal instruction may be used – 'Give me the ball' or 'Show me the football'. However, for some groups of children, especially the very young, such wording as 'Show me...', 'Give me...' or 'Where's the...' might prove confusing, and it might be more appropriate to restrict the verbal demands and combine them with gesture – for example, 'The teacher holds hands out and says "doll" or "Give me the doll".'
3. For the nursery children the decision needs to be made whether to use the actual toys or pictures of toys for test materials. Toy objects are easily handled and are to be preferred with younger children. For the senior pupils, however, it would be impracticable to use the real activity, or even models of the activity, so that pictures would seem to be the obvious choice.
4. Having selected the instructions and test materials, it remains to select a way in which the items will be presented:
   a. The child could be asked to select from a choice of two objects, but chance responses may affect the results considerably
   b. All five items could be presented at once, but this allows the child to guess more correctly with the final items

c   The child could be asked to select from a choice of four objects, in which case if only five items are being tested, it must be decided whether to present each item on more than one occasion or whether other items not being tested should be introduced.

At this stage it is worth specifying whether all the objects are to be changed after each response or, as in the case of the 'objects of the home' test, after each response an item is replaced with another one.

5   Finally, what kind of responses are required? With a physically handicapped child approximations might be accepted – eye pointing to a request such as 'Show me . . .', or perhaps gross approximations of arm pointing.

In devising tests there are no short cuts. If we want to know whether a child *understands* selected vocabulary, care is needed to ensure that one tests only comprehension. At this point we suggest the reader uses the vocabulary for the nursery and senior age-groups and draws up two tests. Obviously, with particular children in mind, the test will vary. (Appendix C illustrates how each might be designed.) Any information gained from the tests should be incorporated with further knowledge about the child's understanding of that vocabulary, through systematic observation and by designing further tests.

Teaching new vocabulary

Assessment is only the first step in the teaching process. It is necessary to use this information to teach what is not known. If, after testing, one discovered that a child did not know the word 'bottle', the obvious next stage would be to teach this word. But, how do we do this? As discussed in Chapter IV, it would be of little use if one taught the child to say 'bottle' and then accepted this as teaching a new word unless the child:

1   *Knew* the function of a bottle
2   Was able to distinguish *bottles from non-bottles*
3   Was able to generalize – that is to realize that a milk bottle, perfume bottle, coca-cola bottle and washing-up liquid bottle are all bottles
4   Was able to realize that bottles are not all of one material (glass), are not all transparent, that some of the properties and functions of bottles are shared by non-bottles
5   Can demonstrate understanding of the word bottle.

Moreover, if in our teaching session the child said 'bottle' only once, this is no true indication that he has learned it. Because we are anxious to cover as much ground as possible in our teaching, there is a great temptation to accept this as the criterion for success. But this may result in superficial teaching and learning. A slower pace with more systematic teaching is more effective in the long run.

There are three main stages involved in acquiring a new vocabulary which fall into a logical order.

1 THE CONCEPT

A concept is usually defined in terms of abstractions or ideas we have about an object or situation. Our approach is less abstract. Our concern is that the child should acquire knowledge and experience of the object or action, and learn about its *functional use and properties* so that he can discriminate the object or action from others, and can generalize it so that it is recognizable in various forms and contexts. He should also be able to classify the objects or actions into groups of the same type and to distinguish the real thing as well as representations of it – that is, toys and pictures from other objects or actions.

2 RECEPTIVE LANGUAGE

This is the stage where the concept is given a label. The object or action with which the child is now familiar acquires a name, so that the child is taught to discriminate and sort on verbal demand. If consistently successful at this stage we can proceed to stage 3.

3 PRODUCTION

Obviously there will be much overlap between this and the previous stage. This is the time to encourage the child to use the label. Imitation of the word (or approximation of the word) will be directly encouraged and once this is occurring consistently, demands will be made for spontaneous production. Spontaneous production of the word by the children takes place during the labelling stage if they are thoroughly involved in the situation. Thus stage 3 stems naturally from 2 and is considerably shortened by thorough and imaginative teaching in the previous stages.

DEVISING PROGRAMMES

Before attempting to teach any new vocabulary, a teacher needs to collect certain information. Vocabulary tests do not provide a full profile of the child's language abilities. Vocabulary cannot be dealt with in isolation from other factors. It is always presented in the context of a situation, of a sentence, and in the context of meaning. One isolated test cannot be relied on to provide the information required to select which vocabulary to teach. Combined with systematic observation and further tests within various contexts, appropriate vocabulary can be chosen. But to know whether or not a child understands a word does not give adequate information as to whether he has established the concept and can generalize it, nor does it tell us whether the child can produce the word.

Furthermore, although it may be discovered that the child does not understand certain vocabulary, this is no indication that he needs to. Has it functional use for him? New vocabulary should be selected for its relevance. It needs to be functional for the child, and preferably able to be generalized to situations outside school. Once the new vocabulary has been selected, there are further factors to be considered. The teaching programmes outlined below presuppose a number of existing skills:

1. The child will need to be able to sit, to look for at least short periods of time and he will also need to be able to make spontaneous movements and sounds.
2. It is essential that the child has object permanence. At the basic concept level even, the child will need to be aware that if an object is out of sight it still exists.
3. In most learning situations the child will be required to point to or pick up objects. For those who cannot do this spontaneously it can be taught by imitation.
4. In most cases spontaneous production of a new word can be taught. The ability to imitate sounds will be necessary although certain children, for physical reasons, are not capable of doing so.

A few children will have major difficulties with some of these prerequisite skills. The teacher must decide whether these need to be taught before beginning the vocabulary programmes and whether they have not been acquired because of the child's handicap. Eye contact may need to be taught with some children. With one child the teacher may feel that a glance in the direction of the object is sufficient while with another child she may want him to look for several seconds and not begin the vocabulary programme until he has achieved this consistently.

Some of the children may have difficulty with the articulatory aspect of expressive language. It will be up to the teacher to decide what approximation to accept. The child might omit initial, middle or final consonants saying 'ky' for 'sky', or for 'apple' he might say 'a/le' and for 'top', 'to'. Or perhaps he substitutes one consonant for another, saying 'poot' for 'foot' or 'tate' for 'take'. It is important that a free speech flow is established, and to avoid restrictive standards of articulation. Correction of articulation requires careful shaping procedures and hence separate programmes, perhaps devised in conjunction with a speech therapist.

THE TEACHING FRAMEWORK

Based on the three stages of concept, reception and production, we devised one clearly defined and effective way of teaching vocabulary. Certain factors are important in devising the teaching framework. It needs to:

1 Require relatively little time in preparation or evaluation
2 Use available resources and facilities
3 Provide assessment and intrinsic evaluation
4 Be enjoyed by teachers and children alike.

The teaching model discussed in Chapter II provides the means to do this. Specifying behavioural objectives and methods for achieving them, suitable programmes can be written. The objectives are the key to teaching, specifying *exactly* what one expects the child to be able to do at the end of the lesson that he could not do before. Any programmes devised will need to allow for small steps of learning.

Marion Blank in *Teaching Learning in the Preschool*[5] points out that a high percentage of correct responses should be ensured. 'If the child were exposed to frequent failure, he would quickly abandon his efforts at learning.' We often expect a child to learn new vocabulary in one step – acquire the concept, label and produce the sound at one and the same time. This does not mean that one must expect every response made by the child to be correct. Learning skills must undoubtedly involve some mistakes. As Marion Blank adds: 'Every lesson, however, should be capable of evoking some error – if it does not, then the lesson is doing little or nothing to facilitate the child's functioning.' She also states that 'the effectiveness of any teaching programme critically hinges on the management of the wrong responses.' Incorrect responses are vital in indicating which aspects of learning are proving difficult. If they occur consistently, it shows that the child is in difficulty, and alternative or extra stages may be necessary.

EXAMPLE: 'BALL'

We might find with one child that he does not understand the word 'ball'. Further investigation may show that the concept is established but, as yet, the child does not connect the label with this now familiar object. The next step therefore, is to provide him with the information that this object has a label – 'ball'. In a situation such as this, the overall objective might be: for the child to point to, or otherwise indicate, a ball from a selection of known objects on request, three out of four times. Note, however, that this objective is based on knowledge of existing skills:

1. The child must be able to point (or something similar) on verbal request – if the child cannot do this, we either teach him to do so or select different, more appropriate, tasks
2. For the child to be able to point to, or otherwise indicate, a ball from a selection of objects he must be able to look at the objects
3. The child must know the objects presented at the same time as the ball.

How will the teacher know the child has been successful in achieving the objective? This might sound absurd – if the child picks up the ball when requested, he must have been successful. But in selecting one object from a group of four, the child has a one in four chance of selecting the correct object by chance. To be certain, the teacher would need to check the behaviour a number of times. The number of correct responses required will be the teacher's decision based on knowledge of the child. The whole programme might take on the following format:

Aim
To develop the child's comprehension of nouns.

Objective 1
For the child to point to, or otherwise indicate, a ball from a selection of known objects on request, to a criterion of three out of four times. (Objects required: doll, brick, car and ball.)

Objective 1A
On request the child will touch, pick up or give the ball to the teacher.

Criterion for success
Three out of four successful responses are required before moving on to objective 1B (this is selected with prior knowledge of the child's abilities).

Organization
Location, time, etc., to be specified by the teacher.

Method
The teacher and the child are seated opposite each other/side by side at a table. Placing the ball on the table in front of the child, the teacher points to the ball and says, 'ball'. The teacher in turn asks the child to:

a   Touch the ball
b   Show me the ball
c   Give me the ball
d   Pick the ball up.

For each successful response the teacher praises: 'Good – ball'. If the child fails, the session is repeated before moving on to objective 1B.

Objective 1B
From a selection of ball and doll the child will, on request, select the ball.

Criterion for success
Three out of four successful responses are required before moving on to objective 1C.

Organization
To be specified by the teacher.

Method
Teacher and child are seated opposite each other/side by side at a table. Teacher places ball and doll on the table in front of the child. Teacher requests:

a   Show me the doll
b   Show me the ball
c   Give me the ball
d   Touch the ball
e   Give me the doll
f   Show me the ball.

The positions of the objects are to be varied after each request. For each successful response, the teacher praises: 'Good – ball'. If the child fails, the teacher should prompt, pointing to and saying 'ball'. This can be followed by 'Show me the ball', then 1B is repeated.

Objective 1C
From a selection of ball, doll and brick the child will, on request, select the ball.

Criterion for success
Three out of four successful responses are required before moving on to objective 1D.

Organization
To be specified by the teacher.

Method
Teacher and child are seated opposite each other/side by side at a table. The teacher

places ball, doll and brick on the table in front of the child. The teacher requests:

a   Show me ball
b   Give me brick
c   Touch the ball
d   Show me the doll
e   Show me the ball
f   Give me the ball.

The positions of the objects are to be varied after each request. For each successful response the teacher praises: 'Good – ball'. If a child fails to respond appropriately, the teacher should prompt saying, 'ball'. This to be followed by 'Show me the ball', then 1C is repeated.

Objective 1D
From a selection of ball, doll, brick and car the child will, on request, select the ball.

Criterion for success
Three out of four successful responses are required.

Organization
To be specified by the teacher.

Method
Teacher and child seated opposite each other/side by side at a table. The teacher places a ball, doll, brick and a car on the table in front of the child. The teacher requests:

a   Give me the doll
b   Show me the ball
c   Show me the car
d   Touch the ball
e   Pick up the brick
f   Give me the ball
g   Show me the doll
h   Pick the ball up.

The position of the objects are to be varied after each request. For each successful response the teacher praises: 'Good – ball'. If the child fails, the teacher should point and say, 'ball'. This to be followed by 'Show me the ball', then the session is repeated.

Evaluation
Can the child now point to or otherwise indicate a ball from a selection of known objects three out of four times? Note that a variety of instructions was used to ask the child to select the ball. If the child is not familiar with all these requests, use those he understands and teach others (if necessary) as a separate programme.

If the child is successful and achieves the objective, it still does not mean that he has acquired complete understanding of the word 'ball'. It means that on request he can consistently indicate ball from a selection of known objects.

Obviously it is easier to teach new vocabulary to the child who has already acquired the concept, as in the case of 'ball'. However, the test results show that much language, especially spatial vocabulary, is not understood, and it would be appropriate to assume that for many the concepts are not even established.

The word 'back' was least known of the spatial vocabulary and further investigation by teachers indicates that most children have not acquired the basic concept. 'Out', on the other hand, was known by 85·8 per cent of the children. We have selected it as an example to illustrate the processes involved in teaching from *concept* through *labelling* to *production*.

EXAMPLE: OUT

What does 'out' mean?

First we must consider that the word 'out' refers to a relationship between the object and a *context*, not to the object itself. Certain contexts commonly relate to 'out':

1 Picking, pulling or pushing *out*
2 Selecting *out*
3 Walking or going *out* (confusion may arise here with 'leaving')
4 Taking objects *out* of containers
5 Getting *out* of a car.

A wide range of skills are associated with these meanings. Finger and thumb co-ordination and precision would be required to take Smarties *out* of a tube, or a strong hand action to tip them *out*. Getting *out* of the car involves changing the bodily position from sitting to standing. There are also more subtle ties of meaning to consider – confusion between 'out' and 'outside'.

There are a vast number of generalizations to contend with. For the child it will be, at first, bewildering and every effort has to be made to ensure that 'out' is emphasized more than other aspects which are inevitably associated. For instance, the situation may require the child to take beads out of a tin four times. In designing a method it would be advisable to anticipate the procedure – will four tins of beads be available, or will the child be expected to wait while the teacher returns them to the tin – that is, puts them 'in'?

How to check whether the child knows 'out'

If the child is instructed to take a pen out of a box and he does, what does it tell us? There are few, if any, alternatives in this situation. What else can the child do but remove the pen from the box? On its own this will tell us very little about the child's understanding of 'out'.

If, after seeing sweets go into a box which is then put in a basket, the child responds appropriately to the instruction 'Take the sweets out', does this mean that he understands 'out'? In most cases the sight and the label of sweets will undoubtedly enhance the chance of success. Did the child respond to a familiar label (sweets) or did he really know 'out'? Did he realize that the sweets were inside one thing which was also in something else?

When checking for understanding and production of vocabulary it is necessary to devise tests and make observations to check on consistency. For example, one might:

1 Check on whether the concept is established:
   a Present the child with a Smartie in a tube
   b Present the child with a box containing objects of varying sizes, shapes and colours
   c Present a variety of containers some of which are full and others partly full
   d Present containers full and partly full of non-continuous substances – for example, bricks or pencils
   e Specifically sit the child in various containers
   f Request imitation of the action 'out' – both self and with objects.
2 Check on whether the child understands the word 'out':
   a Place two boxes in front of the child – one with sweets in, the other empty. Instruct the child to take the sweets 'out'
   b Place a doll in a cot and a doll on the table next to the cot. Instruct the child to take the doll 'out'
   c Put the doll in bed and ask the child if the doll is out of bed.
3 Check whether or not the child can say the word 'out':
   a By imitation – when the child is taking something out, the teacher models the word and asks the child to say it after her
   b The teacher asks the child what he is doing when he is taking something 'out'
   c The teacher demonstrates 'out' and asks the child what action is being performed or what the object is doing.

The programmes are begun at the level indicated by the assessment. For this example, the programme will incorporate all three stages from concept to production of the word 'out'.

A teaching programme for the word 'out'

This programme is very detailed, to allow for all possible problems. Depending on individual children, elements might reasonably be omitted.

Aim
For the child to increase his spatial vocabulary.

Objective 1
The child will consistently use and observe the function of 'out'.

Objective 1A
The child will look towards the teacher when she performs the action of taking something 'out'.

Criterion for success
This needs to be specified by the teacher so that before moving on to objective 1B the child is looking consistently. At first, the teacher may feel that if a child looks on two out of five occasions it is enough. Later, full success might be required.

Organization
Teacher ensures that the tasks are performed in varying ways, co-ordinates lessons with each other.

Method
Positioned near to the child, the teacher will perform the action 'out' by:

a Taking objects out of containers or cupboards
b Going out of a room
c Pouring milk out of bottles
d Taking food out of bags or packets
e Pouring water out of a tap or out of containers.

At the time of performing this action, the child's attention must be sought by calling his name. If looking response is observed in conjunction with the performance of 'out', the teacher will praise the child immediately.

Generalization
Broaden the range of objects, containers and contexts in which the activity is performed.

Objective 1B
The child will allow the teacher to help him perform actions involving 'out'.

Criterion for success and organization
To be specified by the teacher.

Method
The teacher physically helps the child to:

a Take objects out of cupboards and drawers
b Take objects out of containers

c   Take food out of bags or packets
d   Walk out of the room or building
e   Climb out of boxes.

For each successful attempt the teacher will praise the child.

Generalization
As for objective 1A.

Objective 1C
The child will imitate the actions involving 'out'.

Criterion for success and organization
To be specified by the teacher.

Method
Using the same means as in objective 1B, teacher performs 'out' while positioned next to or facing the child. After completing the action, the teacher immediately requests, 'You do it'. For successful imitations the teacher praises the child immediately (the teacher may need to prompt the child to imitate at first).

Generalization
As for objective 1A.

Objective 1D
The child will spontaneously perform the action 'out'.

Criterion for success and organization
To be specified by the teacher.

Method
The teacher:

a   Presents the child with a container filled with various objects
b   Presents the child with a number of containers filled with various objects
c   Presents the child with bottles or buckets filled with sand or water
d   Positions the child in various containers.

Immediately the child performs the action 'out' the teacher praises.

Generalization
As for objective 1A.

Evaluation
By this stage, the initial objective will have been realized – the child will consistently use and observe actions involving 'out'. In other words, he should have established the concept. As a final check it is worth seeking further information. Using a detailed method of observation (see Chapter V), does he use 'out'? If so, when, where, how often, who with and what with? Does he physically perform 'out' with fine motor movements as much as he does with gross motor movements? Is he observant when others are performing 'out' – does he look in the direction of, or comment about, others when they perform 'out'.

If a higher consistency is required, repeat sections or all of the appropriate objectives and re-evaluate his behaviour. If his performance is quite consistent in a generalized way, proceed to objective 2 in which he will be taught that the concept has a label.

Objective 2
On verbal request the child will indicate, or perform the action 'out'.

Objective 2A
When performing or viewing the action 'out', the child will look towards the teacher as she says 'out'.

Criterion for success and organization
To be specified by the teacher.

Method
Seated next to or in front of the child, the teacher first takes an object out of a container and at the same time says 'out'. She then gives the child a container with an object in and requests, 'You do it'. As the child performs the action 'out', the teacher says 'out' and immediately praises the child: 'Out – good'.

Generalization
Introduce a range of containers and objects.

Objective 2b
On verbal request the child will perform 'out'.

Criterion for success and organization
To be specified by the teacher.

Method
Teacher and child are seated opposite each other/side by side at a table.

a The child is presented with two containers, one filled with sand (or alternative) the other filled with bricks. Instruct the child to 'Take the bricks *out*'. Or:
b The child is taken to an open cupboard or drawer and is instructed to take specific objects *out*. Or:
c The child is presented with milk bottles and beakers and is instructed to 'Pour the milk *out*'. Or:
d The child is told to 'Go *out* of the room'. Or:
e The child is positioned in a large box or in a car and is instructed to 'Get *out*'. Or:
f The child is presented with two dolls, one in bed and the other on the table next to it. The child is instructed to 'Take the doll *out* of bed'.

As the child performs the action the teacher immediately says, 'Out – good'. If after giving the instruction the child fails to respond or hesitates, prompt.

Generalization
Widen the range of containers, objects and situations.

TEACHING NEW VOCABULARY

Objective 2C
On verbal request, the child will point to or otherwise indicate, 'out' from other actions.

Criterion for success and organization
To be specified by the teacher.

Method

a The child is presented with two dolls, one in bed and the other at the side. The child is requested to 'Show me the doll that is *out* of bed'. *Or:*
b The child is presented with an empty box next to which are a number of bricks (or alternative). The child is asked 'Are the bricks *out* of the box?' *Or:*
c The child is presented with a box full of bricks and is asked, 'Are the bricks *out* of the box?' *Or:*
d The child is presented with a picture of an object which is in a container and is asked, 'Is the (dog) *out* of the (basket)?'

Generalization
As for objective 2B.

Evaluation
With objective 2, it is worth making an extra check on the child's consistency. If this is felt to be satisfactory, move on to objective 3, where the child will be taught to produce the word 'out'.

Objective 3
In response to a request for information about the relationship of two objects (or groups of objects) one of which is out of the other, the child will spontaneously say 'out'.

Objective 3A
At the request for imitation of the word 'out' while performing or viewing the action, the child will say 'out'.

Criterion for success and organization
To be specified by the teacher.

Method

a The child is asked to perform the action 'out' – for example, 'Take the bricks *out* of the box.' *Or:*
b The child is asked to point to, or otherwise indicate, an object which is 'out' of the container – for example, 'Show me the cup that is *out* of the cupboard.' *Or:*
c The child is asked to reply to a question such as 'Is the doll *out* of bed?'

As the child performs the action and responds as requested, the teacher says, 'Out – you say it.' If the child responds appropriately, the teacher immediately praises: 'Out – good'.

The mini-objectives above are set out in order of difficulty and make increasing demands on the children; these could be regarded as three entirely different objectives and written as such.

Generalization

As with previous objectives use a variety of objects and containers and extend the child's range of contexts.

Objective 3B

The child will imitate the word 'out' while performing or viewing the action, without being requested to do so.

Criterion for success and organization

To be specified by the teacher.

Method

As for objective 3A. As the child performs the action or responds as requested, the teacher says, 'Out'. If the child imitates, the teacher immediately praises: 'Out – good'. If the child fails, repeat objective 3A and follow by 3B.

Objective 3C

While performing the action or referring to the relationship of 'out', the child will spontaneously say 'out'.

Criterion for success and organization

To be specified by the teacher.

Method

The teacher organizes situations which will require the child to:

a Perform the action 'out'
b Refer to which objects are 'out'
c Show by affirmation or negation which objects are 'out'.

When the teacher performs or refers to 'out', the teacher asks what action is being performed or where the object is in relation to others. Ensure that the child produces the word 'out' spontaneously and not simply by imitation or request. If the child hesitates or fails to respond, prompt by repeating objective 3B. Immediately the child responds appropriately, the teacher will praise.

Generalization

As for objective 3A.

Evaluation

Does the child now know 'out'? Has he acquired the concept and can he generalize it? Does he consistently understand 'out' and can he say the word spontaneously in the appropriate context? If the answer to all these is yes, the child can be taught a new word.

This programme for 'out' highlights the necessity to teach by small incremental stages and to ensure that one objective is reached before moving on to another. Ten objectives are specified in this programme, but this does not imply that this word can be taught in ten lessons. Sectional objectives could be attained in one lesson, but the method suggests various ways of realizing the same objective. These have been included primarily to illustrate the need for generalization at each stage. For example, six ways are suggested to achieve objective 2B. We recommend that before moving on to 2C all of these are adopted – spending a lesson on each. Where further practice is necessary, extending the range of objects and contexts not only helps generalize the behaviour, but also introduces variety.

No short cuts should be taken, although changes in the programme to suit individuals will be inevitable. Some children may not be ready to imitate the word; others may not understand all the range of instructions as we suggest them – '*Take* the bricks out', '*Pour* the milk out', '*Go* out'. Some children may be unable to cope with a request of such length as 'Show me the doll that is out of bed.' For children such as these, the word can be taught, but care must be taken to ensure that the instructions or objects do not cause confusion. It is easier for the child if familiar objects are incorporated in the lesson. When the objectives have been reached at each level it is possible to incorporate less frequently used objects.

The above programme suggests one way of teaching a spatial concept using systematic teaching methods. Further examples of teaching programmes for more difficult spatial concepts are given in Appendix D. Each has been used successfully with children from the age of 4 upwards, but we would emphasize the importance of the teacher's role in transforming a written blueprint for action into a sensitive and enjoyable activity. No programme, no matter how carefully written, can ensure enjoyable and effective learning. This depends on the teacher's enthusiasm and imagination.

Despite the teachers' expectations many children did not understand some of the body-part vocabulary, and programmes were written to see how effectively this could be taught. The programme designed to teach the word 'eyebrows' (Appendix D) was used with some success with nursery and junior children, who had not developed the concept. This word was selected simply because the children had no knowledge of it, not because of its utility or functional value. Not only is it possible to adopt the 'eyebrow' programme for other body parts, but also in the same way the basic format of the spatial programmes can be used to teach other spatial words. Care, however, is needed in modifying the instructions.

In the programmes in Appendices C and D we have concentrated upon helping children to acquire the concept and attach a label, although at least one programme, 'on top' and 'underneath' (Appendix D) provides an

236 TEACHING VOCABULARY

adequate model for developing productive language. The emphasis on concept and labelling stages was necessary early on, because of the children's limited linguistic abilities. However, in the course of this work it was found that given an active approach on the part of the teacher, spontaneous production of the words occurred during the labelling stage even with the more limited children. This does not mean that a programme for expressive language is not necessary. It is essential to make sure that children use the vocabulary frequently and in appropriate and varied contexts, and it enables the teacher to pick up the individual child's particular difficulties.

Summary

This chapter began with the results of a small survey, which aimed to assess the ability of children to understand a core vocabulary. The words chosen were those teachers considered relevant and important for the children to know, both in and out of school. The survey paralleled in part the larger survey of language abilities carried out at the beginning of the project, which included the use of the English Picture Vocabulary Test as a measure of receptive vocabulary. The present survey involved some 230 children in six schools for the mentally handicapped, and provided data on the number of children who showed positive evidence of knowledge of words in many categories such as: transport; objects of the home; people; general environment; clothing; body parts; movement; spatial. After discussing the results of the survey, we present a number of suggestions and a worked example designed to encourage teachers to devise assessments of vocabulary relevant to the needs of their own students.

The second part of the chapter provides examples of a number of classroom-based teaching programmes which arose directly from the vocabulary survey, and were mainly carried out by teachers in a number of ESN(S) schools in Clwyd, North Wales. Detailed examples are given in the area of teaching basic knowledge (concepts) as well as comprehension and production of specific words (for example, 'ball' and 'out'), and extended examples of programmes designed to teach knowledge of body parts, and a spatial vocabulary ('near to', 'far away from', 'on top' and 'underneath') are given in Appendix D. The detailed teaching programmes are merely illustrative of the general principles which can be applied in a wide variety of situations.

References

1. M. A. BRIMER and T. L. M. DUNN, *English Picture Vocabulary Test*. Educational Evaluation Enterprises, Bristol, 1962.
2. K. WHELDALL, 'Receptive language development in the mentally handicapped', in P. Berry (ed.), *Language and Communication in the Mentally Handicapped*. Edward Arnold, 1976.
3. D. M. JEFFREE and R. McCONKEY, *PIP Developmental Charts*. Hodder & Stoughton Educational, Dunton Green, 1976.
4. J. K. REYNELL, *The Reynell Developmental Language Scales*. NFER Publishing, Windsor, rev. edn, 1977.
5. M. BLANK, *Teaching Learning in the Preschool*. Merrill, Columbus, Ohio, 1973.

Note. Two teachers using the vocabulary teaching approach advocated in this chapter are featured in 'Teaching new words', one of three published videotapes made by the project. (See note on page viii.)

VII. Non-verbal communication

George and a classroom assistant were observed playing with a large inflatable sofa. By the use of a primitive form of gesture, George successfully communicated to the classroom assistant 'Put that on your head', and also 'No, I don't want that (a plastic bucket); I want this' (the sofa). The meanings, clearly understood by the assistant, were communicated by a combination of pulling and pushing accompanied by excited ritualistic hand-flapping which seemed to indicate 'You're doing fine, keep it up', or else 'That's it, I like it'.

George is typical of many children who were scored by their teachers on the language survey as having limited receptive language and whose productive language was at a level of less than one-word imitation (see Chapter I). A third of the 1400 children were shown to be functioning at less than the one-word imitation level, and our concern grew as we discovered that numerous children were thought by their teachers to have no communication at all. George was scored as having no receptive language, yet he was able to make quite complex demands. He responded to his own name, and demonstrated his understanding of the play with the assistant.

As the survey results show, 18 per cent of pupils move on to the Adult Training Centres without any form of speech, and a fairly high proportion of younger children for a considerable portion of their school life are never in a position to make demands on their environment through speech. But communication could be just as effective if meanings were conveyed non-verbally. With many children we cannot predict at an early stage whether they are ever going to be able to speak; in a sense we can only wait and see. But during this waiting period are we simply to do nothing? Do we wait until the child is 6 or even 16? Undoubtedly we should be doing something, but what? There are few children who are not able to communicate something. For this reason we investigated ways of determining:

>   *Does* the child communicate?
>   *What* does the child communicate?
>   *How* does the child communicate?

A study of two children

We selected two children who were functioning at a non-verbal level and who were either ineffective or failed to make demands on their environment. Many children function at a very basic level of communication, and lack the prerequisite skills for acquiring complex systems of signing or speech. But even a child who is so grossly physically handicapped that he has no voluntary control over his limbs, and who may lack the basic motor skills necessary to perform hand signs, can be taught to express certain meanings by using his face, eyes or voice. A child with no physical handicaps may be intellectually limited, but could be taught to convey simple meanings by the use of his body.

For the first study, therefore, we chose a child who was able to communicate only a limited number of meanings by a limited range of behaviours, but who had certain prerequisite skills:

1. He was able to look towards people and objects
2. He showed a liking for certain objects or activities
3. He displayed at least a few behaviours which could be used for conveying meaning – for example, stiffening of the body, turning the head or arm reaching
4. He functioned below the one-word imitation level.

For the second study we chose a child with little or no productive language but who was able to communicate a wide range of meanings by various behaviours. We were keen to find out which meanings the child needed to communicate, and to adopt the use of a system of signing through which these could be expressed. We chose the Paget–Gorman Sign System (PGSS),[1] a system of hand signs based on a vocabulary of about four thousand words which incorporates grammatical structures such as tenses, plurals, possessives, etc. This has the advantage of being combined in a one-to-one manner with speech so that meanings are communicated by the same structures as in spoken English. We intended to teach selected words and meanings – as one would proceed to teach productive language. The following prerequisite skills were thought essential:

1. Functioning below the one-word level with expressive language
2. Having the concept of and understanding the labels of a limited range of objects
3. Able to imitate hand and arm movements (positions and actions).

We discussed the two children, Ian and Susan, with their class teachers. The Communication Behaviour Rating Schedule (see Appendix E) developed by the project to guide teachers' observations on children's non-verbal communication, provided useful information about their range of communicative behaviours. From this and the teachers' general observations, we were able to devise appropriate teaching programmes. These were drawn up in detail, specifying objectives, methods and modes of reinforcement. Organization and criteria for success were left to the teachers.

Ian

When selected for this study Ian was 14 years 4 months old, a Down's Syndrome child who was exceptionally small, appearing more like a child of about 3. From a few months old, he had been a full-time resident of a large subnormality hospital and for some years a pupil at the special school within the hospital.

Information gathered by his class teacher gave the impression that he was generally a quiet child, who seemed to resent any demands being made of him. He was quite contented when music was played, when he was sung to or when he was sitting on an adult's knee for a chat and a cuddle *–provided no response was required of him*. He also enjoyed being given a drink and being fed. He consistently withdrew and even objected when requested to do anything with his hands that was vaguely messy such as sand play, water play or painting. Furthermore, he demonstrated his dislike of any strenuous activity such as riding a tricycle or physiotherapy. In situations of this sort he appeared lethargic and cried bitterly. Unfortunately, he was thought too frail to be physically persuaded into any of these activities. He would normally be found sitting on the carpeted floor waving his right hand repeatedly with fingers intertwined. This would usually be accompanied by a rocking movement and a low growling sound. He moved location only when placed on the parquet floor, normally cold in comparison to the carpet. He would then shuffle on his bottom until seated on the carpet, where he would resume the manneistic behaviours. He appeared to be uninterested in all toys except a large teddy bear which if placed within arm's reach, he would occasionally touch. This arm reach was only ever observed with his left hand. It was with this hand that he often grasped at adult's clothing to gain attention.

ASSESSMENT

A profile of Ian's language abilities had been recorded in the language survey two years earlier. The results suggested there would be little development over a period of two years, and it was felt that this assessment of Ian would still provide some information. For productive language he had been scored as crying, shrieking and screaming, making long vowel-like vocalizations and also for producing two-syllable babble. For reception, however, we were surprised to discover he had been scored as having *no understanding whatsoever*. He was not even regarded as being at the basic stage of responding to sounds. In view of detailed observations made by his present teacher which demonstrated that he had some receptive language, these results were questioned. His score for production was thought to be an accurate profile of his present level. With the aid of the Communication Behaviour Rating Schedule, Ian's teacher had completed a further assessment to answer the questions: 'Does he communicate?'; 'What does he communicate?'; 'How does he communicate?'

1   Using his face and head he could:
    a   Smile in response to either known or unknown people
    b   Shake his head
    c   Turn his head in response to either known or unknown people.
2   Using his body, or parts of his body, he could:
    a   Rock
    b   Move towards objects
    c   Push objects or people away
    d   Throw objects
    e   Shake objects
    f   Allow objects to be taken from himself.
3   Using his voice he could:
    a   Use combinations of vowel sounds
    b   Hum
    c   Grunt
    d   Produce sounds to music.
4   He also:
    a   Avoided bullies
    b   Reacted when restricted
    c   Showed preference for women.

Ian's teacher also noted that when he was in a good mood he would smile and laugh, although most of the time he was in a rather miserable, lethargic mood and would growl and grind his teeth. If anyone, especially children, came too near him he would make loud noises (vowel sounds) as if shouting.

In all, she felt that Ian 'indicated his mood but did not control his environment in any way'.

Ian had quite a wide range of communicative behaviours, although these were limited to rather basic meanings. He mainly *responded* to people or actions which impinged on his life, and his communications related to infringements on him or his activities. He had sufficient control of his body to reach for an object or push an object away, yet he rarely performed these behaviours. Perhaps it was because he had never experienced the success and satisfaction of making demands and being effective in the environment that he never did so – that *he had not learned to make demands*. Ian certainly had all the prerequisite skills and we felt that this was the direction we should take in teaching him to communicate more effectively.

DESIGN OF THE PROGRAMME

We selected as our aim: to develop Ian's communicative skills in such a way that he points to what he wants.

Ultimately we wanted Ian to be able to point to any object within his environment. Selected objects would be used at first, so this meant that throughout the programme we needed to widen the range of objects in which he showed an interest. Also we did not want Ian to point only when an object was presented in front of him, so we needed to allow for generalization of both object and position. The most important factor was choice. As we eventually aimed for Ian to be able to point to any object he wanted, we were subjecting him to a certain amount of decision-making. We also needed an appropriate reinforcer. As we were hoping to teach Ian to point to what *he* wanted, a suitable reinforcement might be immediately to give him the object he reached for. This would be accompanied by verbal praise.

Observations made by Ian's teacher told us that he was interested in food (Complan), drink and the teddy; and these were selected as suitable objects.

Before deciding how to get him to point, we needed to specify exactly what we wanted him to do. It was necessary to break down the long-term objectives into stages; sub-objectives were also specified in detail:

Objective 1. Ian will reach for a dish of food when it is on the table in front of him but out of arm's reach. This objective is to be achieved by the following objectives:

Objective 1A. Ian will reach for and touch a dish of food when it is placed directly in front of him on the table.

Objective 1B. Ian will reach for the dish of food when it is placed on the table 30 centimetres away.

Objective 1C. Ian will reach for the dish of food when it is placed 45 centimetres away from him on the table.

Objective 1D. Ian will reach for the dish of food when it is placed 60 centimetres away from him on the table.

Objective 1E. Ian will reach for the dish of food when it is placed out of arm's reach. After achieving objective 1, the same objectives are to be used substituting in turn drink and teddy for the food.

Objective 2. Ian will reach towards food (or drink, or teddy) when it is held out of arm's reach and in different positions around him. This objective is to be achieved by the following objectives:

Objective 2A. Ian will reach towards food (or drink or teddy) when it is held by the teacher out of arm's reach at the other side of the table.

Objective 2B. Ian will reach towards the food (or drink, or teddy) when it is held by the teacher out of arm's reach 90 centimetres away from the table in front of him.

Objective 2C. Ian will reach towards food (or drink, or teddy) when it is held 90 centimetres away from the table at either side.

Objective 3. From a selection of food and drink (food and teddy/teddy and drink) held out of arm's reach and in different positions around him Ian will point to one. This objective is to be achieved by the following objectives:

Objective 3A. From a selection of food and drink (food and teddy/teddy and drink) held out of arm's reach and spaced 45 centimetres apart by the teacher, who is facing him, he will point to one.

Objective 3B. From a selection of food and drink (food and teddy/teddy and drink) held out of arm's reach and spaced 45 centimetres apart by the teacher, who is standing at his left/right side, he will point to one.

Objective 4. From a selection of food, drink and teddy, held out of arm's reach and in different positions around him, Ian will point to one. This objective is to be achieved by the following objectives:

Objective 4A. Ian will point towards either drink, food or teddy when they are placed 45 centimetres apart, out of arm's reach on the table/floor in front of him.

Objective 4B. Ian will point to either drink, food or teddy when they are placed over a metre away from him on right/left side.

Method

For each sub-stage of objective 1:

a Teacher sits facing Ian at the table
b Food is placed directly in front of Ian – teacher says 'dinner'

c   When Ian reaches towards the food the teacher says, 'Good boy' and immediately gives him a spoonful of food.

The methods for objective 2 were broadly the same although differences occurred in stage 1 in which the teacher's position was specified – for example, 'Teacher stands 90 centimetres away from the table facing Ian.' For objectives 3 and 4 the table was no longer necessary as we thought it advisable to build in generalization of position. For objective 3B the method states:

a   The teacher stands to the right/left of him one to one-and-a-half metres away
b   The teacher holds the food and drink (food and teddy/teddy and drink) spaced 45 centimetres apart – labels items
c   When Ian reaches towards one item, the teacher says, 'Good boy' and immediately gives him the item.

Objective 4 is similarly dealt with although, in this case, it involves a selection of one from a choice of three objects.

Everything but the criterion for success and the organization were specified in detail. Ian's class consisted of sixteen children and four adults. Together with the teacher, we planned that Ian should have four short sessions each day, which would be administered by two adults at a time. The teacher specified the criterion and organization to suit the people involved.

THE PROGRAMME IN ACTION

Ian's class consisted of children who were profoundly handicapped, and most of the teaching time already consisted of work with individuals. Most children, Ian included, were only capable of being involved in concentrated teaching for short periods. The teacher therefore considered the prospect of working on the programmes four times a day to be quite realistic. She planned for work with other children while the sessions with Ian were in progress.

The programmes with Ian commenced using objective 1A (Ian will reach for and touch a dish of food when it is placed directly in front of him on the table). However, problems arose through expecting him to touch the dish of food. Instead he tended to grasp the teacher's hand or else put his fingers in the food. She immediately moved on to objective 1B, in which the dish was placed a short distance away so that he could reach *in the direction of the bowl*. This meant that neither the teacher's hand nor the dish of food was within easy touching distance.

At first he tended to bang his hands on the table, so for the initial sessions the second adult moved his left hand so that he pointed in the right direction – that is, *he was prompted*. (See Chapter III.) After only a few sessions of presenting a dish containing just a small amount of food, they realized that he responded much better if the dish was seen to be full. Furthermore, the Complan he had previously liked now failed to hold his interest and it was decided to present him with various flavours of Angel Delight.

On the first session of day 4 the results looked promising. This involved objective 1D with the food 60 centimetres away. Although the criterion for success was five successful responses out of ten presentations, he actually reached ten out of ten successful responses. For the second session the criterion was raised so that he was expected to achieve ten out of ten and this he again achieved. The comments for this session stated that he was: 'Slow to respond but, when he is ready, pointing is very clear . . . He banged the table in between his requests for the food but used an arm reach when this did not gain results.' On day 5 objectives 1D and 1E were introduced and for the third session of this day the teacher commented: 'Ian definitely understands the significance of pointing and realizes that he is in control of the situation. He responds only when ready.'

This is the first comment which implied that Ian was becoming really effective in making demands; this was after nineteen sessions. By responding when he was ready, he was establishing his control of the situation. It is worth noting here that the method section specified the exact language to be used by the teacher so as to ensure that he was not swamped with superfluous information. All the adult was expected to say was 'Ian – dinner' (or another object), to gain and direct his attention towards the object, and after he had pointed this was followed immediately by 'Good boy'. The teacher therefore did not need to coax him to respond. On one occasion she had to wait for up to four minutes before he actually responded, but by working in this way Ian was learning and experiencing control.

After twenty-five sessions over a period of only seven days, Ian was already achieving such a high consistency of reaching towards the food that the drink was introduced. To the method section the teacher added that a small amount of drink was to be poured into a cup which he could then drain. Objective 1C was used with a criterion of three successful responses out of five. He responded with five and the teacher commented that: 'He responded as for food. The transfer seems complete.' It was extremely encouraging to find that after only seven full days Ian was able to generalize the pointing strategy. Considering that each session lasted on average for less than five minutes, Ian had acquired this basic strategy of pointing within less than two hours.

From day 8 onwards Ian's sessions were organized so that food and drink were each presented twice daily. Day 11 proved interesting. In the first session, which involved food, the comment was made that Ian 'was reaching before the food was presented.' However, 'when he realized that nothing came of this, he withdrew his hand until he saw the food.'

On the third session of this same day the teddy was introduced for the first time. This involved objective 1B where it was positioned only 30 centimetres away from him, on the floor as opposed to the previous table situation. The teacher planned to 'play with the bear for two or three minutes, letting it tickle and cuddle him; then withdraw it so that he has to reach for it.' For this session it was hoped that Ian would achieve five out of five sucessful responses – he succeeded in doing so. 'Ian enjoyed this play situation and gradually transferred the reaching behaviour he had learnt before to this situation. To begin with he used both hands, then his left hand became predominant.' Once again success was evident. This session was also remarkable in that the teddy itself did not seem to be the object of Ian's demands. From his responses, the teacher felt that the reinforcement was not the object itself but the tickle and cuddle which the teddy gave; this produced an effect of intense anticipation in Ian.

The fourth session on this day turned out to be a minor triumph. Ian was presented on ten occasions with the food which was immediately followed by ten presentations of the drink (objective 2) and achieved ten successful responses for each item. Moreoever, he 'reached out distinctly when the cup was held in a variety of positions'.

The following day, day 12, also provided some interesting information. For the first time objective 3, involving choice, was introduced: from a selection of food and drink (food and teddy/teddy and drink) held out of arm's reach and in different positions around him, Ian will point to one. There were additions to the method: food in bowl in right hand, drinking cup in left; at the table; change cup and bowl over. The criterion was ten correct attempts. The results: thirteen out of thirteen successful responses (six responses to food in right hand; four responses to food in left hand; two responses to drink in right hand; one response to drink in left hand).

On the second attempt Ian did not look and reached for where the bowl had been. He was very cross when given the drink, and watched carefully where the bowl was after this. He only pointed to the drink when he realized that the bowl was empty. Looked into the bowl each subsequent time to check that there was nothing left.

Objective 3 was pursued for the next few sessions using a drink and food. On day 20, however, the teacher presented Ian with two teddies, one pink and the other yellow. For the first part of this session he was allowed to play with the bears without having to point. Then, as they were held in front of him, he was required to choose which he wanted. The result of this was that he met the criterion of ten successful responses, choosing the pink bear six times and the yellow bear four times. The other two sessions which took place on this day involved objective 3 for food and drink and each of these proved so successful that he reached a criterion of twenty clear choices.

On day 21 the teacher made several comments which clearly indicated the extent to which Ian was generalizing the newly acquired means of communication: 'Ian pointed to me quite clearly when he was ready to come off his potty'; 'Ian pointed to some food left in the bowl after the session had been completed'; 'Ian pointed to an anorak which he wanted to wear'.

New toys were introduced from day 30 onwards and, as with previous sessions, he responded well. On day 31 he was presented with various combinations of a jack-in-the-box, a teddy, a flute and an activity board. In each of the two sessions he made ten clear choices. Furthermore, he became much more consistent and spontaneously began to use his right hand to point to objects which were in front of his right side, yet until now this had not been consistent. This was extremely encouraging because it was something we had not anticipated, neither had we built it into the programme. It was something that Ian himself had developed.

As a further combination of two items Ian was presented with two types of food. On each occasion the bowls were identical in shape, size and colour but the food differed in either flavour or in colour and flavour. On day 40, for example, objective 3 was pursued using the choice of chocolate and raspberry Angel Delight. The criterion was for Ian to demonstrate twenty clear choices; he chose the raspberry on sixteen occasions and the chocolate on only four. 'He looked at the colours and immediately pointed to the pink. He did this each time, even when it was moved around. He chose brown by mistake once, and pushed it away. When the pink was finished he chose brown.'

Ian was by now achieving a high level of consistency in making choices. By day 47 his teacher felt that within the classroom it would be possible to watch for him pointing and duly acknowledge this. However, as his 'home life' consisted of a ward of over thirty children, his pointing would generally go unnoticed. While this was being discussed, Ian provided us with a possible direction for further work. The teacher had just been carrying out objective 3, using a choice of chocolate and raspberry Angel Delight. The bowl containing some remaining chocolate was near us on the table. Ian was at the other side of the room and was suddenly heard to make a loud growling sound. As the teacher turned to him in response, Ian pointed towards the bowl of food! Immediately she said, 'Good boy' and walked over to give him a spoonful of the food. She replaced the bowl on the table and once again Ian shouted to attract attention and then pointed for the food. This occurred on five more occasions until the dish was empty. This chance incident had shown how much Ian was now able to generalize the pointing strategy. He could select something from the other side of the room and communicate precisely what he wanted. Furthermore, to gain attention he had spontaneously added vocalization. This occurred after using the programme for only two calendar months. In view of this added vocalization, the teacher slightly amended objectives 3 and 4 so that Ian would be required to vocalize for attention before indicating his choice of object. If used consistently, he would then be able to attract attention while on the wards.

The amended programme began in the first session of day 50 with the following objective: Ian will vocalize to gain adult's attention, then from a selection of two objects held out of arm's reach he will point to one. The method was as follows:

a   Using butterscotch and chocolate, carry out fifteen presentations in the normal way
b   After the fifteenth attempt, put the food down within view, and turn away until he makes a noise
c   When he vocalizes to attract attention, hold bowls and make him point to what he wants.

The criterion was fifteen clear choices, five vocalizations followed by choices. The results met the criterion – ten for butterscotch, ten for chocolate and five vocalizations. The teacher commented that Ian 'chose chocolate five times before eating it. Vocalization coming quickly – looked at my face to see if I was watching and then growled.'

Rather than present the same number of items each session, Ian's teacher felt that it would be better if these were to vary between one object only and a choice of either two or three. The fourth session of day 53 showed Ian's response to a choice of food, drink and a teddy (that is, using objective 4). He made twenty clear choices alternating between food and drink until they were consumed, only then selecting the teddy. For one session during day 56 the food only was presented. Here the adult sat writing with the food on view to Ian, but placed at the side of the desk. On ten occasions Ian vocalized then pointed.

Until day 57, Ian had always shown a preference for food, but on this day he changed his pattern of responses. On each of the twenty presentations he vocalized before pointing to gain attention and selected the radio (which was playing music) fourteen times as opposed to six times for the food and none for the drink. This really was a milestone. Prior to starting the programme, the only toy which he had been observed to show any vague interest in was a teddy. In only five calendar months this had developed to the extent that toys held more interest than food or drink. This occasionally occurred after only two months, but always only showing a preference for the teddy. Now he was showing considerable interest in a range of toys and objects. On day 61 he chose the radio on ten out of ten presentations. 'Although he enjoys playing with the teddy, Ian would have nothing to do with it once the radio was introduced. He took hold of my hand four times and guided it to the switch on the radio while it was in the off position.' Again, on day 64, out of twenty presentations of food and radio he chose the radio twenty times. Furthermore, he used vocalization each time to gain attention before pointing. There were still occasions when he showed a preference for food. On day 69 he selected food nine times and the teddy only once, while on day 70 he chose drink seventeen times and the radio three times. However, in the main, he seemed to be showing less interest in food and drink than formerly.

Before the programmes started Ian was greatly underweight. Perhaps because he had gained a considerable amount of weight during the programme and was now more interested in eating at correct mealtimes, it was understandable that he was becoming less interested in food between meals. Whatever the reason, it is interesting to note his willingness to explore new objects and his ability to express such strong preferences for specific items. After five months, he had been introduced during the sessions to two teddies, a radio, a trumpet, a rattle, ball, flute, bricks, doll, box, jack-in-the-box, button bottle, squeaky horn, cardboard tube, activity board and a car. In at least two sessions involving the radio he was clearly observed to make a distinction between music and talking.

In a matttter of six months we had been able to teach Ian to communicate in a consistent manner. The programme, because of its flexibility, allowed the teacher to progress at the rate she felt appropriate for Ian. Moreover, it allowed her when necessary to deviate, substitute and even make amendments. When Ian vocalized to gain attention, for instance, this was easily absorbed into the work. So successful had this proved that near the end of the programme on day 79 his teacher commented: 'After the first couple of growls, Ian began to experiment with chuckles, shouts, laughs, etc., and was delighted that they also attracted my attention so that he could point.'

The programmes with Ian had undoubtedly proved successful, though there were problems. During the winter months Ian was frequently absent and even when in school was frequently off colour. He had numerous 'off' days when he would refuse to co-operate and had to be coaxed into having any contact with adults at all. However, this did not seem to hamper his progress. His teacher noted that 'slight back-tracking after each absence soon refreshed his memory and enabled us to carry on.' After only two months he was consistently realizing objectives 1 and 2 in which he was required to reach towards food (or an object) held out of arm's reach. He began to use his right hand to point and easily transferred his use of the pointing behaviour to indicate his preference for one of a selection of objects. Furthermore, his vocalization developed to the extent that it was integrated as a major part of the programme.

Before starting the intervention study with Ian, observations had shown that he was a frail, lethargic child who initiated no demands on his environment. After six months of these detailed programmes he changed so much that his teacher was forced to re-evaluate the whole content of her work with Ian. He now made his presence known by demanding attention. He was interested in so many objects that she felt their presentation needed to be controlled for him to establish concepts. She was wary of allowing him to use too many objects at the expense of truly appreciating their individual functions and properties. He had shown special interest in a particular ball and this she developed, still using the principle of vocalization, followed by pointing, leading to the presentation of a variety of objects. Comments from a number of these sessions demonstrate his overall development:

Chose at random but used the balls differently according to their size. Rolled the largest, threw the medium-sized and bounced the smaller one.

When presented with a choice of a ball and a box:

Ian giggled and chuckled each time that he anticipated making his choice. He made me wait to see what he would do with the ball. On two occasions when he chose the box he picked up a ball and put it on the box lid, which was flung as this was tipped up.

On a further session using a variety of balls:

He carried on playing with the ball on his own after the programme. He put the balls on a box and let them roll off by tipping the box. Retrieved the balls himself to repeat the game.

These observations show how the whole child had developed. He was now able to co-operate with and tease an adult and could command attention. He was readily acquiring a number of concepts and for the first time was able to play alone.

Ian very soon realized that he was in charge of the situation and took delight in manipulating and tantalizing every member of staff involved with the programme.

By acquiring a means of communication, basic as it is, he had realized the power of being able to control situations. According to his teacher:

> Ian is now one of the liveliest members of the group. He continues to become more and more extroverted and unless he is unwell is unlikely to become withdrawn. Now that Ian has learned and appreciated the basics of how to control his environment through other people, he is often putting his new skills to the test, using combinations of vocalization, pointing, pushing, pulling and facial expression. He has become more mobile, no longer always waits for people to come to him. Ian's communications are becoming generally more positive – for example, he will now pull down a wet nappy rather than merely sit and moan monotonously. He pushes away an intruder rather than back away and he will climb on to a vacant knee when he wants attention.

FURTHER WORK

The success of the work with Ian had much to do with his teacher who had carried out the work, organized staff and children, and regularly evaluated Ian's performance, so that new objectives could be introduced and necessary amendments made to the programme. When asked how she had felt when first introduced to the programme, she commented, 'It seemed a logical and practical approach which, if carried through systematically, should succeed.'

Before starting the programme, concern was expressed by the other staff involved about the amount of time needed to carry out such detailed programmes. Some questioned whether it was fair to work in such a way that one child would show marked improvement while, for others, improvement would be slight. The teacher felt that a marked improvement in one child was preferable to an all-round slight improvement. She stressed the point that before being involved with this work she had been using a somewhat 'hit and miss' approach towards working with Ian, as she had with many other children, mainly due to the children's lack of communication skills. She was only too glad to be able to pool ideas for developing work, even if only with one child. The one reservation she expressed was that she 'hoped that the staff and timetable would be flexible enough to accommodate the programme without penalizing other children in the class'. After a time it became evident that they need not have worried: 'When a routine incorporating Ian's programmes became fairly well established, this question of working with Ian at the expense of the other children did not arise.'

Indeed by developing a systematic way of working it was possible to ensure an equal amount of teaching time for each child.

The somewhat 'hit and miss' earlier approach to teaching Ian had consisted of 'mainly experimental play situations in an attempt to get some flicker of interest.' It had been extremely difficult to know what to teach, and other adults involved with the class were 'trying to build up their own personal relationships with this rather crotchety little boy.'

After six months Ian developed so rapidly that his teacher was faced with quite the opposite problem – this time the difficulty in deciding what to teach arose from the wide range of possibilities. She felt that further work should, as much as possible, incorporate the vast range of skills he had developed. These included:

1 Using his hands to communicate
2 Using vocalization to communicate
3 Communicating his desire for objects
4 Handling and playing with toys and objects.

The teacher considered her aim for further work to be: to develop global concepts and to work towards labelling objects within each group.

Ian is continually extending his repertoire of vocalization and, on occasions, he will *imitate sound sequences*. For this reason his teacher felt that expressive language could be developed although an additional system of communication (signing) could be used alongside speech. She opted to use the Paget–Gorman Sign System together with productive language; her objectives were as follows:

Objective 1. From a selection of: **a** a variety of balls, or **b** a variety of musical instruments, or **c** an electric organ, Ian will point to what he wants and this object will be named.

Objective 2. From a selection of: **a** a variety of balls, or **b** a variety of musical instruments, or **c** an electric organ, Ian will point to what he wants and this object will be named verbally and by the Paget–Gorman sign.

Objective 3. From a selection of: **a** a variety of balls, or **b** a variety of musical instruments, or **c** an electric organ, Ian will point to what he wants, and then allow his hand to be positioned in the appropriate sign.

Susan

For the second study we selected Susan, a child with virtually no productive language but who nevertheless showed evidence of being able to communicate at a non-verbal level. Our aim in working with Susan was to enhance the effectiveness of her communication by devising ways to teach her some of the principles of the Paget–Gorman system.

Susan was diagnosed as microcephalic and had spent most of her 13 years in a large hospital for the mentally handicapped. A short while before our involvement with Susan, she had been moved into a new class and this had apparently caused her some anxiety. Although she had always been regarded as a timid and withdrawn child, this became much more severe until she began to settle down. Adult intervention with her proved extremely difficult owing to her persistence in covering her face with her hands and turning her body away. A harelip which had been operated upon caused no problems, although her cleft palate did, especially when eating or drinking. As a result these occasions tended to be messy and time consuming. She could sometimes exercise enough control to hold a cup but needed help with a spoon. Susan's physical condition as a whole was frail and her co-ordination poor. She could walk unaided, although assistance was necessary to achieve a standing position. Left to her own devices, Susan chose to sit on the floor where she would remain until moved. She had a pronounced nystagmus which, combined with frequent eye flickering, at times made visual contact difficult. It was thought that eye focusing might be difficult for her. The eye flicker caused her teacher some concern. Although initially it appeared to be involuntary, on numerous occasions the teacher had observed that Susan reacted in this way when adults directed attention to her. It had been thought that Susan might have a partial hearing loss, but she had been observed to turn her head towards the direction of sounds or voices.

ASSESSMENT

Susan's results in the language survey, although the survey had been completed two years earlier, outlined her language abilities. For receptive language, she was scored as only responding to sounds, teacher's voice and her own name. For productive language she was shown to be functioning at a limited level (crying, shrieking and screaming), although it was pointed out that she would imitate one word – 'Mummy'.

Her teacher emphasized the lack of progress in terms of expressive language and confirmed that the results of the language survey still applied, the only reservations being that, because she was so withdrawn, it was difficult to assess the extent to which Susan could interpret visual and auditory stimuli. The information was added that Susan could spontaneously produce one distinguishable word, 'Man', which related to the rhyme, 'This old man'; and on occasions she would quietly make very soft sounds and move her lips while doing so. The teacher added her own reservations as to whether Susan would ever be able to speak, because of her cleft palate, which seemed to be the cause of irregular breathing patterns and constant dribbling.

With the help of the Communication Behaviour Rating Schedule, Susan's teacher was able to account for all those behaviours exhibited by Susan which were a source of communication. We found that Susan was able to communicate via a whole range of behaviours:

1   Using her head and face she could:
    a   Smile, especially in response to a known person
    b   Turn her head – this often demonstrated when she turned her face away from a known person
    c   Cover her face in response to a known person – this she often did by using her hands
    d   Maintain eye contact with both objects and people even if only for limited amounts of time

2   Using her body or parts of her body she could:
    a   Stiffen her arms, body or legs
    b   Shake her head
    c   Kick her legs and stamp her feet
    d   Throw objects
    e   Point
    f   Take adult's hand
    g   Hold out her arms to be picked up
    h   Push objects away
    i   Move towards objects

3   With her voice she could:
    a   Cry or scream
    b   Produce sounds to **i** music; **ii** when given attention; and **iii** when chastized

4   Susan also:
    a   Pulled other children's hair
    b   Reacted when restricted
    c   Avoided bullies.

The teacher added that Susan sometimes used arm pointing to gain attention, but this was often indiscriminate. At times she showed frustration by biting her hand and had been known to display temper, although this had not been observed in the classroom. On occasions when demands were made of her, Susan was frequently obstinate and regularly responded to attention by exhibiting withdrawal – holding her hands up to her face and turning her whole body away. She enjoyed praise and, particularly when there was physical contact, would normally respond by relaxing her body and smiling.

AIMS

Investigating what Susan could communicate, we were forced to make subjective interpretations as to her meanings. Within certain contexts she consistently relaxed her body and made sounds if attention was given to her, and we interpreted this as meaning 'I like it' or 'I am enjoying myself'. When she held out her arms to an adult we felt she was asking to be picked up. When restricted, she would often stiffen her body, put her hands to her face and/or cry, and this was taken to mean that she did not wish to be restricted. Her meanings were mainly interpreted by her teacher, who discussed them with others involved with Susan so that misinterpretations were as far as possible avoided.

Although Susan was able to convey a number of meanings, these were consistently performed in response to the world around her; she would rarely initiate communications with others. Like Ian, she was failing to be very effective in controlling the world about her. Our general aim was for Susan to control and make demands of the world around her. As she had all the prerequisite skills necessary for learning the Paget–Gorman Sign System, our selected aim was: for Susan to use the Paget–Gorman Sign System to communicate nouns. Nouns were selected for the initial work as Susan had shown interest in two specific items – a ball and a drink.

DESIGN OF THE PROGRAMME

The long-term objectives were: when shown a ball, Susan will make the sign 'ball'; when shown a drink, Susan will make the sign 'drink'. We could not make a start in teaching these signs until the unwanted behaviours which occurred when attention was directed to Susan were brought under control. The eye flicker had to be controlled if she was to see and imitate the sign; the habit of putting her hands in front of her face needed controlling before she could make the signs with her hands. Two detailed programmes were drawn up, and the long-term objectives presented in the following order, more immediate objectives being included where necessary:

Objective 1. When in a one-to-one situation with an adult, Susan will put her hands down on her lap when she hears 'Hands down'. This is to be achieved by the following objectives:

Objective 1A. When in a one-to-one situation with an adult, Susan will uncover her eyes when she hears 'Hands down'.

Objective 1B. Susan will move her hands right away from her face when she hears 'Hands down'.

Objective 1C. Susan will put her hands down on her lap when she hears 'Hands down'.

Objective 2. When presented with an object, Susan will look at it.

Objective 3. When shown a ball, Susan will make the sign 'ball'. This is to be achieved by the following objectives:

Objective 3A. When shown a ball, Susan will allow her hand to be held in the appropriate position for 'ball'.

Objective 3B. When shown a ball, Susan will allow her hand to be positioned appropriately for the sign 'ball', and will keep her hand in that position when the teacher removes her own hand.

Objective 3C. When shown a ball, Susan will imitate the teacher's sign for 'ball'.

Objective 3D. When shown a ball, Susan will make the sign 'ball'.

Objective 4. When shown a drink, Susan will make the sign 'drink'. Objective 4 is to be achieved by using objectives 3A, 3B, 3C and 3D, and substituting the word 'drink' for 'ball'.

(The teacher would work on objectives 1 and 2 until Susan was responding consistently, at which point objective 3 could be introduced.)

For Susan to be taught these signs, quite a large amount of classroom time would need to be allocated. We recommended that Susan be taken through a programme at least once a day. The programmes were written so that a minimal amount of time was required for preparation and evaluation. This was necessary in view of the number of hyperactive children in the class who each required personal attention. Fortunately a full-time assistant worked with the teacher so that children were constantly supervised.

After detailed discussions, the programmes were planned to fit in with the time and resources available to the class. For each objective a method was specified in detail. Criterion and organization were left to the teacher. The following is a typical programme:

Objective 3A. When shown a ball, Susan will allow her hand to be held in the appropriate position for 'ball'.

Method
a   Teacher sits facing Susan
b   Teacher holds the ball, puts it in front of Susan (Susan is to look at the ball)
c   Teacher says, 'Ball' and makes the sign for 'ball'
d   Teacher holds Susan's hand in the sign position for 'ball' and says, 'Ball'
e   Teacher lets go of Susan's hand and immediately claps and says, 'Good girl'.

Criterion for success and organization
To be specified by the teacher.

As the objectives changed, so did the elements of the method section. Reinforcement remained constant. As Susan responded extremely well to praise or physical contact, whenever Susan performed the task successfully, she was to be immediately rewarded by a clap and 'Good girl'.

THE PROGRAMME IN ACTION

As there were two adults involved with the class, it was agreed that the programme would be carried out jointly. This had an advantage. Slight differences in preparation and style would be inevitable and provide some degree of built-in variability. Moreover, as the programmes were to be carried out at least once a day, it would be more practical; the teacher could work with other individuals or groups of children while the assistant carried out sessions with Susan. We hoped this would prevent the teacher feeling that she was giving too much time to Susan at the expense of other children.

Objectives 1 and 2 were concerned with controlling Susan's behaviours of putting her hands to her face and looking at objects, and within two weeks these were coming under control. For objective 1 the teacher commented: 'During the past ten sessions over the course of one week, Susan has met objective 1 by putting her hands on her lap 50 per cent of the time.' The teacher considered that this objective should be pursued to reach a higher level of success, but that the method should be changed so that the instruction could be given to Susan at any time when she was observed to display this behaviour. Objective 2, directed at gaining looking responses was achieved after only two sessions where 100 per cent success was evident each time. The teacher felt that Susan could now be introduced to objective 3 – when shown a ball, Susan will make the sign 'ball'.

For the sign 'ball' one hand is positioned as illustrated in Figure 15 below. Having positioned the hand, it is raised in a jerking movement accompanied by the word 'ball'. Teaching this sign, as with all other noun signs, was to be done by small incremental steps:

a   Susan would allow her hand to be held in the appropriate position
b   This would then be extended so that when the teacher released her hand Susan would maintain the sign position
c   She would imitate the sign which, with frequent use, would lead to the stage where spontaneous signs would occur.

Stages **a** and **b** were achieved quickly – 100 per cent success was achieved each time the teacher held Susan's hand in the position for 'ball', and when the teacher released her hand for stage **b**, Susan maintained the sign position adequately achieving 100 per cent success on four out of six sessions for stage **b**. More time was required for objective 3C which specified: when shown a ball, Susan will imitate the teacher's sign for 'ball'. This objective was first pursued in session 21. The teacher specified that Susan was required to make one successful response out of five. Susan achieved two out of five, although the teacher did comment that 'she needed a lot of prompting'. For session 22, the criterion was five out of five, the teacher noting after this session, 'She still needs a lot of prompting to imitate the jerk of the hand. Her hand itself was positioned well and she did jerk it on five occasions. Will repeat the same criterion tomorrow.' It was felt that Susan was successful but that it was necessary to continue with this objective until more consistency was achieved.

In less than three weeks spontaneous signing was achieved, and achieved in just two sessions. Because time and care were exercised in the first three stages, objective 3D was quickly achieved. The teacher's comments on session 27 illustrate this: 'On the first presentation of the ball Susan needed prompting to do the sign, but on the second, third, fourth and fifth presentations she responded with the sign immediately.' In session 28 Susan responded immediately on every presentation of the ball except the third. The teacher felt that the time was now right to move on to the next objective. This did not mean that sessions involving 'ball' would be dropped, for by doing so Susan could easily forget the sign. As objective 4 was worked on, objective 3 would continue to be presented at regular intervals.

For the original programme we had selected two one-handed signs for Susan to learn – 'ball' and 'drink'. However, further observations disclosed that Susan had since become extremely interested in the piano. As the programmes were devised to allow flexibility of use, a new objective, 'piano', was selected and presented before the sign for 'drink'. Objective 4 became: when shown a piano, Susan will make the sign for 'piano'.

A STUDY OF TWO CHILDREN 259

This is a more complicated sign than that for 'drink' or 'ball' – it is a two-handed sign. One hand is held in the basic fist position as for 'ball' (see Figure 15), and at the same time the other hand is held in the claw position; as the arm is moved away from the body the fingers are wiggled as if playing a keyboard (see Figure 16 below). Problems of co-ordination and timing were envisaged. Objective 4A caused no problems. Susan allowed her hands to be held in the sign position, and because one hand position is also the basic position for the 'ball' sign, it was felt that only the other hand position needed to be modelled. The teacher commented on session 30: 'Susan

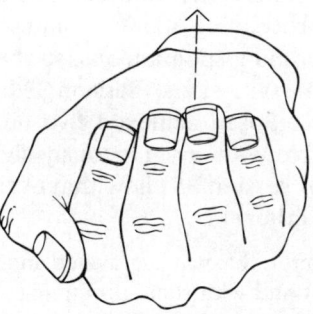

Fig. 15 The Paget–Gorman sign for 'ball'. Hold either closed hand, back downward and fingers forward and inward, at waist level and with elbow on own side (sign for 'thing'); then jerk hand vertically upwards one hand-breadth

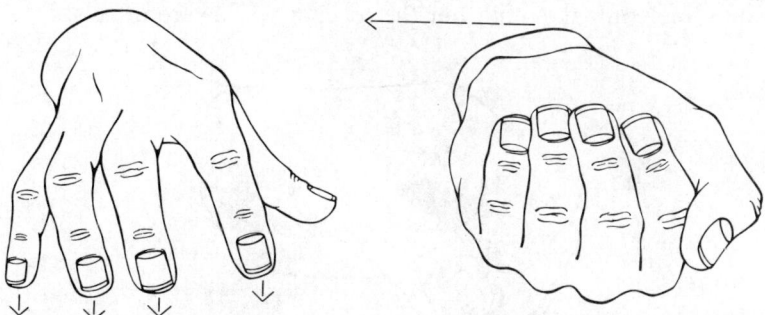

Fig. 16 The Paget–Gorman sign for 'piano'. Hold first hand as 'thing' and put second, clawed hand, back upward and fingers forward and inward on top of first hand; then move second hand horizontally outwards one hand-length, at same time moving all digits simultaneously and independently

allowed one hand to be held and made appropriate movements with the other hand.'

Session 32 was on objective 4B – that Susan would maintain her left hand in the correct position and move her right hand appropriately. The criterion for this session was that 'Susan will allow her left hand to be shaped and will keep it in that position on two out of five occasions. She already makes an approximation with her right hand which we accept. This may be difficult and we prefer her to continue her present approximations if she becomes confused.' Encouragingly, Susan achieved three out of five successful responses. The teacher added the comment: 'Continue tomorrow with shaping hands before proceeding to 4C – imitation of piano sign. The response to "ball" is becoming spontaneous, so this sign will be alternated with "piano" during the next sessions.' Session 33 became a combination of objectives 4B and 3, and Susan achieved five out of five successes with 'piano' and five out of five with spontaneously signing 'ball'.

The teacher's notes for session 35 show that even with distraction Susan was able to achieve the criterion:

Session interrupted by a visitor. Sue was aggravated and annoyed at having to wait, but although under protest and with some prompting, she managed to reach the criterion. After the final reinforcement, i.e. clap and praise, Susan spontaneously came on my knee for a cuddle. For the piano sign Susan still needed the left hand holding and prompting, so continue with the same objective until the sign becomes more spontaneous.

In this session Susan initiated a demonstration of affection – a behaviour she normally exhibited infrequently. The piano sign, it should be noted, was causing some confusion still, but the teacher was aware of this.

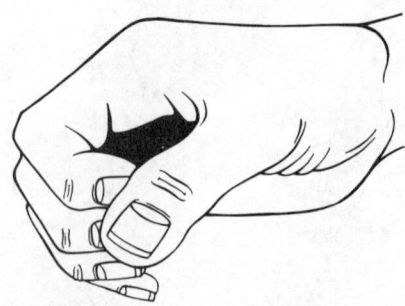

Fig. 17 The Paget–Gorman sign for 'drink'. Hold either O-hand (one of twenty-one standard hand postures), back outward and fingers forward in line with own side

During session 38 the teacher introduced a new objective (objective 5A) which involved Susan allowing her hand to be held in the sign position for 'drink' (see Figure 17). This additional sign was introduced before the previous sign, 'piano', had been established. Although the teacher felt justified in doing this, the situation could have proved extremely confusing. Susan had acquired the sign 'ball' with relatively little difficulty, whereas the more complicated two-handed sign, 'piano', was taking longer. As the third sign, 'drink', was also a one-handed sign, the teacher felt it would help Susan to gain more sense of achievement if a simple sign was introduced. This final objective was not presented at the expense of the earlier ones. The teacher reorganized the programme so that each objective was pursued in turn. For example:

Session 38: objective 5A (drink)
Session 39: objectives 4B and 3 (piano and ball)
Session 40: objective 5A (drink)
Session 41: objective 3 (ball)
Session 42: objective 5A (drink)
Session 43: objective 4B (piano).

Unfortunately, teaching two new signs at one time had resulted in confusion. Susan was obviously mixed up by the variations in signs. Furthermore, the teacher's notes indicate that she had not established a link between object and sign for either 'piano' or 'drink'. On session 38 (concerned with 'drink') the teacher comments: 'Susan tended to want to make the ball sign. She realized that some movement was expected of her.' In session 40 also Susan demonstrated confusion by occasionally making the ball sign while apparently focusing her attention on the drink. During session 44 Susan was expected spontaneously to sign 'ball', a sign which previously she had demonstrated she knew, yet the lesson comments clearly show she was confused.

Susan was more interested in asking for a drink than in wanting the ball . . . It was her insistence on wanting the drink during the session that marred her response to 'ball'. She realized that she must use her hands to communicate but she is using the ball sign for 'drink'. She refused the ball and on being given a drink was evidently very thirsty.

She was at this stage confused to the extent that the one established sign, 'ball', was being misused. It would seem that Susan failed consistently to link any one sign with an object. Under a section of general evaluative notes, the teacher remarks:

In future we will continue with separate alternative sessions for 'drink', 'ball' and 'piano' (each for one day). Reward with clap and 'Good girl' for the sign being taught. Any other recognizable sign performed by Susan during that session will be reinforced by the adult saying 'Good girl' without the clap. This may help Susan to discriminate in future.

The teacher realized how confused Susan had become and began structuring the organization of the programme so that subsequent sessions involved only one sign at a time. Problems were still possible if Susan continued to link signs with wrong meanings. It was questioned whether, instead of reducing the reinforcement when Susan offered a sign other than the one being used, it might prove more effective if she were to be presented with the objects indicated by her signs. After all, one main reason for selecting Susan was that she failed to control or make demands on her environment. Also by consistently matching the appropriate object to the sign made, the connexion between the two would, in time, become established. This was discussed with the teacher and amendments were made. As session 55 showed, this proved more effective.

Session 55 was concerned with objective 5C – when shown a drink, Susan will imitate the sign 'drink'. The teacher specified the criterion for success as one out of five correct responses. The programme was amended in anticipation of Susan's responses:

Ball and toy piano to be out of sight but readily available to give to Susan if she signed either of these instead of the 'drink' sign. To reinforce the correct sign for drink, show a drink and sign 'drink' whenever Susan makes an approximation of this sign. Use clap and 'Good girl' and give Susan a drink.

The results of this session were more encouraging. Susan achieved two out of five successful responses and in her comments the teacher noted: 'Although the first approximation by Susan was not too well shaped, the second attempt was very much better. During this session Susan signed "ball" three times and "piano" twice. On each occasion she was given the appropriate object.'

Session 61 was on objective 4C – imitation of the 'piano' sign – and this was also successful: 'Susan readily wanted to play with the ball although she responded with a good "piano" sign on all but one occasion. She showed more delight when given the ball in response to her own signing.'

By giving Susan the object for which she signed, she became less and less confused. She repeatedly met the criterion set for her and by session 74 was realizing the main objectives: objective 3 – when shown a ball, Susan will make the sign 'ball'; objective 4 – when shown a piano, Susan will make the sign 'piano'; objective 5 – when shown a drink, Susan will make the sign 'drink'. The programmes had proved successful with an added bonus. Susan spontaneously produced the appropriate sign whenever the ball, piano or drink were presented, and she could also do something much more demanding. She could consistently sign for any one of the three objects when they were out of sight. By directly asking for an object when it was not on view, she was demonstrating intent and making quite direct demands on the world around her.

After the Christmas holiday, and three months after the start of the programme, Susan returned to school 'a different child'. To quote her teacher:

On her return to school in the New Year after a two-week holiday Susan seemed so desperate to communicate that her speech development was quite remarkable. She used her signs for 'drink' and 'piano' immediately she entered the classroom. Within a short time during an individual session she began to repeat words quite distinctly. In fact, she imitated thirty spoken words during this short space of time. Her delight and excitement were immeasurable and the more praise she received, the harder she tried to please. This proved to be not just a brief development; each day she would imitate more words, sometimes using signs which had only been taught to other children. She had never been included in any other sign session, but obviously she had observed and retained much of what she had seen. She showed confidence in saying these more familiar words used in sign sessions with familiar objects, but more hesitance with unfamiliar words or objects. Her most complex spontaneous phrase so far has been 'Want to go out.'

Obviously, numerous factors could have been involved in transforming Susan's communicative abilities. However, it is interesting that after being taught three meaningful and relevant signs her total communication had developed to the extent that she began to develop her productive language. This strongly implies that given a means of communication effective for the individual, a person will become much more adept at controlling the world around him. This in turn enables development in other areas of communication – social, cognitive, emotional – to be started for the child. Susan's teacher comments on the effects of the programme:

As the programme developed it became evident that Susan's eye movements could be controlled when she was interested and wanted to look at an object. It was possible to see her turn her head and focus her eyes without any flickering movement. Another noticeable feature was that her balance and posture seemed to be gradually improving. She now walks with more confidence and can get up from a low chair without any support . . . The most noticeable feature about this whole programme has been that, although the odds were against Susan with regard to physical handicap and withdrawn personality, by providing her with the beginnings of a means of communication, there have been dramatic developments in the whole child. Not only has she begun to speak, but her voice projection has improved and she is beginning to sing. Her attempts at self-help skills are developing and after six months she is able to feed herself with a spoon. Susan also seems to need plenty to drink, and since she has been able to communicate this need, we have noticed far less breath odour due to her cleft palate and stale, trapped food.

TEACHER'S REACTIONS TO THE PROGRAMME

On reflection the teacher admitted that she had initially been 'uncertain about the values of a controlled study of this nature'. She felt at first that the programmes were somewhat formal and clinical and was 'uncertain whether objectives 1 and 2 were necessary (hands down and looking at objects) before introducing Susan to the signs'.

Organizing a class of hyperactive children so that one child could receive two individual sessions a day in as constant conditions as possible proved difficult... Many changes of children in the class caused strain when my time was particularly needed to integrate new children to the group. Recording details of each session was time-consuming and was done, at times with difficulty, during each coffee break.

Many favourable points outweighed the problems. For instance, she expressed the view that her involvement had provided her

with a greater insight for developing programmes for every other child, setting demands within the framework of a classroom situation... I was impressed by the consistency of the programme and its effect on the child's responses.

We reminded her of her initial uncertainty about the values of an intensive study of this kind. Her reply was encouraging:

From the point of view of planning an individual programme I have found the method logical, successful and a guideline in assessing what to teach and how to evaluate the levels of success and failure. I have realized the paramount importance of correct assessment, the need for detailed observation and critical analysis. I have also realized how frustration can develop in a child if these criteria are not correctly calculated.

To summarize Susan's total development her teacher expressed delight at the progress Susan had made since the programme was introduced:

To what extent the one-to-one teaching, the development of a structured programme or the various external factors have contributed to her success is very difficult to determine. Susan is a child who responds to affection and praise, as do most children, and a consistent reward of a clap and 'Good girl' provided motivation. I feel it is impossible to conclude that the programme alone is responsible for the dramatic developments in speech, and indeed the development of the whole child, but it could be a most significant factor. Perhaps the most outstanding feature of Susan's progress is the rapid development she has made in terms of speech. Having achieved success in communicating by hand signs, she has spontaneously progressed to using productive language as a parallel form of communication. On occasions, this is combined with signing but in the main now she is using speech, through which she is effectively able to control her environment.

What should Susan be taught next? In one way Susan herself has provided the answer – the development of her productive language, as she is now able to use simple words and short phrases. The teacher made notes when these occurred and made detailed observations to discover where Susan's interests lay. Nouns seemed to present relatively few problems – indeed Susan's vocabulary consisted of these. It was thought that she could make use of more general words such as 'more', 'again', 'another', and through these would have more control of the objects and actions she was now able to communicate. (Chapters IV and VI clearly illustrate how such programmes for teaching new vocabulary may be developed.)

Although quite different programmes were designed and carried out with Ian and Susan, the final results were similar. Both changed from being withdrawn and lethargic children who were equally undemanding, to lively and happy individuals who made their presence known by making frequent demands on the world around them. In each case, the whole child developed. It seems that having acquired an effective means of making demands on and controlling their environment, they became generally more active. Each child showed marked development in all other areas, and gained greater autonomy – an ultimate aim of education for which communication is perhaps the major prerequisite.

Summary

For most of us meaning can be conveyed by a combination of speech and gesture but for one-third of the severely subnormal population this is not possible. For various reasons many of these children lack expressive language; to convey meaning they have to adopt some form of gesture. In time many of these children may acquire some expressive language but it is not possible to predict those who will. Eighteen per cent of those children who leave school at 16+, and even more children who enter at or before the age of 5 years, have no useful expressive language. Not only do these children lack expressive language, but many also have an extremely limited repertoire of non-verbal communication. Can we afford to allow children to spend their childhood, and in some cases go on into their adult life, without any effective means of communication?

Many of this large group of children are capable of learning and using systems of non-verbal communication. With Ian and Susan, we have been able to demonstrate how quickly this can be achieved. With these two children we have shown how important it is for the teacher to be able to assess the communication that exists. The Communication Behaviour Rating Schedule provides a simple means of enabling teachers to identify communicative behaviours exhibited by the child. Combined with observations, this information can provide a detailed account of how the child is able to convey meanings. Having assessed what communication the child has, it is then possible to devise ways of developing it.

We are not advocating that any one system should be adopted and taught wholesale to every non-verbal child in school. Indeed we are primarily concerned with helping the individual child by taking his personal needs and abilities into consideration. We are more concerned with fitting a system to the child, than the child to the system.

There are a number of systems of signing currently available to teachers which will be appropriate for different children. For the purpose of this study we selected just one of these, the Paget-Gorman Sign System which has the advantage of combining the sign with speech. With Ian and Susan it was our intention to teach them to be more effective in making demands on their environment. One of them, Susan, was at an appropriate level of functioning for us to introduce PGSS. Ian was at quite a different level of functioning and for him it was not seen as an appropriate system. It was necessary with him to develop a much simpler, more individualized means of communication. In both cases the success of the work was largely due to the information initially collected which enabled us to identify what meanings the children could communicate and how these could be developed.

The growing interest in active teaching of non-verbal communication systems on the part of teachers, nurses and parents is to be welcomed and encouraged but it would not be right to end this chapter without sounding two notes of caution. First, there is a danger that too many different systems will be developed by teachers and others working in isolation from one another. Apart from the Paget-Gorman system, work is now in progress using the Makaton Vocabulary, Rebus, Premackese, Blissmatics,[2] and many others developed by individual teachers. While we do not advocate that a single system should be taught, we are concerned about the multiplicity of systems. This might lead to a situation where a child who moved from one school to another might find himself taught by a different method. This brings us to what is perhaps the most important point of all about non-verbal communication: the need for complete consistency by all who come into contact with the child. A programme is only as good as the extent to which it can be consistently delivered. Mentally handicapped children, particularly those at the lowest levels of functioning, cannot be expected to learn a non-verbal communication system unless all the key figures with whom they come into contact know the basic signs, can produce them consistently, and can understand and respond to the signs produced by the child. This requires considerable skill in organization, and necessarily involves not only other teachers and adults in the school but above all the child's family. Without the active participation of the family, even the best planned programme may come to nothing. With it, a great deal can be achieved.

References

1. J. A. ROWE, *The Paget–Gorman Sign System*. Spastics Society, 1977. Further details of the Paget–Gorman Sign System are available from Elma Craig, Centre for the Deaf, Keeley House, Keeley Street, London WC2B 4BA. For an excellent review of signing systems currently available, see C. C. KIERNAN, 'Alternatives to speech: a review of research on manual and other forms of communication with the mentally handicapped and other non-communicating populations', *British Journal of Mental Subnormality*, **23**, 1977, 6–28.
2. For a useful overview and critical discussion of these non-verbal communication systems see C. C. KIERNAN, R. JORDAN and C. SAUNDERS, *Starting Off* (Souvenir Press, 1978) and T. TEBBS (ed.), *Ways and Means: a Resource Book of Aids, Methods, Materials and Systems for Use with the Language Retarded Child* (Globe Education, Basingstoke, for Somerset Education Committee, 1978).

Note. The two examples of teaching non-verbal communication described in this chapter are illustrated in 'Communication before speech', one of three published videotapes made by the project. (See note on page viii.)

VIII. Using questions in the classroom

Our concern here is not with teaching a child to acquire new language, but with helping him to use to greater effect the language he possesses. Many teachers bemoan the fact that their children have more verbal ability than they use in most teaching situations. Children are often overheard using quite complex language forms talking to other children or to themselves. Why is this, and what can we do about it? This chapter explores these problems through the use of questions to elicit language from children. We know that teachers use many different kinds of questions throughout the day; in some cases anything up to half of teacher talk consists of questions. But what sort of questions are effective in helping children to use the language abilities they possess fully and productively and in ways which extend their abilities?

Of course, questions are not always productive, as the following example shows:

Teacher　I wonder what we can draw today? (Slight pause.) Can anyone think what we should draw? (Slight pause.) I know! Let's draw a . . .

The question here is not really a true question at all. The teacher knows quite clearly from the start what she wants the children to draw, and has prepared the room and the materials for this. In a sense, her questions are part of her style of interaction.

It is sometimes instructive to record ourselves and count the number of questions we ask in the classroom to which no answer is required. When we do want an answer, children often reply with just a single word. Sometimes, of course, this is all we need:

Teacher　What colour is this?
Child　Blue
Teacher　Are you ready?
Child　Yes

But if we are going to use questions as part of a planned teaching strategy, to

Questioning and picture materials

elicit longer sentences and more complex language, then we need to think hard about the sort of questions we use and the effect they have on the children.

Questioning and picture materials

To highlight some of these problems, we asked the staff of four project schools to get their children to talk about a picture showing two children playing 'shop'. This picture allowed for a wide variety of descriptive language as well as the possibility of more extended discussion. The teachers were each asked to select two children who were using combinations of words in their spontaneous language. The teachers' task was simply to get each child to talk about the picture. We gave no specific instructions and the sessions were tape-recorded and fully transcribed.

THE NEED FOR CLEARLY DEFINED OBJECTIVES

The question is a specific type of demand. Not surprisingly, in the absence of clearly defined objectives to guide the form of the question, vague, haphazard strategies were much in evidence. Teachers were often at a loss to know precisely what they wanted the children to say. Demands for verbal responses were made but often there were no links between one demand and another, and hence no progression towards a defined objective. Because the sessions were random, the dialogue developed in a rather erratic and disjointed manner.

If the teacher is unclear about what she wants the children to do, the children in turn will inevitably be unclear about what to offer. In the following extract a child can be seen to operate primarily at the single-word level.

Teacher   Tell me about the things you can see.
Child   That one.
Teacher   What is it?
Child   Jelly.
Teacher   Jelly do you think?
Child   Eggs.
Teacher   Yes.
Child   Clock.
Teacher   I don't think it's a clock.
Child   What is it then?

When the questions are invented 'off the cuff' like this, the easiest strategy for the teacher is to move around the picture asking 'What's that?' questions. Small wonder that the child mostly answers in single words, although he is quite capable of turning the teacher's statement into a question form in the last exchange. His relatively sophisticated language is again evident later in the session.

Teacher What are these?
Child Nana gets that.
Teacher What is it?
Child I am thinking. I am thinking how it will work. Eggs.
Teacher Eggs. Good.

The teacher in this interchange finally elicits the word 'eggs' and reinforces it with 'Good'. She thus reinforces single-word production even though the boy demonstrates that he is capable of a quite high level of productive language upon which the teacher can build. This contrast between the child's responses and the teacher's demands and his spontaneous language is evident throughout the session.

The final extract shows how easy it is, in a question and answer interchange, to do the opposite of what you intended.

Child Cornflakes, I bought some at the shop.
Teacher You buy them at the shop do you?
Child Yes, sweets, Nana and Jean get them at the shop.
Teacher Nana and Jean get them at the shop?
Child Yes, in that picture.
Teacher What's this?
Child Girl.
Teacher Good, a girl. What has she got on?

Note how the child's contribution becomes shorter until he reaches the one-word level which the teacher immediately reinforces. Difficulties arose here because the teacher had not defined clearly enough what it was the child should say.

ACCEPTING MINIMAL RESPONSES

If a child is known to be capable of producing spontaneous sentences or constructions of three words, what should we expect when asking him to talk about a picture or a similar stimulus? Should we lower our demand level and accept minimal responses when the child is known to have the vocabulary and syntax necessary to offer the information: 'It's a girl eating an ice cream.' It would be pedantic to demand that all oral responses should be delivered in a complex form, when a simpler form conveys the same meaning. However, the child has to learn, not only the forms themselves, but when one is to be preferred to the other. A restricted output may emerge despite the teacher's intentions that the children should use sentences. One of the main reasons for this would seem to be the frequent reinforcement of minimal responses, as the next example illustrates:

Teacher What are these nice things here?
Child   Apples.
Teacher That's right, that's what they are, and what's this?
Child   Cauliflower.
Teacher Oh, good girl, and what are these?
Child   Cornflakes.

This teacher apparently had limited expectations of the child whose responses were praised and immediately followed by new demands. Yet this child was known to be capable of producing spontaneous sentences. It is all too easy to discourage sentence production by unintentionally reinforcing minimal responses. Note what happens in this next extract:

Teacher What's the little boy doing?
Child   Weighing the 'tatoes out.
Teacher Pardon.
Child   Weighing the 'tatoes out.
Teacher He's pouring the potatoes out. Yes, well where is he putting those potatoes?
Child   In a bag.
Teacher And who is holding the bag?
Child   Mummy.
Teacher Is that your mummy?
Child   Yes.
Teacher What's she got on her head?
Child   Hat.
Teacher Can you see anything else in the picture?
Child   Yes . . . cauli.
Teacher Yes. Lovely, that.

Right at the beginning of the dialogue the child demonstrates his ability to go beyond single-word responses by his use of the phrase 'weighing the 'tatoes out'. The response was first corrected and followed by a request for new information. Word *combinations* therefore received no praise but a minimal response 'cauli' was acknowledged with 'Yes. Lovely that'.

Another problem concerns the yes/no response. So often we find ourselves phrasing questions so that the only demand we make of the children is to answer either 'Yes' or 'No'. Frequently this leads to a frustrating interchange in which, no matter how subsequent questions are phrased, there is a tendency for either 'Yes' or 'No' to recur. At the time we wonder how and why it developed and how to break the cycle. The following extract demonstrates how easily this can happen.

Teacher Do you like cornflakes?
Child Yes.
Teacher Do you have them for breakfast?
Child Yes.
Teacher What's this?
Child Yellow.
Teacher What's this? Jam.
Child Jam.
Teacher Do you like jam?
Child Yes.

It is noticeable that the 'Do you?' (or for that matter 'Will you?', 'Have you?', 'Does it?', 'Should it/you?', 'Can it?', etc.) question form used in this interchange is responsible. When the teacher changes to the 'what' format immediately the child has to respond differently. When the teacher returns to the 'Do you?' form again, the 'Yes' response recurs. Thus the child's answer is greatly determined by the form in which the demand is made; altering the form can change the child's response.

FACTUAL CONTENT AND LINGUISTIC STRUCTURE

Talking about a specific stimulus such as a picture involves a complex co-ordination between the factual content of the picture and the linguistic structure with which the content is expressed. These two aspects are closely interrelated: if a child cannot use subject–verb–object structures then he cannot convey certain commonly occurring content elements of a picture, such as 'A boy hitting a ball'. Part of the difficulty in getting mentally handicapped children to talk about a picture, or similar stimulus, lies in helping them to combine these two elements in their responses. Perhaps because teachers expect factual information they tended to ignore the quality of language. In one extract quoted earlier the child was corrected for using a quite sophisticated sentence because the content was not strictly accurate:

Child Weighing 'tatoes out.
Teacher He's pouring the potatoes out. Yes well . . .

In this interchange the child received no praise but instead the information offered was corrected. It is, of course, often necessary to add, delete or rearrange elements of a child's response but at the same time it is easy to acknowledge the effort already made. A child might say: 'Dog run'. It is easy to accept this yet at the same time to correct the syntax by providing a more appropriate model: 'Yes, the dog is running. Good.' Similarly with syntactic or word-order 'mix-ups', if a child were to offer 'Ball hit boy', the teacher could normally provide a more appropriate model response, repeating it with the elements rearranged – 'Yes, the boy is hitting the ball.' Situations in which complex structures are used to convey inaccurate information can be avoided either by first establishing the content elements individually, or by querying only specific aspects of the child's response – 'Yes, she is wearing something, but what is she wearing?' Our aim is to get the children to convey the information using existing language structures. Both aspects are crucial to the child's success and it is vital that failure at one level does not affect success at another.

UNREALISTIC DEMANDS

If the objectives are to be achieved there must be a close match between the demands the teacher makes and the child's ability. A demand should take a child one step further than his present position and will be unrealistic if it is too complex or too simple for that child. Unrealistic questioning demands can confuse the child. Often a number of demands are made all at once in a sort of verbal barrage as, for example, in the following extract:

Teacher   You'd go to the shops, but what do you go to the shops for? We go to the shops to buy things don't we? The money is for buying things. What else can you see in the picture? What would you have for breakfast?
Child   Cornflakes.
Teacher   Cornflakes. What do you use this for? What's this called?

The teacher has been unable to get the child to make more than one-word responses. She begins to pile one complex demand upon another and the child fails to answer. When finally a more realistic demand is made of the child she responds appropriately. Unfortunately this is then followed by two more demands, one immediately following the other. These unrelated demands could be broken down into a simple structure. If a response does not occur to the first demand, 'What do you go to the shops for?', this can be simplified and made more direct – for example, 'What do you buy at the shop?' If again this demand proves too difficult, it may be further simplified so that the responses are directly related to the picture – 'What is this?' followed by 'Can you buy it in a shop?', etc. It is only by a process of continually adjusting demands to appropriate responses that success will occur. These examples illustrate the situation in which responses to the teacher's demands are often much simpler than the child's spontaneous language. It is only by becoming aware of the child's language abilities and planning a set of objectives to match the abilities that the child will be able to offer an optimal level of performance and progress to more complex demands.

REALISTIC DEMANDS AND ACCEPTABLE RESPONSES

The next extract shows this process at work. It illustrates the expertise with which a teacher demands specific information and then pulls it together and instructs the child to do the same:

Teacher   What's the picture about?
Child   Going shopping.
Teacher   Going shopping. Who's going shopping?
Child   A girl.
Teacher   A little girl or a big girl?
Child   A big girl.
Teacher   A big girl. What's she wearing?
Child   Dress.
Teacher   What colour is her dress?
Child   Pink.
Teacher   What, pink and . . .
Child   White.
Teacher   Would you say she is wearing a pink and white dress? Tell me.
Child   She is wearing a pink and white dress.

Demands are linked in a systematic fashion, using a variety of types of questions. Following a single-word response, the teacher proceeds to elaborate on this response and build towards more complex structures. Success is evident when the child offers an eight-word sentence. Because the teacher was precise about what she wanted, the child in turn knew what to offer. This teacher clearly had some overall plan for eliciting language from the child. The complex process of systematically searching out information from a stimulus such as a picture and translating it into grammatical structures is one with which the child needs close guidance. Unless he is instructed how to go about this task, he will be unsure what to do and revert to well-tried, minimal response tactics. Success and progress will depend upon a carefully constructed plan of objectives to guide both teacher and child.

The questioning procedure

Let us assume that we are working with a child who already has spontaneous sentence production but consistently fails to use it when demands (in this case questions) are made of him. We shall also assume that picture materials are to be used, although objects, the classroom, or play activities of other children could equally have been chosen.

A picture is selected which shows a boy standing holding a toy car. Knowing the capabilities of the child, we aim that in response to the teacher's questions he will reply in a full sentence using subject, verb and object. More specifically the objective with this individual picture will be the child's production of a sentence, 'The boy's holding the car.'

STAGE 1. CHECK FOR THE COMPLETE RESPONSE

The first step is to allow the child the opportunity of realizing the objective in an unstructured way. An appropriate instruction might be: 'Tell me about this picture.' If the child is immediately successful, praise is given so that the child knows exactly what responses are acceptable to the teacher.

STAGE 2. OBSERVE THE INCOMPLETE RESPONSE

When the child does not realize the objective but offers some information about the picture, this should be praised before incorporating it in the next demand. If the child offers the information 'Boy car', he has described the subject and object elements of the sentence required, and so he is praised for partial achievement.

STAGE 3. REQUEST FOR MISSING ELEMENTS

In the example above the verb is missing so the teacher asks: 'What is the boy *doing* with the car?' In this way she focuses attention on the missing element. To this the child should respond with an appropriate verb such as 'holding' or 'carrying' which is acknowledged by the teacher who then requires the child to repeat this response, asking him, 'Tell me', and following this by further praise when he is successful.

STAGE 4. COMBINE THE ELEMENTS OFFERED SO FAR

The child has now offered all the elements of the objective and it only remains for him to put them together in sentence form, the teacher asking the child once more: 'Tell me about the picture.'

One teacher illustrates how easily this can be done.

Teacher Tell me about this picture.
Child Boy and car.
Teacher Good. What is the boy doing with the car?
Child Playing.
Teacher Tell me.
Child Playing.
Teacher Good, he's playing. Now tell me about the picture.
Child The boy's playing with a car.
Teacher Good.

Not all children will be as quick or obliging as this boy. Some may offer a one-word response while others, failing to understand the demand, may, like the child below, say nothing.

Teacher Tell me about the picture.
Child (Looks at picture but says nothing)
Teacher (Modifies her demand) Paul. (Gains attention) Who's that? (Points to picture of the boy)
Child Boy.
Teacher It's a boy, good. Tell me? (Repetition)
Child Boy.
Teacher Good. What's the boy got? (Request for object)
Child A ball.
Teacher Yes, the boy's got a ball. Good. What is the boy doing? (Request for verb)
Child Playing.
Teacher The boy's playing. Tell me? (Repetition)
Child He's playing.
Teacher Good. Now, tell me about the picture?
Child The boy's playing – with a ball.
Teacher Good. He's playing with a ball.

After asking her initial question, 'Tell me about the picture', the teacher realizes that this child has failed to understand her demand. Immediately she simplifies it, successfully focusing his attention on the subject, object and verb, and finally obtaining the required sentence.

At first children may find it difficult to know what is expected of them, so praise for appropriate responses is essential. Furthermore, whenever a child's response is appropriate it is useful to ask him to repeat the response using the demand, 'Tell me', followed by suitable verbal praise.

INCORRECT OR NON-EXISTENT RESPONSES

If the child fails to realize what is required of him and does not respond, or offers an inappropriate response, the teacher may have to model the response requiring the child to imitate:

Teacher Tell me about the picture. (Stage 1)
Child   Boy. (Stage 2)
Teacher What's the boy got? (Stage 3)
Child   (No response)
Teacher A ball. (Models response)
Teacher Tell me. (Stage 3)
Child   A ball. (Child imitates)
Teacher Good. So what's the boy got? (Acknowledge and repeat Stage 3)

The teacher models the response, and gets the child to repeat it but ensures that this response is tied to the appropriate question by repeating the original demand.

Putting the procedure into practice

We used this procedure in conjunction with a series of specially drawn pictures. Each set of pictures contained one large picture showing several people involved in varied activities, with some small pictures showing details of the large one. (Examples of pictures used are given in Appendix F.)

A typical session begins with a pre-test using the large picture in which the child is asked only, 'Tell me about this picture.' The child's responses to this instruction are recorded in order to select appropriate objectives. If the child produced only nouns, the immediate objective would be for him to produce utterances which include a person and an object. If the child produced combinations of nouns and verbs, a more adventurous objective would be appropriate, perhaps one which required a combination of a person, an action and an object in one response.

Following the pre-test and the selection of objectives, the smaller pictures (sections of the larger one) are presented in order. Each of these has a specified objective to be realized. Should this be realized as an immediate response to the request, 'Tell me about this picture', a new picture and hence a new objective, is presented. If a child fails to offer an adequate response, the teacher runs through the questioning procedure. The following is a hypothetical interchange over one small picture in which the child offers all the appropriate responses, and the teacher defines the objectives as, 'The child will describe the picture using a subject–verb–object sentence':

Teacher   Tell me about this picture. (Check for the complete response)
Child   A girl. (Partial response, subject only offered)
Teacher   Good. (Praise)
Teacher   Tell me. (Demand for repetition)
Child   A girl. (Appropriate response)
Teacher   Good. (Praise)
Teacher   What is the girl doing? (Extension from what the child offered – request for a verb)
Child   Pushing. (Appropriate response)
Teacher   Good. (Praise)
Teacher   Tell me. (Demand for repetition)
Child   The girl is pushing. (Child combines all the content offered so far)
Teacher   Good. (Praise)
Teacher   What is the girl pushing? (Extension from the last utterance – request for object)
Child   A pram. (Appropriate response)
Teacher   Good. (Praise)
Teacher   Tell me. (Demand for repetition)
Child   The girl's pushing a pram. (Child combines all the information and spontaneously reaches the objective)
Teacher   Very good. (Praise)

Of course this is an ideal dialogue and in practice deviations are normally necessary. There may be difficulty in extracting the required verb, in which case the dialogue may go as follows:

Teacher   Tell me about this picture. (Check for the complete response)
Child   A girl. (Partial response – subject only)
Teacher   Good. (Praise)
Teacher   Tell me. (Demand for repetition)
Child   A girl. (Appropriate response)
Teacher   Good. (Praise)
Teacher   What is the girl doing? (Extension from what the child offered – request for a verb)
Child   A girl. (Incorrect response)
Teacher   Yes, it's a girl. (Acknowledged as relevant)
Teacher   But what is the girl doing? (Demand repeated)
Child   Doing. (Inappropriate response; the child does not understand what is required of him)

Teacher   The girl is pushing. (Teacher models)
Teacher   Tell me. (Asks for imitation)
Child   Pushing. (Appropriate imitative response)
Teacher   Good. (Praise)
Teacher   What is the girl doing? (Repeats original demand)
Child   Pushing. (Appropriate non-imitative response)
Teacher   Good. (Praise for correct verb)
Teacher   The girl is pushing. (Teacher models a combination of information)
Teacher   Tell me. (Demand for imitation)
Child   The girl is pushing. (Child imitates)
Teacher   Good. (Praise)
Teacher   Tell me. (Demand for repetition)
Child   The girl is pushing (Child succeeds)
Teacher   Good. (Praise)
Teacher   What is the girl pushing? (Extension of the response – request for object)
Child   A pram. (Appropriate response)
Teacher   Good. (Praise)
Teacher   Tell me. (Demand for repetition)
Child   Pushing a pram. (Child succeeds)
Teacher   Good. (Praise)
Teacher   Who's pushing the pram? (Demand for the subject again)
Child   The girl's pushing the pram. (Complete response – the objective is achieved)
Teacher   Very good. (Praise)

Here the teacher does not accept imitation alone but uses the instruction, 'Tell me', to elicit a more spontaneous utterance.

After following the programme through, using the questioning procedure when necessary, the large picture is once again presented, accompanied by the instruction, 'Tell me about this picture.' This is in order to discover how much of the learning in the session generalizes to the more complex large picture.

A DETAILED ILLUSTRATION

Carol, aged 13, was one of a group of children involved in an initial investigation into the use of this questioning procedure. The complete transcript below illustrates clearly the change in her responses between the first presentation of large picture A (the pre-test), and the second presentation immediately after the teaching programme on the detail pictures. Note that Carol has a good knowledge of all vocabulary connected with the picture. (Picture A and the detail pictures are reproduced in Appendix F, pages 380–3.)

Pre-test presentation of large picture A

Carol   That's a boy. That's a girl. That's a girl. That's a girl – no, a boy. That's a boy – a girl I mean. That's it, yes, a girl. A boy.

Picture detail a

Objective: The child will use a simple combination of subject–verb–object to say, 'The girl's got a flower.'

Teacher   Tell me about this picture.
Carol   That's a girl.
Teacher   Good.
Teacher   Who's this?
Carol   A girl.
Teacher   Tell me. (Request for repetition to give her confidence and success)
Carol   Tell you? (Does not understand demand)
Teacher   Tell me.
Teacher   A girl. (Teacher models what is required)
Carol   A girl.
Teacher   Good.
Teacher   What's that? (Teacher points to flowers in picture)
Carol   Flowers.
Teacher   Tell me.
Carol   Flowers.
Teacher   Good.
Teacher   Tell me about the picture.
Carol   (No response. Still does not understand the demands)
Teacher   Who's got a flower? (Teacher incorporates the response in a repeated demand)
Carol   A girl.
Teacher   Good.
Teacher   Tell me.
Carol   A girl.
Teacher   Good.
Teacher   The girl's got a flower. (Teacher models the full response)
Carol   Yes.
Teacher   Tell me.
Carol   The girl's got a flower. (Imitation)
Teacher   Good.
Teacher   Tell me about the picture. (Request for spontaneous production)
Carol   (No response. She is still not clear about this latest request for repetition)

Teacher   What's the girl got?
Carol   A flowers. (Teacher accepts flowers)
Teacher   Tell me.
Carol   The girl's got a flowers. (Object achieved – despite plural)
Teacher   Very good girl.

Picture detail b

Objective: The child will use a combination of subject–verb–object to say, 'The boy's got a gun.'

Teacher   Let's see the next one.
Carol   That's a boy.
Teacher   Good.
Teacher   What's he got?
Carol   A gun.
Teacher   Good.
Teacher   Tell me.
Carol   The boy's got a gun. (The objective is quickly achieved this time)
Teacher   Good girl.
Teacher   Let's see the next one.

Picture detail c

Objective: The child will combine a subject and a verb to say, 'The boy's climbing.'

Teacher   Tell me about this picture.
Carol   The boy's climbing up a tree. (More than required. Objective achieved)
Teacher   Very good girl, that's the way.

Picture detail d

Objective: The child will combine a subject and a verb to say, 'The girl is swinging.'

Teacher   Tell me about this picture.
Carol   The girl is, the girl is in the swings. (Verb omitted)
Teacher   Good.
Teacher   What's the girl doing? (Request for the verb)
Carol   Swinging.
Teacher   Tell me about the picture.
Carol   The girl is swinging. (Objective achieved)

Teacher Good, that's the way.
Teacher Let's see the next one.

Picture detail e

Objective: The child will combine a subject and a verb to say, 'The girl is skipping.'

Teacher Tell me about this picture.
Carol The girl is skipping. (Objective achieved. Carol now fully understands the demands of the situation.)
Teacher Good girl. You're doing well aren't you?
Teacher Let's see the next one.

Picture detail f

Objective: The child will use a subject–verb–object combination to say, 'The boy is kicking a ball.'

Teacher Tell me about this picture.
Carol The boy is kicking a ball. (Objective achieved with ease)
Teacher Very good girl.

Picture detail g

Objective: The child will use a subject–verb–object combination to say, 'The girl is pushing a pram.'

Teacher Tell me about this picture.
Carol The girl is pushing a pram. (Objective achieved)
Teacher Good.

Picture detail h

Objective: The child will use a combination of subject plural–verb–object to say, 'The two boys are kicking a ball.'

Teacher Tell me about this picture.
Carol The boy is kicking the ball. (Subject plural missing)
Teacher Good.
Teacher Who are they? (Requests a plural by using 'they')
Carol Two boys.
Teacher Good.
Teacher Tell me about this picture.

Carol The two boys is kicking a balls. (Objective partly achieved; subject–verb–object, though ungrammatical)
Teacher Good girl.

Picture detail i

Objective: The child will use a combination of subject plural–verb–object plural to say, 'The two girls are picking flowers.'

Teacher Tell me about this picture.
Carol The girl and the girl get some flowers. (Plural not in the appropriate form)
Teacher Good.
Teacher Who are they?
Carol Girls.
Teacher How many girls?
Carol Two (Subject plural accurate)
Teacher Good.
Teacher Tell me.
Carol The girl and the girl pick some flowers. (Subject plural not accurate)
Teacher Who are they?
Carol Two girls.
Teacher Good.
Teacher Tell me about the picture.
Carol Pick the flowers. (Subject omitted)
Teacher Who's picking the flowers?
Carol Two girls.
Teacher Good.
Teacher Tell me about the picture.
Carol The two girls got some flowers. (Replaces the required verb)
Teacher Good.
Teacher What are they doing?
Carol Got some flowers.
Teacher What are they *doing*? ('Doing' is heavily stressed)
Carol They're picking.
Teacher Good, they're picking flowers.
Teacher Tell me about the picture.
Carol Tell you about the picture? (Sigh)
Carol Now then.
Carol The two girls pick some flowers. (Objective achieved. Teacher accepts 'pick' in place of 'are picking'.)

Immediately after this session, Carol was given a post-test using the large picture. There is vast improvement in her performance during this post-test when compared with the language she offers during the pre-test.

Carol   The boy's climbing up the tree. The girl is pushing a tripper. Two girls pick some flowers. The two boys kick the ball. The girl with the skipping rope skipping. *And* the girl is swinging. The boy's got a gun.

When the initial demand with the first small picture was made, Carol appeared to be somewhat bewildered and seemed unable to cope with extracting all the required information. However, after only a short time of working through the procedure when person–action–object sentences were required, she coped easily, with no help needed until the more complex demand for plural forms was made. The post-test illustrated a dramatic change in her ability to extract and structure relevant information, in addition to the improvement in verbal output. Now that these objectives and the criteria for success have been realized, new and more complex objectives can be devised.

EVALUATING PERFORMANCE – SUGGESTIONS FOR NEW OBJECTIVES

A further important feature of this procedure is the built-in evaluation, which helps to pinpoint areas of difficulty. The transcripts show Carol's difficulty in the use of plural forms:

The girl's got a flower*s*.
The two boys *is* kicking *a* ball*s*.

She does not make the verb in the sentence agree and does not use the plural article 'some'. This difficulty is not amenable to the questioning procedure since Carol shows she does not *possess* this grammatical skill. A separate teaching programme is needed aimed specifically at teaching plural forms. Subsequently evaluation of success could be made during a further questioning session.

Similarly, the post-tests of other children involved in the initial study showed quite dramatic changes in verbal output. All were capable of producing sentences and they all knew the vocabulary included in the picture. Some were not as adept as Carol at producing subject–verb–object sentences, others were somewhat quicker at interpreting the demands being made of them. But in each case the direction of further work was apparent due to the built-in evauation.

Further applications and developments

It was important to know whether the increase in verbal output would generalize to other pictures or remain specific to one. It would be of little use to pursue a procedure if the effective change was restricted to one set of materials. Changes between pre-test and post-test might be due largely to a 'practice effect'. Not only was the large picture shown twice, for pre- and post-test, but the small sections of this picture were also used. By the time the post-test was administered, the child was quite familiar with the content. Moreover, the whole procedure took no more than twenty minutes, so the results might have been different had there been a longer time between the pre- and post-tests.

The long-term effect of using the procedure also interested us. It would be unrealistic to expect permanant changes in verbal output after one session, but what effect would the procedure have if administered daily over a period of time? We were also concerned with the practical aspects involved in adopting such an approach. Our own rather clumsy initial attempts had emphasized the difficulties a teacher might have. Pictures were the most practical material to use, but it was important to know how adaptable this would be in different situations, such as in cookery, art, during visits or when used to describe objects, events or imaginary situations.

Base-line data were collected from the pupils in four schools, all pre-tested by their own teachers using one large picture. From this pool of subjects a number of children were selected for a series of small-scale studies designed to examine these questions. In these studies we were interested in assessing the change in the children's language following the use of the questioning procedure. To achieve this, a simple categorization system was devised (see Appendix G) which examined three major areas of the children's responses in the pre- and post-tests:

1   Relevance of the response
2   Repetition of information
3   Content – complexity of the responses.

PILOT STUDY

There were two aims for this small pilot study. First, we wished to check on the effectiveness of the procedure (over one session) by comparing one group of children who received the procedure with another who only received general stimulation with play materials for the same period. Secondly, we wanted to know if the effects of the procedure were restricted to the picture involved in the training session or whether the children's performance would improve with a different picture containing different content.

Ten children were selected on the basis of pre-tests and assigned at random to two groups of five each.

Procedure with experimental group

Stage 1 – pre-test. The child was presented with large picture A and instructed to: 'Tell me about this picture.' When the child ceased to offer information, a single prompt, 'Anything else?', was given. This was followed immediately by stage 2.

Stage 2 – teaching session. The child was involved in a structured teaching programme, using the questioning procedure, where behavioural objectives for each of the detail pictures were specified. This was immediately followed by stage 3.

Stage 3 – post-test 1. This was exactly as stage 1, and was immediately followed by a second post-test.

Stage 4 – post-test 2. Large picture B was presented repeating stages 1 and 3.

Procedure with control group

Stages 1, 3 and 4 were identical to the experimental group but stage 2 differed. For the control group stage 2 consisted of a play session of which the mean length of time equalled that of stage 2 for the experimental group. No direction was given by the teacher but communication initiated by the child was responded to.

Results

For the experimental group, the results showed an improvement in the performance of three of the five children. Of the two other children one showed no change between pre- and post-tests while the remaining child performed better on the pre-test. Only one child in the control group showed any improvement, while the performance of three of the children was better on the pre-test. The fifth child in this group showed no change and remained at the one-word response level throughout.

These results suggested that the children in the experimental group showed some improvement in their abilities to extract and offer relevant information about the pictures. Not only was this evident with the large picture A, but also with the second post-test picture B. Thus there seemed

FURTHER APPLICATIONS AND DEVELOPMENTS

some positive evidence that children could generalize from one set of picture materials to another. On the basis of this information, a further study was designed.

MAIN STUDY

The main study was to investigate:

1 The effects of using the questioning procedure over a longer period of time
2 The practical aspects involved in adopting the use of such a procedure
3 How the procedure might be generalized to other situations.

The children involved

By analysing the results of the pre-test administered by class teachers as in the pilot study (that is, for relevance, repetition and content) six children from one school were selected to take part in the main study:

Margaret, aged 14 years
Susan, aged 14 years
Simon, aged 13 years   senior class
Paul, aged 12
Alan, aged 7 years – junior class
Sam, aged 6 years – infant/nursery class.

Preparation

One teacher was asked to use the questioning procedure as a basis for individual programmes with the six children each day for a week. Prior to the start of the study, we met the teacher to discuss the teaching model and the way the questioning procedure might be used with each child. Time was also spent in discussing possible objectives for the children so that when the study commenced the teacher was able to specify her own objectives for each child. A range of picture materials was provided together with skeleton procedure forms (see Appendices F and H) which allowed the teacher time to become familiar with the materials before starting the programme.

The procedure

Week 1. On the Friday of week 1, each of the children was given a pre-test using pictures A and C.

Week 2. Using the questioning procedure, the children were given individual sessions each day for the week. The teacher selected the appropriate pictures and hence language objectives for each child.

Week 3. On the Monday of week 3 each child was given a post-test using pictures A and C.

Pre- and post-test results (weeks 1 and 3)

Four of the six children (Susan, Margaret, Simon and Alan) showed improvement in the language they offered during the post-test. This is especially noticeable in their combined use of two- and three-element utterances. The noticeable difference between the pre- and post-tests lies in the content. Margaret, for instance, increased the number of three-element utterances from three to ten (combination of subject–action–object). She produced fewer two-element responses in the post-test but this was only to be expected in view of the increase of more complex responses. Similarly,

Table 18 Combined scores for pictures A and C

	Number of utterances	Relevant	Not relevant	Non-repetitions	Repetitions and other	Content: number of elements			
						1	2	3	0[a]
Susan									
pre-test	16	16	–	14	2	6	3	6	1
post-test	16	13	3	13	3	–	7	6	3
Alan									
pre-test	30	30	–	29	1	29	1	–	–
post-test	12	12	–	12	–	–	4	8	–
Margaret									
pre-test	11	10	1	9	2	–	7	3	1
post-test	16	14	2	14	2	–	4	10	2
Simon									
pre-test	13	13	–	12	1	4	5	4	–
post-test	16	16	–	15	1	3	7	6	–
Paul									
pre-test	33	27	6	18	11	12	12	3	6
post-test	17	16	1	14	3	9	4	3	1
Sam									
pre-test	20	–	20	–	20	–	–	–	20
post-test	48	41	7	7	41	41	–	–	7

[a] The category '0' covers utterances coded as relevant to picture but not offering information about content, or referring to test situation not to picture, or irrelevant.

Alan changed from twenty-nine one-word responses and produced four two-element and eight three-element replies. Only limited change is noted with Susan, however. There was a shift from one- to two-element responses, but the number of three-element statements remained identical. Simon, too, made limited progress, although all changes were in the desired direction.

Paul and Sam failed to make the kind of progress noted with the other four children. There was an increase in the total number of Sam's utterances during the post-test session together with a startling increase in their relevance to the picture material. Additionally, there was an impact on the content of his language. Sam was the youngest of the children and a number of problems arose mainly because he had few of the prerequisite skills for the programme. His attention span was somewhat limited and it was sometimes difficult for the teacher to get him to look at the picture materials. However, even accounting for this, there was a marked improvement between pre- and post-test scores. While Sam clearly benefited, it would be more appropriate for such children to be helped to develop the prerequisite skills of the procedure, and primarily that of sustained attention. Paul's post-test results showed a marked decrease all round. He not only produces fewer utterances but the content itself deteriorates, only the number of three-element utterances remaining the same.

The teacher who had carried out the prolonged work with these children was asked to comment on the use of the questioning procedure, offer critical comments and raise problems associated with it. She began by expressing an initial reaction: 'My first impression on being presented with the material was that it was straightforward.' However, she went on:

On using the material I discovered that it was not as easy as I had anticipated. This was mainly because I was unfamiliar with the programme and the method and I had difficulty at first in keeping to it. I tended to use my own words – ad libbing – and this confused the child as words which were not required in the sentence were being given. Once I had studied the materials and the programmes carefully, this was no longer a problem . . . I became increasingly aware of giving the children a wrong cue because as a result of this the child picked up trivia.

HOW ADAPTABLE IS THE QUESTIONING PROCEDURE?

The principles involved with a structured procedure of this sort can be generalized to any situation in which a teacher wishes to elicit verbal information from children whose productive language is above the one-word level. The teacher involved in the study thought that she could use this type of programme in the classroom, with a class or group or with an individual child. 'The procedure could be used on any occasion when a teacher might try to get a response from a child. On a visit, in cookery – any time, provided the teacher is familiar with the procedure, appreciates the simplicity and knows her objectives.'

This teacher taught a senior class which included four of the children involved in the study. We asked her to adopt the use of the questioning procedure during any individual or group lesson. The following transcripts give examples of the successful way in which the procedure was used.

Teacher   Now we've got everything weighed. Everything weighed. What will we do next?
Child   Put the flour in the dish.
Teacher   Put the flour in the dish. Good. What sort of dish do we use?
Chorus of children   Saucers.
Teacher   A bowl. So let's say again. What do we do with the flour?
Chorus of children   We put it in the bowl.
Child   We need milk.
Teacher   We need milk. How much milk?
Child   A teaspoonful.
Teacher   Right. So . . .
Child   We need, need a teaspoonful of milk.

Teacher   What did we do yesterday, Julie?
Julie   We went out for a walk.
Teacher   We went out for a walk. Good. Where did we go Susan?
Susan   We went to Werneth Low.
Teacher   We went to Werneth Low. Good. What was the weather like John, yesterday afternoon?
John   Windy.
Teacher   What was windy? The . . .
John   And cold.
Teacher   So . . . The weather was . . .
John   Cold and windy.
Teacher   Good. Tell me again.
John   The wind.
Teacher   The weather . . .
John   The weather was windy and cold.
Teacher   The weather was windy and cold.

Conclusions

We have attempted to highlight some of the problems which arise when we make demands on children through the use of questions. Questions form a major part of teachers' verbal output, and we have seen how easy it is to confuse children through lack of care in their use. These confusions can be overcome by bearing in mind two vital points. First, questions must follow from clearly defined objectives, so that the teacher is quite sure what the desired end-point of the sequence of questions is. If the teacher is uncertain about this, then inevitably the child will be equally confused. Secondly, sensitive questioning must be based on a very careful appraisal of the child's abilities. Unless the teacher is fully aware of what the child is capable of offering, the teacher may ask questions which make either over-simple or unrealistically complex demands.

The questioning procedure does not enable the child to learn new language structures; it is a means of helping him to understand, more easily, the demands of the teacher and the activity in which he is engaged, so that he can use the communicative resources he already has at his disposal in novel contexts.

Occasionally, the procedure may look a little stilted. If we are trying to help children towards functional language, surely there are times when a minimal one-word response is much more appropriate than a complex sentence? This is undoubtedly true from a normal adult's point of view. When we respond to someone with just one word, we usually know that that is all that is necessary for that person, and also that if we wished we could respond in a much more complicated fashion. Indeed, if our initial response proved inadequate, we would certainly do so. We have a vast range of options to choose from to cope with nearly every situation, and we can choose the best one to fit. But this is much less true of mentally handicapped children. They may have no options, and so no choice, and so no notion of what is appropriate to different contexts. The questioning procedure is one way of providing some options and thus opening the way for choice.

IX. Using language curriculum packages

'That looks useful – how much does it cost?'
'Don't think much of the pictures, but it's got some good ideas.'
'Give it five minutes with my lot and it will fall to bits.'
'I can't decide whether I prefer this for the materials, or this for the lessons.'
'Well I need something anyway – I can't do it all on my own.'

These are some of the reactions you might expect from a group of teachers looking at a display of 'curriculum packages' or kits at a teachers' centre. But until a teacher has tried out a particular package with a group of children it will be virtually impossible to come to any firm conclusions about its value. The information available before a teacher decides to invest in a particular curriculum package is often meagre – gleaned from a quick glance through some of the materials and lesson plans and the publisher's notes. This chapter provides more detailed information about four published curriculum packages which deal with language and communication development, and have been used before with ESN(S) children.

Educational evaluation has by now almost become a discipline on its own. The approach we used has been determined partly by constraints of time and resources, and partly by decisions as to what would be of most value to teachers at this stage. The conclusions we come to are not definitive – we do not aim to say that one curriculum package is better than the other, since in every case there are advantages and disadvantages which must be matched against the particular needs of the individual teacher. We do aim to provide certain specific types of information.

Content, method and material

The content and method of a curriculum package represent what we have called the 'programme' aspect. The first concern is to look at *what* a programme attempts to teach, and *how* it tries to do it. We provide many illustrations and try to explain the basic model which underlies the selection of a particular set of objectives. Since most programmes use the same recurring methods, we also look at the basic routines established. We examine these as a set of principles for teaching and illustrate the way they are applied. Throughout this analysis we draw comparisons with our own approach described in previous chapters, and examine the sequence in which various skills are taught. We point out not only what a programme teaches, but also what it does not teach; and look at the extent to which assessment and evaluation of the children's progress is built in to the programme. Although the programme is our main concern, we also examined the materials for their practicality, durability and adaptability.

Implementing a curriculum package

First, we look at what sort of children will be suitable for particular programmes. This is partly covered by the review of content, but we also point to the necessary prerequisite skills. Grouping problems are considered, and other practical and organizational problems discussed, with the various side-benefits certain kits may provide. Initial reactions of teachers and children to the kits are given, with specific examples of individual children's progress and difficulties encountered. Each review concludes with recommendations, based on our own experience, as to the most appropriate way a kit may be used.

The reviews and conclusions are drawn from many different sources, all based around one of the project's teacher working parties. In the initial stages the various kits were passed round, tried out informally and discussed in meetings, and the initial reactions recorded. Each kit was distributed to one or two schools and taught by one teacher to a group of five children, who were tested on a variety of instruments before the teaching began, to record their approximate level of linguistic development. During the teaching, detailed discussions were held at working-party meetings when progress and problems were discussed. The teachers wrote interim reports and kept lesson notes. The reviews and conclusions are the result of the combined experience and expertise of the project team and a group of experienced teachers, some of whom used the kits, while others acted as impartial commentators and observers.

The four curriculum packages reviewed are the *Peabody Language Development Kit* (Level P), *Jim's People* (I, II and III), *Distar Language* (I), and *Language and How to Use it* (Beginning levels).[1]

Peabody Language Development Kit – Level P

The stated aim of the *Peabody* kit is 'to stimulate the receptive, associative and expressive components of oral language development. Concomitant goals are to improve intellectual functioning and enhance future school progress.' The manual defines the target group of children as those with a mental age of 3 to 5 years. Its primary purpose is clearly to help socially disadvantaged children (that is, those children believed to be underfunctioning for primarily environmental reasons) although it is intended also for 'pre-teenaged, trainable mentally retarded children' – that is, ESN(S) children. In common with the other kits not specifically designed for ESN(S) children, there are no suggestions as to possible modifications. The content and methodology apply irrespective of target population.

At first sight, the kit is a highly attractive collection of material, the possibilities of which defy enumeration (the manual provides about six pages of suggestions). It contains cards depicting various words and concepts; colour chips; manikins and accompanying clothes; model fruit and vegetables; records and a xylophone; and three puppets – P. Mooney, whose main functions are as an intermediary for the teacher, and to provide motivation and interest (he has a stick which lights up when pressed, a small bag which he wears and there is a large version which may be worn by teachers or children), Elbert, an elephant who does not know how to listen, and the 'Gasless Goose'.

However, the kit is not merely a set of materials. The manual details a programme of 180 daily lessons and gives general guidelines. The *Peabody* programme is based on the model of psycho-linguistic processes devised by C. E. Osgood,[2] and used in the *Illinois Test of Psycholinguistic Abilities*.[3] Figure 18 shows the programme model in flow diagram form. It distinguishes three types of input to the child: auditory, visual and tactile; and two types of output: vocal and motor. Linking these are three forms of thinking – *associative thinking* which provides the direct link between input and output; *convergent thinking*, which is indirectly linked to input by associative thinking, and includes those processes we call 'logical reasoning', such as deduction, generalization and class concepts; and *divergent thinking* which accounts for those processes often called 'creativity'. Emphasis is on auditory reception, vocal expression and the development of grammatical structures.

The content is derived from this model of language processes. For example, tactile–vocal association is said to be stimulated by lesson 19 part 3, in which children have to feel a shape behind their backs and name it.

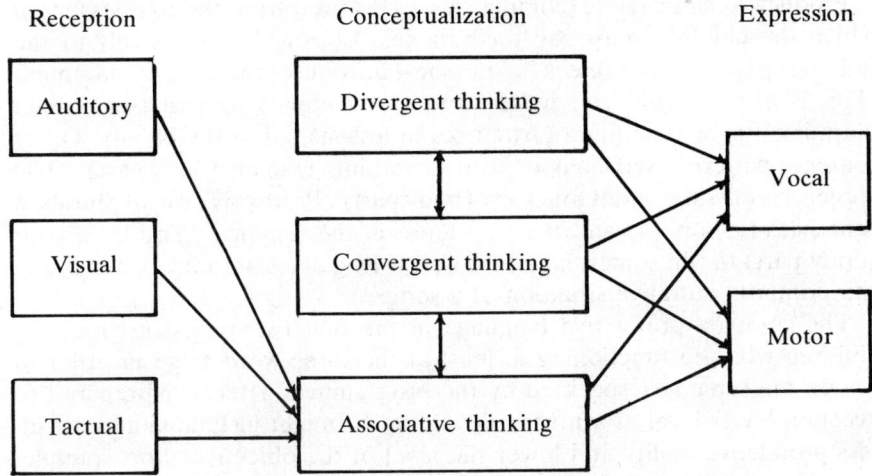

Fig. 18 Model of language processes (*Peabody Language Development Kit* (Level P))

Auditory–motor association is the main process involved in lesson 9, part 4, in which children have to jump over a line when they hear a note on a xylophone. The sort of processes at which the *Peabody* is aimed are primarily cognitive, not social. There is an underlying belief that the development of language aids cognitive development in general. Language is seen mainly as a tool for thought, action and communication with reference to the object world around the child. The social and emotional aspects are not ignored, but form a minor part of the overall programme.

To analyse all 180 lessons would be impractical here. However, it may be useful to take a close look at the first twenty lessons, and then provide a less detailed examination of the first half of the programme.

One of the clearest features of the kit is the use of specific areas of vocabulary in many contexts. Vocabulary is introduced and used to teach a variety of skills. For example, words for various fruits appear first in lesson 4, part 1. In the same lesson, fruit words are used in connexion with a recall game and a hide-and-seek activity, and in lesson 8 they are used in a more complex sentence pattern and in matching three-dimensional models of fruit to pictures. In the first twenty lessons, nine areas of vocabulary are introduced: body parts (six lessons); actions associated with body parts (five lessons); colour and animals (three lessons); fruit, shapes and clothes (two lessons) and transport and noise (one lesson).

Productive language (excluding singing) is used from the first lesson, in which the children must say their names. Lesson 3 extends this to the sentence pattern 'My name is . . .' Lesson 4 introduces the identity statement 'This is a . . .' with fruit words, and this sentence pattern (with slight variations) is repeated in a further seven lessons out of the twenty. Other sentence patterns used include 'I (do something) with my (body part)', 'The (object) is missing' and 'I touch my (body part)'. Productive use of plurals in sentences (lesson 14) and the past tense in the sentence 'You used your (body part) to (do something)' also occur. Negatives are introduced but in the primarily imitative situation of a song.

The complex productive language in the first twenty lessons requires children who are functioning at least at the three-word stage in order to obtain the sentences specified by the programme. A teacher prepared to accept a lower level of syntactic development might include children with less productive ability and lower the level of the objectives, for example, from 'The apple is missing' to 'Apple missing'. From lessons 21 to 90, the productive language required becomes increasingly complex. Negatives, superordinate categories, future tense, prepositions, conjunctions and 'if . . . then' constructions, are all interwoven into sentence forms which themselves grow increasingly complex.

Receptive language is less heavily emphasized. There are, of course, situations in which the teacher talks to the class, who are required only to listen, not to give any response which may be used to assess their understanding. Teacher language which requires no response tends to be complex. For example, in lesson 2, part 2, the teacher says: 'Today P. Mooney is going to let us play a game with the colour chips. We each have a necklace made of chips. A necklace is something you wear round your neck. Let's see how we look in our P. Mooney necklaces.' However, this aspect of receptive language is not strictly speaking part of the programme content. The more important aspects are covered in a number of ways. Lesson 5 uses a 'Simon Says' game in connexion with the understanding of body parts and associated actions. Part of six other lessons out of the first twenty are concerned with understanding single words or specific sounds.

This bias towards productive language is in conflict with the research findings discussed in Chapter IV, which demonstrate that in normal language-learning, understanding very often precedes production. For certain classes of vocabulary the *Peabody* kit requires production before reception. This sequence of development must be seen in the context of the aims and main target population of the kit. The manual emphasizes that the stress is on global language development, rather than specific skills. It is clear in some lessons that the developers would expect at least some children to know the words involved before the lesson, the lesson serving primarily as a reinforcement plus the teaching of the sentence frame. The assumption that some children will know the words is not unreasonable in the case of socially disadvantaged pre-school children, but such an assumption needs to be carefully checked by methods described in Chapter VI with ESN(S) children.

Non-verbal/conceptual abilities are not ignored, although there is again less emphasis on this. Important abilities such as gross motor imitation occur, for example, in lesson 2, part 3 ('Activity time'). The teacher leads the children round the room in a march chanting as they go. Imitation of fine and gross movement occurs again in lesson 10, part 4. Here the actions range from jumping up and down to blinking eyes. Accompanying this imitation, however, is an optional verbal description of the action. Conceptual abilities are tackled, for example, in lesson 8, part 3, in which children are required to match model fruits to pictures of fruits, and lesson 2, part 4, involves colour matching. However, as with the receptive and productive language sections of the programme, the non-verbal and conceptual sections are intermingled with other abilities. Thus, although matching work with fruit occurs in lesson 8, production of these words has already occurred in lesson 4. The introduction stresses that the lessons should be carried through in sequence, but one might hesitate at using lesson 4 before lesson 8, since normally non-verbal/conceptual skills *precede* linguistic use. There is a clear sequence of development, for example, in the complexities of grammatical structures required, but within certain areas of vocabulary the teaching sequence does not accord with the normally accepted developmental sequence.

A further problem in using *Peabody* with ESN(S) children is that the distinction between imitative and productive language is not clearly made, and could lead to children remaining at the imitative level in certain skills. Take, for example, the identity statement, 'This is a . . .', occuring first in lesson 4 when the instruction given is: 'Have the children answer, in unison, using the following sentence pattern: "This is a (banana)." If unable to elicit the correct response say "This is a (banana)", and have the children repeat it, in unison, afterwards.' Thus if the response is not immediately forthcoming, an imitation is acceptable. The sentence pattern next occurs in lesson 5, in which the instruction is less specific: 'Encourage the children to reply using the following sentence patterns: "This is a (head)" or "These are (arms)".' While this instruction seems to be primarily aimed at production, it leaves imitation as a possibility. In lesson 5, part 3, the instruction is clearly imitative ('Encourage the children to repeat in unison'). Lesson 6, part 1, makes the distinction clear but still allows for imitation, and in lesson 7, part 2, the instruction moves on to a clearly productive level: 'Have the children name, in unison, the piece of clothing using the sentence pattern: "This is a (shirt)".' The transition is made, but no procedures specified as to *how* to move a child from imitation to production; the distinction is only implicit and it would be easy for a teacher to accept imitative responses.

The real strength of the *Peabody* programme is as a source of objectives. We are often unaware of the complexities of the language we use, so much so that it would never occur to us to teach words such as 'another' (lesson 22) or the present continuous ending '-ing' (lesson 68). But caution must be exercised in using the kit in exactly the way it suggests, since ESN(S) children may often not have acquired the prerequisite skills.

Similar caution needs to be applied to the methods used. The most striking characteristic apparent to a teacher of ESN(S) children is the speed at which the kit moves. The introduction provides for the use of one lesson over two days' work. If this slower timing is followed, the first twenty lessons will cover eight weeks' work – involving the introduction of nine areas of vocabulary and a considerable number of other skills. Tied to this rapidity is the absence of built-in procedures for checking progress, although in the general introduction the manual says: 'Practice, drill and review are to be encouraged.' Thus, children may go through lesson 4 without achieving successful performance in production of fruit words, and be immediately confronted in the following lesson by new body-part words. The lack of defined criteria for the achievement of objectives is likely to mean that the children are swamped with demands they cannot cope with.

Closely linked to the problem of evaluation is the programme's emphasis on group development and group responding. Teachers of ESN(S) children know how easy it is for a less able child to hide himself among the more capable responses of other children. A common occurrence in the kit is the use of individual children for lower level, non-verbal responses, followed by a group unison response at the verbal level. There are two ways round this problem. First, it is important for the children in a group to differ as little as possible in ability, and to a certain extent in temperament, since personality factors rather than ability may have a lot to do with who is successful in a group. The manual makes no suggestions about the make-up of the group, except for the vast number of children in the '3–5 year mental age range'. Secondly, it would be a simple process to go round the group and check each child individually (this procedure is used in the *Distar* programme).

As with any programme, the *Peabody* kit depends to some extent on the skills of the individual teacher. In the introduction, praise is mentioned as an important part of any lesson and materials such as the colour chips are suggested as token reinforcements, but prompts in the lesson descriptions would encourage appropriate use of reinforcement and enhance the chances of success.

We saw in previous chapters how easy it is for a teacher inadvertently to provide non-verbal cues. Lesson 5, part 4, involves a 'Simon Says' game in which the P. Mooney puppet gives 'simple oral commands' for the children to follow. These involve bodily actions very easily carried out by the teacher while P. Mooney is giving the command. Unless the teacher controls her behaviour very carefully she will not be sure whether the child is learning to imitate bodily actions or to understand simple commands. Non-verbal prompts are essential in the initial stages of learning a new language skill, but they must be progressively withdrawn if a child is to demonstrate mastery of that skill.

The teacher may also provide a missing response and then move on without ensuring that the children produce the response – this is especially easy in a group where there is pressure from the more able children to move on. The lesson outlines fail to describe procedures to correct incorrect responses, or ways of producing responses which have not occurred, except early on where failure to produce a response is followed by modelling and imitation.

Thus the success of the programme depends on a number of teaching skills which are either taken for granted or only briefly outlined in the introduction. Very often these skills become submerged in the daily strain of coping with a group of boisterous ESN(S) children. By far the most appropriate solution would be in-service courses which could be run alongside the implementation of a programme such as *Peabody*.

One final point on method concerns the complexity of language peripheral to the programme objectives, and the use of songs, poems and stories. Lesson 13 contains a story about three shapes, which runs to almost a page, which the children are only required to sit and listen to. The story is grammatically and cognitively very complex, and success would require constant prompting by the teacher to maintain attention. In the same way, the programme uses methods which require often much more sophisticated skills than those being taught. For example, in lesson 15, part 4, the following song is included:

> Bibbety-bob. Here's our job,
> New words to say for work and play.
> (Red) and (orange) are (colours) you see,
> Words we've learnt from P. Mooney.

The most common instruction to the teacher is: 'Lead the children in singing the song'. Adequate performance involves a considerable degree of short-term recall, and the musical skills of pitch and rhythm, in addition to linguistic skills. The title of the lesson is 'Activity – sentence-building time'. It would seem considerably simpler to get the children to say 'red and orange are colours' without requiring additional skills which could easily swamp the main objective. This is not to deny singing a place in the school life of a mentally handicapped child, but it should be separated from the difficulties of language learning.

THE KIT IN USE

The *Peabody* kit was used by one teacher with a group of five children aged 4:10 to 7:0, who ranged in productive language ability from spontaneous grammatical sentences to the pre-one-word level. Reception-scale scores varied from 3 to 9 and EPVT[4] raw scores from 0 to 12. It is clear that for many of the lessons, even at the beginning of the kit, these children were not at an appropriate level of competence. They were selected to discover how much of the programme could be used at a fairly low ability level. Some additional useful comments and criticisms came from another teacher who had previously used the programme with ESN(S) and autistic children in individual situations.

Both teachers and children reacted favourably to the materials in general. In the notes for lesson 1 the teacher remarked: 'Children showed great interest in puppets, record – all equipment very stimulating'; and the children continued to talk about P. Mooney in the class after the lesson. The P. Mooney puppet was found most useful for motivating, encouraging and praising children and the teachers felt that puppets could usefully be used in connexion with other kits. The *Peabody* kit relies much less than the other kits on picture materials, and this was obviously an advantage. Children could hold and manipulate many of the materials (something not possible for the *Distar* and *Jim's People* programmes), although the teacher notes in lesson 19 that one child experienced difficulty in manipulating the shapes. In general, however, the material is attractive, sturdy, easy to handle and, above all, interesting for the children. Occasionally interest fails at certain expected points – in the notes for lesson 13 the teacher remarked: 'Children weren't really interested in story, it was too advanced.' Interest often appeared to be in the material rather than in what it was used for, and the less able children caused more problems: in lesson 20, the teacher noted, two of them chewed at the material while waiting their turn.

Grouping problems were apparent. Clearly the more able children responded appropriately many times when the less able children offered very little, although there may have been considerable benefit in other areas for the less able, notably in social skills. The range of ability in the group, however, matched the range of skills taught by the programme. For example, the teacher commented on lesson 5: 'All children involved to some degree with the lesson.' This lesson involves the introduction and productive use of body-part words and motor imitation of associated actions. While the grammatically more capable children were benefiting from the demands for precise productive language, the less able children were being helped by the less complex, but none the less important, demands for motor imitation. This fortunate combination does not always occur.

The lessons in the manual are not highly adaptable. The manual is inconsistent on this. It stresses the importance of using all 180 lessons in sequence, but provides many suggestions for the non-programme use of the materials. The materials themselves are more adaptable. The kit contains just under four hundred 'stimulus cards' depicting animals, clothing, food, facial expressions, etc. These could prove particularly valuable for use in conjunction with vocabulary programmes such as those outlined in Chapter VI. Many other parts of the material could provide invaluable, controlled stimuli for teaching. A further advantage this material has over the other kits is the ease with which it may be used in class to emphasize and generalize skills learnt in the lesson. Children spontaneously carried over abilities to the classroom. For example, in lesson 2 one child continued to march round the classroom chanting, 'March, march'. The teacher used various other materials in the classroom, for example, for dressing up in the Wendy House after a lesson on clothes. However, she made two specific criticisms. She found the recorded songs too fast for the children to take in what was said; and several children found the colour chips difficult to assemble.

CONCLUSIONS

The kit rests on the assumption that an ESN(S) child, in the mental age-range 3 to 5 years, is equal in ability and intellectual characteristics to a socially disadvantaged child of the same mental age. This assumption has been shown to be untenable, particularly in the field of language development.

The programme is a rich *source* of objectives for a language curriculum, but caution should be exercised in using the programme as laid down by the manual. The teacher found many of the early lessons were too complex and moved at too fast a rate for even the most capable child in her group. However, the programme contained much useful content which could be abstracted to meet the needs of specific children in a class. If a teacher wished to use the programme systematically, as laid out by the manual, extreme care should be taken in selecting the group of children. The teacher should read through the first forty-odd lessons and decide exactly what prerequisite skills the children must have. One possibility is to use the programme as it is given but to build in careful evaluation procedures and move at a pace contingent upon the rate of learning of the group of children. Thus a lesson or part of a lesson would be repeated, with possible variations to avoid boredom and rote learning, until the skills taught by it had been mastered. Lessons might also be broken down into imitative and productive stages. Sentences such as, 'This is a banana' could initially be reduced to 'banana', and built up from there.

Given the careful modifications necessary to the programme to adapt it to ESN(S) children, and some back-up support, the *Peabody* programme has a considerable amount to offer. As a set of materials it is certainly extremely valuable in its own right.

Jim's People

When these reviews were written, *Jim's People* was the only curriculum package then available designed specifically for ESN(S) children. (Bill Gillham's *First Words* (Allen and Unwin, 1979) is a recent useful addition.) *Jim's People* grew out of work carried out at the Hester Adrian Research Centre at the University of Manchester and was developed in conjunction with teachers in the Manchester area.

The kit consists of three boxes (*Jim's People* I, II and III) each containing thirty-two 21cm × 25cm picture cards. The cards are designed to teach specific aspects of language, on their own and in conjunction with other cards. The programme centres on one family, the 'Jim' of the title, accompanied by Stephen, Pat, Ann, Baby, Mum and Dad, and Grandma and Grandad. The names are taught in *Jim's People* I and are used throughout the series. The pictures are clear and designed for specific objectives. This programme is not a collection of materials but a programme of language objectives with materials designed for those objectives.

The short manual outlines the underlying model of the communication process on which the kit is based. The area of concern is divided into understanding, speaking and feedback. The comprehension/production distinction is very clearly made here. Virtually every construction is taught first as understanding and then as speaking. Feedback involves skills very often neglected in kits designed primarily for other groups. In social situations when two people are talking, there is always a large amount of non-verbal communication via facial expression and bodily movements. Successful communication implies that both speaker and listener can understand and produce these social signals. It has been suggested that ESN(S) children may be especially deficient in this. The programme in *Jim's People* II and III covers this vital area systematically.

The programme does not involve social situations but teaches everything through the use of picture materials; thus facial expression is taught in *Jim's People* II, using a number of cards depicting members of the family in various moods. A further feature is that content does not depend on the normal development of language. For example, *Jim's People* I, after teaching family names, then teaches four constructions using both comprehension and production: the possessive ending 's', for example, in 'Jim's shoes'; the simple declarative sentence such as, 'Dad is painting the door', followed by the plural ending '-s' and personal pronouns he/she/they/it. In normal development many of these constructions appear in embryo very early. A child may indicate possession by saying, 'Mummy ball', and plurality by saying, 'More ball', but the adult use of the appropriate ending does not appear until much later. The programme teaches the meaning and the adult forms simultaneously, demonstrating its prime concern with the adult grammatical construction rather than with the meaning it carries. In understanding possessives the distinction is not important. The child can afford to ignore the possessive ending 's' in 'Mum's dress' and take account only of the two words and respond correctly. However, with understanding of plurals the plural ending '-s' is crucial. The teacher using this kit found it necessary to amend this aspect of the programme. Similarly, the instructions for speaking sentences ask the teacher to ensure that 'the whole sentence is spoken, i.e. participle, articles, etc.' Therefore the children should be at a stage when they can produce 'Jim is painting'. The sentence carries an important meaning – that of agent and action – which could be initially expressed as 'Jim paint', since the rest of the information is carried by the picture. It would be unfortunate to lose the valuable and clear material because the child could not grasp the niceties of the adult form. This objective and others could easily be split into an initial stage when the meaning was stressed, then a stage when the appropriate form could be added.

Although it might seem that *Jim's People* does not presume any prior linguistic ability, a child would require some degree of sophistication in auditory discrimination and articulation to be successful. Linked to this point is the size of the steps made by the programme. In productive language, the first stage is single-word production of the family names and the words 'boy' and 'girl', followed by possessives and plurals and then by simple subject–verb and subject–verb–object sentences. *Jim's People* II moves on to much more complex constructions involving, for example, past and future tense. Thus a child essentially at the single-word stage could have only one example of a two-word construction (possessives) before moving on to three- to seven-word sentences. Although such difficulties might not be experienced in comprehension, since the child can ignore much of the adult form and has many non-verbal cues, the load of producing such sentences is very great on a child who has not built up the component parts of such constructions. However, the material does permit more careful programming than the manual suggests. A possible sequence might be as follows:

Stage 1: combination of two names
Cards 1 + 2; 1 + 3, etc. – Jim Pat; Jim Ann
Stage 2: combination of name and object
Cards 1–9 – Jim door; Pat door, etc.
Stage 3: combination of name and verb
Card 19 – Mum wash
Card 28 – Dad paint
Stage 4: combination of verb and object
Card 18 – Wash hands
Card 27 – Paint door.

These steps are mentioned in the manual as a method for achieving the full sentence. We suggest, however, that they should be treated as objectives in their own right. Practice is needed using other materials so that the skills are well established and generalized before moving to more complex constructions.

In general the material exists within the kit for more fine-grained programming of such skills, so what the manual lacks in terms of suggestions for teaching is covered by the materials. Similar instances of large jumps and not enough initial development occur, for example, in the teaching of comparative and superlative adjectives of size – bigger/biggest and smaller/smallest. This sequence is not preceded by any work on the words 'big' and 'small' as simple adjectives, and it is difficult to know how a child could grasp the notion that something can be bigger than something which is also big, if he has not learnt that something big is bigger than something small.

One of the characteristics of *Jim's People* is its simplicity. It selects a limited number of objectives and concentrates on their achievement. This approach to language teaching demands an awareness of what is left out of the package, which will need to be included some time. In the sequences on the past tense in *Jim's People* II, the three example sentences are, 'Dad has shaved', 'Steven has climbed the ladder', and 'Jim has crashed'. These are all basic and simple past-tense forms, but grammatical mastery of the past tense covers a large number of other constructions, each carrying a slightly changed meaning: 'Dad used to shave', 'Dad shaved', 'Dad did shave', 'Dad was shaving'. This is not to deny the importance of what *Jim's People* achieves in teaching one form, but is simply a warning that one construction is only the beginning of the story.

Another, perhaps more crucial, example occurs with question forms in *Jim's People* III, one of which is the 'what' question. The picture used to teach this shows a puzzled looking Jim holding up a spanner and looking at dad – 'What's this for?' There are many different types of 'what' question, demanding different types of response. Under the rubric of 'what' questions come questions demanding explanation: 'What's this for?', 'What's the matter?'; questions demanding the time: 'What time is it?'; questions demanding nominal responses: 'What's that?'; questions involving verbal responses: 'What are you doing?' *Jim's People* covers only one type. Again this is not so much a criticism of the programme, as a pointer towards the complexity of language which no one programme can hope to cover.

Although the manual states that it aims to teach communication skills, it never uses a social communication context in which to teach them. This is particularly relevant to questions in *Jim's People* III and facial expression and posture in *Jim's People* II. An example from the manual will make the approach clear:

This section has been designed to help the learner to understand the use of questions in communication. They will, perhaps, be useful in teaching the type of interrogatory constructions which apply to certain situations. Taking cards 77 [Jim holding a spanner looking at dad] and 78 [Pat asking directions in the street] the teacher could say, 'Show me where Jim is asking what is this for.'

In speaking, the situation is basically the same. 'Presenting the cards separately, the teacher could say, e.g. (77), "Here are Jim and Dad, and Jim's got a spanner in his hand. What is he saying to Dad?"'

The skill being taught is not that of understanding the meaning and function of questions, but the ability to guess at the appropriate question in specific situations. Understanding questions involves learning the appropriate responses to specific types of questions – knowing that a 'where' question has to do with space and direction, and that a 'why' question involves explanation of some sort. Equally, learning to speak questions involves a knowledge of the appropriate form in a certain situation which will elicit the information the child requires. The only way this can be achieved is in a situation in which the child is asked and responds, asks questions, and is responded to.

The manual states that the section on facial expression and posture in *Jim's People* II is designed to teach 'recognition and use of facial expression and postures which denote certain emotions'. Equally important, we felt, was that they should learn to modify their own reactions and emotions to socially acceptable standards. First, recognition is taught as follows: 'The teacher could spread out all or some of the cards on the table and ask the learner, "Show me dad looking pleased" or "Show me where grandma's tired", etc. Or she could ask, "When dad is cross like that, does it make Anne do this or this?" ' Production is taught as follows: 'For example the teacher could present cards 42 and 43, saying, "What is dad doing here?" (Answer: "He's smiling.") "Why is he smiling?" (Answer: "Because he's pleased/happy") etc.' The situation is similar to the question sequences. The child is guessing at the factors obtaining in an imaginary situation, rather than learning the functions of these non-verbal signals in real life discourse.

Jim's People forms a useful set of objectives on which to base a curriculum. All the language skills taught are vital parts of a language curriculum although, as the authors would agree, they are only a foundation. The materials also lend themselves to use for other objectives. A glance at the thirty-two cards in *Jim's People* I suggests their use for a number of areas of vocabulary: colour, clothes, body parts, house and parts of the house, etc. Additionally a number of grammatical skills could be taught – for example, instrumental clauses such as 'with a brush', conjunctions and negatives. Sets II and III also reveal many possibilities not mentioned in the manual.

One of the most striking features of *Jim's People* is that the same basic methods are applied throughout the programme. Choice is one of the crucial elements of the curriculum for ESN(S) children. By choosing between alternatives, the child learns the appropriate response, and by observing the outcomes of the child's choices, the teacher can evaluate precisely what the child is doing. *Jim's People* is very much based on choice. In contrast to *Peabody*, for example, in which responses are very often elicited in isolation, the learner in *Jim's People* has continually to decide between alternatives. Closely tied to this is the built-in assessment and evaluation of progress. For some objectives in *Jim's People* specific tests are suggested before teaching; for some, generally involving more simple constructions, the teaching is organized so that the demands made during teaching serve as assessment and evaluation procedures. There are thus clear indications at each step as to the child's progress and whether he is ready to go on to the next objective. This basis of choice implies that one of the prerequisite skills for *Jim's People* is the ability to chose between stimuli. Although this is obviously a fundamental skill, the teacher concerned discovered that one of her children experienced difficulty at this level.

The total reliance on pictures carries with it two main problems. Pictures are not ideally suited to certain objectives, particularly those concerned with the linguistic representation of spatial concepts. An extreme example of this is in the teaching of the words 'towards' and 'away from'. In this sequence, the pictures show a car driving towards and away from traffic lights. Not only are spatial relationships involved here, but movement is also crucial to the meaning: the child must infer movement from a static picture. We would suggest that different, three dimensional materials are used before using pictures. Other occasions arose when the teacher felt that three-dimensional material would be valuable; specifically, the suggestion arose for a parallel set of figures or puppets of the family. These could prove invaluable as an extension of the programme. They would have the motivating force of the puppets in the *Peabody* kit, and they could be integrated into all the programme objectives as an initial step towards the use of pictures. It would, of course, be easy to find materials in any classroom to meet the requirements of most of the *Jim's People* objectives.

There are, in all, only ninety-six pictures in *Jim's People*. A certain amount of overlap is necessary, and this can cause problems. In the plural sequences in *Jim's People* I, one of the words used is 'door'/'doors', illustrated by the cards depicting individual family members, each standing to the side of a large door. It was found by the teacher that these cards in particular acquired 'names' and it was difficult to draw children's attention to the specific aspect of the picture concerned with the current objective. Because there are relatively few cards for each sequence, individual cards may easily become associated with individual objectives, increasing the chances of rote-learning. The problem is particularly acute in the prepositions and questions sequences in set III, with only one card to illustrate each preposition or question form. A child may quickly learn to distinguish pairs of prepositions in terms of the difference between pictures, rather than learning them as generalized concepts. It would be a mistake to rely on one set of materials to teach any of the objectives.

THE KIT IN USE

Jim's People was used by two teachers during the course of the study, each of whom taught very different children. Teacher A taught a group of five ESN(S) children aged between 5:7 and 13:6 in a school for the ESN(S). This group varied in ability from the production of two-word utterances to the use of grammatical sentences, with EPVT (pre-school version) raw scores varying between 7 and 33. Teacher B taught four children selected from a class of junior age, autistic, largely ESN(S) children. These children ranged in age from 4:2 to 9:2, and in productive language ability from imitating single words to producing grammatical sentences. Because of the children's particular problems, they were taught on an individual basis. Both teachers followed the manual's recommendations and taught ten-minute lessons although, as with other kits, daily lessons proved impossible for practical reasons.

Both teachers and children responded positively to the materials. Teacher A lists her reasons for liking the pictures as follows:

1   They were bright and cheerful and attractive both to myself and to the children.
2   They were clearly defined and lacking in unnecessary detail.
3   The subject matter would be of interest to young ESN(S) children, primarily because they relate to Jim's family and home and experiences encountered.

It was apparent that the children looked forward to the lessons. There were the inevitable times when children were not interested, but these tended to occur immediately following a long break between lessons, and were associated with specific children.

The material is very much teacher-oriented. The cards were not strong enough to be handled by the children except in controlled individual sessions, so there was a danger of loss of interest and involvement. The teachers found it necessary to sort out the cards and order them before the lesson. The cards are identified only by a number on the back and, since they are often face-down, teachers suggested it might be useful to have them identified in writing on the back. There has to be somewhere to lay out up to four 21cm × 25cm cards, so working at a table would often be helpful.

Apart from the positive response to the pictures, both teachers found the flexibility offered by the kit a great advantage. This, of course, is dependent on the teacher's skill in exploiting it, as teacher A commented: 'The complete freedom of usage which the kit contains must presume adaptability, but it should be stressed that the teacher using the kit in this way must be a resourceful and imaginative person ready to take the initiative.' Flexibility in planning the programme across a series of lessons is well illustrated in the contrast between the use and rate of learning adopted by the two teachers. Teacher B progressed slowly with her children with special learning problems, taking nine ten-minute lessons to teach the names 'Jim' and 'Pat' to one child. Comments on this child's progress indicate a steady growth in interest and response. Teacher A described her approach as follows: 'I worked fast, kept my language clear and to the point. Changed cards often. Made many demands which they coped with well.'

This teacher moved through the programme much faster, covering all the sequences in *Jim's People* I between January and May, despite long intervening periods of absence, holiday, etc. Flexibility within lessons was also felt to be possible, so that different children within a group could have different sub-objectives specified for them (see organizational techniques for achieving this in Chapter III). One particular possibility is setting 'understanding' objectives for some children and 'speaking' objectives for others, working on the same basic sequence. Another possibility mentioned by teacher A is helping one child simply to choose one picture in preference to another within a lesson containing more complicated objectives for other children.

As discussed already, much of the *Jim's People* material is a basis for, rather than a complete, language programme. Using the kit made this apparent in a number of ways. First, the limited number of pictures and associated overlap led to problems (for example, in teaching plurals as already mentioned). Secondly, on occasions the teacher found it necessary to elaborate on the lesson, not by expanding to new objectives, but by using different methods and materials. For example, the possessive sequence was extended by teacher A to children's own body parts and clothes. Teacher A expressed a strong desire to extend the programme much further, and to use the kit in the classroom, integrated with other activities: 'so that concepts taught in the ten-minute sessions daily could be reinforced through drama, PE, classroom activities, both structured and free play ... even to choose visits that would coincide with particular concepts.' Examples of spontaneous generalizations occurred, but such occasions were relatively uncommon, and the need for planned generalization is obvious.

Particular learning problems tended to occur with speaking sequences, especially in the plurals section when the '-s' ending proved exceptionally difficult for many children. Teacher A overcame this by adding the phrase 'lots of' in the initial stages. One or two children had articulation difficulties, and although the kit does not, on the face of it, expect any productive language ability before starting on the programme, articulation difficulties may impede the development of the grammatical structures which the kit emphasizes.

It is clear that *Jim's People* is not without its problems and drawbacks; however, appropriate use of its flexibility generally overcomes these.

CONCLUSIONS

Jim's People and *Peabody* represent to a large degree two sides of the same coin. What *Peabody* lacks in programme content it makes up in material, and conversely what *Jim's People* lacks in material, it recovers in content. *Jim's People* covers a number of important language skills with an emphasis on grammar, and has materials specifically designed for teaching these skills. It is probably best seen as a basis around which to structure a language programme, by extending the objectives to other areas of experience and by using a variety of methods. *Jim's People* assumes the ability to interpret two-dimensional picture material, and the ability to select between alternatives, both of which skills may be taught as separate pre-programmes. The programme requires a level of articulatory ability which will not conflict with the speaking sequences. Again pre-programmes could be designed to help with specific difficulties, particularly in co-operation with speech therapists.

Some sequences, particularly the initial naming sections, may not need as refined steps as the manual suggests, but others, particularly the sentence sequences, will need to be broken down further. Built-in assessments will help in deciding the level of operation as will other observations. Prompts may be necessary, such as 'lots of' in the plural sequence, in the initial stages of teaching a new concept. Sequences such as those on comparatives and superlatives and prepositions may need some prerequisite work at a non-verbal level. Finally, implementation of *Jim's People* will require generalization and extension, with the use of other materials and methods to ensure that learning does not become restricted to a limited number of pictures in one situation.

The main advantage of *Jim's People* is undoubtedly its essential simplicity based on an objectives approach to teaching, which provides the teacher with a basis for the assessment, teaching and evaluation essential to a successful language curriculum.

Distar Language I

As the reviews of *Peabody* and *Jim's People* have shown, curriculum packages are an amalgam of materials and programmes. In *Distar* the emphasis is on the programme – every single picture has been devised to teach one aspect of language, and it would be extremely difficult to use the materials for any other purpose. *Distar* is based on the work of Carl Bereiter and Siegfried Engelmann described in their book, *Teaching Disadvantaged Children in the Pre-school*.[5] The *Distar* manual states that the programme 'is not designed for children of a particular age, racial or ethnic group. It is designed to teach basic language concepts to children who, for whatever reason, have not learnt these concepts.' Nevertheless it is quite clear that it is primarily a programme for the disadvantaged pre-school child. But, as with other similar programmes, it potentially offers a great deal to severely mentally handicapped children. Two extracts from Bereiter and Engelmann's book will make the conceptual basis of the kit explicit:

So far as the learning situation is concerned, language is a self-consistent representation of reality that deals in true and false statements.
The disadvantaged child masters a language that is adequate for maintaining social relationships and for meeting his social and material needs, but he does not learn to use language for obtaining and transmitting information, for monitoring his own behaviour, and for carrying on verbal reasoning. In short, he fails to master the cognitive uses of language, which are the uses that are of primary importance in school.

While *Distar* acknowledges the existence of the social uses of language, the emphasis is entirely on the use of language as a tool for logical thought.

Most British teachers' initial reaction to *Distar* is one of alarm at the precise teaching instructions. Virtually everything the teacher has to say and do is written out in the eight books which make up the kit. Each page contains one or more small pictures, and instructions next to each picture as to what the teacher must say and do and the responses expected of the children. A good example of the format of a *Distar* lesson is the first lesson which teaches polar adjectives:

Task 3 *Teaching 'Long'*
Teacher demonstration. Point to each car in order [the page contains four long and two short cars].
Point. 'See this car? This car is long.'
Point. 'This car is not long.'
Point. 'This car is long.' (etc.)
Individual activity. Call on each child. 'Find the car that is long.'
'Find another car that is long.'
Group activity. Point to each car. 'Is this car long?' Accept yes or no answers.

This extract illustrates some of the primary principles on which *Distar* is based. The first phase, *demonstration*, is a minor part of the sequence and only occurs in the first lesson of teaching a new objective. (Compare this with the amount of demonstration and 'teacher talk' in *Peabody*, where many sections of lessons require virtually no response from the children other than attention.) The second phase in the sequence, the *demand*, is crucial. *Distar* is based on the achievement of precise behavioural objectives, and it is through the teacher's demands that these are realized. Every single demand in the programme is spelt out alongside an exact specification of the *response* expected. *Reinforcement* and *correction* is generally written down as an instruction at the beginning of each page: 'Praise the children for correct responses. Correct mistakes immediately.' The teacher's guide provides detailed help on the appropriate use of praise and correction procedures. Finally, *repetition* is used for every objective. Often almost unnoticed changes to the lesson occur, such as changing the positions of otherwise identical pictures. In some lessons the work is repeated using different pictures. The extract above is followed by a lesson on 'long' and 'not long', using dogs and snakes instead of cars. In this way the programme introduces subtle changes in context and thus aims towards generalized language skills, an advantage it has over *Jim's People*, for example. Repetition in a different and often more realistic context occurs with stories at the end of every lesson. These stories are very similar in format to the lessons and involve the children by demanding responses taught in previous and current lessons.

The content reflects the logical bias of the model: thus the first sets of objectives are concerned with teaching identity statements: 'This is an x'; and action statements: 'This x is y-ing'. The identity statements in lessons 1 to 16 (called the pre-programme) shows how *Distar* builds up a skill through a series of sub-objectives. Lesson 2, on object identification, involves the production of five single words using two sets of pictures differing in minor respects from each other. Lesson 3, on teaching full statements, uses some of the same vocabulary and introduces one new word:

Point. 'Everybody, what is this?' 'Boy.'
'Yes, this is a boy. Say the whole thing.'
'This is a boy.' 'Again.'

The same identity statement objective is used in the following seven lessons with many repetitions in each. Lesson 10 turns the statement into a teacher question, 'Is that an x?', and demands the response, 'Yes'; lesson 11 introduces 'No' by requiring the teacher to point, for example, to a tree and ask, 'Is this a car?' New vocabulary is introduced on its own in lesson 14, followed by teaching the negative identity statement, 'This is not a boy', dependent on the earlier teaching of 'No'. Lessons following this which are concerned with identity statements use combinations of all these objectives. Similar sequences of objectives are used throughout the programme to teach polar adjectives, prepositions, pronouns, same and different, plurals, superordinate categories, if . . . then constructions, etc. There are, in all, twenty-two different sets of objectives taught.

The production/comprehension distinction which forms one of the bases of *Jim's People* is recognized by *Distar* for many sets of objectives, but not in all cases, notably not in teaching identity and action statements in the first part of the programme. *Distar* therefore shares with the other kits a very large step at the beginning of the programme. The first thing a child must do is produce five nouns: tree, boy, car, dog and shoe; and three verbs: standing, sitting and running. Following this, in lesson 3, children are required to produce sentences such as 'This is a car' and 'The boy is running'. *Distar* is therefore not a beginning language programme. Because *Distar* contains no pre-linguistic, non-verbal work, a teacher using *Distar* might introduce her own tests of her group's ability to deal with several concepts non-verbally before using the *Distar* lessons. Separate programmes could be devised as a preparation for the kit lessons (see Chapter VI).

Another very noticeable feature is the separation of 'thinking' and 'complete statement' operations. These words, which the guide uses, are perhaps inappropriate since both operations demand productive language, but the essential distinction is between linguistic decision-making at a conceptual or semantic level and placing the outcome of these decisions in a syntactically complete and correct sentence frame. An example from lesson 29 will make this distinction clear:

'Is the pot over?' 'Yes.' (Thinking)
'Yes the pot is over.' 'What is the pot over?'
(Point to the bottle). 'The bottle.' (Thinking)
'Yes the pot is over (wait) . . . the bottle. Say it with me.'
(Point) 'The pot is over (wait, point) the bottle.' (Complete statement).

The two decisions as to the relative position of the pot and what the pot is over are made separately, and then combined into the full statement. In this way, there is less danger that a child's possible lack of syntactic ability will impede his conceptual and semantic development. In fact, the thinking/full statement distinction affords one possible adaptation of the kit for ESN(S) children. It would be possible to omit the complete statement sections of the kit, at least in the first instance, to establish the various concepts. Following this, syntactically incomplete statements might be accepted, such as 'Pot over bottle', and finally the articles and function words could be introduced. However, it is important to emphasize that the final objectives are equally important whether or not the steps towards them are broken down, and that these possible adaptations have not been rigorously field-tested and evaluated. It is up to the individual teacher to try out and amend such ideas on the basis of her own group's progress.

On occasions the constraints of logic take over from the constraints of everyday life. Book C of the programme devotes most of its pages to lessons on parts of various common objects. The trouble arises in dividing up objects – for example, according to the programme a spade has a handle and a scoop, a cup has a handle and a bowl, and a torso has shoulders, a chest and an abdomen. Many other examples of exceedingly rare words, even in an adult's vocabulary, could be given. The programme is concerned here to give the child 'an opportunity to learn that an object can be viewed in more than one way: as an object and as the sum of the parts.' This is a significant skill, but it is questionable whether many of the examples chosen are going to be of great benefit. A more realistic selection of examples, such as a car which has doors, wheels and a roof, could have the advantage that the children would be likely to know these words already and thus the lesson could concentrate on the part/whole relationship.

Similar improbable examples occur in other objectives. The examples used to teach 'If . . . then' constructions show how the programme uses *arbitrary* situations to teach an *abstract* concept. The first lesson on 'If . . . then' uses the sentence, 'If a lady has long hair, she has a black eye', and incidentally points out that this does not imply that other ladies do not have black eyes. There is, of course, nothing in a child's experience which suggests that this connexion is likely, but sentences such as 'If he gets kicked, then he cries' are associated with a reasonably high degree of probability. While it might be an eventual objective to have children dealing with abstract, arbitrary events, teaching might well be more successful if it is initially rooted in the child's non-verbal experience.

Distar does not teach communication; it teaches a variety of language skills but not how to fit these skills into the day-to-day interaction in the world outside the *Distar* lesson. This is a problem it shares with the other kits to a certain extent, but the rigidity of *Distar* makes the problem more acute. In *Distar* lessons children make responses; they do not initiate demands or statements. A child who completes *Distar* should be able to describe a picture of a bottle as 'tall and full', but could he then ask someone in the classroom to pass him 'the tall, full bottle'?

The programme suffers from a number of disadvantages as a result of its precision. A lesson routine is quickly established (the pre-programme is in part intended to acquaint the children with this routine). Breaks therefore do not go unnoticed. The teacher who used *Distar* discovered that any deviation from the daily lessons was likely to lead to problems in re-establishing the routine. But this is a relatively minor difficulty in comparison to the difficulties that may arise for the children in generalizing the skills they have learnt, and for the teacher in adapting or modifying the programme to suit her own needs.

We have already touched on one aspect of generalization, but other more basic types of generalization need attention. Children must first of all learn to associate what they have acquired in lessons with different stimuli in different settings. Next they must learn that the skills they have acquired need not be dependent upon particular stimuli and settings. The most obvious example here is the separation of 'thinking' and 'full statement' operations which characterizes every *Distar* lesson. The manual goes to the extent of discouraging the acceptance of full statements as responses to the 'thinking' stage. Thus children learn to give full statements only in response to, 'Say the whole thing'. The teacher can carry over this cue to her everyday classroom activities, but to what extent will the children expect to be asked to 'Say the whole thing' elsewhere? The teacher using *Distar* confirmed this, since progress in the *Distar* lessons was not always paralleled by progress at other times. The programme manual mentions generalization problems, and gives one or two brief examples of how objectives can be extended, but it does not discuss this in very much detail. It cannot be stressed enough that generalization needs as much care in planning and recording as initial teaching. It should not be seen as something which happens incidentally.

Adaptation is another difficulty caused by the rigidity of *Distar*. Certain simple adaptations are easily made, such as altering Americanisms to suit UK usage, but major changes would be very difficult. Such changes as reducing the size of some of the steps (easily done with *Jim's People*) would require alteration to the point at which the materials in the kit would cease to be appropriate. Equally, *Distar* does not provide the sort of materials which can be adapted for other purposes.

These disadvantages do not imply that *Distar* is completely inflexible. It is highly flexible in different respects. First, more than any other programme, *Distar* has exact built-in assessments, with precise instructions on courses of action depending on the outcome of these short tests. A placement test at the beginning of the programme decides where the group is going to start. Similar tests throughout the programme indicate whether or not the children need to repeat a particular set of lessons. Since different skills are taught in different books, it is also possible to vary the speed at which a group moves through different books without losing the cumulative approach whereby later lessons depend on earlier skills.

The placement test at the start of the programme is also useful for grouping. *Distar* is intended to be used with every child in a normal classroom of twenty-five or more children, in which groups of children of similar ability can be formed and taught at different times. This is the second source of flexibility. Different groups can move at different rates, but more important, the group membership need not be fixed. Since all groups use the same routine, the outcome of assessments can be used to reallocate children to groups more appropriate to their progress and achievements. (The manual stresses the importance of homogeneous groups to the success of the programme.) Of course, this is less of an advantage in one class of ESN(S) children, since only about two groups of five each could be formed, but in the use of the programme across a school, particularly by a 'floating' teacher or language specialist, flexibility in grouping could be of major significance.

The programme makes a useful distinction between group and individual responses. The manual argues that group responses allow economies of time, but they also have the potential advantage of helping co-operation and, in the initial stages of learning a skill, of allowing imitation between children. Individual responses following every group activity allow the teacher to evaluate individual progress. Similar teaching strategies have already been discussed; *Distar*'s particular approach is one useful compromise between the organizational difficulties of individual teaching and the need to monitor individual progress.

Distar has more than one objective per lesson. As a random example, lesson 21 teaches identity statements, the polar adjectives 'full'/'not full' and 'long'/'not long', action statements, parts (recognizing parts of wholes) and ends with a story. (Compare this with the recommendation in *Jim's People* not to teach more than one skill in one lesson.) A mixture of objectives is used to ensure ease of changing between skills, and because of a belief that disadvantaged children must progress more quickly than normal children if they are ever to catch up. This mixing of content had disadvantages used with ESN(S) children. A full lesson usually took thirty to forty minutes to complete, and confusion often arose between objectives. The obvious way round this is to teach one lesson in two daily sessions, which solves the lesson length problem and may help the confusion problem.

The teachers' guide to the programme is outstanding. It contains detailed notes on each set of objectives, discussing why and how it is taught, and particular problems. There is a sizeable section on general principles of teaching, discussing problems such as prompting, reinforcement and pacing. The appendices summarize the specific concepts taught and where they can be found. As with *Jim's People*, the materials are all pictures with one or two exceptions, and the limitations of such material which were discussed in the review of *Jim's People* apply equally to *Distar*. The *Distar* pictures have additional disadvantages. The initial impression they give is somewhat dull and cluttered. All are black and green on a white background, and many are quite small. Some pages have up to ten illustrations which the teacher must draw attention to individually, but others contain only one. Pages with a number of drawings cause problems for children with attention difficulties, and it would be difficult to solve this drawback other than by a complicated series of different shaped masking cards. Every lesson ends with each child being presented with a small line-drawing, a 'Takehome', which acts as a reward for working hard. Each 'Takehome' has a teaching sequence printed on the back which the child must complete to be awarded the picture. 'Takehomes' also provide a useful link between the kit lesson, the rest of the school day and home; parental co-operation can more easily be enlisted if the family can see exactly what the child has been doing.

THE KIT IN USE

The teacher who used *Distar* was a 'floating' teacher with special responsibility for language development throughout the school. The five children in her group were from different classes and came together only for *Distar* lessons. The group was aged between 11:10 and 14:8 at the start of the programme and scored raw scores on the EPVT (pre-school version) of 26 to 36, representing a vocabulary age-range from 4:10 to beyond the test norms. Four of the children were judged to be using grammatical sentences, but one child scored considerably lower at the level of imitating single words, although his EPVT and reception-scale scores were similar to the rest of the group. The scores on the placement test, which ranged from 22 to 26, indicated that the group should start the programme at lesson 25.

The initial reactions not only of this teacher but most others were guardedly positive towards the programme but critical of the materials. One teacher noted these points among others:

I was impressed with the layout generally – its precise aims and objectives were there and one could examine and summarize its success or otherwise following each lesson. The actual pictures provided, on which the lessons were based, were dull and uninteresting. Also rather vague in design, being depicted in green or black. Too much content on one page . . . ideally one picture, one page.

The children generally reacted positively; disruptions tended to be from children who were disruptive in other situations. In the first few lessons the teacher noted:

> The children were interested and on the whole co-operated well, except that they tired towards the end. In the group activities the children enjoyed answering together, a bit too noisily perhaps . . . The children were really fascinated by the 'parts of a match' lesson and coped well.

Comments in the lesson notes of the first few lessons show how experience with the programme changed the teacher's opinion from reservation to enthusiasm:

Lesson 25: 'It will be interesting to see if this specialized work with a small group with much concentrated effort will modify the general behaviour of certain children.'

Lesson 27: 'I do like the way lessons are designed to achieve specific objectives . . . The children are getting the idea and I think the kit may well prove more valuable than at first sight.'

Lesson 29: 'Gradually getting used to precise method of presentation.'

Lesson 39: 'I like the balance of group and individual activity . . . it really helps to decide whether they are learning or chanting meaninglessly in the group.'

The notes on the children's responses show quite clearly the progress that was made, as a group as well as individually. For example, the teacher noted that she felt only one child had not grasped anything of the concept 'over' after four lessons, and in lesson 34 only one child failed the review lesson on parts. By lesson 37, the teacher recorded that: 'The children are beginning to learn that "Say the whole thing" means a complete statement is required from them.' And in the following lesson: 'Follow-up becomes more important now because the children are making whole statements quite readily in *Distar* lessons.' For the final comment on group progress, when the teacher recycled the lesson 25 to 40, partly because of a misuse of the story book on her part, she noted: 'Although the children do not seem to be aware of having done the work before, they have learnt from it and are giving better responses and covering the ground more quickly.'

The teacher who used *Distar* was not a class teacher so she asked for feedback on generalization from other teachers and noted the following comments on one child after lessons 38 and 40:

> Mrs H. asked him the questions on the 'Takehome' I had just given him . . . He did not get one right although he answered correctly for me. She immediately got a book and asked him to tell her about the picture. Instead of his usual labelling response, he did make one or two statements . . . It seems as if only the *Distar* 'Say the whole thing'

will trigger the right response – the children do not carry over the knowledge gained in the lesson to other situations.

Generalization for these children certainly presented a problem, and the teacher's comments emphasized the importance of detailed planning for this aspect of learning.

Many other comments in the teacher's notes reinforced points discussed in the review of *Distar*'s methods. The adaptations she made were those which the programme format allows. Americanisms were replaced by UK equivalents but, more significantly, lessons were cut in half and covered over two sessions, which even then generally took thirty minutes to complete. Occasionally specific sections of lessons in which the teacher felt progress had not been made were repeated. Routines, as suggested, proved vital to this group. Difficulties were always encountered after a few days' break, as shown by the teacher's comment on lesson 36: 'A week since the last lesson. The procedure seems to have lost some of its swing for all of us – a good case for trying to get a lesson in *daily*.'

CONCLUSIONS

Distar represents the current ultimate in precision in curriculum packages, and it is best used for that – with regular daily lessons in small groups moving towards the achievement of highly specific objectives. But it would be a disservice to the programme to suggest that this is all it has to offer. *Distar*'s distinct approach lies not in its content but in the methods; such methods could easily be used in any classroom situation. Many of the *Distar* principles have been advocated in previous chapters. Once a teacher has become acquainted with these basic methods of *Distar* by reading the guide, and practising and using the kit, similar teaching sequences could be used with a wide variety of materials and in many different settings. Obviously the first consideration will be to adopt the same objectives as the kit uses to ensure generalization, but later on, new objectives, perhaps selected from the *Peabody* or any other kit, could be taught.

As with other programmes care must be exercised when implementing the kit to ensure the appropriate selection of children, and in making any necessary adaptations. Selecting the group is made much easier in *Distar* by the built-in placement test, but although this test tells you where children should start in the programme, it does not tell you which children are not suitable at all. Because of the initial jump to quite complex productive language, it is important to ensure that the jump can be made without too much difficulty, and that the children selected will not have articulatory problems which might impede their progress. Adaptations to individual lessons are not easy to make, but the programme format facilitates breaking down the lessons into shorter sections and repeating individual sections. Characteristics such as the arbitrary or uncommon nature of many examples cannot be avoided in the lessons, but separate pre-programmes using the basic *Distar* routines could easily be devised and slotted in at the appropriate stage.

Language and How to Use it – Beginning levels

If *Distar* lies at one extreme of the programme–materials continuum, then *Language and How to Use it*, represents the opposite extreme. This package differs in many respects from the other three reviewed.

The kit contains a large variety of mostly pictorial materials: matching cards; cards which depict a story in sequence; flat geometric shapes in various colours; pictures showing plural objects; pictures to be used with incongruous sentences; picture jigsaw puzzles; pictures with missing parts, etc. In addition, there is a teacher's manual. The kit is intended for 5- to 6-year-old normal children, and as well as being designed to teach language, also contains work on creative drama, pre-reading, pre-writing and number.

The other packages reviewed have to a varying extent been based around a series of lessons to be followed through in sequence, which in turn are based on a particular theoretical standpoint. *Language and How to Use it* has a totally different approach. The introduction to the manual states: 'This book is a handbook for ready reference and a source book for ideas. It is in no sense a curriculum for the kindergarten to be followed in sequence ... Skip round from chapter to chapter, as the children seem ready for various lessons.' The manual and materials are largely independent; many suggestions in the manual involve materials not in the kit, and all the materials could be used without reference to the manual.

Perhaps the feature that distinguishes *Language and How to Use it* most clearly from the other three packages is the absence of any overall approach to language. *Peabody, Jim's People* and *Distar* all base their programmes on certain ideas about the nature of language and its development. *Language and How to Use it* seems to be based more on practice than theory, and the lack of a theoretical basis is noticeable in the contradictions and occasionally strange opinions about language. The introductory section of the manual virtually ignores meaning, and places its emphasis on syntax and pronunciation, to the extent that it suggests classifying children into the following five groups:

1   'Children who readily understand what you say to them and who respond appropriately, expressing ideas in language very like your own.'
2   '... similar to the first group, but these pupils speak with pronunciations characteristic of younger children.'
3   'Children whose pronunciation reflects a foreign language that has been spoken in the home.'
4   'Children who use pronunciation and idioms of a certain section of the country.'
5   'The classroom to which you are assigned may be in a poverty area where there are many disadvantaged children. You may encounter in your group several of the saddest children of all, those who have never heard any language except repressive speech.'

This suggests that the aim is to produce children speaking the standard English of the 'educated person'. (However, the action following this classification is not specified.) The introduction also seems to be interested in the social and emotional aspects of communication: 'Direct your attention first towards communication. Your goal is to understand the idea the child is trying to express, and to frame the idea you want him to get in language he can understand.' Perhaps the contradiction is solved by the following quotation, again from the introduction, which may clarify the theoretical basis of the kit: 'Standard English, at the beginning levels of instruction, is better caught than taught.' It seems that the lesson suggestions and ideas put forward in the manual are based on the following assumption: children come to school at the age of 5 able to express and understand a certain amount, but without the form of language necessary to communicate with 'educated people'.

There are three chapters concerned with **a** large language units, **b** vocabulary and concepts, and **c** syntax. 'Large language units' deals with storytelling and listening to stories, interpreting pictures, and getting information from, and getting used to, books. The introductory suggestions on storytelling would be very difficult to apply directly to ESN(S) children since they are at a highly complex level, but more important they are imprecise. Behavioural objectives associated with this section are defined by the manual as 'specific behaviours you can hope for in most of the children at the conclusion of the activity.' Unfortunately many of these 'objectives' are by no means specific behaviours as the second story-telling objective illustrates: 'Take part in general discussion on the action or characters of a story.' The section concerned with vocabulary and concepts contains work on names, common classroom objects, categories, shape, colour, polar opposites, comparatives and superlatives, etc. It also contains work on 'following directions' and 'orientation in the classroom', strangely placed under this heading. The central idea of this work is revealed in the opening remark suggesting that vocabulary is seen in terms of other vocabulary. According to this viewpoint, words are not defined by the objects or concepts they refer to, but by a verbal definition. Obviously verbal elaboration is an important aspect of language development for normal 5- to 6-year-olds, and many such children may pick up words purely on this basis. However, such a basis needs to be approached with extreme care with ESN(S) children.

Take the lesson concerned with common classroom objects. First, the comprehension/production distinction is made: children have to identify common objects on the basis of instructions such as, 'Come and show me the pencil.' Following this, the children are required to identify the object themselves. This reasonable approach, however, gives way to a variety of demands which diverge from the original objectives: 'What is a pencil for?'; 'What colour is this pencil?'; 'What is it made from?'; 'Which is the sharpened end?'; 'Why is it sharpened?'; 'What is on the other end?'; 'What is the eraser for?' With ESN(S) children, both teacher and children will lose themselves in this flood of demands, and neither will emerge from the lesson knowing exactly what has been achieved. Similar criticisms may be levelled at much of the content of this section. The work on syntax has perhaps more to offer, particularly in the way of ideas which can be modified. Suggestions include work on completing incomplete sentences from memory; asking questions; subject–verb (past tense)–object sentences; tense; location; cause and condition; etc.

One useful approach is the incongruous sentence idea. The teacher holds up a picture of, for example, a cake on a plate and reverses the word order to 'The plate is on the cake.' Children are required to say what is wrong with the description and to put it right. This method could easily be used in many situations in which word order carries vital aspects of meaning. Subject–verb–object sentences, such as 'The boy is riding a bicycle', could be transformed to 'The bicycle is riding the boy.'

Nearly all the content in the manual is taught in a more carefully programmed way by the other three packages. (Of course, this does not apply to the pre-reading, pre-writing and number work which is not our main concern here.) The teaching approach would need extensive adaptation to prove successful with handicapped children – particularly, much smaller steps towards final objectives, and extensive simplification to avoid verbal bombardment. The use of suggestions in the manual would need to be very carefully built in to other language programmes so that the prerequisite

LANGUAGE AND HOW TO USE IT

skills for various activities were already developed. The suggestion to skip from chapter to chapter could not be applied with any certainty to mentally handicapped children.

Several suggestions are made on recording children's language, keeping a notebook, etc. These are rather unsystematic but nevertheless useful, particularly from the perspective of recording free-language samples. As with *Jim's People*, there is a constant danger of 'double standards' in the classroom – that children will use different sorts of language when interacting mainly with the teacher, and in free situations when interaction is more often between children. Recording and analysing free-language samples is important.

The language materials are as follows:

> Two sets of three picture-sequence cards
> 'One picture tells a story' (four picture cards)
> 'Cafeteria' (twelve small cards showing pictures of food)
> Colour matching and naming (fifty coloured discs in ten colours)
> Seventy-two geometric forms in three colours and four shapes
> Learning the plural form of nouns (eight picture cards)
> Map game (simple directions to follow)
> 'That's silly' – word order (six picture cards to be used with nonsense sentences to show the importance of word order)
> 'That's silly' – incongruities (four picture cards to be used with incongruous sentences which children correct)
> Face masks (to be used in dramatizing one of the recorded stories)
> 'Snap' (three packs of thirty-six cards in eighteen matching pairs)
> Picture puzzles (four jigsaw puzzles of increasing complexity)
> Identifying missing parts (six sets of four picture cards for discrimination)
> Pictures with incongruities (four pictures to stimulate visual perception and conversation)
> Learning capital letters, small letters, and numerals (two sets of thirty-six cards)
> Learning safety signs (twelve cards with pictures in two sets)
> Listening activities record (songs, finger games, mood music, story for dramatization, sound discrimination story, etc.)

THE KIT IN USE

Language and How to Use it was used by a 'floating' teacher who withdrew a group of five children aged 7:4 to 9:3 from their classes. The inevitable organizational difficulties involved meant that lessons could not take place daily, so the experience of the kit with this group of children was limited. However, the materials were also used throughout the school for classroom activities and we drew on both experiences here.

Lessons selected from the manual involved story-telling from pictures, identifying common objects, comparative and superlative size adjectives, and identifying and classifying various kinds of foods. In most cases the teacher found the ability level demanded far exceeded this particular group. As a generalization, the teacher concluded:

> It is far more appropriate to children aged 11 to 14 ... it is scaled too low for many of the 14- to 16-year-olds, who usually have a wide experience both at home and school, while their language needs structuring – i.e. the language level is appropriate, the experience level is not.

Even so, the lesson notes reveal that persistent effort in the story-telling lessons resulted in the more able children improving, albeit in a general manner.

Lesson 1: 'Level too high for these children to participate fully.'
Lesson 3: 'Again too high for this type of child, but it seemed to draw some spontaneous response from Peter and Ian.'
Lesson 4: 'They are beginning to understand what is expected of them.'

This progression perhaps shows how persistence with one specific aim in mind can be effective, rather than demonstrating the effectiveness of the kit with this group.

With other lessons, the teacher appreciated the flexibility offered, in that the manual gave general guidelines only. In a later picture-story lesson she noted: 'Pictures are very clear and can be used at a level below that indicated in the handbook providing the lessons are restructured to the needs of the particular children.' For a lesson on 'describing common objects' a similar comment was made: 'Another not too highly structured lesson which gives the teacher provision to scale the expectation level down to suit individual children.' These comments support the view that the kit is best seen as a set of flexible materials which can be adapted to a wide range of ability.

Using language curriculum packages – general issues

FINDING THE RIGHT GROUP OF CHILDREN

When a teacher devises her own programmes she can design them for her particular requirements; thus the curriculum is matched to the children. This desirable situation is reversed when a curriculum package is used. The programme, or at least its basis, is fixed and so the children must be matched to the curriculum. The teacher must be acutely aware of the skills and abilities of her children. It is not enough to be aware only of the abilities in the area with which the package is concerned, since various other abilities – notably perceptual and social skills – need to be considered. The teacher also needs to be aware of those skills which are not taught, but are assumed by the kit. The manuals do not always specify these prerequisites in detail. The rate of progress through the package will be a significant factor in determining the necessary abilities of the group to be taught. Rate of learning is much more in the hands of the teacher, of course, but every package will have a limit to flexibility in this respect determined largely by the size of the incremental steps towards terminal objectives.

Finding children appropriate to a package, therefore, involves a complex matching procedure, and in most cases this match will not be perfect. Children may have some of the necessary skills but not others. One common situation would be a child with the necessary cognitive and language skills but without the more general social skills necessary for working in a group. This matching procedure is further complicated by any adaptations the teacher might make, particularly in the rate of progress, since these adaptations are likely to make the package suitable for different, and possibly more, children. This problem can be tackled in several ways. Continual use and experience of a package will make teachers increasingly aware of the prerequisites, and those children who are likely to be suitable. More important, the matching procedure will be made significantly easier if a package is integrated with the rest of the curriculum and its use planned well in advance. In this situation the children could be prepared for a package with a series of teacher devised programmes to teach the prerequisite skills.

Finding the right children does not always mean the same as finding the right group. Several packages stress the importance of achieving a homogeneous group, particularly those which emphasize group responding. But not only is it important to have children of similar abilities; one also needs children compatible with each other socially. Group structure can have a large influence on children's progress, especially if the group is not as homogeneous in ability as might be wished for. Many instances of children hindering or helping each other were noted throughout teaching the four packages studied; indeed children occasionally reinforced each other for achievement of objectives. Thus the more able children can occasionally take on a teaching role, and this may be one way of involving such children when they might otherwise be waiting for less able children to respond.

ORGANIZATION AND INTEGRATION

There is generally a recommendation in manuals to conduct daily or twice-daily lessons, and curriculum packages used on a regular basis at a distinct period during the day unavoidably lose the flexibility of normal class teaching. There are the obvious and inevitable absences which cause more problems the less flexible the package becomes. The more a package is based on a series of cumulative lessons, the more difficult it becomes to cope with absences. And there are inevitable breaks in the daily routine during term-time.

Special problems arise when packages are used by a 'floating' teacher with direct responsibility for language throughout the school. As the two 'floating' teachers involved in this work discovered, they spent quite long periods deputizing for other members of staff who were off work. If such a situation seems likely, a flexible package not dependent on strict routine might be the appropriate choice. The second major concern for 'floating' teachers will be co-ordination with the class teacher, on whom the 'floater' is dependent for much of the information on assessment and generalization to other situations. It is vital that the class teacher should know exactly what has been taught and how, and that the 'floating' and class teachers discuss the best way of establishing and extending the objectives of the package.

Co-ordination between 'floating' and class teacher is only one aspect of the more general issue — the extent to which a particular package should be integrated into the rest of the curriculum. Our use of the four packages in this study was largely on an ad hoc basis, but it became clear that there were many possibilities for a much more widespread and systematic exploitation of the potential offered by packages. The planned inclusion of a package into the general curriculum means that programmes can be devised specifically to lead children towards the programme in that package. An additional advantage is that a package could form the basis for structured co-ordination between classes, so that a child moving to another class would continue where he left off. The more complicated possibility is the use of more than one package in the school, co-ordinating packages with each other. Sections could be selected out of one kit which might act as prerequisite programmes for a more advanced package. Since there is considerable overlap between packages, the same objective could be taught using different kits, thereby gaining in generalization and flexibility.

Another aspect of integration with the rest of the school curriculum concerns the inevitable question: 'What happens at the end of a programme?' Obviously packages may occasionally lead into each other, but it is more likely that the teacher will be left to devise her own follow-up. The follow-up and other language work that a teacher does will naturally depend on the objectives of the package. No one curriculum package covers everything that needs to be taught at any one stage. A large overlap in objectives between packages illustrates the concentration on certain specific aspects of language development. While most kits teach many of the fundamentals of language, they rarely programme the *use* of the fundamentals.

Even within the cognitive aspects of language, no kit can possibly cover the entire spectrum of skills and abilities. Packages must be selective and their selections are based on the model of language they adopt. The most apparent generalization that may be made is that none of them go low enough down the ability range, particularly with regard to the initial stages of productive language. Only *Jim's People* was designed specifically for mentally handicapped children, and even this package takes a large leap from a limited number of two-word constructions to subject–verb–object sentences.

Conclusions

Although the four packages reviewed present many problems and difficulties, it is the advantages we wish to stress here – disadvantages can generally be overcome. Because no teacher has the time or physical resources at her disposal to devise programmes to teach everything she might wish to teach, she must rely to some extent on commercially available programmes. Undoubtedly the greatest advantage of a structured curriculum package was neatly summed up by one member of the working party: 'They stop you floundering.' While the packages we have reviewed do not cover everything, what they do cover is dealt with in a generally clear and structured way.

But curriculum packages can have benefits beyond the actual programme. Not only do they provide a structure for teaching, they can also act as an invaluable source of objectives and methods to be fitted in to other lessons. Language packages can be used to a varying extent as a set of materials for achieving objectives other than those set out in the kit. Perhaps the best approach to a language curriculum package is to ask: 'What can I get out of it?' The fact that the programme may be unsuitable for one particular group of children does not imply that it has nothing to offer. The materials are an obvious aspect. Less obvious are the benefits to be derived from careful selection from the objectives and methods, and adaptation of these to suit particular needs. If a package is used as such, then adaptations are also likely to be necessary. Careful pacing to suit a particular group of children is vital. The steps towards many objectives may need to be broken down into smaller steps, but it is most important to remember that an adaptation should not imply the abandonment of the objective, simply that it will take longer to get there.

After the children have been selected, the adaptations decided upon, the implementation and organization problems resolved, the final question remains: 'Is it working – are these children learning?' Success does not depend only on the programme but involves a complex interaction between the programme and many other factors. Perhaps the most vital of these is the teacher's enthusiasm. The increased effort a teacher puts into something she supports will have an effect on the children. Success with a programme will also depend partly on general teaching skills. The abilities to reinforce, to shape up specific behaviours and fade out prompts all contribute to a successful outcome.

Finally, it is worth recalling two factors which influence outcome. First, children who do not have the prerequisite skills the programme expects will have much more difficulty achieving objectives. Secondly, we may expect at least an indirect effect on success as a result of the use of programme methods and objectives in generalization programmes outside the kit lessons.

References

1. LLOYD DUNN, J. O. SMITH and KATHRYN HORTON, *Peabody Language Development Kit.* American Guidance Services, Minnesota, 1968. Distributed in the UK by Educational Evaluation Enterprises, Bristol and NFER Publishing, Windsor. BARBARA THOMAS, SHEENA GASKIN and PETER HERRIOT, *Jim's People*. Hart-Davis Educational, St Albans, 1973; rev. edn, 1977 (available from Learning Development Aids, Wisbech, Cambridgeshire). SIEGFRIED ENGELMANN and JEAN OSBORN, *Distar Language.* Science Research Associates, Henley-on-Thames, 1969. MARION MONROE, *Language and How to Use it.* Scott, Foresman, Glenview, Illinois, 1970.

2. C. E. OSGOOD, 'A behaviouristic analysis', in C. E. Osgood (ed.), *Contemporary Approaches to Cognition*. Harvard University Press, Cambridge, Mass., 1957.

3. S. A. KIRK, J. J. MCCARTHY and W. KIRK, *The Illinois Test of Psycho-*

linguistic Ability. University of Illinois Press, Urbana, Illinois, 1968 (distributed by NFER publishing, Windsor).
4. M. A. BRIMER and L. M. DUNN, *English Picture Vocabulary Tests*. Educational Evaluation Enterprises, Bristol, 1962.
5. C. BEREITER and S. ENGELMANN, *Teaching Disadvantaged Children in the Pre-school*. Prentice-Hall, New Jersey, 1966.

X. Postscript

This is a good moment for stock-taking in special education. The world of education has been conducting a 'great debate' about the competence of children and the skills of teachers. A concern with what is taught and with effective methods of teaching is even more evident in special education. The work of the Committee of Enquiry into the Education of Handicapped Children and Young People (chaired by H. M. Warnock), and the publication of the its report, *Special Educational Needs* (HMSO, 1978), have stimulated a fundamental reappraisal of the needs of all handicapped children and engendered much discussion about how these needs can be met.

But mentally handicapped children are still comparative strangers to the world of special education. Few would deny that the transfer of responsibility from health to education authorities in 1971 has been a marked success. Of course, much more might have been achieved if local education authorities had not had to cope with a severe resources crisis, not to mention the problems presented by the reorganization of local government and the transformation of teacher education and teacher supply. We mention these wider issues of policies and services partly because they are again being debated in the context of the Warnock Report, and partly because they have, somewhat paradoxically, distracted attention from the central question of special education – that of curriculum development.

Our concern in this report has been with what teachers do, and with ways in which teachers can develop their professional skills. Although we have looked at only one small corner of the curriculum, we hope that the work will be seen to have relevance beyond the language and communication curriculum, and beyond the field of mental handicap.

The Warnock Report rightly emphasizes that progress in special education depends on teachers who are appropriately trained and equipped with a range of specialist qualifications. Only a small minority of teachers working with handicapped children have a specialist qualification at the present time; the proportion is lowest in the ESN(S) field. Because the government has not yet responded to the Warnock Report, it is impossible to know how much financial support will be available to implement the crucial recommendations concerning teacher training. But many local education authorities are already considering the implications of the report, particularly for in-service training, and are beginning to collaborate with universities and colleges in mounting courses to meet the wide range of need.

We hope that the work reported here will provide both encouragement and source material for teachers on in-service and other training courses. In a sense, this book can be read as a report of an in-service course in curriculum development. A small number of teachers worked with us intensively, but this work affected all the nineteen schools in which they taught, as well as schools which took part in other ways.

Instead of attempting to summarize our conclusions, we would like to make a number of specific suggestions for action that might be taken by teachers, psychologists and advisers concerned with ESN(S) children, trying to set these in the context of current developments in special education, and particularly the need for in-service education.

Teacher workshops

First, we want to convey our enthusiasm about teacher workshops. These can take a variety of forms, but essentially consist of a small group of teachers meeting regularly to devise and try out teaching methods. The teachers can all be from the same school, or they can come together from different schools, meeting either in a school or a teachers' centre. It may be useful to recruit one or two non-teachers – for example, a speech therapist, psychologist, adviser or someone from a college of education or university department with knowledge of the particular topic the teachers wish to study. This will depend on the objectives established by the teachers themselves. The important point is that teachers should discuss their own priorities and come to their own decisions about what they want to do.

They may wish to conduct a language survey similar to the project's described in Chapter I. They may prefer to develop other instruments, as ours are rather crude; on the other hand, by using our questions they would be able to compare findings. For example, they may wish to compare their data with ours in respect of the language abilities of school-leavers, and to make comparisons within their own school between one set of leavers and another. Above all, the value of a language survey of this kind is to pinpoint those areas where curriculum development is most urgently needed, and to relate the findings of the survey to subsequent teaching programmes. Teachers may prefer to begin by sharing existing methods and skills with one another, or by holding regular sessions within their own schools to discuss their problems in teaching particular children – a kind of case conference, probably without the child, but illustrated with tape recordings and possibly even video recordings.

Teacher workshops involving teachers from different schools are a direct and practical way of developing professional skills. We hope that each education authority will consider their potential for in-service training and for decreasing the sense of isolation experienced by many teachers in special schools. We would encourage teachers to set up such workshops, and to ask their authorities not only to support them but also to provide them with basic recording equipment if at all possible. Ideally, a small portable video-recording system should be available. Such systems are now increasingly in use in teachers' centres and also in the larger schools. They can be used for a wide variety of purposes; teachers can record and discuss their own teaching and that of their (consenting) colleagues; one-to-one and group-teaching situations can be recorded for later replay and group discussions; they can be used for detailed observation of a child or group of children; or monitoring the response to particular kinds of teaching. They can also be used to record programmes 'off air' for later replay at leisure (bearing in mind the terms of educational broadcasting recording concessions and retention rights). We look forward to the day when VTR becomes standard equipment in teachers' centres and at least in the larger schools. We believe it will pay for itself many times over in leading to the development of professional skills.

Teacher workshops represent a welcome change from the more traditional type of in-service training in which groups of teachers are brought together by an adviser or a college to listen passively to lectures by 'experts', but with little opportunity either for discussion or for critical evaluation of the relevance of the suggestions to the classroom. The advantage of the workshop approach lies in its continuing commitment. Teachers go back to their classrooms to try out ideas and methods that have been suggested, and then report progress at later workshop meetings. Furthermore, teachers provide a working link between the workshop and colleagues in their own schools. A related advantage of workshops is that they make it easier for teachers to put into practice in their own classrooms ideas which have arisen in group discussions. The more traditional type of course, whether it is a one-year advanced diploma course or a series of study days, rarely carries with it any kind of commitment that the teacher returning from such a course will have the opportunity or even the encouragement to try to put into practice what he has learned. But with the workshop, the initial involvement of heads and other colleagues makes it more likely that such opportunities will be made available, or can be created. The commitment by the school is continued and increased as a result of the workshop itself and the development of ideas arising from it.

Sharing knowledge and skills

We have been struck in the course of our work by the lack of opportunities for teachers from different schools to share ideas and experiences. Many teachers have never visited other special schools, or set foot in an Adult Training Centre, residential home or hospital for mentally handicapped children, nor are they given opportunities to experience at first hand the day-to-day work of people such as Adult Training Centre instructors, further education staff, careers officers for the handicapped, nurses, residential or field social workers.

Teachers' workshops represent one approach to the problem of professional isolation, but much can be achieved by a systematic attempt to provide opportunities for teachers not only to visit both special and ordinary schools but also to work in them for brief periods. Staff exchanges for specified periods are admittedly not easy to organize and are not always convenient either for the school or for the staff, but they do provide opportunities for the broadening of experience and skills. We hope, therefore, that individual heads, as well as advisers and others with responsibility for professional development, will plan to provide such opportunities for teachers and collaborate with their colleagues in other departments, including health, social services and employment.[1]

Where the teaching of language and communication skills is concerned, teachers in special schools have much in common with their colleagues working in other kinds of school. Indeed, those who are having to think systematically about the teaching of English as a first language have a valuable contribution to make to the work of colleagues in special and ordinary schools who work with children experiencing different kinds of difficulties in developing language skills. The Bullock Report[2] rightly emphasized the many ways in which language skills lie at the very foundations of literacy; it also stressed the importance of receptive language skills and of helping children to listen and to learn to listen. Teachers working with mentally handicapped children are faced every day with the task of helping each child to lay these foundations and to build on them. Other children who have made a start in learning their own language still experience difficulties in using language as a tool for communicating and for thinking and will benefit from attempts to help them to become more skilled in doing so. Here again, teachers of ESN(S) children have much to contribute but also much to learn from opportunities to share knowledge and skills with colleagues teaching children with a range of difficulties in language and learning. These opportunities need to be created and developed.

Schools as resource centres

The Warnock Report suggests that a number of special schools should in future function as resource centres, providing skilled help and specialist materials not only to their colleagues in other special schools but also to teachers working with handicapped children in ordinary schools.

Because the teaching of language and communication skills represents common ground to teachers working in a variety of settings, ESN(S) schools have a special contribution to make in developing specialist methods and materials of interest to staff working not only with ESN(S) children but also children with other kinds of language difficulties. For example, there is a growing interest in methods of teaching non-verbal communication and a need for teachers to be able to study the various methods and manuals now becoming available.[3] Similarly, the commercially produced language kits reviewed in Chapter IX are already being supplemented by new materials, some of which are specifically designed for ESN(S) children (for example, Bill Gillham's *First Words* (Allen and Unwin, 1979), and the increasing range of handbooks in the Human Horizons Series published by Souvenir Press). Resource centres can provide not merely a library where teachers can inspect the range of materials now becoming available, but also opportunities to discuss these with colleagues who have used them. There should also be videotapes of the materials being used with children. In the same way, developmental and assessment charts should be available.

Special education outside schools

The Warnock Report envisages that a number of teachers will in future be working outside special schools, sometimes as advisory teachers, sometimes as peripatetic teachers working in the homes of children who are still too young to attend school. For example, a number of teachers are working as 'home visitors' with very young handicapped children and their families long before the child is due to go to any school. In some parts of the country, teachers are informed whenever a handicapped child is born or identified, and begin to work with the child in his own home. No matter how young the child, we believe that the approach outlined in this report is of some relevance, though the content of what is to be taught to a very young child will require modification in the light of particular needs. An educational approach in the broadest sense is relevant for a handicapped baby just a few weeks of age; some educators are now working with newborn Down's Syndrome infants, assessing levels of development, and planning with the family to help the baby to achieve the next steps in his development, however small.

We hope that teachers will be able to find ways of seeing very young children, and that every student training to teach mentally handicapped children has the opportunity of developing a close relationship with a handicapped infant and his family. Special education can begin at birth, and teachers can play a leading part in providing educational help even for a very small baby.

At the other end of the age-range, teachers in ESN(S) schools have much to contribute to the further education development of children and young people who have left school. For example, they can act as advisers and consultants to further education colleges and Adult Training Centres and to staff of hospitals and hostels. Because language and communication skills are critical for successful adaptation to the community, young people will continue to need skilled and systematic help to enable them to develop their abilities and to use them to the full in the whole range of living and learning situations that they will encounter outside school. Indeed, we now need to extend to adults some of the methods of teaching language skills that are showing good results with children. Unfortunately, very little published material is available on the teaching of language and communication skills to adults. Although the principles are perhaps not fundamentally different, both content and method would need to be adapted to the needs of older people. Furthermore, adults are particularly vulnerable to under-stimulation and to the absence of demand, which in turn leads to levels of performance which are much lower than they need be. We suspect that under-estimation by staff and under-functioning by the mentally handicapped may be even more common with adults than with children.

Partnership with parents

Many schools have now moved beyond the traditional 'parents' evening' and 'open day' type of contact with families, and established a real educational partnership with parents in which parent and teacher each learn from the other. These have taken a wide variety of forms, depending on local needs and circumstances. Some parent–teacher workshops have been held weekly over a period of six or more months; parents are helped to make a detailed assessment of their own child, using one of the existing developmental charts or checklists. In this way, parents and teachers can compare notes, and discuss reasons for possible discrepancies between behaviours shown by the child in one setting and not in another. Above all, such joint assessments should lead to common teaching objectives, and to full partnership in achieving them. It makes sense, for example, for parents and teachers to be fully in partnership not only in the teaching of self-care skills but also in respect of language and communication objectives. These can also be achieved by a variety of other means – by home–school diaries, exchange of detailed records, regular visits of teachers to the home, toy libraries, and so on.

The need for a detailed working partnership between parents and teachers is particularly important where language and communication abilities are concerned. These lie at the heart of the relationship between parent and child. Parents naturally want to do everything they can to foster the child's ability to communicate but are often uncertain about how to start. But partnership with parents has to be on a basis of equality. In practice, this means that language objectives need to be developed jointly rather than unilaterally, and on the basis of an assessment of the child's existing skills and needs, as shown both at home and in school. Teachers should be given opportunities to observe the child's communication abilities at home, just as parents need opportunities to observe their child's response to teaching and to other children.

We now see language and communication as one expression of the child's social development and as growing out of his relationship with other people. Communication begins when a baby first smiles at his mother and language is much more than speech. It includes listening to sounds and words and responding non-verbally as well as verbally to what others say. We are also beginning to understand how language is rooted in certain kinds of play, such as symbolic play when a child makes one thing stand for or represent another. This is why no programme of language teaching can get very far without studying the child at home or without a true partnership with parents and families.

References

1. For fuller discussion of in-service education in a post-Warnock context see P. MITTLER, 'Developing staff skills', *Apex,* **3**, 1978, 20–2, and *People not Patients: Problems and Policies in Mental Handicap*, Methuen, 1979.

2. Department of Education and Science, *A Language for Life*, Report of Committee of Inquiry appointed by Secretary of State for Education and Science under Chairmanship of Sir Alan Bullock. (Bullock Report). HMSO, 1975.
3. C. C. KIERNAN, R. JORDAN and C. SAUNDERS, *Starting Off.* Souvenir Press, 1978. T. TEBBS (ed.), *Ways and Means: a Resource Book of Aids, Methods, Materials and Systems for Use with the Language Retarded Child*. Globe Education, Basingstoke, for Somerset Education Committee, 1978.

Appendices

Contents

A The language survey – additional tables 341
B Words used in vocabulary survey 346
C Example of tests for play and pastime vocabulary 349
D Examples of detailed programmes for teaching body-part and spatial vocabulary 350
E Communication Behaviour Rating Schedule 372
F Pictures used in the questioning procedure tests 380
G Categories for analysis of utterances in questioning procedure tests 385
H Questioning – skeleton procedure form 388

Appendices

Appendix A The language survey – additional tables

Table A1 Number and percentage in major diagnostic categories

Category	Number	Percentage
Down's Syndrome	393	34·3
Cerebral Palsy	104	9·1
Hydrocephaly	65	5·7
Microcephaly	54	4·7
Autism/psychosis	28	2·5
Phenylketonuria	14	1·2
Other categories	26	2·3
Undefined diagnosis	461	40·2
Total	1145	100·0
Missing information	236	–

Table A2 Distribution of social class

Social class	Number	Percentage	Percentage of national population
I	38	8·0	3·6
II	87	18·3	16·1
III	251	52·8	49·5
IV	72	15·2	22·6
V	27	5·7	8·2
Total	475	100·0	100·0
Missing information	906	–	–

Table A3 Distribution of English Picture Vocabulary Test (EPVT) (pre-school version) raw score and vocabulary age

Score	Frequency	%	Equivalent vocabulary age	Score	Frequency	%	Equivalent vocabulary age
0	6	0·7	⎫	26	12	1·3	4:10
1	37	4·1		27	17	1·9	4:11
2	39	4·3		28	19	2·1	
3	49	5·4		29	14	1·5	
4	42	4·6	Pre-norm	30	8	0·9	
5	39	4·3		31	21	2·3	
6	41	4·5		32	25	2·8	
7	20	2·2	⎭	33	24	2·6	Post-norm
8	25	2·8	3:0	34	20	2·2	
9	26	2·9	3:1	35	33	3·6	
10	23	2·5	3:2	36	26	2·9	
11	35	3·9	3:4	37	21	2·3	
12	18	2·0	3:6	38	21	2·3	
13	25	2·8	3:7	39	18	2·0	
14	22	2·4	3:8	40	21	2·3	
15	14	1·5	3:9				
16	12	1·3	3:11	Total	908	100·1[a]	
17	15	1·7	4:0				
18	20	2·2	4:1	Untestable	386		
19	10	1·1	4:2	Missing	87		
20	18	2·0	4:3				
21	10	1·1	4:4	[a] Error due to rounding			
22	12	1·3	4:5				
23	14	1·5	4:7				
24	15	1·7	4:8				
25	21	2·3	4:9				

Table A4 Averages and standard deviations on the production and reception scales and EPVT (raw score), for males and females

	Male			Female		
Scale	Average	Standard deviation	Number	Average	Standard deviation	Number
Production scale	7.9	4.0	803	8.5	4.0	547*
Reception scale	6.2	3.5	805	6.5	3.4	548
EPVT raw score	18.6	12.9	527	16.9	12.4	380*

* $p < 0.05$

Table A5 Averages and standard deviations for Down's Syndrome and non-Down's Syndrome children

	Down's Syndrome			Non-Down's Syndrome		
Scale	Average	Standard deviation	Number	Average	Standard deviation	Number
Production scale	8.8	3.3	387	7.8	4.3	741***
Reception scale	6.6	3.0	389	6.1	3.7	742*
EPVT raw score	15.8	12.1	310	19.3	12.8	451***

* $p < 0.05$, *** $p < 0.001$

Table A6 Averages and standard deviations on the production and reception scales and EPVT (raw score), for children living at home, in hospital, in hostels and in other forms of care

	Production scale			Reception scale			EPVT raw score		
Type of care	Average	Standard deviation	Number	Average	Standard deviation	Number	Average	Standard deviation	Number
At home	8.5	3.9	1050	6.6	3.4	1051	18.4	12.7	755
In hospitals	5.9	4.0	142	3.9	2.9	142	13.5	13.0	50
In hostels	8.4	4.0	54	6.7	3.3	55	20.9	11.0	37
Other forms	8.1	4.0	47	6.5	3.6	47	15.9	10.0	30
	***			***			*		

* $p < 0.05$, *** $p < 0.001$

Table A7 Averages and standard deviations on the production and reception scale and EPVT (raw score), for children living with both natural parents and those living with others

	Both parents			Others		
Scale	Average	Standard deviation	Number	Average	Standard deviation	Number
Production scale	8.5	3.9	834	8.2	4.0	147
Reception scale	6.7	3.4	935	6.7	3.6	147
EPVT raw score	18.4	12.5	672	18.9	13.9	104

Table A8 Averages and standard deviations on the production and reception scales and EPVT (raw score), for children with 0–5+ siblings

Number of siblings	Production scale			Reception scale			EPVT (raw score)		
	Average	Standard deviation	Number	Average	Standard deviation	Number	Average	Standard deviation	Number
0	6·9	4·2	120	5·4	3·3	120	18·0	13·7	67
1	8·1	3·9	316	6·2	3·5	316	17·6	12·5	204
2	7·9	4·1	342	6·2	3·5	343	18·4	12·4	215
3	8·6	3·8	183	6·7	3·3	182	19·2	13·5	133
4	9·3	3·6	112	7·5	3·3	114	19·1	13·0	91
5+	8·9	3·4	105	6·7	3·4	105	17·7	12·0	80
	***			***					

*** p < 0·001

Table A9 Averages and standard deviations on the production and reception scales and EPVT (raw score), for children in social classes I–V

Social class	Production scale			Reception scale			EPVT (raw score)		
	Average	Standard deviation	Number	Average	Standard deviation	Number	Average	Standard deviation	Number
I	8·6	3·6	37	6·4	3·0	37	18·2	11·7	27
II	8·4	3·6	87	6·6	3·4	87	20·0	11·9	55
III	8·4	4·1	250	6·7	3·6	250	20·7	11·9	177
IV	8·5	4·0	71	6·2	3·4	70	18·0	12·9	44
V	8·5	3·2	27	6·0	3·0	27	19·6	12·1	19

Appendix B Words used in vocabulary survey

Body parts

Arm	Tongue	Neck	Hair
Bottom	Shoulders	Tummy	Head
Knees	Lips	Mouth	Thumb
Nails	Legs	Feet	Nose
Hand	Chest	Eyes	Eyebrows
Elbow	Teeth	Cheeks	Fingers
Back	Ears	Chin	
Toes	Face	Eyelashes	

Colour

Orange	Blue	Yellow	Red
Green	White	Black	

Spatial

On	Between	Front	Short
Thin	Far away	Middle	Out
Under	Long	Fat	Back
Empty	Bottom	Top	High
Behind	Inside	Near	Full
Side	Corner	Low	In
Down	Little	Off	Big

Movement

Run	Stop	Walk	Jump
Hop	Skip	Quickly	Bend down
Sideways	Turn round	Stamp	Slowly
Fall down	Backwards	Sit down	Lie down
Roll over	Crawl	Curl up	Stretch
Clap	Stand up	Kick	

Personal objects

Soap	Toilet roll	Nail brush	Face cloth

Sponge   Brush   Comb   Tooth paste
Towel   Tooth brush

Objects of the home

Table cloth	Plate	Tray	Sugar bowl
Bottle	Plug	Pan	Knife
Tea towel	Telephone	Mirror	Iron
Fork	Cup	Kettle	Teapot
Dish cloth	Radio	Lid	Saucer
Glass	Spoon	Milk jug	Pillow
Beaker			

Clothes

Cap	Anorak	Tie	Shirt
Trousers	Shoes	Underpants	Socks
Hat	Coat	Dress	Cardigan
Skirt	Blouse	Tights	Vest

Transport

Car	Train	Boat	Lorry
Bus	Bike	Van	

General environment

Building	Traffic lights	Church	Telephone box
Dog	Zebra crossing	Wall	
Shop	Cat	Post box	

People

Baby	Girl	Footballer	Dustbinman
Man	Nurse	Boy	
Policeman	Fireman	Lady	

House

Door	Garden	Fence	Chimney

APPENDIX B

Garage   Roof   Window   Tree
Gate   Flower   Kitchen   Upstairs
Bathroom   Living room   Bedroom   Downstairs

Furniture

Sink   Table   Fridge   Chair
Cooker   Television   Settee   Lamp
Armchair   Carpet   Sideboard   Mat
Bed   Wardrobe   Dressing table Cot
Chest of drawers Bath   Toilet   Wash basin

Appendix C Example of tests for play and pastime vocabulary

Games and sports test for a senior group

Items required: individual pictures of a game of football, a game of cricket, a game of tennis, a running race and people swimming. Place the pictures of swimming, football, and cricket in front of the child. As each item is tested, replace with a new item as directed.

		tick if correct
	'Show me cricket'	☐
Replace with tennis	'Show me swimming'	☐
Replace with running	'Show me football'	☐
Replace with cricket	'Show me running'	☐
Replace with swimming	'Show me tennis'	☐

Toy test for nursery-age group

Items required (using real toys): small teddy bear, ball, car, doll, gun. Place ball, car and doll on the table in front of the child. As each item is tested, replace it with a new item as directed. When making the verbal request the teacher is to hold hand out in order to receive object.

		tick if correct
	'Give me the doll'	☐
Replace with gun	'Give me the car'	☐
Replace with teddy	'Give me the gun'	☐
Replace with car	'Give me the ball'	☐
Replace with doll	'Give me the teddy'	☐

If the child is unable to respond to 'Give me', this should be taught using familiar objects different from the ones used in the test.

Appendix D Examples of detailed programmes for teaching body-part and spatial vocabulary

Body-part vocabulary – eyebrows

AIM

For the child to understand and produce the word 'eyebrows'.

OBJECTIVE 1

In response to an instruction such as 'You do it', the child will imitate the teacher by appropriately pointing to the eyebrows of self, another child, a doll and a picture of a face.

OBJECTIVE 2

In response to an instruction such as 'Show me . . . eyebrows' (child's own, another child's, doll's, or person in picture), the child will point appropriately.

OBJECTIVE 3

In response to a question such as 'What are these?', the child will spontaneously say, 'Eyebrows'.

REINFORCEMENT

The teacher will select appropriate reinforcement for the child. Reinforcement must be immediate.

CRITERIA FOR SUCCESS

For each programme the teacher will specify an appropriate criterion for success which may involve:
1   Number of successful responses to be obtained by the child. For example, in the first session for one objective the child may be required to make two successful responses out of five. In the last session for the same objective the child may be required to make ten out of ten successful responses.

BODY-PART AND SPATIAL VOCABULARY PROGRAMMES

2 Approximations from the child which will be regarded as successful – for example, specification as to whether the child is required to touch the body part concerned, whether or not the child is required to point to both parts in the case of eyebrows, shoulders, feet, etc.
3 Specification as to length of time between the instruction and the response.
4 Specification as to clarity or approximation of the child's productive language.

ORGANIZATION

For each programme the teacher will specify the organization involved, such as:
1 Where the programme will take place
2 Position of child/children
3 Time of day.

OBJECTIVE 1

In response to an instruction such as 'You do it', the child will imitate the teacher by appropriately pointing to the eyebrows of self, another child, a doll and a picture of a face.

Objective 1A

The child will allow his hand to be held to touch own and teacher's eyebrows.

Criterion for success and organization

To be specified by the teacher.

Method

a The teacher sits facing the child.
b The teacher touches own then child's eyebrows. (Ensure that the child is looking.)
c The teacher holds the child's dominant hand and with it touches the child's eyebrows. Reinforce.
d The teacher holds the child's dominant hand and with it touches own eyebrows. Reinforce.

Objective 1B

The child will allow his hand to be held to touch another child's eyebrows.

Criterion for success and organization

To be specified by the teacher.

Method

a   Teacher sits next to child.
b   Another child stands in front of child.
c   Teacher points to other child's eyebrows.
d   Teacher holds child's dominant hand and with it touches other child's eyebrows. Reinforce.

Objective 1C

The child will allow his hand to be held to point to the eyebrows of a doll.

Criterion for success and organization

To be specified by the teacher.

Method

a   The teacher sits next to the child.
b   The doll is placed in front of the child.
c   The teacher points to the doll's eyebrows.
d   The teacher holds the child's dominant hand and with it points to the doll's eyebrows. Reinforce.

Objective 1D

The child will allow his hands to be held to point to the eyebrows of a face on a picture.

Criterion for success and organization

To be specified by the teacher.

Method
a   The teacher sits next to the child.
b   Picture of face is placed in front of child.
c   Teacher points to eyebrows on picture.
d   Teacher holds child's dominant hand and with it touches the eyebrows. Reinforce.

Objective 1E

The child will put eyebrow pieces into face jigsaw.

Criterion for success and organization

To be specified by the teacher.

Method
a   Teacher sits at table next to child.
b   Jigsaw is placed in front of child.
c   Teacher touches eyebrows on face jigsaw.
d   Teacher holds child's dominant hand and with it touches eyebrows on face jigsaw. Reinforce.
e   Teacher takes eyebrow pieces out – child handles them.
f   Teacher puts eyebrow pieces in jigsaw.
g   Teacher instructs child to 'Take them out'. Reinforce.
h   Teacher instructs child to 'Put them in'. Reinforce.

Objective 1F

The child will imitate the teacher by touching his own eyebrows.

Criterion for success and organization

To be specified by the teacher.

Method
a   Teacher sits facing child.
b   Teacher touches own eyebrows.

c   Child to imitate. Reinforce.
(Teacher may need to prompt the child to touch his own eyebrows.)

Objective 1G

The child will imitate the teacher by touching the eyebrows of another child.

Criterion for success and organization

To be specified by the teacher.

Method

a   Teacher sits next to child.
b   Other child stands in front of child.
c   Teacher touches eyebrows of the other child.
d   Child to imitate. Reinforce.
(Teacher may need to prompt the child to point to the other child's eyebrows.)

Objective 1H

The child will imitate the teacher by touching the doll's eyebrows.

Criterion for success and organization

To be specified by the teacher.

Method

a   Teacher sits next to child.
b   Doll is placed in front of child.
c   Teacher touches the doll's eyebrows.
Child to imitate. Reinforce.
(Teacher may need to prompt the child to touch the doll's eyebrows.)

Objective 1I

The child will imitate the teacher by touching the eyebrows of the face on the picture.

Criterion for success and organization

To be specified by the teacher.

Method

a Teacher sits next to child.
b Picture is placed in front of child.
c Teacher touches eyebrows on face.
d Child to imitate. Reinforce.
(Teacher may need to prompt the child to touch the eyebrows.)

Objective 1J

In response to an instruction such as 'You do it', the child will imitate the teacher by appropriately pointing to the eyebrows of self, another child, a doll and a picture of a face.

Criterion for success and organization

To be specified by the teacher.

Method

a Teacher points to own eyebrows then says, 'You do it'. Reinforce.
b Child to touch his own eyebrows.
(Same for another child, a doll and a picture of a face.)

OBJECTIVE 2

In response to an instruction such as 'Show me (child's own, another child's, doll's, or person's in picture) eyebrows', the child will point appropriately.

Objective 2A

In response to 'Eyebrows – show me', the child will imitate the teacher by appropriately touching his own eyebrows.

Criterion for success and organization

To be specified by the teacher.

Method

a Teacher points to own eyebrows and says, 'Eyebrows'.
b Teacher instructs child, 'Eyebrows – show me'. Reinforce.
(Child to touch his own eyebrows.)

Objective 2B

In response to 'Eyebrows – show me', the child will imitate the teacher by appropriately touching the eyebrows of another child.

Criterion for success and organization

To be specified by the teacher.

Method

As for objective 2A

Objective 2C

In response to 'Eyebrows – show me', the child will imitate the teacher by appropriately touching the eyebrows of a doll.

Criterion for success and organization

To be specified by the teacher.

Method

As for objective 2A

Objective 2D

In response to 'Eyebrows – show me', the child will imitate the teacher by appropriately touching the eyebrows of a picture of a face.

Criterion for success and organization

To be specified by the teacher.

Method

As for objective 2A

Objective 2E

In response to an instruction such as 'Show me your eyebrows', the child will point automatically.

Criterion for success and organization

To be specified by the teacher.

Method

a   Teacher instructs child to 'Show me your eyebrows'. Reinforce.
b   Teacher instructs child to 'Touch your eyebrows'. Reinforce.
c   Teacher instructs child to 'Point to your eyebrows'. Reinforce.
d   Teacher asks the child, 'Where are your eyebrows?' Reinforce.
(Teacher may need to prompt the child at first.)

Objective 2F

In response to 'Show me (name of another child) eyebrows', the child will point appropriately.

Criterion for success and organization

To be specified by the teacher.

Method

As for objective 2E.

Objective 2G

In response to 'Show me the doll's eyebrows', the child will point appropriately.

Criterion for success and organization

To be specified by the teacher.

Method

As for objective 2E.

Objective 2H

In response to 'Show me his eyebrows', the child will point appropriately to the picture.

Criterion for success and organization

To be specified by the teacher.

Method

As for objective 2E.

Generalization

The teacher may also involve the child in drawing eyebrows on face, colouring eyebrows in on drawing, putting eyebrows in a jigsaw.

OBJECTIVE 3

In response to a question such as 'What are these?', the child will spontaneously say, 'Eyebrows'.

Objective 3A

In response to an instruction such as 'You say it', the child will imitate the word 'eyebrows'.

Criterion for success and organization

To be specified by the teacher.

Method

a Teacher points to own eyebrows and says, 'Eyebrows'.
b Teacher instructs the child, 'You say it'.
c Reinforce the child when he says it. If the child fails, say, 'Eyebrows – tell me'. Reinforce, then repeat from **a**.
(Same with another child, doll and picture of a face.)

Objective 3B

In response to a question such as 'What are these?', the child will spontaneously say, 'Eyebrows'.

Criterion for success and organization

To be specified by the teacher.

Method

a Teacher points to own eyebrows and asks, 'What are these?'
b Reinforce the child when he says 'Eyebrows'. If the child fails, the teacher says, 'Eyebrows – tell me'. Reinforce, then repeat from **a**.
(Same with another child, doll and picture of a face.)

Spatial vocabulary – 'near to' and 'far away from'

AIM

To develop an understanding of the concepts 'near to' and 'far away from' in such a way that the children will be able to move self, place objects and discriminate between objects in positions 'near to' or 'far away from'.

OBJECTIVE 1

The child will, on verbal request, move to parts of the room, hall, playground which are 'near to' or 'far away from' teacher.

OBJECTIVE 2

The child will, on verbal request, place objects in positions which, in the context of the activity, are 'near to' or 'far away from': a specified person; a specified object.

OBJECTIVE 3

The child will, on verbal request, discriminate between standard objects placed 'near to' or 'far away from' self.

ORGANIZATION

To be specified by teacher throughout.

OBJECTIVE 1

The child will, on verbal request, move to parts of the room, hall, playground which are 'near to' or 'far away from' teacher.

Objective 1A

The child will, on verbal request from teacher, move to a position 'near to' the teacher.

Method

a Children all seated near to each other.
b Teacher moves away three to four metres and sits down.
c Say, '(Name) you come and sit here'. (Prompt if necessary.)
d When child does so, reward and say, 'You sit down *near* me'. (Give some stress to the word 'near'.)
e Repeat procedure with rest of children ensuring reward for correct performance.

Criterion for success

Consistent and successful completion of behaviour.

BODY-PART AND SPATIAL VOCABULARY PROGRAMMES

Generalization

Ensure that this type of sequence is used in a number of different situations both in and out of the classroom, hall, playground, etc.

Objective 1B

The child will, on verbal request from classroom assistant, move and take up a position 'near to' her. (It is *essential* that, with the exception of the occasional prompts on initial learning, the teacher avoids any gestures or non-verbal cues during the teaching.)

Method

a Children all seated by teacher (as at end of objective 1A).
b Classroom assistant three to four metres away.
c Assistant says, '(Name) you come and sit here'. (Prompt if necessary.) As child does so, reward and say, 'You sit down *near to me*'. (Emphasize 'near to me'.)

Generalization

As for objective 1A.

Objective 1C

The child will, on verbal request from teacher, move to a position 'near to' her.

Method

a Children all seated in group with assistant.
b Teacher three to four metres away.
c Teacher says, '(Name) come and sit *near to* me'. (Prompt if necessary.) Reward and say, 'That's right, sit *near to* me'. (Emphasize 'near'.)
d Repeat with other children ensuring reward for successful performance.

Criterion for success

Consistent and successful completion of behaviour.

Generalization

As for objective 1A.

Demonstration

The teacher/assistant will, on verbal request from teacher/assistant, move to a position 'far away from' and then return to a 'near to' position.

- **a** The teacher, assistant and children are seated together at one side of the room.
- **b** Teacher to children, 'I'm going to ask Mrs/Miss (name) to go far away from us.' To assistant, 'Mrs/Miss (name), would you go far away from us?')
- **c** Assistant to teacher, 'Yes, I'm going far away from you.' She does so and sits down.
- **d** Teacher to children, 'I'm going to ask Mrs/Miss (name) to sit near to us.' Teacher to assistant, 'Mrs/Miss (name), would you sit near to us?'
- **e** Assistant, 'Yes, I'll sit near to you.' Moves back to group saying, 'Now I'm near to you.'
- **f** Repeat sequence **a** to **e**, this time with the teacher moving 'far away from'.

Objective 1D

The child will, on verbal request from teacher/assistant, move to a position 'far away from' and then return to a 'near to' position.

Method

- **a** Teacher, assistant and children all seated together at one side of the room.
- **b** Teacher to children, 'This time I'm going to ask (child's name) to go far away from us.' Turns to child in question, '(Name) you go far away from us and sit down.' (Assistant prompts if necessary.) Reward if successful.
- **c** Teacher to group, '(Name) is far away from us.'
- **d** Teacher to child, '(Name) now sit near to us.' Reward when child returns and sits down.
- **e** Continue with other children.

BODY-PART AND SPATIAL VOCABULARY PROGRAMMES

f Continue till all children will respond correctly.
g It is important that different locations in the room are selected as being 'far away from'. It may be useful, therefore, if the teacher and classroom assistant take occasional turns at going 'far away from' so as to widen the possible number of locations.

Criterion for success

Consistent and successful completion of behaviour.

Generalization

As for objective 1A. Once the children are responding consistently, further practice can be given through objective 2.

OBJECTIVE 2

The child will, on verbal request, place objects in positions which, in the context of the activity, are 'near to' or 'far away from': a specified person; a specified object.

Objective 2A

The child will, on verbal request from teacher/assistant take a standard object, (teddy, ball, doll, brick, toy car) and place it 'far away from' or 'near to' the teacher.

Materials

Standard objects – teddy bear, ball, doll, brick, toy car.

Method
a Teacher, assistant and children seated in group to one side of the room.
b Teacher to one child in group, '(Name) you take teddy far away from us.' (Prompt if necessary by assistant.)
c Reward for successful completion.
d Teacher to same child, '(Name) bring teddy near to me.' (Prompt by assistant if necessary.)
e Reward if successful.

f Select a second child and repeat sequence with different standard object.
g Repeat same procedure with remaining children varying the standard objects.
h Give further practice as necessary with standard objects in random order.

Criterion for success

Consistent and successful completion of behaviour.

Generalization

As for objective 1A.

Objective 2B

As objective 2A but objects to be placed 'near to' assistant on returning to group.

Objective 2C

As objective 2A but objects to be placed 'near to' a specified child in the group on return.

Objective 2D

The child will, on verbal request, take a standard object, place it 'far away from' and return it 'near to' a specified object.

Materials

Standard objects. A chair is placed close to the teacher and group of children.

Method

Procedure as for objectives 2A, 2B and 2C, but teacher suggests on returning to group that the child places the standard object 'near to' the chair. Gesture may be used to indicate which chair.

Objective 2E

As objective 2D but table substituted for chair. The table may be placed somewhat further away from the group than the chair was. (Perhaps a metre or so further.)

Criterion for success

Consistent and successful completion of behaviour.

Generalization

As for objective 1A. It is also possible to vary the demands made of the child on returning to the group by requesting that the standard object be placed 'near to' a variety of prominent classroom features (for example, door, window), so long as these are relatively close to the group.

At this point in the programme the children should, without hesitation, move to, or take objects to, positions which are 'near to' or 'far away from'. If this is the case it should be possible to move on to objective 3 which involves discriminating between objects placed 'near to' or 'far away from' the child.

OBJECTIVE 3

The child will, on verbal request, discriminate between standard objects placed 'near to' or 'far away from' self.

Materials

Pairs of standard objects (teddy, ball, doll, brick, toy car).

Method

a Teacher and children seated together.
b Assistant, with children watching, places one teddy about a metre from the group, and the other at the far end of the room but still on view.
c The teacher says to child, '(Name) give/bring me the teddy near to us.' (Prompt if necessary.)
d Reward if successful.
e Assistant places both teddy bears out of sight.

f   With children again watching, assitant places two balls, one 'near to' the group, the other in a 'far away from' location (different from last object).
g   Repeat sequence with different child, this time selecting 'ball far away from us'.
h   Assistant removes the two balls.
i   Repeat procedure with remaining children using different standard objects, varying position of target object alternately.

Criterion for success

Consistent and successful completion of behaviour.

Generalization

Further practice with a wide range of non-standard objects. It should now be possible to transfer the child's skill with these two concepts to 'table-top' situations – for example, toy farmyard and animals: 'Put the pig near to the fence'; 'Put the pig far away from the other pigs', etc.

Spatial vocabulary – 'on top' and 'underneath' (production)

AIM

To develop the child's productive language ability relating to selected spatial vocabulary.

OBJECTIVE 1

The child will say, 'On top' or 'Underneath' when asked where a specified standard object has been placed by the teacher in relation to a box.

OBJECTIVE 2

The child will say, 'On top of the box' or 'Underneath the box' when asked to state the position of a standard object in relation to a box.

OBJECTIVE 3

The child will say, 'On top of the (object)' or 'Underneath the (object)' when asked to state the position of a standard object in relation to another object.

OBJECTIVE 4

The child will say, 'On top of the (object)' or 'Underneath the (object)' when asked to state the position of a classroom object in relation to another suitable object.

OBJECTIVE 1

The child will say 'On top' or 'Underneath' when asked where a specified standard object has been placed by the teacher in relation to a box.

Materials

Standard objects – doll, ball, toy car, teddy bear. In addition, a sealed cardboard box approximately 38cm × 30cm × 15cm supported on several books will be necessary.

Objective 1A

The child will say 'On top' when asked where a standard object (on top of the box) has been placed. (Cardboard box, supported off the table by books to enable objects to be placed underneath easily, is placed on the table. Standard objects within teacher's reach but out of children's vision.)

Method

a   With children watching, teacher picks up toy car, places it on top of the box and turns to one of the children saying, 'Where's the car?'
b   If child successful – that is, says 'On top' – reward.
c   If fails, prompt, teacher saying, 'On top, tell me.'
    With correct response, reward.
d   Teacher replaces car with doll on top of the box.
e   Teacher to second child, 'Where's the doll?'
f   If successful – that is, says 'On top' – reward.
g   If fails, prompt, teacher says, 'On top, tell me.'
    With correct response, reward.
h   Repeat sequence with all children, changing the standard object each time.

Criterion for success

Consistent successful production of 'on top' by each child.

Generalization

Practice and variety can be given by use of a selection of non-standard objects.

Objective 1B

The child will say 'Underneath' when asked where a standard object (underneath the box) has been placed.

Method

Procedure as for objective 1A, but object placed underneath box on each occasion.

Criterion for success

Consistent successful production of 'underneath' by each child.

Generalization

As for objective 1A.

Objective 1C

The child will say 'On top' or 'Underneath' when asked where a standard object has been placed.

Method

Procedure as for objectives 1A and 1B, but presenting the 'on top' and 'underneath' positions alternately.

Criterion for success

Consistent and successful production of 'on top' and 'underneath' by each child.

Generalization

As for objective 1A.

OBJECTIVE 2

The child will say 'On top of the box' or 'Underneath the box' when asked to state the position of a standard object in relation to a box.

Materials

As for objective 1.

Objective 2A

The child will say, 'On top of the box' when asked to state the position of a standard object in relation to a box.

Method

Procedure similar to objective 1A except that the demand for the child is changed to 'On top of the box'.

Criterion for success

Consistent and successful production of 'On top of the box'.

Generalization

As for objective 1A. At a particular stage of development a child may not be able to produce the full response. The teacher may well, therefore, adopt a different objective – for example, 'On top box'.

Objective 2B

The child will say, 'Underneath the box' when asked to state the position of a standard object in relation to a box.

Method

Procedure similar to objective 1B except that the demand for the child is changed to 'Underneath the box'.

Criterion for success

Consistent and successful production of 'Underneath the box'.

Generalization

As for objectives 1A and 2A.

Objective 2C

The child will say, 'On top of the box' or 'Underneath the box' when asked to state the position of a standard object in relation to a box.

Method

Procedure similar to objectives 2A and 2B, except that the position of the standard object will be alternated between the two positions.

Criterion for success

Consistent and successful production of 'On top of the box' or 'Underneath the box'.

Generalization

As for objective 1A.

OBJECTIVE 3

The child will say 'On top of the (object)' or 'Underneath the (object)' when asked to state the position of a standard object in relation to another object.

Method

Procedure similar to objective 2C except that the standard objects will be placed 'on top of' or 'underneath' a variety of classroom objects and furniture.

Criterion for success

Consistent and successful production of 'On top of the (object)' or 'Underneath the (object)'.

Generalization

As for objective 1A.

OBJECTIVE 4

The child will say, 'On top of the (object)' or 'Underneath the (object)' when asked to state the position of a classroom object in relation to another similar object.

Method

Procedure as for objective 3, but any suitable classroom object substituted for standard objects.

Criterion for success

The child should at this point produce consistent and successful responses of the kind required.

Generalization

Opportunities should be offered to the child to extend the range of objects used. It may be that the use of two-dimensional materials – drawings and other materials – could be introduced to extend the programme. For example: a picture of object 'on top of/underneath' concrete object; pictures of objects 'on top of/underneath', etc.

Appendix E   Communication Behaviour Rating Schedule

Many children lack expressive language but still use primitive forms of communication; in a number of cases these children may have a high level of understanding. The main problem is to discover the exact meaning of their communication. Unfortunately, teachers have to rely on direct observations. Together with a group of teachers, therefore, we set out to draw up an organized format through which the questions raised about these children's communication might be answered.

From observations of a large number of children attending special-care classes, we became aware of the vast range of behaviours they used in order to communicate. All the children were functioning at below the one-word level and therefore relied on a non-verbal means of communication. We listed these behaviours under a number of headings, to form a concise checklist – the Communication Behaviour Rating Schedule. We also provided a space at the side of each behaviour for the teacher to try to evaluate the meaning of the communication.

The Communication Behaviour Rating Schedule (CBRS) was used by members of one of the project working parties to assess all children in their schools who were at or below the one-word imitation level. From the results it was evident that even the most limited children were able to communicate by a range of behaviours. By using the schedule, and picking up those communication behaviours and meanings expressed by the children, the teachers were sensitized to a system of observation. For each individual they were answering the questions: 'Does the child communicate?'; 'What does the child communicate?'; 'How does the child communicate?' The last question is perhaps the most important. It is crucial to know how a teacher interprets the behaviour the child is offering. The teacher needs to be as objective as possible with subjective material. More adequate interpretations of the child's meanings inevitably lead to feedback for the child, and in this way the child learns that his behaviour can produce an effect on the environment. In turn, through these interactions, meanings can develop.

The Communication Behaviour Rating Schedule is not a development scale nor is it based on a developmental model; it cannot therefore be used on its own as a guide for teaching. It is not a test, neither is it a procedure for gathering data on a collection of children. It is basically a checklist which can be used in conjunction with specific observations as a means of looking in detail at an individual child's non-verbal communication. It includes a wide range of possible behaviours a child might use to communicate. There will undoubtedly be children who display behaviours which are not included;

incorporated under each section is a space for new behaviours to be added.

The success of the CBRS has been due to the way it has sensitized teachers to recognize that, despite gross mental and physical handicaps, children are able to communicate, even if on a limited basis. Recognizing this may help teachers change their attitudes and expectations of their children. In Chapter VII, the study of Ian and Susan shows that before their teachers were involved with this teaching programme they were only partly recognizing the communication abilities of the children, and were making demands on them which were at a level well below their capabilities. This is evident in the tremendous change in both children in only a short space of time. Yet Ian was 15 years old and Susan 13 before they acquired even their basic systems of communication. Each child had been grossly under-functioning over a long period of time.

COMMUNICATION BEHAVIOUR RATING SCHEDULE

NAME OF CHILD ....

DATE OF BIRTH ....

NAME OF TEACHER ....

DATE OF TESTING ....

CLASS ....

SCHOOL ....

Please indicate the child's ability to see, hear and walk by ticking the most appropriate of the statements in each of the following sections. If the child has any artificial aids (e.g. glasses, calipers), please assess the child when the aid is in use:

(a) No difficulty in seeing ☐
     Some difficulty in seeing ☐
     Great difficulty in seeing ☐
     No usable vision ☐

(b) No difficulty in hearing ☐
     Some difficulty in hearing ☐
     Great difficulty in hearing ☐
     No usable hearing ☐

(c) No difficulty in walking ☐
Limps or walks unsteadily ☐
Walks when assisted ☐
Unable to walk, but crawls, uses wheelchair, etc. ☐
Unable to walk, bed-/crib-bound ☐

Please indicate the degree and type of spasticity, if any, by ticking the most appropriate of the statements listed below:

(a) Not spastic ☐
Mildly spastic ☐
Moderately spastic ☐
Severely spastic ☐
(b) Diplegia ☐
Hemiplegia ☐
Paraplegia ☐
Quadriplegia ☐
Triplegia ☐
Other (please specify) ....

HANDS AND ARMS

What is the child communicating?

Pull ☐	
Push ☐	
Point ☐	
Shake ☐	
Throw (objects) ☐	
Stiffen arms ☐	
Relax arms ☐	
Pinch	
(a) self ☐	
(b) children ☐	
(c) adults ☐	
Scratch	
(a) self ☐	
(b) children ☐	
(c) adults ☐	
Pull hair of	
(a) self ☐	
(b) children ☐	
(c) adults ☐	
Hit	
(a) self ☐	
(b) children ☐	
(c) adults ☐	

Push
  (a) children
  (b) adults

Additional behaviours

BODY

What is the child communicating?

Stiffen
Relax
Wriggle
Jerk
Rock

Additional behaviours

LEGS AND FEET

Kick
Stiffen legs
Relax legs
Stamp

Additional behaviours

VOICE

What is the child communicating?

- Squeal
- Cry
- Shout
- Hum
- Scream
- Click tongue
- Sucking sound
- Imitates other children's
  - *(a)* distress sounds
  - *(b)* sounds of pleasure
- Produces sounds
  - *(a)* to music
  - *(b)* to own voice (on tape recorder)
  - *(c)* for attention
  - *(d)* when given attention
  - *(e)* when refusing object
  - *(f)* when chastized

Additional behaviours

HANDS

What is the child communicating?

- Pushes objects away
- Pushes people away
- Takes adult's hands
- Allows objects to be taken from self
- Covers ears/eyes with hands
- Holds out arms to be picked up
- Places adult's hands on activity/object
- Takes objects from
  - *(a)* child
  - *(b)* adult

Holds objects out to child/adult ☐
Puts arms round
   (a) child ☐
   (b) adult ☐
Objects to hands being held ☐
Objects to hands being messy ☐
Pulls at clothes/body for toilet ☐

Additional behaviours

FACE AND HEAD

What is the child communicating?

Smile ☐
Suck ☐
Mouth object ☐
Shake head ☐
Turn head ☐
Smile in response to
   (a) known person ☐
   (b) unknown person ☐
Turn face away in response to
   (a) known person ☐
   (b) unknown person ☐
Cover face in response to
   (a) known person ☐
   (b) unknown person ☐
Bang head on floor/wall ☐
Bang head with hands ☐
Bite
   (a) self ☐
   (b) children ☐
   (c) adults ☐
Kiss
   (a) self ☐
   (b) children ☐
   (c) adults ☐

Eye contact with
  (a) objects
  (b) people

Additional behaviours

LEGS AND BODY

What is the child communicating?

Moves towards
  (a) object
  (b) child
  (c) adult
Follows
  (a) object
  (b) child
  (c) adult

Additional behaviours

SOCIAL

What is the child communicating?

Shares objects/activities
Chases in fun/games
  (a) children
  (b) adults
Torments other children
Avoids bullies

Shows preference for
  (a) children
  (b) women
  (c) men
Reacts when restricted

Additional behaviours

Appendix F Pictures used in the questioning procedure tests

Picture A

Details of picture A

d

e

f

Details of picture A

g

h

i

Picture B

Picture C

Appendix G   Categories for analysis of utterances in questioning procedure tests

The child's language from the pre- and post-tests is transcribed into utterances.

A   Relevance of the utterance

How much of what the child says is relevant to the picture?

1   Those utterances which directly provide information about the picture, for example:
'The girl's swinging'
'Ball'
2   Those utterances which refer to the picture but offer no information about the content, for example:
'Look at that'
'What is this?'
3   Those utterances which offer no information about the picture but which refer to the testing situation, for example:
'No more'
'Finished now'
0   Those utterances which are irrelevant to either the picture or the testing situation, for example:
'It's making a noise' (lawnmower outside)
'I'm tired'
'Brick on the floor'.

Example

	Relevance
Someone playing football	1
And a girl picking flowers	1
There	2
A boy climbing on a tree	1
A girl wheeling a barrow	1
Pram	1
That	2
A boy playing with a gun	1
And swinging	1
No	3

In the text, categories 1 and 2 are termed relevant; others are termed irrelevant.

B Repetition of utterances

How often does the child repeat utterances? Is the content repeated or is more information added? (We are not specifically concerned with repetition of syntactic form; the content is important.)

1 Those utterances which are the initial reference to an aspect or aspects of the picture, or which add new information which has not been given previously
2 Those utterances which are not the initial reference to an element of the picture that is duplicated, for example: types of people
3 Those utterances which are exact repetitions (except for those which apply to **B**2)
0 Those utterances which are not applicable, that is those scored as **A**2, **A**3 or **A**0.

Example

	Repetition
Someone playing football	1
And a girl picking flowers	1
There	0
A boy climbing on a tree	1
A girl wheeling a barrow	1
Pram	1
That	0
A boy playing with a gun	1
And swinging	1
No	0

In the text, categories 1 and 2 are termed non-repetitions; categories 3 and 0 are termed repetitions.

C Content of utterances

The complexity of a response was scored in terms of the number of unique elements it contained. The picture used in this study primarily contained people, their actions and objects. Responses which contained information about only one of these groups were scored 1; responses which contained a combination of two of these groups were scored 2; and responses which

ANALYSIS OF UTTERANCES IN QUESTIONING TESTS

combined all three groups were scored 3. Utterances coded under relevance as 2, 3 or 0 are coded 0 here. The following pre-test gives examples of the relevance and content categories.

	Group
Apple tree	1
Boy, dog	2
Girl riding a horse	3
Boy fishing	2
Cow	1
Pussy cat	1
Holding a bottle	2
Squirrel	1
Walk	1

Appendix H Questioning – skeleton procedure form

NAME ....

AGE ....

SCHOOL ....

(*Title of picture*)

Transcript of talk about picture ... before programme.
'Tell me about this picture.'

Transcript of talk about picture ... after programme.
'Tell me about this picture.'

SEQUENCE 1
Subject/object – possessor/possessed

Objective: when presented with the picture the child will say:
....
Criterion: will accept: ....
- (i) Teacher says, 'Tell me about this picture.'
  If criterion is reached, praise and move to next picture.
- (ii) Teacher says, 'Who's this?'
  If correct response is given, praise and say, 'Tell me.'
  If fails, model and repeat.
- (iii) Teacher says, 'Who's that?'
  If correct response is given, praise and say, 'Tell me.'
  If fails, model and repeat.
- (iv) Teacher says, 'Tell me about this picture.'
  If criterion is reached, praise and move to next picture.
- (v) Teacher says, 'Who's got a baby?'
  If correct response is given, praise and say, 'Tell me.'
  If fails, model and repeat.
- (vi) Teacher says, 'What's the lady got?'
  If correct response is given, praise and say, 'Tell me.'
  If fails, model and repeat.

(vii) Teacher says, 'Tell me about this picture.'
   If criterion is reached, praise and move to next picture.
   If fails, repeat *(v)* and *(vi)*.

Sequence 2
Subject/verb

Objective: when presented with the picture the child will say:
....
Criterion: will accept: ....
(i) Teacher says, 'Tell me about this picture.'
   If criterion is reached, praise and move on to next picture.
(ii) Teacher says, 'Who's this?'
   If correct response is given, praise and say, 'Tell me.'
   If fails, model and repeat.
(iii) Teacher says, 'What's the lady doing?'
   If correct response is given, praise and say, 'Tell me.'
   If fails, model and repeat.
(iv) Teacher says, 'Tell me about this picture.'
   If the criterion is reached, praise and move to next picture.
   If fails, model and repeat from *(ii)*.

Sequence 3
Subject plural/verb/object (single/plural)

Objective: when presented with the picture the child will say:
....
Criterion: will accept ....
(i) Teacher says 'Tell me about this picture.'
   If criterion is reached, praise and move on to next picture.
(ii) Teacher says 'Who are they?'
   If correct response is given, praise and say 'Tell me.'
   If fails, model and repeat.
(iii) Teacher says 'How many ladies?'
   If correct response is given, praise and say 'Tell me.'
   If fails, model and repeat.
(iv) Teacher says 'What are the two ladies doing?'
   If correct response is given, praise and say 'Tell me.'
   If fails, model and repeat.
(v) Teacher says 'What are the two ladies carrying?'
   If correct response is given, praise and say 'Tell me.'

If fails, model and repeat.
(vi) Teacher says 'Tell me about this picture.'
If criterion is reached, praise and move on to next picture.
If the child fails, model and repeat from *(ii)*.

Project team, consultative committee and participating schools

Project team

Peter Mittler	*Director*
Ken Leeming	*Deputy director*
Judith Coupe	*Research associates*
Will Swann	
Ann Rawson	*Project secretary*

Consultative committee

M. Gore (Chairman)	Headmaster, Melland School, Manchester
N. L. Dodsworth	Headmaster, Bramcote Hills County Secondary Boys School, Nottinghamshire
Miss J. Davenport	Headmistress, Woodhouse Park Infants School, Manchester
A. Gorton	Assistant Education Officer, Cheshire
M. Griffiths	HM Inspectorate of Schools
R. Heavey	Headmaster, Mill House Day Special ESN(S) School, Newton le Willows, Lancashire
Miss W. M. Johnson	Headmistress, Woodhouse Park J. M. School, Manchester
C. Mowforth	Remedial teacher, Berkshire
R. Nicholls	Headmaster, Tesdale Special School, **Abingdon**, Oxfordshire
T. Pascoe	Headmaster, Borocourt Hospital School, Berkshire

392 SCHOOLS PARTICIPATING IN PROJECT

Miss M. Skeffington   Lecturer in the Education of Handicapped Children, University of Manchester

Dr Joan Tough   Director, Schools Council Communication Skills Project, Institute of Education, Leeds University

K. G. Tucker   Assistant Director of Education, Liverpool

M. Ward   Schools Council Research Team

Schools participating in the project

Beacon School, Stockport
The Birches, Manchester 14
Brentwood School, Altrincham
Cranage Hall Hospital School, Holmes Chapel, Nr Crewe
Crosby Meadow, Manchester 9
Crow Wood Hospital School, Widnes
Dee Banks School, Chester
Dee Side School, Neston
Glengarth Nursery School, Marple, Stockport
Hartford Hill School, Northwich
Leacroft, Manchester 10
Loushers Lane School, Warrington
Moss Brooke School, Widnes
Park Lane School, Macclesfield
Pictor School, Sale
Piper Hill School, Manchester 23
Springfield School, Crewe
Stanley School, Eastham, Wirral
Werneth Grange School, Hyde

In addition to the nineteen project schools, the project team worked closely with a number of other schools for particular purposes:

Delyn School, Mold, Clywd
Glanaffron School, Queensferry, Dee Side, Clwyd
The Laurels, Chadderton, Oldham
Mill House School, Newton le Willows, Lancashire
Powys School, Gwersyllt, Wrexham, Clwyd
Tirionfa School, Rhuddlan, Clwyd
Ysgol y Graig, Llysfaen, Old Colwyn, Clywd

Index

ability, language
  age and 23–8, 37, 342
  in identifiable groups 29–33
  survey of 9–39, 238, 240–1, 253, 331, 341–5; as assessment technique 33–4; conclusions 35–8; as curriculum planning guide 34–5; questionnaires 9–10, 17–18; results 18–22, 34–5; structure and scope 9–12, 16
  tests of, following questioning procedure 285–9
  use of, in classroom 268, 270, 274, 285
  see also vocabulary tests
abstractions 135, 145, 210–11, 214, 222
academic aims
  in curricula 56–7
  parents' 52, 53
  teachers' 48
action, teaching 120, 123–4, 130–1, 136, 142, 149
adjectives 135, 139, 304
Adult Training Centres 56, 60, 335
aesthetic autonomy 64
AINSWORTH, M.D.S. 114
age of children 11, 68
age and language ability 23–8, 37, 342
aim, autonomy as ultimate 61
aims
  curriculum 40–66, 56–8, 159
  of education 45, 55; techniques for achieving 2

objectives and 69–70, 225–7, 230–4 242–3, 255–7, 350–71
  parents' 50–4; and teachers', compared 47
  teachers' 40, 42–50
ARGYLE, M. *The Psychology of Interpersonal Behaviour* 15
articulation
  assessment of 15, 17–18, 20–1, 36
  problems 159, 223–4, 309–10
ASHTON, P. 44, 55, 61
assessment 71, 99, 164
  definition of 42
  techniques 33–4, 106, 164–6
  see also ability, language; reception of language; production of language; vocabulary tests
assistants, classroom 78
attributes 135–6, 143
AUSTIN, J. L. *How To Do Things With Words* 108
autistic children 308
autonomy, development of 58–9, 61–4

babies, teaching xii, 334–5
Bayley Mental and Motor Scales 27
behaviour, child's
  categories of 81–2
  definition 44
  factors in 176–7
  modification 67–8, 77, 255–7, 263
  observation 167–72, 174–6, 186
  problems 140, 165–6, 186, 188–92, 194–7, 253, 255

394 INDEX

behavioural communication 239–41, 254–5
see also Communication Behaviour Rating Schedule
behavioural principles and methods 2
BELL, S. M. 114
BEREITER, C., and ENGELMANN, S. *Teaching Disadvantaged Children in the Pre-school* 311
BLANK, MARION *Teaching Learning in the Preschool* 85, 99–100, 224
BLOOM, LOIS 95
body parts
  teaching 88–9, 90–1, 350–66
  vocabulary 207, 235; tests 207–9, 346
BOWERMAN, M. 95
BRICKER, W. A. and D. D. 98
British Abilities Scale 33
BROWN, R. 95
BRUNER, J. S. 97
Bullock Report (*A Language for Life*) 333

CARR, J. 27
cause and effect, teaching 155
checklists 164, 202, 372
Cheshire Education Committee 3
child-centred approach 71
choice 63–4, 306
CHOMSKY, NOAM *Syntactic Structures* 94
CLARK, EVE 96
class
  size of 11, 36
  see also social class
classroom
  observation 173–95
  organization 43, 77–80
  using questions in 268–91
clauses 146–54
cleft palate 253–4, 264
clothing vocabulary test 205, 207, 216, 347
cognition 95–6, 103–5, 295
colour 211, 216–17, 297, 346

combination of words 133–5, 142–4, 151–4
commissive language 109
Committee of Enquiry into the Education of Handicapped Children and Young People 330
communication 93, 100–3
  lack of means of 60, 265–6
  as parents' aim 53
  pre-linguistic 96–8, 104, 111–14
  as teachers' aim 50
  see also language; medium of communication; non-verbal communication
Communication Behaviour Rating Schedule 240–1, 254, 266, 372–9
comprehension see meaning; production of language; reception of language; vocabulary tests
concepts, teaching 222, 224, 236, 252, 297
conjunctions 154
context 95, 96
control demands 83–4
controlling others, language for 114, 156–7
Coupe, Judith 5
criterion-referenced tests 213
CROMER, R. 95–6
crying 114
CUNNINGHAM, C. C. 27
curriculum
  aims 40–66, 56–7, 159
  content 9, 93–163; one-word level, at or below 110–31; one-to-two-word level 131–44; extending meaning and structure 144–59
  educational approaches 99–100
  framework 93–4, 95, 110, 160
  objectives, need for xii
  organization and integration 326–7
  packages 55, 60, 99, 144, 292–329, 334; content 294–5, 301–3, 307, 309–10, 311–12, 315–17,

320–3; evaluation of 292–3, 297–302, 304–7, 309–10, 313–15, 317, 319–20, 322–3, 327–8; matching children to 324–6; methods 295–300, 303–7, 311, 316, 319; in use 300–1, 308–10, 317–19, 323–4; *see also specific packages*
planning, guide to 34–5
production of language in 60, 111–21, 154

decision-making, education for 57
declarations 109
demand–response–feedback sequence 86, 87, 90
demands
  child's 111, 114–15, 138, 242, 245, 265
  teacher's 81–4, 312
  see also questions
demonstration 362
demonstration/prompt 82, 86, 87, 299
Department of Education and Science 45
development
  age and 23
  language, research trends in 94–7
  planning for 2–3
developmental charts 213, 215
diagnostic categories 341
dialogue, teacher–child 99, 113, 226–227, 229–34
  see also demands; questions; response
directive language 108–9
disappearance, teaching 117, 130–1, 142–3, 148
discovery, language for 157–8
Distar Language 99, 298, 300, 310–19
DONALDSON, MARGARET 96
Down's Syndrome children 12, 27, 30, 36, 37, 98, 186, 240, 335, 343

Educating Mentally Handicapped Children (DES) 99

education
  aims of 2, 45, 55
  further 335
  life-related 48, 55, 57
  special 330–1, 334
emotional aims
  in curriculum 57–8
  parents' 52
  teachers' 48–9
emotions, language for 158
ENGELMANN, S. 311
English Picture Vocabulary Test (EPVT) 10, 14, 16, 22, 37, 203, 211, 213, 216, 236
  age and 26–8, 37, 342
  Down's Syndrome and 30, 343
  family background and care 30–2, 344–5
  scoring 17–22, 32
  sex differences 29, 343
  social class and 32–3, 345
environment
  general, vocabulary test on 205–6, 347
  normal 100
existence, teaching 118
expressive language 108–9, 123, 158, 236
  lack of 238–9, 265–6
expressive meaning 111–14
eyebrows 350–9

facial expression 159, 306, 377–8
family background and language ability 30–2, 38, 344–5
feedback following response 82, 85–90, 302–3
'floating' teachers 326
forms of language 108–9, 130, 137–8
FRANKENA, W. K. 63
functional approach to non-verbal concepts 139
functional generalization 142, 222–3
functions of language 108–9, 155–9
further education 335

games in teaching 148–50, 153, 180, 349
generalization 109, 140–2, 221–3, 228, 245, 248, 358, 361, 365–6, 368–9
  in language kits 284–5, 287, 309–10, 312, 315, 319
gestural imitation 127–8
gestures 102, 106–7, 238
  assessment of 15, 21–2, 36–7
  vocalization with 248–51, 264–5
  see also pointing; signs
GILLHAM, BILL *First Words* 334
group teaching 79–80, 90

HALLIDAY, M. A. K. 96
hand grasping 180–2
handicaps, autonomy and 61
HARING, N., and SCHIEFELBUSCH, R. L. *Teaching Special Children* 77
Helping the Retarded (Perkins, et al.) 77
Hester Adrian Research Centre, Manchester University xii, 3, 12
home
  children living at, language ability of 30–1, 36, 344
  objects, vocabulary test 205, 346–348
  visitors 334–5, 336
hospital children 29–31, 36, 38, 138 159, 240, 344
hostel children 30–1, 344
How To Do Things With Words (Austin) 108
HUGHES, J. M. 44, 50, 56, 57, 60
Human Horizons Series 334
HUNT, J. MC V. 125, 126–7

Illinois Test of Psycholinguistic Abilities 294
imagination, language for 157
imitation 74, 86, 126–8, 279, 297–8
incongruities 322–3
incontinence 196–7, 200

independence 49, 52, 58–9
  see also autonomy
individual communication system 22
initiating role, child in 156
inquiry, language for 157–8
instrumental meanings 135, 143
intelligence tests 12, 33, 213
intervention observation 105–6, 167, 170, 172, 177–82, 184–5, 187, 193–5, 198–202

Jim's People language kit 55, 99, 159, 300, 302–10, 315, 317

kits see curriculum packages

language 93
  about language 158–9
  form and functions of 81–2
  kits see curriculum packages
  representative 109
  see also ability; development; production of language; reception of language; teaching; vocabulary
Language and How to Use It 320–4
A Language for Life (Bullock Report) 333
learning by ESN(S) children 35
Leeming, Ken 5
leisure 60
lessons see plan; planning
location 135, 143, 152–3

MACDONALD et al. 98
MCMASTER, J. 42, 99
Mager's 'Hey Dad Test' 42–3
Manchester Teachers' Centre 4
MARSHALL, A. 28
matching 139
meaning
  agent 105–6, 119–20, 122, 124, 130–1, 136–7, 142
  alternative 213–15, 228
  development of 95
  expressive 111–14

generalization of types of 140–1
instrumental 135, 143
interpretation of 96
new 135–6; prerequisites for 139–40
relational 111, 114–18, 125; extending 132–3, 143
substantive 111, 118–21; combining 132–5, 142–4
teaching 103–6, 108, 109–25; prerequisites for 123–4, 129, 143, 152
medium of communication 102, 106–7
personalized 22, 107
teaching 125–8
methods, teaching 73–7, 112–60
definition of 43
prerequisites for 140
see also non-verbal communication; objectives; observation; vocabulary teaching
microcephalic child 253
MILLER, J. F. 98
miming 79
MITCHELL, D. R. 50–1
Mittler, Peter 5
money, teaching of 57
moral aspects of education 48, 52
moral autonomy 63–4
MOREHEAD, D. M. and A. 126
mother, working with 188–95
mother–child interaction 97, 112, 114, 192–3, 194
motivation 184–5
motor imitation 128
movement vocabulary tests 209, 346

negatives 148–9
NESBIT, M. 57, 59–60
non-verbal communication 18, 60, 96, 98, 106–7, 111–14, 138–9, 238–67, 334
behaviours 239–41, 254–5; *see also* Communication Behaviour Rating Schedule

individual system 22, 107
language kits and 297
prerequisites for 239, 242
productive language following 264–5
teaching: aims and objectives 242–243, 255–7; methods 243–52, 257–267; systems 266–7
see also gestures; pointing; signs
normative tests 213
nouns, vocabulary
teaching 225–8; non-verbal 255–264
tests 204–9
nursery age-group, language ability of 28
nursery rhymes 209

object meanings, teaching 120–1, 124, 130–3, 137–8, 142–3, 144
objectives, teachers' 80, 178, 180, 291
aims and 69–70, 225–7, 230–4, 242–3, 255–7, 350–71
defining 42–3, 67–92, 151, 153–4
language kit as source of 298, 301, 306, 316, 327
methods of achieving 73–7, 90, 130, 280–3
planning and organization 69–73, 77–80, 80–92
syntactic 151
observation
classroom 173–95
effect of, on teacher 5
forms 168–9, 171, 176, 191, 199
framework for 167–72
levels of 166–7
methods of 164–202
by mother 188–92
outside the classroom 188–201
periods 172–3, 176, 202
records 173, 198, 202
in residential home 195–201
see also intervention observation

occupational education *see* work aims
OSGOOD, C. E. 294
outside activities 55, 56–8, 100, 188–201

Paget–Gorman Sign System 107, 239, 252–3, 255, 259, 261, 266
parallel bars 184
Parental Involvement Project Charts 213
parents
  aims of 50–4; and teachers', compared 47
  language ability of children living with 344
  teaching approach, child's age and 27–8
  working with xii, 50–1, 104–5, 188–95, 335–6
parent–teacher workshops 335–6
Peabody Language Development Kit 55, 99, 294–302
people vocabulary test 205–6, 347
PERKINS, E. A. *et al. Helping the Retarded* 77
PETERS, R. S. 63
physical aims 49
physical education 54, 59
physical autonomy 61–2
PIAGET, J. 63, 95, 126
pictures
  incongruous 323
  objects and 139–40
  questions on 269–89, 305–6, 389–91
  used in questioning tests 381–5
  see also curriculum packages
plan, lesson
  evaluation and modification 81, 89–92
  implementation 80–9
planning
  curriculum 34–5
  development 2–3
  lessons: methods 73–7; objectives 69–73, 80–92; organization 77–80
play 54, 60, 128, 336
pleasure, expressions of 112–13
plurals 146, 284, 303, 307, 309
pointing 245–8
  vocalization with 248–51
possession 134, 143, 309
possessives 147–8, 303
PREMACK, D. 98, 107
prepositions 135, 139, 143
production of language
  assessment of 13, 17–19, 24–5, 29, 31, 34, 36; *see also* vocabulary tests
  comprehension and 212–13, 222, 229
  in curriculum 60, 111–21, 154
  non-verbal communication and 263
  teaching kits and 296, 302–3, 322
  see also teaching
project *see* Schools Council Education of Severely Educationally Subnormal Pupils Project
pronouns 150
prosthetics 62–3
psychologists, assessment by 33
Psychology of Interpersonal Behaviour (Argyle) 15
punishment 193

questioning procedure 275–91
  categories for analysis of utterances in 386–8
  pictures used in 380–4
  skeleton form 388–90
  tests of effectiveness 285–9
questionnaires
  language 9–10, 17–18; results 18–22, 34–5
  personal information 10, 29
questions 152–3, 158
  in the classroom 268–91
  eliciting minimal response 270–2, 274–5
  full-sentence responses to 274–84

pictures and 269–89, 305–6, 388–90
  unrealistic 273–4
reception of language 60, 102, 212–13, 222
  assessment of 13–14, 17–18, 19–20, 25–6, 31, 34, 36
  production of language and 212–13, 222, 229
  teaching 121–3, 154, 156; language kits and 296, 302–3, 322
  see also meaning; vocabulary tests
record keeping 89, 126, 168–71, 173, 198, 202, 212, 264, 323
recurrence, teaching 116, 122, 125, 130, 132–3, 142–3
reinforcement
  of correct responses 73–4, 91, 112–13, 193, 197–9, 242, 246, 260, 262, 264–5, 275, 277–83, 312, 350
  of minimal response 270–1
rejection, teaching 117–18, 148
repetition 275–83, 312, 387
representative language 109
research trends 94–9
residential care
  language ability and 30–1, 344
  problem child in 195–201
  see also hospital children; hostel children; observation
resource centres 334
responses 67, 82, 85, 100, 312
  accuracy of 272–3
  categories for analysis of 385–7
  feedback after 82, 85–90, 302–3
  full-sentence 274–84
  group and individual 316
  minimal 270–2, 274–5
  see also reinforcement
Reynell Language Development Scale 215

schools
  ESN(S), as resource centres 334
  size of 11, 36
  special education outside 334–5

SCHIEFELBUSCH, R. L. 77
Schools Council Education of Severely Educationally Subnormal Pupils Project 3–5
  consultative committee 391–2
  schools participating 392
  scope 3–4
  team 5, 391
screaming 188–90, 192, 194–5, 196, 200–1
SEARLE, J. 108–9
sentences 145, 154–5, 271, 274–84
  incongruous 322–3
sex differences in language ability 29–30, 36–7, 343
sex ratio of children 11
shopping 57
signs 126, 239, 252, 255–63
  voice production and 264–5
  see also Paget–Gorman Sign System
SIMPSON, P. F. 44
situational generalization 141
skills
  age and 23
  teaching 50, 54–5, 58, 59, 72
SKINNER, B. F. *Verbal Behaviour* 94
social aims 47–8, 51–2, 53, 56
social class 12, 341
  language ability and 32–3, 36, 38, 345
social interaction, language for 157, 311
Social Science Research Council (SSRC) Language and Communication project 3
sorting 139
sound production 170, 174, 177–8, 180–1, 377
spastic child 173, 374
spatial vocabulary
  teaching 228–36, 359–71
  test 210–11, 215, 346
special education 330–1, 334–5
Special Educational Needs (Warnock Report) xi, 330

speech *see* production of language; voice production
sports, in vocabulary tests   349
standardized tests   213, 215
STEVENS, M.   99
stimulation   67, 73
structure of language   102, 107–8, 131, 145
subject–verb–object (SVO) construction   151–2
Swann, Will   5
symbolic play   128
symbols   102, 104–5, 126
syntactic objectives   151
Syntactic Structures (Chomsky)   94
syntax   95, 102, 322

teacher workshops   331–3
teachers   5, 335
  assessment by   33–4
  children acting as   79
  'floating'   326
  sharing knowledge and skills   333–4
  style   43–4, 90
  training   330–2
  working outside schools   334
  see also aims; objectives
teaching
  group   79–80, 90
  language   19, 54, 55, 60, 94–5, 109–10, 333–4; research into   97–9
  model   40–4, 67–9
  sequences   86–9, 98, 136, 145
  see also reception of language; methods; non-verbal communication; vocabulary
Teaching Disadvantaged Children in the Pre-school (Bereiter and Engelmann)   311
Teaching Learning in the Preschool (Blank)   85, 99–100, 224
Teaching Special Children (Haring and Schiefelbusch)   77
terminology   40, 42–4
tests   164–5, 202, 213, 285–9; *see also* vocabulary tests

time, child's understanding of   149
TOUGH, JOAN   99
toys in vocabulary tests   349
training, teacher   330–2
transport vocabulary test   204, 347
TREVARTHAN, C.   96

understanding *see* meaning; production of language; reception of language
UZGIRIS, I.   125, 126–7

Verbal Behaviour (Skinner)   94
verbs   120, 149–50, 209–10, 305
video-recordings   viii, 5, 68, 332, 334
vocabulary
  knowledge survey   4
  selection of   213–14, 219–20, 223, 236, 346–9
  teaching   221–36, 350–7; aims and objectives   225–7, 230–4, 350–71; language kits and   295, 301, 306; methods   226–8, 230–4, 351–71; prerequisites for   222–3
  tests   203–12, 222–3, 229, 236; designing   212–21; guessing in   216–17; instructions in   215–221; materials   216–17, 220; words used in   346–9
  see also English Picture Vocabulary Test
vocal imitation   127
vocalization with gestures   248–51

walking   182–4
  frame   185
Warnock Report (*Special Educational Needs*)   330, 334
WHELDALL, K.   212
WILSON, J.   63
work aims   50, 53, 59–60
workshops
  parent–teacher   335–6
  teacher   331–3

YODER, D. E.   98